Dilemmas of Reconciliation

Cases and Concepts

Dilemmas of Reconciliation

Cases and Concepts

edited by
Carol A.L. Prager and Trudy Govier

Wilfrid Laurier University Press

[WLU]

We acknowledge the financial support of the Government of Canada through the Book Publishing Industry Development Program for our publishing activities.

National Library of Canada Cataloguing in Publication Data

Dilemmas of reconciliation : cases and concepts /
Carol A.L. Prager, Trudy Govier, editors.

Includes bibliographical references and index.
ISBN 0-88920-415-2

1. Reconciliation.   2. International relations—Moral and ethical aspects.
3. Political ethics. I. Prager, Carol A.L. (Anne Leuchs), 1939– II. Govier, Trudy, 1944–

JA79.D44 2003   172'.4   C2003-901846-6

© 2003 Wilfrid Laurier University Press
Waterloo, Ontario, Canada   N2L 3C5
www.wlupress.wlu.ca

Cover design by Leslie Macredie; text design by C. Bonas-Taylor.
Cover etching *What Is This Hubbub?* (c.1810-1813) by Francisco Goya y Lucientes.
Photograph: © National Gallery of Canada. Permission courtesy of National Gallery of Canada, Ottawa. Purchased 1933.

∞

Printed in Canada

Contents

Case Studies

Conclusion

Introduction[1]

Carol A.L. Prager

The twentieth century's tens of millions of mass human rights abuses (increasingly associated at century's end with international interventions to stop them and to rebuild political communities afterward) have led to an intense focus on reconciliation. (The horrifying civilian toll resulting from the terrorist attacks in New York and Washington, DC, on September 11, 2001, although not comparable in all respects to the issues under consideration here, reminds us that in the twenty-first century the more things change, the more they remain the same.) Practical politics and life underscore the necessity to move on, but how is this possible, or even conceivable, when unspeakable cruelty has been inflicted by hundreds of thousands of ordinary human beings on millions of others, sometimes, as in ethnic cleansing, with the explicit intent to make future reconciliation impossible? This is a central question that contributors to this volume address.

The study of reconciliation per se is quite recent.[2] The voluminous Holocaust literature[3] has been more concerned with how a horror of such evil and magnitude could have occurred in our time than with how reconciliation could be achieved, although the most thoroughgoing reconciliation measures have been taken by the German government, as the eminent Holocaust historian Michael R. Marrus documents in this volume. Following upon the Second World War's Nuremberg War Crimes Tribunal, contributor Justice Richard J. Goldstone played a key role in establishing the United Nations War Crimes Tribunal for the former Yugoslavia, where he served as chief prosecutor,

Notes to introduction are on pp. 24-26.

and, subsequently the United Nations War Crimes Tribunal for Rwanda. Meanwhile it became clear that war crime trials, critically important as they were, could complicate reconciliation and were unable to address the societal cleavages left in the wake of massive human rights abuses. It became obvious, moreover, that war crime trials could not (and, perhaps, should not) try all war crimes. Again, Richard Goldstone, through the Goldstone Commission, played a large part in establishing the South African Truth and Reconciliation Commission. Other reconciliation commissions and tribunals (such as the Guatemalan and Cambodian ones Jim Handy and David Chandler refer to) appeared or were planned. As the perplexities involved in achieving reconciliation became apparent, scholars increasingly turned their attention to themes of restorative justice, acknowledgement, forgiveness, restitution, and reparations.[4] Most recently, the World Conference against Racism, Racial Discrimination, Xenophobia and Related Intolerance raised the issue of reparations for the slavery practised by European powers during the seventeenth century, a practice declared by the conference to be a crime against humanity.

This collection begins with an overview by Michael R. Marrus. He asks whether and in what sense people might be capable of forgiving the past. Marrus describes efforts to deal with the Holocaust under four headings: political, legal, material, and cultural. Politically, there has been explicit acknowledgement by the German state of its collective responsibility for gross wrongdoing. That acknowledgement, Marrus says, is essential for any reconciliation among Germans, Jews, and the other Holocaust victims. There have been trials of prominent perpetrators in one international tribunal and in four different national ones, and they have been significant, although it would be a mistake, argues Marrus, to regard any such trials as lessons in history. No legal proceeding is designed to offer a full and accurate history of events; rather its purpose is to determine the guilt or innocence of particular individuals, under specific procedural rules. As of June 1999, Germany had paid the equivalent of some $60 billion in reparations. Since then the German government has addressed the issue of slave labour, but that of confiscated works of art has yet to be dealt with. Within Jewish communities, efforts to pursue material compensation are controversial, with some individuals claiming that it risks trivializing Holocaust wrongs. Culturally, Marrus notes the body of literature, drama, and scholarship about Holocaust wrongs, and the monuments, that have been established to acknowledge them. Issues arise here too: there is, for example, the danger of a kind of "Victim Olympics."

Perspectives and Approaches

Philosopher and policy analyst David Crocker contributes to an understanding of what reconciliation can mean by describing eight goals of a normative framework for reckoning with past wrongs. Crocker argues that for societies seeking something like reconciliation in the wake of serious wrongdoing, the most significant goals are (1) investigating the truth about the relevant past events; (2) providing a public platform for victims to tell their stories about what happened to them; (3) establishing some measure of accountability and appropriate sanctions for the most significant perpetrators of wrongdoing; (4) complying, and showing compliance with, the rule of law; (5) appropriately compensating the victims of wrongdoing; (6) contributing to institutional reform and long-term development; (7) reconciliation of previously opposed groups and individuals; and (8) deepening and strengthening the quality of public deliberation.

Philosopher Trudy Govier, focusing on a crucially important element of reconciliation, notes numerous references to acknowledgement in recent discussions of reconciliation and transitional justice. She cites the Final Report of South Africa's Truth and Reconciliation Commission and the 1996 Canadian government report on Aboriginal Peoples. These and other sources claim that acknowledgement of past wrongs is fundamentally important for reconciliation, but they do not explain what acknowledgement is or why it might play a central role. Govier's essay begins to answer these questions. First, she explores acknowledgement by contrasting it with various forms of denial, self-deception, and ignoring. She discusses both individual and collective cases, concentrating particularly on the 1996 Canadian report on Aboriginal Peoples. Then she addresses the importance of acknowledgement from the point of view of victims. Using the idea that identities are significantly social, Govier proposes a theory as to why acknowledgement is so fundamentally important to victims.

Philosopher Susan Dwyer focuses on how reconciliation should be understood in political contexts. Some commentators have expressed considerable skepticism about reconciliation as a political goal, fearing that talk about the need for reconciliation implies a condoning of serious injustice. Dwyer comments on the quest for national reconciliation in South

Africa, where there has been a tendency to think of reconciliation in terms of Christian religious teachings and forgiveness, partly due to the leadership of Archbishop Desmond Tutu. Urging close attention to the distinction between macro (large group) and micro (individual) contexts, she cautions against applying a richly emotive and essentially personal conception of reconciliation to those political contexts in which we explore national reconciliation. She resists the idea that reconciliation at the macro level requires apology and forgiveness, and proposes an alternative conception in terms of the reconciliation, or compatibility, of narratives about the past. The importance of Dwyer's insights is apparent today in Burundi, where attempts to reconcile after massacres and civil war have been thwarted because, while there are Hutu and Tutsi accounts of what has happened since Burundi's independence, there are no history books to mediate between them. In this case, UNESCO has undertaken the task of producing one.[5]

Marc Forget, a mediator and activist who works in Canada and abroad with the Quaker Committee for Jails and Justice, turns to the social implications of criminal abuse, providing an account of restorative justice alternatives that emphasize social and historical contexts. Restorative justice alternatives, such as community sentencing and victim-offender mediation, recognize that crime does not simply involve individuals but also families and larger social groups, and underscore the importance of acknowledgement, restitution, and the building of better relations between victims and offenders. Such processes are relevant in the aftermath of political conflicts, and have been used by Forget and others in such places as Nicaragua and South Africa. From the point of view of restorative justice, traditional legal process and, in particular, retributive conceptions of punishment are open to a number of criticisms. When conflicts are brought to courts, both victims and the immediate community lose power to take part in the resolution of their own conflicts. This phenomenon is largely responsible for the frustration and rage that many victims feel when the judicial process, in seeking a legal determination of guilt, must attend carefully to the rights of the accused offender and only minimally acknowledges the needs and suffering of victims. Such frustration also characterizes the aftermath of violent political conflicts. Forget describes striking individual cases in which mediated communication has led to restitution, rehabilitation, and lasting cooperation between victims and offenders.

Like Dwyer and Forget, philosopher Larry May, who has recently completed a law degree and has written extensively on issues of collective responsibility, draws attention to the group aspects of human rights abuses. While restorative justice processes are, to some extent, exemplified in truth commissions, international legal proceedings—as in the special tribunals for Rwanda and for the former Yugoslavia—are also a centrally important element of post-conflict processes. May argues that international crimes should generally be seen as group-based, in the sense that such crimes are committed by collectivities against individuals who are group members, for example, women, members of an ethnic group, or a political class. It is, moreover, crucial for the authority and credibility of such tribunals that there be a distinction between international crimes and domestic ones, that is, the latter falling within the jurisdiction of domestic courts. May explores in depth the crime of mass rape, describing how and why it has recently come to be understood as an international crime. The treatment of offenders in cases of mass rape is enormously significant for reconciliation, because this is one of the most common, serious, and profoundly disturbing offences that a group can commit against another.

Political scientist Thomas Keating then turns to the roles and responsibilities of outsiders in the contexts of conflict, reconciliation, and relevant Canadian foreign policy. Citizens and policy-makers are sometimes willing to intervene in the affairs of other countries to try to limit civil violence, and yet one must obviously be cautious about such intervention. It is enormously difficult for outsiders to intervene constructively, so as to build within a country a capacity for sustaining non-violence and better relationships. The post-Cold War period exhibits intense and apparently intractable civil conflicts in virtually every region of the world. Media coverage and public acceptance of humanitarian principles create pressure to intervene, and one might cite such public pressure as evidence of the emergence of a caring global community. In this light, Keating discusses the frustrating attempts of Canada and the United Nations to intervene in Haiti.

Finally, as a political scientist and political philosopher, I turn to the relationship between understanding and judging, on the one hand, and reconciliation on the other. Considering the tendency to judge too quickly before attempting to understand and explain, I concentrate on issues of individual and group responsibility. Because atrocities in the Holocaust and other contexts are so terrible to contemplate, we have a tendency to judge actions too readily, protecting our sensibilities and our sense of our own immunity and virtue. We pull back and think that the people involved must be moral monsters, utterly different from us. I argue that while such a response is itself explicable and understandable, ultimately it works against anything like healing and reconciliation. Judgement crowds out the even more essential element of understanding. How do human individuals come to commit cruel and atrocious actions in such contexts as the Holocaust? It is not enough to stand back from such questions because, with regard to cruelly immoral actions, the Holocaust was by no means unique. It is precisely because mass cruelty happens so often that we have to try to understand it. Complex issues about individual responsibility for atrocious acts emerge from the extensive Holocaust literature, but are not to be found only there. Recoiling from the contemplation of terror and abuse, we may not want to understand—fearing, perhaps, that if we understand we will be led to forgive something that should not be forgiven. But such attitudes cannot be constructive when it comes to prevention or reconciliation. In the end, I speak of gaining from my reflections a tragic sense of life. The complexities of judging and understanding guilt and responsibility provide another dilemma of reconciliation.

Case Studies

In order to examine the reconciliation attempts discussed in the previous section, we turn to a series of telling case studies. Roger Epp, who teaches political theory at Augustana University in Camrose, Alberta, provides the first—an exploration of the state of the hoped-for reconciliation between Canadian Aboriginal and non-Aboriginal populations, especially in light of their particular rural experience of the Canadian prairie. The relationship between these two groups raises profound questions about identity, history, and community, and has generated complex and highly charged politics, as well as many legal cases. Epp sets his discussion in the context of the substantial report issued in 1996 by Canada's Royal Commission on Aboriginal People. The report was extremely thorough and its work was widely commended, although there has been little progress in the implementation of its recommendations. The federal government has largely taken a passive stance on the issues, and there seems to be a kind of backlash, evidenced in some opinion polls and recent commentary, to conceptions of aboriginal rights and self-government. Theoretically, critics of reconciliation negotiations and processes argue that we should move forward from the present and not from the past, which is a minefield of grievances and unfixable wrongs that will lead to contention and struggle. Taking exception to this view, Epp advances the notion of birthright as providing a historically grounded perspective on such reconciliation issues; Epp's idea is, however, at total variance with current Lockean contractarian conceptions. Epp also importantly observes that Canadian society's responsibilities for reconciliation efforts fall disproportionately on non-native rural communities, which often find themselves competing with native Canadians for scarce resources. Resentments can occur, Epp notes, as in the conflicts over fishing rights in Burnt Church, New Brunswick. He argues that the most significant work of national reconciliation in the Canadian context will proceed in small face-to-face initiatives with participants who live and work in close proximity.

Wilhelm Verwoerd, a South African philosopher who for several years worked as a staff researcher for that country's Truth and Reconciliation Commission and is a defender of the TRC and its work, sets forth and responds to fundamental criticisms, making use of political cartoons to illustrate his points. Under the leadership of Archbishop Desmond Tutu, the TRC was the most ambitious truth commission ever held. It featured public hearings in which some seven thousand victims told stories of suffering, special sector hearings exploring how law, business, the churches, and media had functioned so as to prop up apartheid; and individualized conditional amnesty for perpetrators who fully disclosed information about politically motivated crimes. Its widely discussed final report presents an indispensable tool for the understanding of a major contemporary attempt to contend with the dilemmas of reconciliation. And yet, Verwoerd points out, there is an anomaly in the current understanding of the TRC. Internationally, its work has been seen very positively, but the Commission has been strongly criticized within South Africa. In terms of *justice*, the criticism was that perpetrators were going unpunished and victims were denied an opportunity to proceed against perpetrators in the courts. On these grounds, it was alleged that there was no true justice in the TRC. In terms of *truth*, there were concerns as to how much truth about apartheid had become known, whether the Commission was biased in favour of the African National Congress, and how truth could provide a basis for reconciliation. In terms of *reconciliation*, people came to wonder how it was that exposing truth could lead to healing and reconciliation. Even when sus-

tained efforts are launched under inspired moral leadership, national reconciliation is bound to be a prolonged and messy business.

Historian James Handy, who has extensively studied the Guatemalan
case with particular attention to the situation of the Mayan people, provides
historical background and discusses the progress toward reconciliation of
Mayan and non-Mayan Guatemalans. He reports that the Guatemalan
truth commission and relevant accords have had only the most modest
impact. Although there have been advances, both the Catholic Church and
the truth commission have had to powerfully condemn renewed violence by
the military against the Mayan people, and few of the steps needed to
address that violence have been taken. Despite good intentions and articu-
lations of human rights values, social and economic inequality and political
repression persist. Issues at stake involve the very identity of the Guatemalan
nation, raising the question of the extent to which it is founded on, and can
constructively include, the Mayan people. In the case of Guatemala the role
of human rights abuses in attempts to define membership in political communities is highlighted.

David Chandler, an internationally recognized scholar of Cambodia
during the Khmer Rouge period of 1975-79, considers the Cambodian
case, again exemplifying intransigence in dealing with a bloody past.
Under the Khmer Rouge, some 1.7 million Cambodians were killed.
Today Cambodia faces, in an acute form, the dilemma of confronting the
past while simultaneously struggling to construct a workable democratic
society. The current regime has wished to "move on" to some form of
national reconciliation that would work on a basis of generalized innocence and imposed forgetfulness. People are conditioned to see themselves
as victims both by their own experience and by government propaganda,
resulting in a standard reading of history according to which Cambodian
individuals and groups were not really agents in their own right. Popular
memory and the Museum of Genocidal Crimes have helped to shape
Cambodians' contemporary understanding of their recent history as one
in which perpetrators seem to come from somewhere else and everybody
was an innocent victim. At one point, Prime Minister Hun Sen urged
Cambodians to "dig a hole and bury the past"; this was no mere off-the-
cuff remark, but rather an expression of serious policy. Surviving documents offer vivid and detailed evidence of appalling wrongs, committed,
for example, in S-21, a prison notorious for its torture and executions, by
a regime that saw enemies everywhere and ruthlessly sought to eliminate

every one of them. Centralized power was linked by the Khmer Rouge to the production of its own history, which may explain the extraordinary documentation of a rat's nest of forced confessions. Some trials have been held, but as of June 2001 the possibility of systematically bringing top Khmer Rouge leaders to trial seemed remote, although given rapid changes in Cambodia and the existence of international parties urging some form of trials or a truth commission, that situation could change.

Finally, Janet Keeping, a lawyer with the Canadian Institute of Resource Law and its director of Russian Affairs, explores the concept of national reconciliation as it might apply to post-communist Russia, another intractable case replete with the dilemmas of reconciliation. Noting different conceptions of national reconciliation in terms of narrative or of the building of trust, Keeping proposes that, in the Russian context, one could understand reconciliation as some capacity to build together a more decent society. The Russian case is especially complex because there is such a multitude of disruptive and politically controversial events, resulting in a widespread and intense sense of grievance, but one that is not focused on any specific set of events or situations, or on any particular groups of perpetrators and victims. Because there are too many layers of grievance, resentment, and anger, and no good focus for a single kind of rupture that might be reconciled, it is difficult to talk meaningfully about any processes of national reconciliation in Russia. The fact that, without their empire, Russians have lost any clear sense of what it means to be Russian serves to compound this question. There is considerable evidence to suggest that Russians articulate grievances without any expectation of finding practical responses to them and tend to have low expectations of themselves and their country. Nevertheless, one can cite, both in university contexts and in aspects of regional and federal relationships, examples of developing trust, facilitating cooperation between individuals and institutions that would have been suspicious of each other during Soviet times.

Tensions Surrounding Reconciliation

The emphasis on dilemmas in the title of this volume suggests the presence of pervasive tensions, a fact recognized by Wilhelm Verwoerd in the context of South Africa's reconciliation process and by Sue Dwyer in her observation that "reconciliation is fundamentally a process whose aim is to lessen the sting of a tension." It is useful, when considering dilemmas of reconciliation, where rationales, approaches, and historical cases dramatically exemplify trade-offs between values and/or realities, to think in such terms. Here I will discuss some of the interwoven tensions arising out of these essays that point to the need for further analysis and/or identify enduring strains affecting reconciliation that will have to be accepted and managed. This exploration will be followed by a discussion of grounds for optimism and pessimism about the prospects for reconciliation and the events that give rise to the need for it.

A point that bears repeating is that since the historical sequences giving rise to demands for reconciliation are extremely complex, the processes of reconciliation are going to be at least as complex. As Richard Goldstone, Michael Marrus, Roger Epp, and others observe, the dilemmas of reconciliation must be viewed in their historical, social, psychological, legal, and philosophical dimensions. Moreover, Wilhelm Verwoerd identifies an inherent "messiness" in the notion of reconciliation. In fact, the contributions to this volume demonstrate that the problems involved in understanding the dilemmas of reconciliation are so daunting that anyone in search of rigour and clarity would probably head off in the opposite direction were it not for their enormous intrinsic importance. As Albert Camus profoundly wrote, "We can no longer choose our problems; they choose us."[6]

"What" Must Be Reconciled?

Richard Goldstone, David Crocker, Sue Dwyer, Janet Keeping, and Roger Epp draw attention to a basic question around which much else revolves. What precisely is it that must be reconciled? As David Crocker puts it, "it matters what a particular transition is from and to." Different circumstances of human rights abuses impose different conditions on the effectiveness of reconciliation processes. Absolutistic nationalisms at work in Bosnia and Kosovo seem particularly intractable because they make agreement on a single historical narrative virtually impossible. At the same time, as a recent study by the World Bank makes clear, the cause of most intrastate violence (often involving mass human rights abuses) can be traced to competition for valuable commodities, such as diamonds in Sierra Leone and oil in the Sudan. Reconciliation in such cases might revolve around somewhat different issues. Again, the aftermath of Stalinism and totalitarianism in Russia raises its own obstacles to reconciliation given the "incoherence" of Russian public opinion, as Janet Keeping observes, and the extraordinarily long list of grievances clamouring for reconciliation. There are so many inadequately articulated issues that Keeping sees them less as "disputes," and more as "grievances," indeed, grievances upon grievances, that lead to no particular form of redress and result in "gridlock." Under these circumstances perhaps all that can be hoped for is a kind of muddling through that is enhanced by the slightest movement forward. The legacies left in the wake of revolutionary projects such as the Cambodian and the Chinese under Mao can also be diffuse, on the one hand, but formidable, on the other. The perpetrators may not be the only ones who want to "dig a hole and bury the past."[7]

There are even more fundamental questions about "what" needs to be reconciled that claim our attention. What is the nature of the crimes that demand reconciliation? How can these crimes be understood and explained, if they can be understood at all? In what ways does their genesis place inherent limitations on the process of reconciliation? Roger Epp shows that the way in which issues of reconciliation are conceptualized makes all the difference. Reconciliation with Canadian Aboriginals, he contends, must proceed from the deep appreciation of history recognized by the notion of birthrights, rather than by an ahistorical Lockean contractarian framework. Further, as Sue Dwyer asks, are we morally obliged to attempt to reconcile? Michael Marrus cites Rabbi Leon Klenicki's powerful phrase, "the triumphalism of pain," underscoring how suffering can be used to trump "rational" argument and discussion. Marrus also points to the phenomenon of new generations using their forbears' suffering as a potent form of identity, leading to new rounds of demands for apologies and acknowledgement of past suffering. This tendency, moreover, can work against understanding. I have explored, for example, the dark space between understanding and judging crimes against humanity.

In this murky place we confront an enduring and tragic fact of human existence, that inflicting evil is so much easier than recovering from it. At the same time, as Marc Forget reminds us, this need not mean that the impact of the harm on perpetrators is negligible. In a similar vein, one of Verwoerd's eloquent political cartoons emphasizes the fact that amnesty does not so much signify forgiveness as a recognition of the humanity of the perpetrator. This is an area that might fruitfully be further explored. At the same time research reveals that where there has been aggression on both sides, both former enemies' accounts involve significant distortions of the historical record. Rwanda, the Balkans, Northern Ireland, and especially today the Middle East exemplify this phenomenon. One is left wondering if the two or more sides are describing the same events.

The complex nature of the "what" casts doubt on the likelihood of agreeing, in many if not most cases, upon on a single narrative, the importance of which is emphasized by Sue Dwyer and others. As James Handy and Roger Epp point out, this is a besetting problem in Guatemala and in many aboriginal grievances. Where agreement on a single narrative is not possible, the usefulness of the broader, historical, more loosely defined Durkheimian notion of *conscience collective,* as Marrus points out, might be explored.

The Ideal vs. the Possible

Perhaps the most important tension links the ideal and the possible. Is reconciliation by means of truth and reconciliation commissions, for example, necessarily inferior to justice as determined by war crime tribunals? Sue Dwyer and other contributors argue no for different reasons. Dwyer states that comprehensive war crimes trials are, for a multitude of reasons, not possible; I note many reasons, including the power of group aspects of abuses to diminish individual moral freedom.

A conflict also arises between what we believe with good reason ought to work in reconciliation attempts and what actually does work. As Jean Bethke Elshtain writes: "Maybe there is a political version of forgiveness that must, not all of the time but most of the time, step back from full reconciliation and certainly from absolution."[8] Verwoerd's discussion of the criticisms of the South African Truth and Reconciliation Commission ("justice-based, truth-based, and reconciliation-based") expressed through political cartoons, identifies a host of paradoxes and ambiguities. It is logical, for instance, to think that the truth-telling demanded by victims is required for reconciliation, and on the individual level and in some historical cases, including the South African, there is some evidence that this is the case. A less intuitive point, however, is that too much truth-telling can be counterproductive and instead of healing societal cleavages can generate more, as Verwoerd notes. Similarly David Chandler writes, "We are entitled to ask if opening old wounds, on a national basis, is more beneficial for at least some of the wounded than covering them over and hoping they will heal....Moreover, there is no sure way of knowing whether the Germans or the Japanese, the excavators or buriers of their respective pasts, are en masse, psychically better off." Chandler's insights help account for the fact that the UN has had enormous difficulty in setting up Cambodian war crime trials because the regime had insisted on appointing more than half of the panel's judges. More recently the UN made the concession that three of five judges will be appointed by the Cambodian government.

Govier makes a strong case for the powerful role acknowledgement can play in reconciliation on the ground that "acknowledging...wrongs will assist victims to heal, will mark a separation from the wrongdoing of the past and a commitment to reform, and may constitute a first step toward reconciliation." She refers to "the second wound of silence" cruelly enforcing the lesson that accompanied the infliction of harm that the victim simply doesn't matter. The statement by Manes Sperber also comes to mind: "Without confession and sincere repentance their forgetting is nothing more than a continuation of their crime."9 Richard Goldstone similarly emphasizes the importance of acknowledgement, while Michael Marrus draws attention to the unprecedented, comprehensive acknowledgement by German leaders of Germany's responsibility for the Holocaust. On the other hand, Dwyer, "scrupulously avoid[ing] the language of healing," warns "that any conception of reconciliation...that makes reconciliation dependent on forgiveness, or that emphasizes interpersonal harmony or fellow-feeling, will fail to be a realistic model for most creatures like us."

The values on which reconciliation rests are liberal, Enlightenment, humanistic values such as liberty, human rights, and democracy. In this regard, Larry May makes a convincing case for mass rape being subsumed by *jus cogens*, a category of norms recognized by "civilized nations" that are universally binding whether or not explicitly agreed to. Like David Crocker, who proposes a normative framework for reconciliation embracing eight desiderata, we can usefully envision its ideal components, but, as Crocker also notes, we also need to reflect on what is good enough in the real world. Some form of acknowledgement, as Govier argues, would seem crucial. But, at the end of the day, the "good enough" often defies generalization. It can, however, be related to what Michael Marrus called "coming to terms with," a more comprehensive notion that may or may not entail explicit reconciliation processes, but involves "political, legal, material, and cultural ways of reckoning." In the case of the Holocaust, for example, "the coming to terms with" politically extended to collaborationist regimes, while the cultural category includes the kind of scholarly analysis in which contributors to this volume are engaged. While "coming to terms with" may include a certain pragmatism and appreciation of the importance of the passing of time, it does not rule out the possibility of continued denial, such as that of the Japanese, who refused, until October 2001,[10] to take responsibility for atrocities committed against the Chinese during the Second World War.[11]

An appreciation of what "coming to terms with" in specific contexts can mean is most likely to be found among those closest to actual situations. While scholars can indefinitely dispute legal and ethical points, ordinary people and political leaders tend to be more practical. Sometimes mere survival is a cherished victory. After the tortuous struggle for reconciliation seemed to hit a stone wall with the defeat of the Referendum on the Indigenous Accord, Mayan leaders, Jim Handy reports, could still exclaim: "We are alive, despite it all, against the odds, we are alive!" As Desmond Tutu observed: "Forgiveness is not some nebulous thing. It is practical politics. Without forgiveness, there is no future."[12] In the process of "coming to terms with," Handy, Dwyer, Marrus, and others emphasize the key role played by practical and material help that gives people a stake in whatever resolution is achieved. Such material help has been important in Kosovo, the Middle East conflict, and has been essential in post-Milosevic Yugoslavia. Its continuing importance in what has been called peace- or nation-building has been emphasized by Tom Keating and others.

The fact that reconciliation is a long process that is not terminated by the conclusions of war crime trials or of truth and reconciliation commissions must also be faced. Reconciliation is never achieved once and for all, but occurs with alternate bouts of forward movement and the stasis of anger and grieving. Moreover, prosperity can paper over lingering animosities but adverse economic conditions can expose them again. Succeeding generations in Germany, Italy, and France, for example, have wanted to reach their own conclusions about the traumatic historical events of the Second World War, especially as new archival sources become available. The collapse of the Soviet Union unleashed new anger and questioning about Russia's Stalinist past.[13]

Contributors such as Crocker and Govier link reconciliation with democracy. For them, the more democratic a society, the greater the likelihood of reconciliation being achieved. Indeed, reconciliation may be seen as a stepping stone toward greater democracy, as David Crocker

notes. There are good reasons for identifying a resonance between reconciliation and constitutional democracy, such as the affirmation of the rule
of law, the moral worth of all individuals, transparency, and so forth. As
Tom Keating points out, the effort to "support the emergence of participatory and pluralistic societies with a well-functioning and responsible
government administration acting under the rule of law and respect for
human rights" has been at the heart of the Canadian initiative to promote
"human security." At the same time, as Keating also notes, liberal democracy remains elusive in our world, and the case of Haiti underscores how
the efforts of outsiders to nurture it can go terribly wrong.[14] Thus, popular elections do not necessarily signify that a democratic society in any
meaningful sense has been ushered in, nor do democratic governments
preclude wide-scale, serious human rights abuses. As Czech crimes against
Germans and ethnic Hungarians in the immediate post-Second World
War period demonstrated, democracy is no guarantee of decent, legal, and
humane policies.[15] Democratic Australia all but exterminated its Tasman-
ian population. A more complete understanding of the relationship
between reconciliation and democracy would be enormously interesting
and useful. Does reconciliation succeed to the extent that democratic elements are present? Does it contribute to the development of democracy?
What, if any, reconciliation is possible in the absence of democracy?

The Universal vs. the Local

The closely related tension between the universal and local is a related
theme. Local political and cultural differences often assert themselves in the
context of reconciliation and must be taken into account for many reasons,
including the fact that any reconciliation process must first and foremost be
meaningful to the parties. In his essay in this collection, Roger Epp argues
that reconciliation between Canadian Aboriginals and non-Aboriginals is
frustrated because of the qualitatively different lenses through which they
see their shared history. Indeed, difference is not only at the root of demands
for reconciliation, which are typically expressed by minorities that have been
abused (although majorities can also be targeted for abuse), but is often a
result of communal violence. Hence, the principles at work in reconciliation
might not be the Enlightenment ones, but ones that could be termed "Neo-
Enlightenment."[16] As Elazar Barkan writes:

> The present debate over rights…is partially a result of expand-ing…elementary Enlightenment rights to new peoples, groups, and cultures around the world. These principles have been appropriated by a world that concurrently rejected the Euro-pean claim for "natural" superiority and traditional privileges. Instead the poor, the weak, and the disadvantaged have come to demand intellectual, moral, and political equality. These demands for political and economic justice, which go beyond the traditional legal principles, inform Neo-Enlightenment that increasingly includes compensation for past deprivations and historical injustices.…Neo-Enlightenment morality takes the liberal framework of individual rights as a core value and adds to it a vague and variable set of local circumstances and tradi-tions. This view accepts that certain abstract (liberal) tenets have come to constitute the moral spectrum within which political disagreements are debated; yet it underscores the necessity of considering local particularities and identities.[17]

Neo-Enlightenment values lead to a tension that precariously links universal norms, such as *jus cogens*, with local groups and facts. Thus, on the one hand, minority victims appeal to universal human rights. On the other, when, for instance, the government of a former colonial territory is accused of human rights abuses, it may attempt to defend itself by reject-ing criticism based on universal norms as expressions of neo-colonialism. The former Yugoslavia initially rejected the legitimacy of the UN War Crimes Tribunal for the former Yugoslavia, hoping to come to terms with past policies and deeds through public discourse, Yugoslav courts, a possi-ble truth commission, and the acknowledgement that Yugoslavia has something momentous to answer for.[18]

Here aspects of the "what" again come into play. The banality of wide-scale, systematic human rights abuses can often be traced to the apparent universal need to define group membership.[19] Thus Stalin, Pol Pot, Mao Zedong, and Rwandan Hutus massacred political or ethnic groups in a frenzied attempt to eradicate them. North and Latin American societies, as James Handy and Roger Epp point out, were determined to reject the claims of Aboriginal peoples and, in the process, almost destroyed the peo-ples themselves. Hitler's project was the creation of a "racially pure" soci-ety through the extermination of non-Aryan peoples. More recently Slo-bodan Milosevic set out to ethnically cleanse "greater Serbia" of Croatians, Muslims, and Kosovars.

The anticolonial account, according to which regional characteristics and differences must be taken into consideration in the application of universal norms, can take on the form of extreme cultural relativism. Richard Goldstone insists on "the increasing emptiness of claims for cultural relativism, particularly in the human rights field," pointing out that the rulers who defend cultural relativism the loudest are the ones with the most appalling records of human rights abuses.

Individual vs. Group

Many questions arising from these essays are entwined with another tension between individual and group responsibility. On the one hand, in every case individuals are the instruments of human rights abuses, and Western philosophy upholds a strict norm of individual accountability. On the other, massive human rights abuses are not only, or perhaps even primarily, the expression of individual cruelty, but of calculated political programs, orchestrated by political leaders to marginalize or exterminate groups, and/or, as in the cases of Cambodia and the Soviet Union, to transform societies. Richard Goldstone, Michael Marrus, Sue Dwyer, Larry May, and others explicitly recognize that the wide-scale abuses that lead to demands for reconciliation are not exhausted by the individual level of analysis. As Goldstone points out, we want to reinforce the idea of individual accountability but avoid the notion of collective guilt. "[While] it is individuals who did these things, there is also a countervailing set of circumstances that are missed completely when you focus on just one war criminal after another," he writes. When particular individuals bear primary responsibility for abuses, war crime trials seem the appropriate approach, but when group factors are powerfully in play, other approaches, such as truth and reconciliation commissions, also recommend themselves. The operating principles of truth and reconciliation commissions generally hold that a stronger case for amnesty can be made for those who committed wrongs for political reasons and whose actions did not include gratuitous cruelty but were proportionate to political objectives. Thus, the "political" can undercut individual responsibility in significant ways. As Chandler observed, in their conception of the Khmer Rouge revolution its leader saw "the energies of the revolution...[as]...collective, impersonal ones, overriding the individualism that Party documents criticized in pre-revolutionary culture."

When confronted with the group aspects of mass violence, we may encounter limits to the value of insights taken from the individual level of analysis. Dwyer distinguishes between micro- and macro-level reconciliation. Not only individuals but also societies must take responsibility for the harm they do. The very different policies of Germany and Japan regarding their atrocities during the Second World War, as analyzed by Ian Buruma in *The Wages of Guilt*, are instructive. While the Germans have repeatedly acknowledged their responsibility for the Holocaust and paid reparations, until very recently the Japanese have refused to do either. (In July 2000 Germans finally dealt with the outstanding issue of slave labourers by agreeing to reparations of US $5 billion.) Certainly, individual responsibility has a crucial place in accounting for atrocities and in the reconciliation process, but more attention might well be devoted to what that place is and how it is related to group-level accounts.

Finally, the group figures in the nature of the atrocities themselves. Larry May sees this group basis, exemplified by mass rape, as an essential pre-condition for jurisdiction of international courts such as the International Criminal Court. For May, international crimes are defined as those committed by political groups and/or are crimes against individuals defined by group membership. Typically, the particular abuses giving rise to demands for reconciliation are calculated to impose such harm, shame, and humiliation on victims as group members that ever living together again would be inconceivable. An example is the repeated raping of Muslim women by Serbs so they would bear Serb children, an experience designed to throw the women, husbands, and communities into profound disarray, pain, and conflict. The participation of so many "ordinary" individuals in such crimes may lend credence to Romain Gary's observation that "inhumanity is part of being human."[20] Should one wonder, then, as Sue Dwyer[21] points out, that there may be cases where reconciliation is psychologically impossible—at either the individual or group level?

In his paper "Crime as Interpersonal Conflict" Marc Forget draws attention to a related group aspect as he focuses on restorative justice. He argues that in their individualism modern systems of justice lose track of the fact that legal systems leading up to the modern Western one viewed crime as harm inflicted, not on the state, but on individuals and their families. Such crimes, therefore, were matters for "restorative justice" among the families involved. In the ancient Roman world, Forget notes, much of what we consider crime today was treated as a civil matter. The inflicting of harm on individuals and groups was anticipated, so a system of restorative justice, by which individuals, families, and communities could be reconciled, had to be established. Indeed, perpetrators' instinctive understanding of crime as interpersonal and interfamilial underlies much of the deliberate cruelty we see in human rights abuses. Importantly, "restorative justice" also takes into account the circumstances affecting the perpetrator. Philip Gourevitch has underlined the importance of this insight in Rwanda.[22]

Again, the group figures in the issue of national self-determination, the importance of which Keating emphasizes. National self-determination and sovereignty are at the root of the legal and ethical controversy over humanitarian intervention to stop human rights atrocities, with most international lawyers weighing in against such interventions. Intervention is, at best, a right belonging to outsiders under clearly circumscribed circumstances, but is not an obligation. For the most part, countries must determine their own destinies, often by civil wars in which atrocities, tragically, are universally committed. Hence the inevitable conflict between international norms and self-determination. (This conflict also intersects the tension between the universal and local.) The importance of national self-determination and sovereignty is heightened when a decision on international intervention is reached, and in the nation building that often follows efforts at reconciliation. One has to ask whether solutions that are foisted from outside on political communities are always superior to solutions that may evolve over a longer time by a political community left to itself. Judging from Janet Keeping's account, Russia may be a case in point. Similarly, the demands by outsiders to establish reconciliation processes and to build peace can also be seen as interference in national self-determination, a point raised by Chandler in the Cambodian case. Would the Guatemalan "coming to terms with" be more advanced today if there had been international intervention?

War Crime Trials vs. Truth and Reconciliation Commissions

The tension between war crime trials and truth and reconciliation commissions is a recurrent theme in this collection. Truth and reconciliation commissions can speak to special group aspects of violations: the influence of constructed stereotypes as in Nazi Germany, Rwanda, and elsewhere; coercion to participate in atrocities as in Rwanda; the tendency to follow orders and go along as in the case of Nazi Germany, which Richard Goldstone reminds us is an all-too-human trait; the larger political projects that horrific atrocities are part of, and so forth. At the same time, truth and reconciliation commissions may seem second-best to victims who crave a more precise justice, such as that in principle available in war crime tribunals, which insist on strict individual responsibility and are retributive. War crime trials target those who acted with the greatest moral freedom, but they are difficult to carry out because of the scope of the crimes, the difficulties in getting evidence, and the lack of judicial personnel, especially in places like Cambodia where judges were targeted by the Khmer Rouge.

For many reasons, political or other considerations often impose trade-offs between peace and justice, a point noted by David Crocker: "I believe," he writes, "there are times when (at least) legal punishment has to be delayed or even foregone in favour of other goals such as democracy or reconciliation." In the last days of Milosevic's rule, the international community had to weigh the aggressive pursuit of one of the most infamous indicted war criminals against the wider loss of life. Further, as Dwyer points out, some attempts at reconciliation are predicated "on a return to a previous state of harmony," where there is, in fact, no previously existing harmony that can be returned to.

Another confounding consideration is a disjunction between leaders and the ordinary person. The leadership may be more sympathetic or more opposed to reconciliation. An example of the first is the German government, which took the lead, as Marrus points out, in making real and symbolic apologies and providing reparations to victims of the Holocaust. In Northern Ireland, however, the people are ahead of their leaders, who sometimes seem to frustrate their desire for peace. Yet the argument has been forcefully made by some contributors that harm that is not recognized as such by all concerned, and addressed in significant ways, may be expected to create more harm in the future.

Grounds for Pessimism

No doubt, the surest route to reconciliation is to have no calamities that require it. Because we do not inhabit that world but one in which potent forces that can lead to massive human rights abuses abound, what can the future realistically hold? On the dispiriting side, philosophers, psychologists, theologians, and others acknowledge that evil is integral to the human condition, and this recognition supports a tragic sense of life.[23] If so much harm inflicted on others, individually or collectively, costs the perpetrator(s) so much less than it costs the victim, it seems impossible to envisage a permanent solution. When normal human provocations to lash out are placed in the context of the current emphasis on unlimited possibilities and cutthroat economic competition, it is hard to see many people or nations free of the desire, at some time or other, to harm others. On the individual level such diffused anger is increasingly expressed in "road rage," "air rage," or even the battering to death of one parent by another at his child's hockey game.

Moreover, while globalization might hold out the hope that group membership will decrease in importance, paradoxically the reverse seems to be true. Pressures toward globalization seem to trigger reactions on the part of groups (national and other) determined to maintain and enhance the significance of their group identities. Today radical Islam provides the most spectacular example. Indeed, as other forms of belonging become less salient, victimhood itself may be cultivated as a form of identity, as Michael Marrus and Ian Buruma suggest.[24]

Finally, when we are faced with the persuasive desiderata for effective reconciliation outlined by David A. Crocker, it is clear that in practice, the best that can be achieved consists more or less of half measures. But half measures, as Goldstone and Keating argue, can do more harm than good. As the latter points out, the Haitian case must be everyone's nightmare of the backfiring of attempts to do good. The pursuit of justice, moreover, might entail unacceptable trade-offs. An example is Turkey's recent warning to the United States that the passage of a House of Representatives' resolution blaming Turkey for genocide against the Armenians would endanger an agreement allowing the US to use a Turkish airbase in any future crisis involving Iraq.[25] Nor should the pervasive tendency to manipulate and pervert ethical norms, as in the Middle East and Northern Ireland, be overlooked.[26] In international affairs, politics generally trumps ethical consistency. There are thus two problematic issues that must be borne in mind: the continuing spewing forth of harm, on the one hand, and the capacity to contain, or redress it, on the other. It is the improvement of the latter that at least provides whatever reasons for optimism there may be.

Grounds for Hope

As new norms of legitimacy evolve in the international realm, more responsible decisions can be expected from political leaders. As Richard Goldstone maintains, "I think when victories have been won, it's very hard to move backward. I think there is a sort of inexorable movement forward." Thus, the British seizure of Pinochet in response to a Spanish indictment for crimes against humanity has changed for all time the law regarding jurisdiction over war criminals. Although the British House of Lords ultimately ruled that Pinochet was medically unfit to stand trial, the British courts succeeded in stripping Pinochet of his immunity from prosecution, underscoring the fact that those accused of crimes against humanity will have few places to hide. Commentators now refer to the "Pinochet effect"—the possibility of seizing authors of mass human rights abuses in whatever jurisdiction they may be. Important precedents and experience can accumulate rapidly. It is becoming much more difficult for states that perpetrate massive, systematic human rights abuses to rationalize their behaviour in terms of international norms. A good human rights record, moreover, is increasingly an important element of a state's legitimacy and status in the international community, and loans from international financial institutions increasingly depend on it. The importance of human rights records can be seen in the European Union's isolation of Austria after the election of Jorge Haider, whose sympathy with the perpetrators of the Holocaust was deemed beyond the pale. Turkey's exclusion from the European Union for its human rights record is another example. Even more stunning is the acknowledgement of genocide in Kosovo by the ardent nationalist and new Yugoslav president Vojislav Kostunica,[27] and his willingness to see Slobodan Milosevic tried for war crimes. Finally, and strikingly, at long last, there has been the apology by Japanese prime minister Junichiro Koizumi for his country's brutal aggression toward China during the Second World War. Political leaders prepared to ignite human rights catastrophes are fewer because they fear the impact of being ostracized. The support of one hundred and thirty-nine states for an International Criminal Court also underscores the extent to which the norms of responsibility for human rights abuses have taken root.

Many of the issues surrounding reconciliation after wide-scale human rights abuses are in a brisk state of development, as Richard Goldstone points out. In the past decade or so, considerable progress has been made on diplomatic and legal fronts, such as the creation of the tribunals for Yugoslavia and Rwanda, as well as progress toward the establishment of the International Criminal Court. We see this in the attention given to these bodies by scholars, and in a wider appreciation of their importance among political leaders, and the leaders' own desire to be seen acting decently. Because it is hard to imagine a time when the wellsprings of mass atrocities will run dry, the need for reconciliation will continue to exceed the imperfect, ad hoc, tension-ridden reconciliation processes available. Although there are well-founded grounds for both optimism and pessimism, progress, associated with the assimilation of new international norms and a principled and resolute refusal to become immobilized by pessimism, can be expected to lumber forward, thus providing grounds for the optimism of Richard Goldstone.

Acknowledgements

This volume grew out of the international interdisciplinary conference, "Dilemmas of Reconciliation," held in June 1999 under the auspices of the University of Calgary's Humanities Institute. The collection, however, has evolved since the conference and is not simply the publication of its proceedings.

There are many organizations and individuals the editors would like to thank for their support, participation in the conference, and help in the publication of this volume. Jane Kelly, the Institute's director, provided leadership, inspiration, and concrete help at all stages, and Gerry Dyer tirelessly, graciously, and with awe-inspiring efficiency oversaw every aspect of the conference's organization. Ashis Gupta provided enthusiastic assistance and organized the highly successful literary evening that accompanied the conference.

Special thanks for their generous financial support go to the Canadian Federation for the Humanities and Social Sciences, the Canadian Centre for the Study of Foreign Policy, the Kahanoff Foundation, Petro-Canada, and PanCanadian. Several faculties, many academic departments, and granting bodies of University of Calgary, including the University's Conference Office and Special Projects Fund, also generously supported the conference.

We also want to thank Gretchen Macmillan, Kerry Buck, Thomas Scheff, Suzanne Reitzinger, Jean Slick, Cynthia Brown, Bea Medicine, and Kathleen Mahoney for their stimulating participation in the conference.

We owe a special debt a gratitude to Michael R. Marrus who stepped in at the last moment to give the conference's keynote address. Stephen R. Randall, dean of the Faculty of Social Sciences, generously supported the conference and presided over its banquet with aplomb.

We wish to express our appreciation to Brian Henderson, director of Wilfrid Laurier University Press, the Press's editorial board, and two anonymous readers, all of whom provided valuable comments on the manuscript. Carolyn Andres worked cheerfully and efficiently in the preparation of the final manuscript.

David A. Crocker's paper is an amended version of "Reckoning with Past Wrongs: A Normative Framework," originally published in *Ethics and International Affairs* 13: 43-64.

Susan Dwyer's paper "Reconciliation for Realists" was originally published in *Ethics and International Affairs* 13: 81-98.

Notes

1 Trudy Govier provided the summaries for the papers contained in the Introduction.

2 Probably the best place to start is Martha Minow's excellent *Between Vengeance and Forgiveness: Facing History after Genocide and Mass Violence* (Boston: Beacon Press, 1998). Also very useful are the following: Michael Ignatieff, *The Warrior's Honour: Ethnic War and the Modern Conscience* (Toronto: Viking, 1980); Elazar Barkan, *The Guilt of Nations: Restitution and Negotiating Historical Injustices* (New York: W.W. Norton, 2000); Mark Osiel, *Mass Atrocity, Collective Memory, and the Law* (New Brunswick, NJ: Transaction, 1997); Nicholas Tavuchis, *Mea Culpa: A Sociology of Apology and Reconciliation* (Stanford, CA: Stanford University Press, 1991), and Belinda Cooper, ed., *War Crimes: The Legacy of Nuremberg* (New York: TV Books, 1999). Publication of new titles in reconciliation studies achieved even greater momentum in the year 2001 with the publication of, for example, Andrew Rigby, *Justice and Reconciliation: After the Violence* (Boulder, CO: L. Rienner, 2001); Nigel Biggar, ed., *Burying the Past: Making Peace and Doing Justice after Civil War* (Washington, DC: Georgetown University Press, 2001); Michael Hadley, ed., *The Spiritual Roots of Restorative Justice* (Albany: State University of New York Press, 2001); A. James McAdams, *Judging the Past in Unified Germany* (New York: Cambridge University Press, 2001); Eric K. Yamamoto, *Race, Rights, and Reparation: Law and the Japanese American Internment* (Gaithersburg, MD: Aspen Law & Business, 2001).

3 The Holocaust literature is vast. But see, for example, Michael R. Marrus, *The Holocaust in History* (Toronto: Lester & Orpen Dennys, 1987); Christopher R.

Browning, *Ordinary Men: Reserve Battalion 101 and the Final Solution in Poland* (New York: HarperCollins, 1992); Primo Levi, *The Drowned and the Saved* (New York: Summit Books, 1986); Daniel J. Goldhagen, *Hitler's Willing Executioners: Ordinary Germans and the Holocaust* (New York: Knopf, 1996); Lawrence L. Langer, *Preempting the Holocaust* (New Haven, CT: Yale University Press, 1998); Saul Friedlander, *Nazi Germany and the Jews: The Years of Persecution, 1933-1939, Vol. I* (New York: HarperPerennial, 1997); Michael Berenbaum and Abraham J. Peck, eds., *The Holocaust and History: The Known, the Unknown, the Disputed, and the Reexamined* (Bloomington: Indiana University Press, 1998), Omer Bartov, *Murder in Our Midst: The Holocaust, Industrial Killing, and Representation* (Oxford: Oxford University Press, 1996); and Tzvetan Todorov, *Facing the Extreme: Moral Life in the Concentration Camps.* Trans. Arthur Denner and Abigail Pollak (New York: Metropolitan Books, 1996).

4 A voluminous literature is growing up here, too. See, for example, Robert D. Enright and Jo Anna North, eds., *Exploring Forgiveness* (Madison: University of Wisconsin Press, 1998); Trudy Govier, *Dilemmas of Trust* (Kingston and Montreal: McGill-Queen's University Press, 1998); Donald Shriver, *An Ethic for Enemies: Forgiveness in Politics* (Oxford: Oxford University Press, 1995); Heather Strang and John Braithwaite, eds., *Restorative Justice and Civil Society* (Cambridge: Cambridge University Press, 2001); Michael L. Hadley, *The Spiritual Roots of Restorative Justice* (Albany: State University Press of New York, 2001); Erik Luna, *Reason and Emotion in Restorative Justice* (Wellington, NZ: Victoria University, 2000); Heather Strang and John Braithwaite, eds., *Restorative Justice: Philosophy to Practice* (Aldershot, UK: Ashgate, 2000); Mark S. Umbreit and Robert B. Coates, *Multicultural Implications of Restorative Justice* (Washington, DC: US Department of Justice, Office for Victims of Crimes, 2000); Susan Jacoby, *Wild Justice* (New York: Harper & Row, 1983); Herbert Lottman, *The People's Anger: Justice and Revenge in Post-Liberation France* (London: Hutchinson, 1996); and Trudy Govier, *Forgiveness and Revenge* (London: Routledge, 2002).

5 Andrew England, "Blame Clouds Burundi History," *The Washington Times*, September 27, 2001.

6 Cited by Roger W. Smith, "Human Destructiveness and Politics: The Twentieth Century As an Age of Genocide," in Walliman and Dobkowski, eds., *Genocide and the Modern Age: Etiology and Case Studies of Mass Death* (New York: Greenwood Press, 1987), 21.

7 David Chandler, "Coming to Terms with the Terror and History of Pol Pot's Cambodia (1975-1979)," in this volume.

8 Jean Bethke Elshtain, "Epilogue: Is There Room for Forgiveness in International Relations?" in *New Wine and Old Bottles: International Politics and Ethical Discourse* (Notre Dame, IN: University of Notre Dame Press, 1998), 40.

9 Manes Sperber, in *The Sunflower: On the Possibilities and Limits of Forgiveness* (rev. ed.), ed. Simon Wiesenthal (New York: Schocken Books, 1998), 246-50; 248.

10 Philip P. Pan, "Koizumi Tries to Assuage China," *The Washington Post*, October 9, 2001.
11 Ian Buruma, *The Wages of Guilt: Memories of War in Germany and Japan*. (Farrar Straus Giroux, 1994).
12 Desmond Tutu, in *The Sunflower: On the Possibilities and Limits of Forgiveness* (rev. ed.), ed. Simon Wiesenthal (New York: Schocken Books, 1998), 268.
13 See Istvan Deak, Jan T. Gross, and Tony Judt, eds., *The Politics of Retribution in Europe: World War II and Its Aftermath* (Princeton, NJ: Princeton University Press, 2000), vii-xii.
14 The fact that they continue to go wrong has been documented by David Gonzalez in "Human Rights Group Cites a Setback in Haiti," *The New York Times*, September 27, 2001.
15 Mark Mazower, *Dark Continent: Europe's Twentieth Century* (New York: Vintage Books, 1999), 8-9.
16 Elazar Barkan, *The Guilt of Nations: Restitution and Negotiating Historical Injustices* (New York: W.W. Norton, 2000), 310-12.
17 Barkan, 311-12.
18 Steven Erlanger, "The Serbs Ask a Chance to Judge Their Own Guilt," *The New York Times*, Week in Review, October 15, 2000.
19 Roger W. Smith, "Human Destructiveness and Politics," in Walliman and Dobkowski, eds., *Genocide and the Modern Age*, 21-39.
20 Cited by Tzvetan Todorov, in *The Sunflower: On the Possibilities and Limits of Forgiveness* (rev. ed.), ed. Simon Wiesenthal (New York: Schocken Books, 1998), 265.
21 Sue Dwyer, "Reconciliation for Realists," in this volume.
22 Phillip Gourevitch, talk given July 11, 2000 at Banff, Alberta.
23 Robert Waelder, *Progress and Revolution: A Study of the Issues of Our Age* (New York: International Universities Press, 1967), 116. Waelder cites Charles L. Sanford's contention: "The demonic view of history is...extremely immature, not to say irrational....The more mature tragic sense of life is held by relatively few people. It probably contributes little in the short run to the making of history, because, keyed to the understanding of human limitations rather than human potentiality, it is not aggressive. It transcends a simplistic moralism by seeing elements of good and evil intermixed in human character and events."
24 Ian Buruma, "The Joys and Perils of Victimhood," *The New York Review of Books* 46, April 8, 1999, 4-9.
25 Molly Moore and John Ward Anderson, "Turkey Warns of Retaliation if U.S. Makes Genocide Charge," *Washington Post Foreign Service*, October 6, 2000, A22.
26 John O'Sullivan, "Peace? Not in Our Time," *Chicago Sun-Times*, October 24, 2000.
27 "Kostunica Admits Yugoslav Genocide," *The Times* (London), October 24, 2000.

Overview

Michael R. Marrus

Can the past be forgiven? Can people who have been traumatized live with memory and each other again? What do they need to be healed? Our task in this volume is to seek a more informed sense of which strategies and approaches to reconciliation are being employed, how effective or problematic the strategies have proven to be in various contexts, and what ethnic and political issues arise from the use of these strategies.

Attempting answers, I draw on the field that I know best, which is the Holocaust, the destruction of European Jewry during the Second World War, widely recognized as the benchmark, a defining moment in the drama of good and evil. I want to emphasize that as I draw upon the history of the reaction to the Holocaust following the Second World War, I will limit myself to collectivities, peoples, societies, countries, nations, and civilizations, rather than referring to individuals. In doing so, I want to identify four different strategies or ways of reckoning with this particular catastrophe: political, legal, material, and cultural. Each of these operates, to one degree or another, on a therapeutic level often referred to as "coming to terms" with the Holocaust. What I want to discuss is what we mean by "coming to terms" in these four different contexts. In what follows I will offer some thoughts about each of them.

First, as to the political, I think it's extremely important to engage in the necessary and important work of comparison. We must recognize that with the destruction of European Jewry, great catastrophe that it was, we have nevertheless a quite remarkable and full acknowledgement of Ger-

Notes to overview are on p. 36.

man responsibility—or rather non-Communist German responsibility—
for the murder of European Jews, together with the attendant acknowledged obligation to make restitution. This did not come immediately, of
course, for Germans were not allowed to express themselves collectively,
for some time after the war. But there was a key step early on, hedged
though it was with qualifications, as to German culpability. It came from
none other than Chancellor Konrad Adenauer of West Germany, in his
speech to the Bundestag on September 27, 1951. "In the name of the German people," Adenauer said, "unspeakable crimes were committed, which
require moral and material restitution." (The word he used was *Wiedergutmachung.*) "These crimes concern damage to individuals as well as to Jewish property whose owners are no longer alive. The government of the
Federal Republic will support the rapid conclusion of a law regarding its
just implementation."

And so the government did, and the law was passed. The result produced a quite different set of circumstances than that which was obtained,
let us say, for the Roma people or for the Armenians, who still await a
comparable acknowledgement from the Turkish government of its political responsibility for the genocidal attacks upon them by the Turks in
1915. The action of the German government was extremely important,
qualified and unsatisfactory as it was in certain respects. Various German
personalities subsequently refined that acknowledgement. But it was
there. It was, moreover, articulated with extraordinary eloquence by the
German president Richard von Wiezsäcker, who made a speech to the
same Bundestag on May 8, 1985, on the fortieth anniversary of the end
of the Second World War. This is surely one of the most important German statements made on the Holocaust since the end of the war for its
degree of refinement and subtlety. Wiezsäcker, himself the son of a convicted war criminal, referred to the need for Germans "to look the truth
straight in the eye without embellishment or distortion." "At the root of
the tyranny of the Third Reich was Hitler's immeasurable hatred against
our Jewish compatriots." Anyone at the time who opened his eyes and ears
and sought information could not fail to notice that the Jews were being
deported. The nature and the scope of the destruction they faced may
have exceeded human imagination, but in reality there was, apart from the
crime itself, the attempt by too many people, including those of my generation, who were young and were not involved in planning the events
and then carrying them out not to take note of what was happening.

There were many ways of not burdening one's conscience, of shunning responsibility, looking away, keeping quiet." "When the unspeakable truth of the Holocaust became known at the end of the war, all too many claimed that we had not known anything about it or even suspected anything. There is no such thing as the guilt or innocence of an entire nation." Wiezsäcker made a critical distinction between guilt and responsibility: "Guilt is like innocence, not collective, but personal." But younger Germans did have a responsibility to keep alive the memories. Anyone who closes his eyes to the past is blind to the present. Whoever refuses to remember inhumanity is prone to new risks of infection. The Jewish nation remembers, and will always remember. "We seek reconciliation, and there can be no reconciliation without remembrance. Reconciliation with the Jewish nation had to pass through the memory of the Holocaust." Wiezsacker set a standard, I think, for political acknowledgement and, remarkably, perhaps with no small influence of his example, there has been acceleration in Germany of acknowledgements of various sorts, of apologies read into the public record.

In my own work I have followed especially closely the French apologies: apologies from the French government, from the Roman Catholic hierarchy, the doctors, professors, the police union, etc. Within the Catholic Church, Pope John Paul II has set a high standard for apologies. I am among those who have appreciated the recent document "We Remember," issued under the authority of the Vatican, which actually used the Hebrew word *teshuva* preferring its meaning, "repentance," to an apology. We have seen in recent years a great wave of apologies, leading many to think, with some acuteness and critical perception, that perhaps apologies are becoming cheap or superficial since they are being advanced by people who almost invariably had themselves no part in the wrongdoing.

The legal coming to terms with the Holocaust refers to the trials of perpetrators principally, and also to the trials of collaborators in the Holocaust. This was a significant impulse from 1945, from the time of the Nuremberg Trials before the International Military Tribunal, which first raised the issue of the European Jews in the postwar proceedings against Nazi war criminals. Indeed, tracing this process from its origins in 1945, I would like to identify five different kinds of such trials.

The first instance, of which there is only one example, is international, referring to the Nuremberg Trials, presided over by the four principal Allies—Great Britain, France, the Soviet Union, and the

United States. There were also trials by the various victorious powers in their own zones of occupation, as well as, third, trials by successor regimes—France, Belgium, the Netherlands, Eastern Europe, Romania, Hungary, Poland. Much less known were the trials of Jews by Jews: Jews accused of having been *Kapos*, of having supervised the oppression of fellow Jews; Jews who had roles in the Jewish Council—the *Judenrat*— or the Jewish police in the ghettos of Eastern Europe. The famous Kastner trial in Israel in the mid-1950s provided yet another example of trials of Jews by Jews. Finally, third-party proceedings against war criminals were held in Great Britain, France, Australia, and in the United States. Though each of these kinds of trials makes sense as part of the quest for justice following the Holocaust, their complexity and quality varied in many instances.

From a critical perspective, one can identify, along with the quest for justice, an additional expectation related to the outcome of these trials. Courts benefit from great prestige in Western, liberal societies; hence trials are seen as the vehicle by which the collectivity allocates responsibility for criminal actions, registers abhorrence for criminal actions, and explains criminal actions. The expectation is that the trials will represent history or will provide a kind of record or account. In reference to the subsequent proceedings after the international military court, Robert Kempner, one of the young prosecutors at the Nuremberg Trials said, "these trials are the greatest history seminar in the history of the world!" Kempner's understanding was that the trials would provide a lasting historical record and validate a historical understanding of the catastrophe that had befallen the Jewish people. However, despite good intentions there are frequently obstacles in the path of those goals. Here I offer five different kinds of trial obstacles—often huge obstacles—that arise in the course of these proceedings and frustrate and disappoint those who expected them to provide that kind of validation and historical account.

First of all, such trials provide not one coherent account but at least two—and often more coherent accounts—of what happened. There is the account of the prosecution and there is the account of the defence, which onlookers hear at the same time. According to Continental legal procedure, there are often many different accounts, as interested parties present their interpretations of a particular issue. And so the narrative account that emerges from such proceedings is complex, to say the least, and often highly conflicted.

Second, much of what happened, whether it is the big picture or whether it is crucial elements related to the crimes being described, cannot be presented at trials because of the rules of evidence or the focus of particular trials. Trials present, therefore, what appears to most of us as a highly truncated version of reality.

Third, as any historian knows, what emerges from the proceeding depends upon the questions asked. In trials, the questions are usually defined in an indictment, and indictments, as lawyers know, are framed in order to guide the prosecution, not to elicit the most complete and satisfactory historical accounts. Indictments depend upon a legal framework; they are defined by the availability of evidence, by a determination of what charges are most likely to result in convictions. Clearly, the trials directed in this manner are unlikely to yield the most comprehensive or satisfactory historical account.

Fourth, speaking as a historian, it seems to me that legal processes do not generally open the door to discussion and to issues of long-term causation, to comparisons, to connections with related phenomena—the very substance and stuff of historical accounts.

Finally, the judgements at the ends of trials are typically disappointing from the vantage point of those who anticipate a ringing declaration of the character, scope, and nature of these crimes. Legal judgements are (and how, often, can they not be?) legalistic, that is, limited to the legal questions, however important. Indeed they are vitally important to the questions of guilt or innocence. In short, my own sense is not to look to trials to validate our general understanding of the Holocaust or to promote historical explanations or historical understandings. I agree on this narrow point with Hannah Arendt, who wrote in her book *Eichmann in Jerusalem*[1] that the purpose of a trial is "to render justice and nothing else. Even the noblest of ulterior purposes can only distract from the law's main business: to weigh the charges brought against the accused, to render judgement and to mete out punishment."

Now I turn to the third way of reckoning, the material. I am referring, of course, to indemnification or to restitution. We had, as a result of the Holocaust, the commitment of Konrad Adenauer and his associates—however qualified, however insufficient, however inadequate. Accompanying the acceptance of political responsibility, Germany has, over the years, paid out the equivalent of $60 billion in reparations, both for the indemnification of individual Nazi victims as well as collective indemnification of the Jewish people. Of course there have been other forms of reparations and indemnification. Collaborationist governments have offered their own material reckoning. And now neutral governments, the Swiss most particularly, are on the line and in the news. However, all kinds of outstanding claims remain. The World Jewish Restitution Organization, together with local Jewish organizations, has outstanding claims, currently being debated and deliberated with Austria, Belarus, Belgium, Croatia, the Czech Republic, Estonia, France, Germany, Hungary, Italy, Latvia, Lithuania, Moldavia, Norway, Poland, Portugal, Romania, Russia, Serbia, Slovakia, Sweden, Switzerland, and Ukraine. The total amount of the claims runs into the billions of dollars. New kinds of claims are now coming on stream. Some claims relate to works of art; other claims relate to reparations for slave labour. There are claims against American companies whose former German subsidiaries are accused of involvement in slave labour, or otherwise assisting the German war machine. More recently, someone in Canada whose parents were sent to Auschwitz by train is bringing suit in the French courts against the French State Railway System. There are also new vehicles for restitution, such as class-action lawsuits. American politicians, seeking ethnic votes, have added their voices, as have lawyers seeking contingency fees.

While acknowledging the claims of justice, you will be correct in detecting my own sense of exasperation with some of these trends. There are certainly all kinds of divisions within the Jewish world about the appropriate course of action to take. Indeed, there seems to be nothing like this issue, this material reckoning, to promote and to exacerbate divisions. Who gets what? Jewish organizations are pitted against lawyers for individual claimants. Local Jewish interests oppose the World Jewish Congress and the World Jewish Restitution Organization. Individual claims clash with the New York-based Jewish Claims Conference, which was established in 1951 to channel reparations to Holocaust survivors. Still others offer a thoroughgoing critique to the effect that pursuing such claims will promote a kind of trivialization of the memory of the Holocaust. Put most crudely, there is a fear that, in the end, it will all be seen to boil down to money. "No people can present the world with an unlimited number of moral demands," says Efraim Zuroff of the Simon Wiesenthal Center, who urges that Jewish energies should go rather to bringing war criminals to justice. Israel Guttmann, the most senior Israeli historian of the Holocaust, agrees, but urges rather that Jews should concentrate upon historical analysis. "In principle," he writes, "restitution is just. But I'm worried that this demand will create the impression that our histori-cal account with Europe is associated with this one issue. We're talking about the destruction of a whole civilization."

I turn finally (I am opening up issues rather than closing them down or resolving them) to the cultural reckoning with the Holocaust. This is a huge, sprawling subject that extends from scholarship and the arts to Holocaust-related institutions. Let me offer a *tour d'horizon*, and begin with scholarship. I think that the quite extraordinary range of scholarship that we associate with the Holocaust provides a kind of benchmark in itself for how, through study and scientific historical analysis, one can come to terms with the catastrophe in a particular and measured, respon-sible way. And yet let us also recognize that this approach is quite recent. When I studied history in the late 1950s and early 1960s, the Holocaust did not appear in historical scholarship. One could study the history of Germany or the history of the Second World War without a word being spoken about the destruction of European Jewry. I would trace the begin-ning of the wave of historical scholarship to the early 1960s with the appearance of Raul Hilberg's book *The Destruction of European Jews*,[2] which probably remains the most important book ever written on the sub-ject, as well as to the controversy provoked about the same time by Han-nah Arendt's *Eichmann in Jerusalem*.[3] In the following decade, the 1970s, the scholarship began to flow. And flow it did, to the point that now I contend in my book *The Holocaust in History*[4] that the Holocaust has actually entered into the mainstream of historical understanding. You can no longer study Nazi Germany, as one once could, without fully coming to grips with the Holocaust, and so it is with the various collaborationist regimes all across Europe. So it is, for that matter, with the course of the Second World War—including the story of the anti-German Allies. So it is with the history of the Western Allies. As a historical subject, the Holo-caust has unquestionably "arrived."

Who among us can also doubt that the Holocaust has "arrived" in the popular media? It's all around us, in fact. Saul Friedlander has described a tendency toward kitsch in the portrayal of Nazism and the Holocaust—with all of the attendant vulgarization and popularization.[5] Where are we, one may ask, when Steven Spielberg becomes the principle interpreter of the Holocaust for much of the global community, much of which has only heard of the murder of European Jewry from his films? Who can deny the hazards of popularization that derive from the arrival of this theme into the popular media?

And then there are the monuments, the memorials, and the museums—expressions and institutional embodiments of collective memory. I think one has only to mention the topic to acknowledge that this is an area fraught with disagreement, controversy, and contention. What is the latest German debate about what is appropriate as a monument for the Holocaust? Few lay people can keep up with the disagreements, which are profound and overwhelming for most people who struggle to follow the many, often bitterly contentious arguments.

Much of the popularity of Holocaust themes was quite unexpected. The most unexpected of all, perhaps, is the relatively recent United States' Holocaust Memorial Museum. In the first six years it received twelve million visitors. The carpet wore out. Queues circle the building. Two million people a year visit this museum, and of the twelve million who have visited, we are reliably told that 8.6 million were non-Jews. A recent survey found that 94 percent of the visitors described their experience as very favourable. This is a reception administrators of other museums could only dream of. What does this mean that the Holocaust becomes a cultural icon of such extraordinary prominence?

Philip Gourevitch has quite rightly, it seems to me, called attention to the disturbing underside of this phenomenon. He describes watching boisterous groups of children going through the exhibits of terrible atrocities. "What does this mean in their experience? What kind of lasting effect will it have? I don't think we really know," he writes.[6]

Gourevitch describes disturbingly an aspect of all of this—one hesitates to even pronounce the word—its "trendiness." "At different moments in time," he claims, "particular historical events and personalities come to exert a special fascination on the public imagination." Today it is the Holocaust that is invoked; yesterday it might have been Napoleon. "Fashions in popular history invariably tell us more about our own times than about the piece of the past that has suddenly been turned to as a mirror. As Americans observe the bloody unravellings of the post-Cold War world, the Holocaust Museum provides a rhetorical exercise in bearing witness to dehumanization and mass murder from a seemingly safe distance." Gourevitch's point is that people can steep themselves in the most ghastly atrocities and come away with a sense of how extraordinarily evil people were then and how fantastic the suffering was of the

Jews then, but somehow derive from this, at least as his argument would seem to have it, that there is a kind of insulation that derives from this emphasis on the Holocaust.

To conclude: I think that in each of these ways of reckoning with the Holocaust—political or legal or material or cultural—there is an effort to construct out of this grievous wrong what is commonly called a collective memory. This is what the French sociologist Emile Durkheim called a collective conscience. The legal scholar Mark Osiel calls it "the stories a society tells about the momentous events in its history," speaking of "the events that most profoundly affect the lives of its members and most aroused their passions for long periods of time."[7] The construction of these collective memories seems to be an undoubted and important part of our culture. I think they do something for the victims and I think they do something for society.

For the victims there are two aspects, one looking in and one looking out. Looking outward, the victim group, that is the Jews, makes a claim upon society for a publicly validated acknowledgement of its suffering. Advancing such a claim seems to be, in itself, a very deep impulse. Related to this, I believe, is the quest to validate one's standing in society. I think this is what Jews and other groups that have been victimized are trying to do in creating this particular collective conscience. And looking inwardly, as Ian Buruma reflects in a way that makes a lot of sense to me, "can be a way of coming out, as it were, of nailing the colors of one's identity to the mast. The only way a new generation can be identified with the suffering of previous generations is for the suffering to be publicly acknowledged, over and over again."[8]

This process raises important questions for society as a whole, as well as for particular groups. I see some obvious benefits, but there are some obvious warnings for all of us. The benefit, of course—and perhaps it has been cited so often that we take it for granted—is the repetition of the universal lesson: never again. To steep people in the memory of the Jewish catastrophe is a way, if not to assure, then at least to register a resolve that it will never happen again. Will this work? The jury is still out, of course. Buruma, at least, leaves us with a warning. The warning comes from the emphasis within groups to focus on their suffering as a badge of authenticity. "This tendency to identify authenticity in communal suffering," he writes, "actually impedes understanding among people, for feelings can only be expressed but not discussed or argued about. This cannot result in mutual understanding, but only a mute acceptance of whatever people wish to say about themselves, or in violent confrontation."[9]

Have we heard this before? I certainly have, as someone who lectures on the Holocaust. Let me leave it to you, to those who know particular cases much better than I do myself, to judge how salutary it is to anchor identity in suffering. I'm not sure what to draw from this. People have written about competition among victim groups, in which one group after another seeks to anchor its identify in its particular suffering and to promote its experience of victimization as being more horrible than the next, more worthy of study, more important to get into the curriculum—unique. It is a baneful trend.

Rabbi Leon Klenicki, who is deeply involved in Christian-Jewish dialogue reconciliation uses the expression the "triumphalism of pain." *The triumphalism of pain.* This is perhaps too negative a note on which to end, but perhaps a negative note is appropriate to this ghastly subject in which some people see too many rays of hope.

Notes

1 Hannah Arendt, *Eichmann in Jerusalem: A Report on the Banality of Evil* (New York: Viking, 1963).
2 Raul Hilberg, *The Destruction of European Jews* (London: Allen, 1961).
3 Hannah Arendt, *Eichmann in Jerusalem: A Report on the Banality of Evil* (New York: Viking, 1963).
4 Michael R. Marrus, *The Holocaust in History* (Toronto: Lester & Orpen Dennys, 1987).
5 Saul Friedlander, *Memory, History, and the Extermination of the Jews of Europe* (Bloomington: Indiana University Press, 1993).
6 Philip Gourevitch, "What They Saw at the Holocaust Museum," *New York Times Magazine*, February 12, 1995.
7 Mark Osiel, in Ian Buruma, "The Joys and Perils of Victimhood," *The New York Review of Books* 46, April 8, 1999, 4-9.
8 Ibid.
9 Ibid.

PERSPECTIVES AND
APPROACHES

Reckoning with Past Wrongs: A Normative Framework

David A. Crocker

Many nations and some international bodies today are deciding what, if anything, they should do about past violations of internationally recognized human rights. These abuses—which include war crimes, crimes against humanity, genocide, rape, and torture—may have been committed by a government against its own citizens (or those of other countries), by its opponents, or by combatants in a civil or international armed conflict.[1] Some of these societies are making a transition to democracy and some are not.

The challenge of "transitional justice," a term increasingly used, is how incomplete and fledgling democracies, such as South Africa, Guatemala, South Korea, the Philippines, Argentina, Chile, or El Salvador, should respond (or should have responded) to past evils, without undermining its new democratic regime or jeopardizing its prospects for equitable and long-term development. This focus on new democracies has much to recommend it, for it is important that new democratic institutions, where they exist, be protected and consolidated, and that reckoning with an evil past not imperil them.

However, nations other than new democracies also have occasion to decide what they "should do about a difficult past,"[2] and their choices are of intrinsic moral significance as well as relevance for new democracies. For present purposes, countries can be roughly divided into three types: post-conflict societies, such as Bosnia, Cambodia, and Rwanda, which aspire to make a democratic transition but are at present taken up with

---

Notes to chapter 1 are on pp. 58-63.

ongoing security issues following ethnic strife and massacres; authoritarian and conflict-ridden societies, such as Yugoslavia, Indonesia, and Peru, in which both an end to civil conflict and the beginning of democratization may depend on negotiated agreements between the government and its opposition with respect to treatment of human rights violators; and mature democracies, such as the United States, Germany, Japan, France, and Switzerland, which are reckoning with past evils such as slavery, war crimes, collaboration with the Nazi extermination efforts, or failures to prevent human rights abuses.[3] The fashionable focus on new democracies tends to limit what such societies may learn from other attempts to reckon with past rights abuses and to diminish the moral challenge facing non-democratic and mature democracies as they reckon with an unsavoury past.

Even in the context of societies making a democratic transition, the term "transitional justice" may be misleading. This is because, like the term "accountability," transitional justice singles out one morally urgent feature from a complex that has many pressing goals or obligations.

Means and Ends

Societies and international bodies have employed many means in reckoning with human rights abuses that a prior regime or its opponents have committed. Many discussions assume that there are only two possible responses: trials and punishment or forgetting the past. For example, upon coming out of hiding and surrendering to the Cambodian government in late December 1998, Khieu Samphan, a former top leader of the Khmer Rouge, urged Cambodians to "let bygones be bygones." During its control of Cambodia from 1975 to 1979, the Khmer Rouge is estimated to have killed between 1.5 and 1.7 million people, including most of the educated class, and to have destroyed much of Cambodian culture. Although he was to backtrack a few days later, Cambodian Prime Minister Hun Sen initially agreed with Khieu Samphan and remarked that Khieu Samphan and another high-placed defector, Nuon Chea, should be welcomed back "with bouquets of flowers, not with prisons and handcuffs" and that "we should dig a hole and bury the past and look ahead to the 21st century with a clean slate."[4]

When trials are judged as impractical and forgetting as undesirable, truth commissions have been advocated (and in some twenty countries employed) as a third way. However, in addition to these three tools, there are a variety of other measures, such as international (ad hoc or permanent) criminal tribunals; social shaming and banning of perpetrators from public office ("lustration"); public access to police records; public apology or memorials to victims; reburial of victims; compensation to victims or their families; literary and historical writing; and blanket or individualized amnesty (legal immunity from prosecution).

To decide among the diverse tools, as well as to fashion, combine, and sequence them, a society, sometimes in cooperation with international institutions, ideally should (1) consider what lessons it might learn from other societies; (2) examine its own capabilities and limitations; and (3) set clear objectives for its efforts. The first task is best accomplished by those who will be key actors in their nation's attempts to reckon with an evil past. The second responsibility most obviously falls on historians, social scientists, and legal scholars who are adept at identifying a society's distinctive historical legacies, institutional strengths and weaknesses, and political constraints. The last task, that of identifying goals and standards of evaluation, must be taken up by philosophers and applied ethicists, but not by these alone; citizens, political leaders, policy analysts, and social scientists also have a responsibility to make moral judgements, engage in ethical analysis, and set forth ethically based recommendations.

Although philosophers and other ethicists have not entirely ignored the topic of reckoning with past wrongs, it is legal scholars, social scientists, policy analysts, and activists who have made the most helpful contributions. It is understandable that much of the work on transitional justice has been of an empirical and strategic nature. Fledgling democracies need effective institutions and strategies for addressing prior human rights violations; establishing such arrangements and policies requires a grasp of what works and why. Legal and human rights scholars have focused on what national and international law permits and requires with respect to prosecuting gross human rights violations.[5] They have also reported and assessed the progress of the Bosnian and Rwandan international criminal tribunals, crafted the terms of an agreement on a permanent international criminal tribunal, and argued for the implementation of that agreement.[6] Investigative reporters have described what particular countries and the international community have done and failed to do in their efforts to reckon with past human rights abuses.[7] Principal actors or advisers have written about their experiences and assessed their achievements.[8] Historians and social scientists have addressed the issue of why certain countries decided on particular approaches and the motivations for and consequences of those choices.[9]

However, there are also large and pressing ethical questions. How should "success" with respect to reckoning with past wrongs be conceived? Are the ends that societies seek to achieve and the means they adopt to achieve them consistent and morally justified? Questions such as these should not be overlooked or swamped by legal or strategic considerations.

To be sure, moral concerns are often implicit in the existing work on transitional justice, and moral norms of various kinds underlie the institutions and policies that societies have already established to reckon with an evil past. Indeed, one task of ethical analysis with respect to past human rights abuses is to identify and clarify those operative values for which reasonable justification can be given. Michael Walzer's attempt to fashion a new moral theory (with historical illustrations) concerning just and unjust wars between nations can be adapted to the forging of a normative framework to assess what should be done when a society reckons with human rights violations.[10]

When political actors or scholars do explicitly pose ethical questions with respect to addressing past wrongs, they usually do so in relation to only one goal, such as penal justice, truth, or reconciliation, or one tool, such as trials, truth commissions, or amnesties.[11] However, the full range of conceptual and moral issues underlying the many ends and means of transitional justice has not received the sustained analysis it deserves.[12]

Cross-Cultural Goals

To fashion and evaluate any particular tool to reckon with past evil in a particular society and to combine it with other tools requires not only knowledge of that society's historical legacies and current capabilities but also a grasp of morally important goals and standards of assessment. What goals and norms should be used, where should they come from, and how might they be promoted? In recent conference papers and writings, I have formulated eight goals that have emerged from worldwide moral deliberation on transitional justice and may serve as a useful framework when particular societies deliberate about what they are trying to achieve and how they should go about doing so.[13]

In the present essay I employ these eight goals to identify and clarify the variety of ethical issues that emerge in reckoning with past wrongs, widespread agreements about resolving each issue, leading options for more robust solutions of each issue, and ways to weigh or trade off the norms when they conflict. My aim is both to show that there are crucial moral aspects in reckoning with the past and to clarify, criticize, revise, apply, and diffuse eight moral norms. The goals that I propose are not a recipe or "one-size-fits-all" blueprint but rather a framework for exploration by which societies confronting past atrocities can decide—through cross-cultural and critical dialogue—what is most important to accomplish and what are the morally best ways to do so.

Before setting forth morally urgent ends, two opposing (but dialectically related) goals should be ruled out: vengeance, and disregarding the past in favour of the future. I will not repeat my arguments set forth elsewhere that countries should reject these goals.[14] Two remarks about both goals and a new example about implementing them, however, are in order. First, various tools may be employed to realize each of these morally undesirable ends. Vengeance can be carried out privately (by individuals or groups) or officially (in reprisals and kangaroo courts). A nation can overcome an evil past and attempt to move to a better future by forgiving and forgetting (letting bygones be bygones), outright denial (for instance, that the Holocaust occurred), or rationalization of the past as a necessary evil. Second, attempts to realize each of these goals often lead—either precipitously or eventually—to efforts to achieve the other: the side that has wreaked revenge often attempts to protect itself from counter-revenge by calling for "forgive and forget"; silence about the past may incite revenge for both the original act and its burial.

Both tendencies are illustrated by the case of the thousands of atrocities committed by Croat Nazis (Ustashi) against Serbs, Jews, and Gypsies during the Second World War, especially in the Jasenovac concentration camp. There is good reason to believe that the breakup of Yugoslavia and the Serb violation of Croat rights during the war between Croatia and Serbia in 1991-92 can be partially explained (not justified) by the genocidal practices of the Croats during the Second World War and by the failure of postwar Croats and the Tito government to hold either investigations or trials. Serbian philosopher Svetozar Stojanovic observes:

> The communist victor [Tito] in Yugoslavia never seriously looked into Ustashi genocide as an issue or a problem. Instead of carrying out de-Nazification through education...he lim-

ited himself to the liquidation of captured Ustashis. It is true that Pavelic and the other main criminals had, however, fled abroad, and the new authorities did not endeavour to organize their trial (at least in absentia) like the one in Nürnberg, although they more than deserved it. The karst pits into which Serbs were thrown alive by Ustashis in Herzegovina remained concreted over, and their relatives were not allowed to remove the bodies and bury them. These "concreted pits" have become a metaphor for the communist illusion that enforced silence is the best way to deal with terrible crimes among nations. Perhaps that was why, not only due to his personal nonchalance, Tito never visited Jasenovac.[15]

Goal 1: Truth

To meet the challenge of reckoning with past atrocities, a society should investigate, establish, and publicly disseminate the truth about them. What Alex Boraine calls "forensic truth," or "hard facts,"[16] is information about whose moral and legal rights were violated, by whom, how, when, and where. Given the moral significance of individual accountability, the identity of individual perpetrators, on the one hand, and of moral heroes who sacrificed personal safety to prevent violations, on the other, should be brought to light.

There is also what has been called "emotional truth"—knowledge concerning the psychological and physical impact on victims and their loved ones from rights abuses and the threat of such abuses. The constant threat of such abuses, especially in contexts of physical deprivation, can itself cause overwhelming fear and, thereby, constitute a rights violation. David Rohde makes this point clearly in his agonizing account of the aftermath of the takeover of Muslim Srebrenica by General Ratko Mladic and his Bosnian Serb forces:

> During the trek [the "Marathon of Death" in which thousands of male Bosnian non-combatants and a few soldiers fled Srebrenica], it quickly became clear that the threat to the column was as much psychological as it was physical. Shells abruptly whizzed overhead. Gunfire erupted with no warning. Corpses littered their route. A Serb mortar had landed ahead of them at 1 p.m. and killed five men. A human stomach and intestines lay across the green grass just below the intact head and torso of a man in his twenties. Mevludin [Oric, a Bosnian Muslim

soldier] had seen such things before; the others hadn't. The image would slowly eat at their minds. Some men were already saying it was hopeless. It was better to kill yourself, they said, than be captured by the Serbs.[17]

Fear also had devastating consequences for the Muslim women and children, herded together in Srebrenica, whose husbands and fathers were taken away and tortured during the night of July 12, 1995:

> She [Srebrenica resident Camila Omanovic] could see what was happening around her, but it was the sounds that haunted her. Screams suddenly filled the night. At one point, she heard bloodcurdling cries coming from the hills near the base. She later decided the Serbs must be playing recordings to terrorize them. Women gave birth or cried as their husbands were taken away. Men wailed and called out women's names....Panic would grip the crowd. People would suddenly rise up and rush off in one direction. Then there would be silence until the cycle of screams and panic started all over again. Nearly hallucinating, Camila could not sleep....But it was the fear that didn't let her sleep. A fear more intense than anything she had ever felt. A fear that changed her forever.[18]

Finally, there is less individualized and more general truth, such as plausible interpretations of what caused neighbours to brutalize neighbours, governments (and their opponents) to incite, execute, or permit atrocities, and other countries or international bodies to fail to act in time or in the right way.[19]

Knowledge about the past is important in itself. One way to make this point is to say that victims and their descendants have a moral right to know the truth about human rights abuses. Moreover, without reasonably complete truth, none of the other goals of transitional justice (to be discussed presently) are likely to be realized. Appropriate sanctions are impossible without reasonable certainty about the identity of perpetrators and the nature of their involvement. Public acknowledgement must refer to specific occurrences, while reparations presuppose the accurate identification of victims and the kinds of harm they suffered. If reconciliation in any of its several senses is to take place, there must be some agreement about what happened and why. Former enemies are unlikely to be reconciled if what counts as lies for one side are verities for the other.

Yet truth, while important, sometimes must be traded off against other goods. Since the truth can harm people as well as benefit them, sometimes it is better that some facts about the past remain unknown. By deepening ethnic hostility, too much or the wrong kind of truth might impede democratization and reconciliation. Disclosures that satisfy a victim's need to know may incite violence when publicly revealed. The most effective methods for obtaining the truth might violate the rule of law, personal privacy, or the right not to incriminate oneself. Or such methods might be too costly in relation to other goals. Some truths about the past would be irrelevant to reckoning with past injustices. The general point is that apparently justified efforts in limiting the pursuit or the disclosure of truth imply the need to balance truth against other goals.

Even given that truth is one important good that can be traded off in relation to other goods, many issues remain to be resolved. First, can one plausibly argue that there is one truth about the past and, if so, how should we understand this ideal in relation to the frequently diverse views about the content of this truth? How should a truth commission address diverse interpretations of the past when they emerge in the commission's work or in public reaction to it? My own view is that disagreements should be reduced as much as possible and those that remain should be clearly identified as topics for further public deliberation.[20] Second, to whom and at what cost should the truth be made known? Third, how should we assess truth commissions and other investigative bodies, investigative reporting and historical writing, national trials, international criminal tribunals, and the granting of public access to police files? Given their different standards of evidence and proof, how much and what sort of truth can be reasonably expected from each of these approaches? What are the merits of each method both in reducing disagreement and accommodating or respecting remaining differences? To what extent, if any, might a truth commission impede rather than promote international and domestic judicial determination of individual guilt and innocence? What ethical issues emerge from the various methods of collecting and interpreting information about past abuses?[21]

My general belief, which I cannot develop or defend in this essay, is that there are many different but complementary ways of obtaining reasonable knowledge about the past and that no one means should be overemphasized. Trials, for example, owing to subpoena power and adversarial cross-examination, are usually superior to truth commissions in establishing truths relevant to the guilt or innocence of particular individuals; truth commissions tend to be better than trials in describing the larger institutional patterns contributing to rights violations; historical investigations— often with the advantage of fuller documentation, more ample opportunities to check sources, and greater hindsight than is possible in either trials or truth commissions—are best at sifting evidence and evaluating explanatory hypotheses. Not only can these tools complement each other but each one can make use of others. Truth commissions often make recommendations to legal proceedings. Historians provide expert testimony in trials and sometimes are members of truth commissions. Investigative reporters and forensic experts have been enormously important in uncovering atrocities and dispelling rumours and false propaganda.[22]

Goal 2: Public Platform for Victims

In any society attempting to reckon with an evil past, victims or their families should be provided with a platform to tell their stories and have their testimony publicly acknowledged. When victims are able to give their accounts and when they receive sympathy for their suffering, they are respected as persons with dignity rather than—as before—treated with contempt. This respect enables those once humiliated as victims to become empowered as citizens. Those once reduced to screams or paralyzing fear now may share a personal narrative. The public character of the platform is essential, for secrecy about human rights abuses, enforced through violence and intimidation, was one of the conditions that made possible extensive campaigns of terror.

Among the unresolved questions that remain is the weight to be given to this goal when the public character of testimony would put former victims, perpetrators, or reporters at substantial risk. After disclosing to the press that the Argentine military did indeed kill some suspected "subversives" and their children by pushing them from airplanes into the sea, a military officer was brutally attacked and his face carved with the initials of the reporters to whom he revealed the truth. Another problem surfaces when a victim's public testimony is not followed up by efforts to heal wounds and compensate for harms.[23] Finally, unless there is independent investigation or cross-examination of accusers, alleged perpetrators may be treated unfairly and due process compromised.

48 · DAVID A. CROCKER

Goal 3: Accountability and Punishment

Ethically defensible treatment of past wrongs requires that those individuals and groups responsible for past crimes be held accountable and receive appropriate sanctions or punishment. Punishment may range from the death penalty, imprisonment, fines, international travel restrictions, and the payment of compensation to economic sanctions on an entire society and public shaming of individuals and prohibitions on their holding public office.

Many questions about responsibility and punishment remain to be answered. How, for example, can accountability be explained and fairly assigned? How should we understand the degrees and kinds of responsibility with respect to the authorization, planning, "middle management," execution, provision of material support for, and concealment of, atrocities? Consider also journalist Bill Berkeley's observation about a Hutu official found guilty (by the International Tribunal for Rwanda) of "nine counts of genocide, crimes against humanity, and war crimes, including rape":

> Jean-Paul Akayesu was neither a psychopath nor a simpleton. He was not a top figure like the former defense minister, Theonoste Bagasora, Rwanda's Himmler, who is now in custody [of the International Tribunal for Rwanda] in Arusha, nor a lowly, illiterate, machete-wielding peasant. He was, instead, the link between the two: an archetype of the indispensable middle management of genocide. He personified a rigidly hierarchical society and culture of obedience, without which killing on such a scale would not have been possible.[24]

Should those who actually commit (minor) abuses be ignored or pardoned in favour of holding their superiors accountable, or should the moral guilt and cumulative impact of those who "merely" followed orders also be recognized? What is needed is a theory—relevant to judging past rights abusers—that identifies those conditions that make an agent more or less blameworthy (and praiseworthy). Recent work suggests that a perpetrator's moral guilt is proportional to what he knew (or could reasonably know) and when he knew it; how much freedom (from coercion) or power (in a chain of command) he had to commit or prevent evil; and what personal risks he ran in performing or forgoing a rights violation.

For which crimes should people be held accountable when a country or the international community is reckoning with past evil?[25] Is it morally justifiable to hold people accountable either for an act that was not illegal at the time it was committed or for one that a government subsequently pardons?[26] Further, an ethics of reckoning with past wrongs would address violations such as war crimes, crimes against humanity, genocide, torture, and rape. This list implies both that Chile erred in restricting its official truth commission to investigating only killings and disappearances and that the International Criminal Tribunal for the former Yugoslavia achieved moral progress when it convicted persons of rape in the wars in Croatia and Bosnia.

Should the list of human rights violations be extended further than "physical security rights"? Should it include civil and political rights, such as the right of free speech and the rights not to be discriminated against on the basis of race, ethnicity, religion, or gender, and economic rights, such as the right not to be hungry or the right to employment? I return to this issue when I address what long-term economic and political development should aim for so as to protect against a recurrence of past atrocities.

Two additional questions with respect to accountability must be addressed. How should "sins of commission" be morally compared to "sins of omission"? How does the United Nations' failure to bomb the Serbs attacking Srebrenica in July 1995 compare with the atrocities committed by the Serbian forces? To what extent are groups—particular police units, political parties, religious bodies, professional associations (e.g., of doctors or lawyers), independence movements (e.g., the Kosovo Liberation Army), governments, and alliances (e.g., the UN, NATO)—and not solely individuals responsible for rights violations?[27] Without a suitably nuanced and graded view of accountability or responsibility, a society falls into the morally objectionable options of, on the one hand, whitewash or social amnesia[28] or, on the other hand, the demonization of all members of an accused group.

Similar questions may be asked with respect to sanctions, whether criminal (punishment), civil, or non-legal (social shaming, individual lustration, or economic sanctions on an entire society). What types of sanctions are appropriate for what violations, and on what bases? Can justice be achieved through social shaming and moral censure rather than imprisonment? If trials and legal punishments are to be pursued, what purposes can or should they serve? Should a theory of criminal punishment include a retributive element and, if so, how should it be understood, and can retribution be distinguished from revenge?

Legal philosophers and scholars who have addressed reckoning with past political wrongs, such as Carlos Nino and Jaime Malamud-Goti, have tended to reject retributivism in favour of a deterrence or rehabilitation approach.[29] Retributivism, however, is having something of a revival, and I believe that it captures some important intuitions about penal justice. One task facing ethicists is to consider which retributive theory is best in itself and in reckoning with past atrocities. This inquiry would also consider whether the most reasonable approach to punishment would be a "mixed theory" in which a retributive principle, however understood, is coupled with other justifications or functions of punishment, such as protection, deterrence, rehabilitation, and moral education.[30]

Goal 4: Rule of Law

As they reckon with past wrongs, democracies—whether new or mature—should comply with the rule of law, and societies (or their democratic oppositions) that aspire to become democratic should lay the groundwork now for eventual rule of law. The rule of law is a critical part of Nuremberg's complex legacy and is important for any society dealing with an evil past. I here follow David Luban's analysis of rule of law, which itself draws on Lon Fuller.[31]

The rule of law includes respect for due process, in the sense of procedural fairness, publicity, and impartiality. Like cases must be treated alike, and private revenge must be prohibited. Rule of law is especially important in a new and fragile democracy bent on distinguishing itself from prior authoritarianism, institutionalized bias, or the "rule of the gun."

Again, however, there is an ongoing debate on what rule of law should mean and how it should be valued in relation to other goals. Can "victor's justice" be avoided and legal standards applied impartially to both sides in a former conflict? If so, at what cost? Can those suspected of rights abuses justifiably be convicted when their acts—even though prohibited by international law—were permitted by local law, covered by amnesty laws, or performed in obedience to higher orders? In what way, if any, does the ideal of procedural fairness apply to truth commissions, when alleged perpetrators have no right to cross-examine their accusers? (In South Africa, for example, an investigative arm of the TRC determined the reliability of all testimony—whether by victims, alleged perpetrators, or those seeking amnesty.) What if violations of due process result in fuller disclosures or more accurate assignment of responsibility?

Some advocates of due process, sceptical that victor's justice can be avoided, contend that the only ethically justified way to reckon with past political wrongs is to bury the past and move on to a better future.[32] But rule of law, like other ideals, is capable of more or less institutional embodiment. Safeguards fairly protecting both defendants and victims have been developed in local and national jurisdictions and in jurisdictional decisions. Upon learning that one British Law Lord had failed to disclose a relationship to the human rights group Amnesty International, the British Law Lords set aside their initial decision to permit Pinochet's extradition to Spain to stand trial on charges of genocide and other rights abuses. The Pinochet case also shows the lack of both international and Chilean consensus on the issue of when, if ever, a court in one country has the moral or legal right to prosecute alleged human rights violators who are citizens or (former) leaders of other countries. Apart from the question of its impact on Chile's development achievements, international and Chilean opinion is divided about whether Chile's sovereignty would have been violated if Pinochet had been brought to justice in a foreign country.[33] This question cannot be answered merely by appealing to international law and therefore requires moral reflection, for international law points in different directions and is itself evolving in relation to the Pinochet case.

The International Criminal Tribunals for both Rwanda and the former Yugoslavia have slowly developed and improved the fairness of their procedures. An enormous challenge in implementing the plan for a permanent international criminal court will be to devise fair procedures, including procedures for determining whether international or national courts have jurisdiction.

Goal 5: Compensation to Victims

Compensation, restitution, or reparation, in the form of income, property, medical services, or educational and other opportunities, should be paid to individuals and groups whose rights have been violated. One way of reckoning with past wrongs is by "righting" them—by restoring victims to something approaching their status quo ante.

But if compensation is pursued, pressing questions abound. Who should provide the compensation? Is it fair to use general taxes, when arguably many citizens were not responsible for violations? Or does mere citizenship in a nation that violated rights imply liability? Do German (and

US) corporations that used slave labour during the Second World War owe compensation to the victims or their survivors? What moral obligations, if any, do foreign governments and international civil society have in making reparations to victims of rights abuses? Might requiring guilty perpetrators to provide reparations to their victims be a means for punishing perpetrators or promoting reconciliation between violator and victim?

What form should reparation take and how should compensatory amounts be decided? Is compensation more justified in the form of cash, giving the victim the freedom to decide on its use, or as goods and services related to basic needs? Should compensation be the same for all, even though victims suffered in different degrees and ways, have different numbers of dependents, and have differential access to services depending on where they live? Given the other goals of reckoning with past wrongs, what portion of public resources should be devoted to compensatory justice? What should be done about those victims (or their descendants) the nature or extent of whose injuries—whether physical or psychological—does not become apparent until years after their rights have been violated?

Should groups—for instance, specific Mayan villages in Guatemala or Muslim villages in Bosnia's Drina Valley—as well as individuals be recipients? Is South Africa justified in considering public memorials, such as museums and monuments or days of remembrance, "symbolic compensation" for damage done to the entire South African society?[34]

Recent events suggest that nations and the international community are beginning to answer these questions. Following Chile's example, South Africa is implementing a nuanced "reparation and rehabilitation policy" that defends reparation on both moral ("restoration of dignity") and legal grounds and provides several types of both individual and communal reparation. Individuals are compensated both through monetary packages that take into account severity of harm, number of dependents, and access to social services and through services such as reburials and providing of headstones.

There is widespread approval of recent agreements to compensate Holocaust victims and those who worked as slave labourers for German companies during the Second World War. Early in January 1999, two Swiss banks—but not the Swiss government—signed an agreement for $1.25 billion in payments to resolve all class action suits and individual claims against the banks. (To be sure, some Swiss claim that they are being unfairly singled out.) The fund will compensate Holocaust victims for a variety of harms, including the loss of bank deposits and insurance policies and the looting of assets by the Nazis.[35] Similarly, the German government has agreed to set up a "compensation fund" (the Remembrance, Responsibility and the Future fund) of $1.7 billion, to be financed by German banks and other corporations (and perhaps by the government), to compensate Holocaust survivors for the companies' role in stealing assets, financing the building of the Auschwitz concentration camp, or making use of slave labour.[36] While these agreements are also prudent ways for the banks and companies to terminate the legal claims against them, the basic principle of the agreements reflects considered judgements about compensatory justice. As German Chancellor Gerhard Schröder remarked, the fund is to fulfill "the moral responsibility of German firms with regard to such issues as forced labourers, Aryanization and other injustice during the Nazi regime." These cases illustrate "the quest," as journalist Roger Cohen puts it, "to find a balance between remembrance and forward-looking themes."[37]

Goal 6: Institutional Reform and Long-term Development

An emerging democracy fails to make a sustainable transition unless it identifies the causes of past abuses and takes steps to reform the law and basic institutions—government, economic life, and civil society—in order to reduce the possibility that such violations will be repeated. More generally, reckoning with past political wrongs requires that societies be oriented to the future as well as to the past and present; they must take steps to remedy what caused human rights violations and protect against their recurrence. Basic institutions include the judiciary, police, military, land tenure system, tax system, and the structure of economic opportunities. One temptation in post-conflict or post-authoritarian societies is to permit euphoria—which comes with the cessation of hostilities and the launching of a new democracy—to pre-empt the hard work needed to remove the fundamental causes of injustice and guard against their repetition.

In both Guatemala and South Africa, for example, among the fundamental causes of repression and human rights abuses were racism and deep disparities in economic and political power. A society, whether it already is or whether it aspires to be democratic, must try to remove such fundamental causes of human rights abuses, and to do so in a way that will consolidate its democracy and promote equitable development in the future.

Questions remain, however, with respect to how democratic consolidation and economic development should be conceived. Are free and fair elections sufficient (or necessary) for the former?[38] Are increasing rates of per capita GNP necessary or sufficient for the latter? What should be the fundamental goals of economic and social development?[39] How might past injustices be addressed such that democratic and just development may be promoted and protected? What role, for example, might compensatory transfers to victims play in increasing social equity? When reckoning with past injustices does not coincide with or contribute to ameliorating present ones, how much should be spent on the former at the expense of the latter? Development ethicists should join scholars of transitional justice to explore the links between addressing past wrongs and advancing future rights.

Goal 7: Reconciliation

A society (or an international community) seeking to surmount its conflictual or repressive past should aim to reconcile former enemies. There are, however, at least three meanings of reconciliation, ranging from "thinner" to "thicker" conceptions. In the most minimal account, which almost everyone agrees is at least part of what should be meant by the term, reconciliation is nothing more than "simple coexistence,"[40] in the sense that former enemies comply with the law instead of killing each other. Although this modus vivendi is certainly better than violent conflict, transitional societies can and arguably should aim for more: while former enemies may continue to disagree and even to be adversaries, they must not only live together non-violently but also respect each other as fellow citizens. Mark J. Osiel calls this kind of reconciliation "liberal social solidarity,"[41] while Amy Gutmann and Dennis Thompson term it "democratic reciprocity."[42] Among other things, this implies a willingness to hear each other out, to enter into a give and take about matters of public policy, to build on areas of common concern, and to forge principled compromises with which all can live. The process of reconciliation, so conceived, may help prevent a society from lapsing back into violence as a way to resolve conflict.

More robust conceptions of reconciliation have sometimes been attributed to the truth commissions of Chile and South Africa—reconciliation as forgiveness, mercy (rather than justice), a shared comprehensive vision, mutual healing, or harmony.[43] (Both of these commissions include the word "reconciliation" in their name.) Given the depth of hostility between past opponents and objections to coercing mutuality or contrition, these thicker conceptions of reconciliation are more difficult to defend than the thinner notions. An essential task of the ethics of transitional justice is to consider the advantages and disadvantages of going beyond the first or second conceptions of reconciliation to some version of the third notion.[44]

Goal 8: Public Deliberation

Any society reckoning with past atrocities should aim, I believe, to include public spaces, debate, and deliberation in its goals, institutions, and strategies. It is unlikely that in any given society there will be full agreement about the aims and means for dealing with past abuses. And, even if there were agreement, trade-offs would have to be made. All good things do not always go together; sometimes achieving or even approximating one end will come at the expense of (fully) achieving another. Legal sanctions against former human rights violators can imperil a potential or fragile democracy in which the military responsible for the earlier abuses still wields social and political power. In order to protect witnesses or secure testimony from alleged perpetrators, a truth commission's interrogation of witnesses or alleged perpetrators sometimes may have to take place behind closed doors. Testimony by victims and confessions by perpetrators may worsen relations among former enemies, at least in the short run.[45] What is spent on a truth commission or on high-profile trials and punishments will not be available to eradicate infrastructural causes (and effects) of rights violations. A truth commission's exchange of truth for amnesty may preclude achieving penal justice. What can be aspired to, especially but not exclusively in a new democracy, is that disagreements about ends, trade-offs, and means will be reduced if not eliminated through public deliberation—both national and international—that permits a fair hearing for all and promotes both morally acceptable compromises and tolerance of remaining differences.[46] This public dialogue may be one of the ingredients in or conditions for social reform that replaces a culture of impunity with a culture of human rights. In non-democratic Cambodia, for example, many citizens are disclosing what they suffered under Khmer Rouge tyranny, debating what should be done, and agreeing which Khmer leaders should be tried:

Countless unburdenings…are taking place among Cambodians today as the country seems to be embarking, spontaneously, on a long-delayed national conversation about its traumatic past.…The comments also suggest an emerging political assertiveness among people better informed and more aware of their rights.…The seemingly near-unanimous view is that Khmer Rouge leaders should be put on trial, if only to determine who is really to blame for the country's suffering—and even if any convictions are followed by an amnesty.…With popular emotions stirring, he [Kao Kim Hourn of the Cambodian Institute for Cooperation and Peace] said, "internal pressure on the government has begun to build up." He added: "National Reconciliation at all costs? Bury the past? Forgive and forget? No. I don't think that is the case now."…Despite the violent power politics that has persistently stunted the establishment of democracy and human rights, a fledgling civil society has begun to emerge, addressing everything from education to flood control.[47]

Contextualizing Goals and Tools

Although each of the eight goals specified above has prescriptive content, each also allows considerable latitude in devising policies sensitive to specific historical and local facts. Different means may be justified for achieving particular ends, and the selection of means—constrained by local institutional capacities—will have consequences for the priority ranking that any given society assigns to the goals overall. In particular circumstances, the achievement of one or more of the goals would itself be a means (whether one that is helpful, necessary, or the best) to the realization of one or more of the others. For instance, truth may contribute to just punishment, fair compensation, and even reconciliation. When perpetrators are judicially directed to compensate their former victims, steps may be taken toward both retribution and reconciliation.

In summary, I have employed the eight goals to identify the moral aspects of reckoning with past wrongs, the areas of emerging international agreement, and the topics for further cross-cultural reflection and deliberation. Moreover, I propose that the eight goals be employed—and in turn evaluated—as criteria for evaluating the general "success" of various kinds of tools, such as truth commissions,[48] and designing and assessing a package of tools for attaining transitional justice in particular countries.

I recognize that different local conditions have a crucial bearing on the best that can be done in particular contexts. For example, it matters what a given transition is from and what it is to. Were prior violations perpetrated or permitted by a dictatorship, or did they occur in the context of a civil war, ethnic conflict, or attempted secession? If one of the latter, has the previous conflict been brought to a negotiated end, or was one side unilaterally victorious? How long was the period of violations, and how many people were perpetrators and victims (or both)? Does the particular society have a history of democratic institutions, or was it a long-standing dictatorship? Does the emerging society perpetuate, albeit in a new form, the ruling party, judicial system, and military apparatus of the old regime? What are the strength and potential of democratic governance, the market, and civil society? What is the general level of well-being among citizens, and are there continuing ethnic conflicts or radical economic disparities between segments of society? Each of these factors highlights the dangers of supposing that there is a recipe or single set of policies for reckoning with past wrongs that will be ethically defensible and practically feasible. These factors also indicate that sometimes the best that can be done is to approximate one or more of the eight goals initially or postpone attempts to realize them until conditions are improved. And sometimes excruciatingly difficult trade-offs will have to be made.

Concluding Remarks

It might be claimed that—regardless of its structure and content—it is neither possible nor desirable to formulate a general, cross-cultural normative framework and that the best that a society can do is to generate various tactics of its own for reckoning with past evil. However, policies and strategies that are designed and implemented solely under pressure of immediate circumstances and without proper attention to the relevant ethical questions are likely to be ad hoc, ineffective, inconsistent, and unstable. Moral questions have a habit of not going away. They may be trumped in the short term by certain strategic and prudential imperatives, and some measure of peace can be established without paying close attention to them. Long-term peace, however, cannot be realized if resentment, bitterness, and moral doubts about the just treatment of perpetrators and victims of human rights abuses linger in the minds of citizens. A general framework inspired and shaped by lessons learned from a variety of contexts can encourage each society reckoning with an atrocious past to realize in its own way as many as possible of the goals that international dialogue agrees are morally urgent.

It might also be argued that much more is needed than a normative framework or "vision." This is correct. But, while far from sufficient, it is essential to be clear on morally based objectives as we reckon with a society's past wrongs. The eminent Costa Rican philosopher Manuel Formosa nicely puts the general point: "It is clear that the new society will not come about just by thinking about it. But there is no doubt that one must begin by setting forth what is important; because, if we don't, we will never achieve it."[49]

Notes

I am grateful to David P. Crocker, Stacy Kotzin, Mauricio Olavarria, and my colleagues at the Institute for Philosophy and Public Policy and the School of Public Affairs—especially Susan Dwyer, Arthur Evenchik, Peter Levine, Xiaorong Li, Judith Lichtenberg, and other participants in the Transitional Justice Project—for helpful comments on earlier versions of this essay. This present essay is a slightly updated version of an article that appeared in *Ethics and International Affairs* 13 (1999): 43-64. Thanks to the journal's editors, Joel Rosenthal and Deborah Field Washburn, for permission to reprint the original article, which their suggestions improved, in the present context.

1 The best multidisciplinary collections on transitional justice are Neil J. Kritz, ed., *Transitional Justice: How Emerging Democracies Reckon with Former Regimes*, 3 vols. (Washington, DC: United States Institute of Peace Press, 1995); Naomi Roht-Arriaza, ed., *Impunity and Human Rights in International Law and Practice* (New York: Oxford University Press, 1995); and A. James McAdams, ed., *Transitional Justice and the Rule of Law in New Democracies* (Notre Dame: University of Notre Dame Press, 1997).

2 Timothy Garton Ash, "The Truth about Dictatorship," *New York Review of Books* (February 19, 1998), 35.

3 For these broader issues, see Ash's essay and Juan E. Méndez, "Accountability for Past Abuses," *Human Rights Quarterly* 19 (1997): 256-58, and "In Defense of Transitional Justice," in McAdams, ed., *Transitional Justice*, 22-23, n. 4.

4 Seth Mydans, "Under Prodding, 2 Khmer Rouge Apologize for the Reign of Terror," *New York Times*, December 30, 1998, A1; and "Cambodian Leader Resists Punishing Top Khmer Rouge," *New York Times*, December 29, 1998, A1, A8. *Violence*, (Boston, 1998). See David Chandler, "Will There Be a Trial for the Khmer Rouge?" *Ethics & International Affairs* 14 (2000): 67-82.

5 See Steven R. Ratner and Jason S. Abrams, *Accountability for Human Rights and Atrocities in International Law: Beyond the Nuremberg Legacy* (Oxford: Clarendon Press, 1997); and Aryeh Neier, *War Crimes: Brutality, Genocide, Terror and the Struggle for Justice* (New York: Times Books, 1998).

6 Ruth Wedgwood, "Fiddling in Rome," *Foreign Affairs* 77 (November-December 1998), 20-24.

7 Lawrence Weschler, *A Miracle, a Universe: Settling Accounts with Torturers* (New York: Pantheon, 1990); Roy Gutman, *Witness to Genocide* (New York: Macmillan, 1993); Tina Rosenberg, *The Haunted Land: Facing Europe's Ghosts After Communism* (New York: Random House, 1995) and "Defending the Indefensible," *New York Times Magazine*, April 19, 1998, 45-69; David Rohde, *Endgame: The Betrayal and Fall of Srebrenica, Europe's Worst Massacre since World War II* (Boulder, CO: Westview Press, 1997); Marguerite Feitlowitz, *A Lexicon of Terror: Argentina and the Legacies of Torture* (New York: Oxford University Press, 1998); Roger Cohen, *Hearts Grown Brutal: Sagas of Sarajevo* (New York: Random House, 1997); Chuck Sudetic, *Blood and Vengeance: One Family's Story of the War in Bosnia* (New York: W.W. Norton, 1998); Bill Berkeley, "Aftermath: The Pursuit of Justice and the Future of Africa," *Washington Post Magazine*, October 11, 1998, 10-15, 25-29; and Philip Gourevitch, *We Wish to Inform You That Tomorrow We Will Be Killed with Our Families: Stories from Rwanda* (New York: Farrar, Straus & Giroux, 1998).

8 See, for example, the essays by the following authors, in Neil J. Kritz, ed., *Transitional Justice*, vol. 1, who took part respectively in attempts to reckon with past wrongs in El Salvador, Argentina, and Chile: Thomas Buergenthal, Carlos Nino, and José Zalaguett.

9 See A. James McAdams, ed., *Transitional Justice*; and Mark Osiel, *Mass Atrocity, Collective Memory, and the Law* (New Brunswick, NJ: Transaction Books, 1997).

10 See Michael Walzer, *Just and Unjust Wars: A Moral Argument with Historical Illustrations*, 2d ed., (New York: Basic Books, 1977), xxvii.

11 See, for example, Donald Shriver, *An Ethic for Enemies: Forgiveness in Politics* (New York: Oxford University Press, 1995); Pablo De Greiff, "Trial and Punishment, Pardon and Oblivion: On Two Inadequate Policies for the Treatment of Former Human Rights Abusers," *Philosophy and Social Criticism* 12 (1996): 93-111; "International Criminal Courts and Transitions to Democracy," *Public Affairs Quarterly* 12 (1998): 79-99; Lyn S. Graybill, "South Africa's Truth and Reconciliation Commission: Ethical and Theological Perspectives," *Ethics & International Affairs* 12 (1998): 43-62; and T.M. Scanlon, "Punishment and the Rule of Law," in Harold Hongju Koh and Ronald C. Slye, eds., *Deliberative Democracy and Human Rights* (New Haven and London: Yale University Press, 1999).

12 One exception to this judgement is Ash, "The Truth about Dictatorship." Although he neither clarifies nor defends his ethical assumptions and although his particular assessments can be disputed, Ash insightfully consid-

ers four general measures—forgetting, trials, purges, and historical writing—with lots of variations and examples, especially from East and Central European countries. See also Martha Minow, *Between Vengeance and Forgiveness: Facing History after Genocide and Mass Violence*, (Boston: Beacon Press, 1998) and Tina Rosenberg, "Confronting the Painful Past," afterword in Martin Meredith, *Coming to Terms: South Africa's Search for Truth* (New York: Public Affairs, 2000), 325-70.

13 David A. Crocker, "Transitional Justice and International Civil Society: Toward a Normative Framework," *Constellations* 5 (1998): 492-517; "Civil Society and Transitional Justice," in Robert Fullinwider, ed., *Civil Society, Democracy, and Civic Renewal* (Lanham, MD: Rowman & Littlefield, forthcoming); and "Truth Commissions, Transitional Justice, and Civil Society," in Robert I. Rotberg and Dennis Thompson, eds., *Truth v. Justice: The Morality of Truth Commissions"* (Princeton: Princeton University Press, forthcoming); "Retribution and Reconciliation," *Report from the Institute for Philosophy & Public Policy* 20, 1 (Winter/Spring 2000): 1-6. My list of objectives has benefited from the work of Méndez and Zalaquett as well as from that of Margaret Popkin and Naomi Roht-Arriaza, who formulate and employ four criteria in "Truth as Justice: Investigatory Commissions in Latin America," *Law and Social Inquiry* 20 (1995): 79-116, especially 93-106.

14 Crocker, "Transitional Justice and International Civil Society," 495-96.

15 Svetozar Stojanovic, *The Fall of Yugoslavia: Why Communism Failed* (Amherst, NY: Prometheus Books, 1997), 77-78; see also 89-92.

16 Alex Boraine, "The Societal and Conflictual Conditions That Are Necessary or Conducive to Truth Commissions" (paper presented at the South African Truth and Reconciliation Commission Conference, World Peace Foundation, Somerset West, South Africa, May 28-30, 1998).

17 Rohde, *End Game*, 226.

18 Ibid., 230-31.

19 For investigations of what the United States and other Western powers could and should have done to prevent the Holocaust, see Richard Breitman, *Official Secrets: What the Nazis Planned, What the British and Americans Knew* (New York: Hill and Wang, 1999); and Istvan Deak, "Horror and Hindsight," a review of *Official Secrets* by Richard Breitman, *The New Republic*, February 15, 1999, 38-41. For consideration of the same issues with respect to the failure of the United States, the UN, and the European Union to intervene militarily in Croatia and Bosnia in 1991-95, see Mark Danner, "The US and the Yugoslav Catastrophe," *New York Review of Books* 44 (November 20, 1997), 56-64.

20 See my "Truth Commissions, Transitional Justice, and Civil Society."

21 See, for example, Patrick Ball, *Who Did What to Whom? Planning and Implementing a Large Scale Human Rights Data Project* (Washington, DC: American Association for the Advancement of Science, 1996); and Patrick Ball, Paul Kobrak, and Herbert Spirer, *State Violence in Guatemala, 1960-1996: A*

Quantitative Reflection (Washington, DC: American Association for the Advancement of Science, 1999).

22 See Mark Danner, "Bosnia: The Turning Point," *New York Review of Books* 45 (February 5, 1998): 34-41, for a compelling argument that rejects Serb claims that it was Muslims themselves who were responsible for the mortar attack that killed 68 Muslims in a Sarajevan market on February 5, 1994.

23 Suzanne Daly, "In Apartheid Injury, Agony Is Relived but Not Put to Rest," *New York Times*, July 17, 1997, A1, A10.

24 "Aftermath: Genocide, the Pursuit of Justice and the Future of Africa," *Washington Post Magazine*, October 11, 1998, 14, 28.

25 See Michael Walzer, *Just and Unjust Wars: A Moral Argument with Historical Illustration* (New York: Basic Books, 1977), 304-27; Neier, *War Crimes*, 229-45; and Mark J. Osiel, "Obeying Orders: Atrocity, Military Discipline, and the Law of War," *California Law Review* 86 (October 1998): 943-1129.

26 Peter Quint, *The Imperfect Union: Constitutional Structures of German Unification* (Princeton: Princeton University Press, 1997), 194-215. Cf. Anne Sa'adah, *Germany's Second Chance: Trust, Justice, and Reconciliation* (Cambridge: Harvard University Press, 1998).

27 Larry May and Stacey Hoffman, eds., *Collective Responsibility: Five Decades of Debate in Theoretical and Applied Ethics* (Lanham, MD: Rowman and Littlefield, 1991).

28 See Carlos Nino, *Radical Evil on Trial* (New Haven: Yale University Press, 1996), 210-28; Neier, *War Crimes*, 210-228; and Peter A. French, ed., *The Spectrum of Responsibility* (New York: St. Martin's Press, 1991).

29 Nino, *Radical Evil on Trial*, and "A Consensual Theory of Punishment," in A. John Simmons et al., eds., *Punishment: A Philosophy & Public Affairs Reader* (Princeton: Princeton University Press, 1995), 95-111; and Jaime Malamud-Goti, "Transitional Governments in the Breach: Why Punish State Criminals?" in Kritz, ed., *Transitional Justice*, vol. 1, 193-202.

30 See, for example, Simmons et al., eds., *Punishment*; Lawrence Crocker, "The Upper Limit of Punishment," *Emory Law Journal* 41 (1992): 1059-1110 and "A Retributive Theory of Criminal Justice" (unpublished mss.); Michael Moore, *Laying Blame* (Oxford: Clarendon Press, 1997); Jean Hampton, "The Moral Education Theory of Punishment," *Philosophy and Public Affairs* 13 (1984): 208-38; Herbert Morris, "Persons and Punishment," *Monist* 52 (1968): 475-501; George Sher, *Desert* (Princeton, NJ: Princeton University Press, 1987); James Rachels, "Punishment and Desert," in Hugh LaFollette, ed., *Ethics in Practice: An Anthology* (Cambridge, MA and Oxford: Blackwell, 1997); and David A. Crocker, "Retribution and Reconciliation."

31 David Luban, "The Legacies of Nuremberg," in *Legal Modernism* (Ann Arbor: University of Michigan Press, 1994), 335-78. Cf. Lon L. Fuller, *The Morality of Law*, rev. ed. (New Haven: Yale University Press, 1977), 33-39.

32 See, for example, Stephen Holmes, "The End of Decommunization," in Kritz, ed., *Transitional Justice*, vol. 1, 116-20; and Jon Elster, "On Doing

What One Can: An Argument against Post-Communist Restitution and Retribution," in ibid., 556-68.

33 Warren Hoge, "Law Lords in London Open Rehearing of Pinochet Case," *New York Times*, January 19, 1999, A1. Both the international and the Chilean consensus has evolved since this essay originally appeared in the spring of 1999. In January 2000, Pinochet was extradicted from Britain to Chile. Even if Pinochet never stands trial in Chile, the effect of the Spanish and British actions have been to "establish that even former heads of state do not enjoy impunity for crimes against humanity, and may be tried outside the country where the crimes were committed"; ("New Twist in the Pinochet Case," *New York Times*, January 15, 2000, A18).

34 *Report of the [South African] Truth and Reconciliation Commission*, vol. 5, chap. 5, para. 27-28 and 85-93.

35 David A. Sanger, "Gold Dispute with the Swiss Declared to Be at an End," *New York Times*, January 31, 1999, A1.

36 Roger Cohen, "German Companies Adopt Fund for Slave Labourers under Nazis," *New York Times*, February 17, 1999, A1. Cohen observes that "since World War Two the German government has paid out about $80 billion in aid, most of it to Jews who survived concentration camps or fled."

37 Ibid.

38 See Robert A. Dahl, *Democracy and Its Critics* (New Haven: Yale University Press, 1989), especially chaps. 8, 17, and 18; and Larry A. Diamond, "Democracy in Latin America: Degrees, Illusions, Directions for Consolidation," in Tom Farer, ed., *Beyond Sovereignty: Collectively Defending Democracy in the Americas* (Baltimore: Johns Hopkins University Press, 1996), 52-104.

39 See, for example, David A. Crocker, "Development Ethics," in Edward Craig, ed., *Routledge Encyclopedia of Philosophy*, vol. 3 (London: Routledge, 1998), 39-44; Amartya Sen, *Development as Freedom* (New York: Alfred A. Knopf, 1999); and Martha C. Nussbaum, *Women and Human Development: The Capabilities Approach* (Cambridge, UK: Cambridge University Press, 2000).

40 Charles Villa-Vicencio, "A Different Kind of Justice: The South African Truth and Reconciliation Commission," *Contemporary Justice Review* (forthcoming).

41 Osiel, *Mass Atrocity, Collective Memory, and the Law*, 17, n. 22; see also 47-51; 204, n. 136; 263-65.

42 Amy Gutmann and Dennis Thompson, "Moral Foundations of Truth Commissions" in Rotberg and Thompson, eds., *Truth v. Justice*.

43 See David Little, "A Different Kind of Justice: Dealing with Human Rights Violations in Transitional Societies," in *Ethics & International Affairs* 13 (1999): 65-80.

44 See Susan Dwyer, "Reconciliation for Realists," in *Ethics & International Affairs* 13 (1999): 81-98.

45 See Gilbert A. Lewthwaite, "In South Africa, Much Truth Yields Little Reconciliation," *Baltimore Sun*, July 30, 1998, 12; and Phylicia Oppelt, "Irreconcil-

able: The Healing Work of My Country's Truth Commission Has Opened New Wounds for Me," *Washington Post*, September 13, 1998, C1, C4.

46 See James Bohman, *Public Deliberation: Pluralism, Complexity, and Democracy* (Cambridge: MIT Press, 1996); and Amy Gutmann and Dennis Thompson, *Democracy and Disagreement* (Cambridge: Harvard University Press, 1996).

47 Seth Mydans, "20 Years On, Anger Ignites against Khmer Rouge," *New York Times*, January 10, 1999, A1.

48 See, for example, Priscilla B. Hayner, "The Past as Predator: The Role of Official Truth-Seeking in Conflict Resolution and Prevention," in *International Conflict Resolution: Techniques and Evaluation* (Washington, DC: National Research Council, forthcoming).

49 Manuel Formosa, "La alternativa: Repensar la revolución," *Seminario Universidad*, Universidad de Costa Rica, October 23, 1987, 5.

2

What Is Acknowledgement and Why Is It Important?

Trudy Govier

Introduction

In an intriguing work on intractable conflict between nations and groups, Thomas Scheff theorizes that a major underlying cause of such conflict is to be found in cycles of humiliation and rage. Toward the end of his book *Bloody Revenge*, Scheff suggests that acknowledgement of feelings may have an important role to play in the resolution of such conflicts. He mentions apologies as a form of acknowledgement and suggests that a greater acknowledgement of human interdependence and less denial would have positive effects on some ongoing conflicts.[1] Joseph Montville, director of a program on preventive diplomacy, also claims that acknowledgement of wrongdoing, often expressed through formal apology, is profoundly important for the healing of victims and their reconciliation with perpetrators.[2] Michael Ignatieff makes similar claims about apology and acknowledgement at the end of *The Warrior's Honour*, his book about the horrifying breakdown of moral codes characteristic of ethnic violence, especially in Yugoslavia. Ignatieff boldly claims that had President Tudjman of Croatia officially apologized to Serbs for the violence committed by the fascist Ustache during the Second World War, the fears of Serbs living within Croatia would have been soothed and the brutal Balkan wars of the nineties would not have happened. The apology would have served to acknowledge past wrongdoing and suffering and announce a break from it.[3] In her recent work *Between Vengeance and Forgiveness*, Martha

---

Notes to chapter 2 are on pp. 87-89.

Minow also emphasizes the importance of acknowledgement of past wrongs when discussing trials, truth commissions, reparations, and apologies as different ways of responding to and attempting to recover from gross human rights violations.[4]

In the introduction to his book, *A Miracle, A Universe*, which discusses Latin American experience in dealing with torturers after democratization, Lawrence Weschler describes a conference at which participants struggled to come to terms with the concept of acknowledgement. Weschler says:

> Fragile, tentative democracies time and again hurl themselves toward an abyss, struggling over this issue of truth. It's a mysteriously powerful, almost magical notion, because often everyone already knows the truth—everyone knows who the torturers were and what they did, the torturers know that everyone knows, and everyone knows that they know. Why, then, this need to risk everything to render that knowledge explicit? The participants...worried this question around the table several times—distinctions here seemed particularly slippery and elusive—until Thomas Nagel, a professor of philosophy and law at New York University, almost stumbled upon an answer. "It's the difference," Nagel said haltingly, "between knowledge and *ac*knowledgement. It's what happens and can only happen to knowledge when it becomes officially sanctioned, when it is made part of the public cognitive scene." Yes, several of the panelists agreed. And that transformation, offered another participant, is sacramental.[5]

The *acknowledgement* of past wrongs and those who had suffered from them was a primary goal of South Africa's Truth and Reconciliation Commission. In his introduction to the Commission's final report, Archbishop Desmond Tutu alluded to Ariel Dorfman's well-known work *Death and the Maiden*, which deals with a torture victim's temptation to enact revenge on the man who tortured her. She has him tied up when he admits that what he did was wrong. Then "his admission restores her dignity and her identity. Her experience is confirmed as real and not illusory, and her sense of self is affirmed," Tutu says. Later in this report, in a chapter explaining the mandate of the Commission, there are further references to acknowledgement. A central purpose of the TRC was to "acknowledge the tragedy of human suffering wherever it has occurred," whether victims were black or white.

The work of the TRC was based on the assumption that there is a potentially healing power in being able to tell one's story, in having the importance of that story recognized by a public body, and in being thereby publicly acknowledged as one wronged, with a credible and important story to tell. As human beings with stories to tell, some seven thousand South Africans appeared before the TRC, where they were respectfully heard and treated as human beings with dignity and meriting respect.[6] Some linked the work of the Commission to an African concept known as *Ubuntu*. The saying *umuntu ngumuntu ngabuntu* means that people are people only through other people. For many people, being denigrated and disrespected by others meant scarcely maintaining status as human beings. In such cases acknowledgement may be expected to have tremendous power and an impact both on the healing of human beings wounded by past abuse and on their potential reconciliation with those who have wounded them.

But it is not necessary to look as far as South Africa to find statements about the importance of acknowledgement. Such statements are also to be found in the Canadian Royal Commission on Aboriginal Peoples, issued in 1996.

> While we assume the role of defender of human rights in the international community, we retain, in our conception of Canada's origins and make-up, the remnants of colonial attitudes of cultural superiority that do violence to the Aboriginal peoples to whom they are directed. Restoring Aboriginal nations to a place of honour in our shared history, and *recognizing* their continuing presence as collectives participating in Canadian life, are therefore fundamental to the changes we propose.[7]

In its survey of relations between Aboriginal peoples and those who came after them to settle in their territory and found the nation of Canada, the 1996 report notes that official Canadian history tends to ignore and negate Aboriginal people's view of themselves and their encounter with settler society. The report calls for *acknowledgement* of Aboriginal peoples and cultures, the wrongs done to them, and their contribution to Canadian history and society:

> Before Aboriginal and non-Aboriginal people can get on with the work of reconciliation, a great cleansing of the wounds of the past must take place. The government of Canada, on behalf of the Canadian people, must acknowledge and express deep

regret for the spiritual, cultural, economic and physical violence
visited upon Aboriginal people, as individuals and as nations, in
the past. And they must make a public commitment that such
violence will never again be permitted or supported.[8]

Later in the context of a discussion of compulsory relocations of many
native communities, the Commission called again for acknowledgement,
seeing it as highly significant for the healing of Aboriginal peoples and
their potential reconciliation with mainstream Canadian society.

> The commission is of the opinion that governments ought to
> *acknowledge* that the practice of relocating Aboriginal commu-
> nities, where these relocations failed to adhere to the standards
> we recommend, has contributed to the violation of Aboriginal
> people's rights as human beings…many Aboriginal communi-
> ties continue to feel a deep sense of grievance about relocation.
> Healing will begin in earnest only when governments *acknowl-
> edge* that relocation practices, however well-intentioned, con-
> tributed to a denial of human rights. *Acknowledging* responsi-
> bility assists in the necessary healing process because it creates
> room for dialogue about the reasons for relocation and the fact
> that these reasons were often based on ignorance and erro-
> neous assumptions about Aboriginal people and their identity.
> Aboriginal people need to know that governments accept
> responsibility for relocations and recognize their effects.
> Recognition and responsibility are the necessary first steps to
> overcoming the many adverse effects of relocations.[9]

The Canadian Royal Commission on Aboriginal Peoples cited the
Canadian Human Rights Commission, which said in 1991 and reiterated
in 1994 that the situation of Aboriginal peoples is the single most important human rights issue confronting Canada. The Human Rights Commission recommended government apologies for various aspects of
native/white relations, including relocations, the appallingly brutal system
of residential schools, the treatment of veterans, and the exploitive failure
to take treaty commitments seriously. It called for these apologies *as a form
of acknowledgement* and a step toward compensation for "the affront to
dignity, self-respect and self-determination" implicit in many relocations.
Apologies would serve a broad educative function, acknowledge serious
affronts to human dignity, and express commitment that the mistakes of
the past would not be committed again.

The Commission found that in many fundamental aspects, relations with mainstream (largely white) Canadian society has been disastrous for Aboriginal peoples and should be a source of outrage and shame to non-Aboriginal Canadian society. The Report calls for respect for Aboriginal Canadians as individuals, and for respect for their cultures and contributions to Canadian history and society. It calls repeatedly for *acknowledgement* of the dignity and worth of these peoples and the wrongs done to them by governments and the broader society over several centuries.

Acknowledgement and Denial

The concept of acknowledgement strikes me as a fascinating one that merits more attention than it has received and more than I can give it here. Conceptually, acknowledgement is closely related to confession, admission, avowal, and recognition; however, following recent discussions of justice and past wrongs, I concentrate on acknowledgement in particular without exploring the conceptual niceties of connections and distinctions between acknowledgement and these other notions.[10] In this paper, my interest is in trying to understand what constitutes acknowledgement, and in particular in reflecting on the significance of acknowledgement for victims, perpetrators, and communities in the wake of wrongdoing. In such contexts, denial on an individual or collective level is open to serious moral criticism because in effect we choose to ignore serious harms to other people.

Lest these comments be taken to castigate anyone in particular, let me say that I suspect that most of us find ourselves in several roles with regard to the commission of serious wrongs. We are victims, or affiliates of victims, of some wrongs; perpetrators, or affiliates of perpetrators, of others; and bystanders with regard to others. In the Canadian situation, for instance, one might be a Holocaust survivor or child of a survivor, in this respect a victim, and nevertheless one might also be a beneficiary and, through affiliation with church or state institutions, a perpetrator with regard to Canadian social wrongs against Aboriginal peoples.

There would appear to be relatively little written in either psychology or philosophy about acknowledgement as such, and the conception of acknowledgement seems abstract and even rather vague. We can see from the statements cited above a widely held conviction that acknowledgement is something of great importance in the context of addressing wrongdoing. And yet (as exemplifed by the conference discussion described by Lawrence Weschler) participants arrived at the notion of acknowledgement only with difficulty. They were hard-pressed to articulate what acknowledgement amounts to, and to differentiate it from knowledge. We have seen in reports of the South African Truth and Reconciliation Commission and the Canadian Royal Commission on Aboriginal People the expressed conviction that acknowledgement matters a great deal to wronged peoples, and should serve as an important first stage of reconciliation and the healing of victims of wrongdoing.

I thus arrive at the questions that set the theme for this paper. What is acknowledgement? And why it is important?

Acknowledgement is not the same thing as knowledge, because we may know things that we do not acknowledge. A woman may know that she is short-tempered and prone to yell at her children without ever acknowledging to them that she has these failings. They may know it without ever expressing it to her, and so on. A man may know that he is eighty-two years old and people eighty-two years old have a short time left to live; thus in some sense he knows that he has a short future—and yet he may not acknowledge this. That is to say, he may not admit it to himself, spell it out to himself, avow it as an aspect of his identity, or admit it to other people. He has chosen to ignore or deny the fact of his age and not take it into account in when planning and conducting his relationships and practical affairs. Though he has the evidence and intellectual capacity for this knowledge, he does not articulate to himself what he knows; he does not avow or admit this consequence to himself or others. That is to say, he does not acknowledge that he probably has only a short time left to live. Rather, he is in a state of *denial* or *avoidance* with regard to this implication.

At the conference described by Weschler, participants discussed a situation in which people knew that certain individuals had been torturers under a military regime. And yet those facts were not publicly acknowledged—that is to say, they were not openly admitted and discussed. Acknowledging them would mean spelling them out, publicly stating that these were facts—and by implication, taking some action in the light of those facts.

Much of what we know or are in a position to know, we would also acknowledge, or would be willing to acknowledge. But some of what we know or are in a position to know, we do not acknowledge and would not be willing to acknowledge. The issue of acknowledgement arises when we know or are in a position to know unwelcome things that we do not wish to spell out or publicly admit. We can also acknowledge pleasant things— but the issue of doing so does not usually arise, because we have little or no temptation to deny such things. The difference between knowledge and acknowledgement lies in explicit verbal spelling out or other form of marked awareness.[11] The mother who *knows* that she is sometimes bad-tempered with her children might go beyond her own knowledge to *acknowledge* to them her irritability. She might, for instance, say to them something like, "I know I've been crabby this past week, and I've been yelling at you, and I'm sorry." In articulating such an acknowledgement, the mother would have first recognized and conceptualized her feelings and behaviour and then have admitted her failings openly to her children. In this kind of acknowledgement what is first involved is an admission to oneself; that is followed by an admission to others. Those who have been hurt by her behaviour are likely to be reassured by her acknowledgement that it is she who has failed. (She has, for instance, implied that it was not the children's behaviour that was responsible for her actions and reactions.)

This example suggests why we might expect acknowledgement to make a powerful difference in contexts of wrongdoing. Acknowledgement is a necessary condition of willingness to make restitution and commit to positive change. Only a person who acknowledges her irritability will attempt to overcome it; and admitting a failing to those who have suffered from it indicates to them that one is separating oneself from what was done and is resolved not to do it again. The implication of the mother's acknowledgement of her irritability towards her children is that she is going to try to change. Often, acknowledgement to oneself and then to others constitutes a fundamental stage in moral progress. In the treatment of alcoholics by Alcoholics Anonymous, one begins by saying, "I am———, and I am an alcoholic." To address and attempt to resolve a problem, one must first acknowledge that one has it. That means admitting explicitly and publicly that this problem is attached to oneself, part of oneself, part of who one is.

In such cases, acknowledgement is knowledge and, further than knowledge, a kind of *avowal* that amounts to a spelling out or marking of what we know. A person who acknowledges something, X, admits or allows that X is attached in some way to himself. Typically he would also acknowledge X to others. But in order to do so sincerely, he must first acknowledge X to himself.

One way of trying to understand acknowledgement is to contrast it with what it is not—which is to say, with various forms of denial. There are many forms of denial, and many ways of failing to acknowledge something that is wrong. We may redescribe it, seeking to prove to ourselves that it is something other than it is. We may emotionally detach ourselves from it; we may ignore it; or we may deceive ourselves about it.

One opposite to acknowledgement is self-deception. A person may be an alcoholic, may have considerable evidence that he is an alcoholic, and sufficient evidence about his own drinking habits and needs that, were such evidence to apply to anyone else, he would readily conclude her to be an alcoholic. He may experience serious family and working problems as a result of his drinking; yet he may not be prepared to admit to himself or anyone else that he is an alcoholic. He may ignore relevant facts because he is unwilling to avow this trait as an aspect of himself; "alcoholic" is not a label he is willing to accept as describing himself. Such a man can be said to be "in denial" or to be deceiving himself about his alcoholism. He is in a position to know, and in some sense even does know, and take account of the fact, that he is an alcoholic. Yet he does not acknowledge this.

In his 1969 book *Self-Deception*, Herbert Fingarette used the notions of *disavowal* and *lack of acknowledgement* as the basis for an account of self-deception. He said that the self-deceiver is engaged in the world in a way he is not prepared to accept as part of his personal identity and thus does not spell out, admit, or avow. There is a gap between the way he is engaged in the world and the story he tells himself and others about himself. In that work, Fingarette said:

> A person may avow or acknowledge as his an action, a feeling, an emotion, a perception, a belief, an attitude, a concern, an aim, or a reason. In avowing them as his, a person is identifying himself as one who feels, suffers, perceives, believes, etc., thus and so....In speaking of avowal and acknowledgement, we are concerned with an acceptance by the person which is constitutive, which is *de jure* in its force, which establishes something as *his for him*.[12]

We might deny, or deceive ourselves about, such central aspects of ourselves. And we may also, collectively and individually, deny or deceive ourselves about central aspects of our societies. Fingarette spoke of acknowledging, or failing to acknowledge, *engagements in the world*. Engagements that we are not prepared to acknowledge are those which we are not willing to accept as part of ourselves, personal frailties or inadequacies, or—most pertinently for the present topic, acts of wrongdoing for which we have shared responsibility or with which we have been significantly affiliated. If one wished to extend this account to contexts of social wrongs, one might say that past wrongs such as slavery, forced assimilation of indigenous peoples, abuse, and discriminations are to be considered as previous engagements in the world that whole societies are unwilling to acknowledge.

In a 1998 paper on self-deception, Fingarette takes a slightly different position. He argues that as the mind normally works, we attend to some aspects of the world while not attending to others. For example, a person who is writing a letter by hand will attend to what he is saying, but not to the way in which his fingers are holding the pen. Yet though he is not attending to the position of his fingers, he can intelligently take account of that and adapt their position if his fingers slip.

> My attention is focused on my thoughts at the moment and on the task of choosing words to express them adequately. Once I have the words in mind, and have elected to write them down, the writing itself is "automatic."
>
> The crux of the matter, if we generalize, is that we can take account of something without necessarily focusing our attention on it. That is, we can recognize it, and respond to it, without directing our attention to what we are doing, and our response can be intelligently adaptive rather than merely a reflex or habit automatism.[13]

To function in this world, we must be able to take account of data that are not the focus of our attention. What we learn in learning to write is to write without attending to the way we hold our pen or place our paper, or the manner in which we shape the letters. We can write without paying any attention to such things, even though there is a sense in which we are aware of them, and can make appropriate adaptations if necessary. Attention is always selective; we cannot attend to everything. In this later work, Fingarette claims that self-deception is a matter of motivated selective attention. He says that *when we deceive ourselves we turn our attention away from unwelcome information and fail to attend to it. We can nevertheless take some account of that information, which, of course, is one of the things that enables us to turn our attention away from it.* We deceive ourselves when we ignore, that is, fail to attend to, information that is unwelcome to us because it is emotionally painful or traumatic. Fingarette says:

> Suppose, for example, that I have done something shameful. I take account of my conduct and its significance for me. However, just because this particular shame is deeply wounding to me, given my sense of self, I avoid focusing my attention on the event, or at least on its shameful features. I thus damp down the effect on me and avoid a traumatic wound to my self-esteem. *There is a price. I lose the opportunity to appraise the conduct with the clarity and depth that are afforded by close attention.* I also have less reliable recall, and can thus more readily rationalize what happened and what I have done about it. For all these reasons, I cannot deal with the matter as effectively as I otherwise might. I shall be less creative and less subtle about handling the matter, tending to reach into my past for evasive techniques already worked out. This may not be the wisest policy in the long run, but, being all too human, we sometimes do such things because of fear in the short run.[14]

As individuals, we are often aware that certain acts are shameful and this awareness permits a certain selectivity in our attention. We can exploit it to take account of the acts as we wish to, which often means turning our attention away from them, not attending either to what we did and ignoring our fleeting feelings of guilt or to our embarrassment about them.

Fingarette argues that the combination of unfocused but nevertheless intelligent awareness of some things and lack of attention to other things should not be regarded as especially mysterious. Such a combination is absolutely characteristic of the way in which we function in the world, and necessary for our functioning: we cannot attend to everything. (Fingarette is making this remark about individuals, but it would appear that one can say the same thing about societies.) When we deceive ourselves in this way, our selective attention is in principle entirely similar to the selective attention involved in holding a pen. What is distinctive about self-deception as a form of selective attention is the *motive* involved, which is to protect ourselves from unwelcome feelings or facts—from things we do not wish to acknowledge. Notably, *there are potential costs in lack of acknowledgement.* Most notably, a problem not acknowledged is one we cannot hope to resolve. If we do not acknowledge it, we cannot even attempt to resolve it.

We are enabled to deceive ourselves because others refrain from bringing unpleasant truths home to us. Self-deception may be a social thing, and is often the result of collusion or complicity among people.[15] Groups may be said to deceive themselves when their members generally deny, avoid, or ignore unpleasant aspects of their histories. In a recent article on the vital art of *ignoring*, Annette Baier notes this important fact, and says:

> These phenomena, of sensible selective attention, of selective recall, of imperfect record keeping or cover-up of our own past selective control, are normal human phenomenology, both for individuals and for groups. Nations attend to some calls on their attention more than to others, write selective histories, and rewrite them as establishments and ideologies change. Also, social mechanisms of many kinds assist individuals in their individual self-deceptive activities, especially when these are coordinated with the maintenance of the preferred collective memory, that is needed for a group's current self-esteem. War veterans' memories of what slaughter they participated in or witnessed may be uncomfortable memories both for them personally and for the national record. Psychiatric services help soothe and play down such memories as could be disruptive. In a free nation, the press, the film industry, and the book trade can serve as important curbs on this smoothing over of the blemishes on our shared past, can serve to revive uncomfortable memories and to stir up painful awareness of what we would understandably prefer to forget, or to continue to ignore.[16]

Both as individuals and as groups, we may choose to ignore certain unpleasant things that we would rather not acknowledge, because we wish to avow these things as aspects of our identity. Individuals can deny; groups can also deny. And yet in both cases, what we deny may be something we need to avow and acknowledge—because only by so doing can we begin to make necessary changes.

Choosing to Ignore

The phenomenon of ignoring is of considerable interest. Interestingly, we cannot ignore something unless we have some awareness of it. Consider, for example, the case of the cobwebs above my dining room light. To ignore them, I have to know they are there. I may notice them while I am cleaning and decide to ignore them because I cannot easily reach them. *If I did not notice them at all, did not see them, had no awareness of them, I could not ignore them.* By definition, we do not pay attention to what we ignore, but necessarily, we have to have some awareness of something in order to ignore it. If I continue to ignore the cobwebs, I will not notice when they grow, or attract dust or entrap small flies. Then as an effect of my ignoring them, there will be many things I will not know about them. However, in order to ignore them, I do have to know that they exist. Eventually, these cobwebs will grow so large that I can no longer ignore them. Could the same be said about resentment, anger, and alienation as the result of past wrongs?

There are many things we quite properly fail to attend to—the small cobweb in the corner, the colour of a colleague's shirt, the mailman's jacket, the size of the pages of a book. We cannot attend to everything, and no harm is done. As both Fingarette and Baier allow, there are many cases and many respects in which ignoring things is quite simply necessary. Neither as societies nor as individuals can we attend to everything. *What sorts of things should we attend to? What sorts of things can we properly ignore?* When we say of something that is not attended to that it is *ignored*, we are already suggesting that it is the kind of thing that very well might have been attended to. Suppose I get a red patch on my leg and decide to ignore it, paying no further attention to it. If it grows, I may have trouble ignoring it. If it spreads over my entire leg and my skin begins to itch, I am likely to find the condition impossible to ignore. It seems appropriate, to speak of *ignoring* in this context, because my bodily condition and health are matters where I am expected to take responsibility.

To ignore some things, to fail to acknowledge, is sometimes highly risky, as is suggested by the common expression "ignore this at your peril." Consider, for instance, the man who decides to ignore his doctor's diagnosis of adult-onset diabetes and the prescription of diet, exercise, and medication that went along with that diagnosis. He was told he had this problem of glucose intolerance, told what to do about it, and warned of the complications that might arise if he did nothing about it. He could be said to *know* he had this problem because he had been given this diagnosis by a reliable authority, one that he himself had been willing to regard as reliable in the past. Certainly he was in a position to know it. Yet he ignored the advice. He did not acknowledge to himself or to others that he was a diabetic, because he did not want to believe it and act on the implications. He did not want to restrict his diet, conform to a regime of exercise, and regularly monitor his blood sugar levels. Because he ignored the advice, there was much that this man did not know—whether those levels were higher in the morning than the evening, raised by eating ice cream, dangerously high, or normal or low, for instance. He did not know that the tingling in his hands and feet and the itchiness of his skin were side effects of his diabetes. Eventually, he experienced serious circulatory problems, developed sores that would not heal, and had to have his feet amputated. At that point, it had become impossible to ignore the diabetes any longer.

To concentrate on one thing, or on some range of things, we must ignore many others. In our selective attention we implicitly distinguish between those things that matter to us and those that do not. Sometimes it is even a duty to ignore certain information. We may, for example, serve in a role that requires impartiality. (For example, if a man is a member of a hiring committee, knows one job applicant is the cousin of his brother-in-law, and ignores this connection when judging the application, his ignoring amounts to admirable impartiality.) To ignore information or phenomena can be perfectly all right, it can be neutral, it can be a duty, or it can be culpable. We speak of culpable ignorance and we may also speak of *culpable ignoring*.[17] We are correctly said to culpably ignore things if we ignore things we *should have, and could have, paid attention to*. But to say this is not to answer the more general question of what, as individuals and as societies, we should attend to and not ignore.

When we have failed to acknowledge a problem and the problem grows worse as a result of our lack of attention to it, we may cry, like the diabetic in denial, "but we didn't know." As a result of our ignoring and our denial, the protestation will have some elements of truth. But at a more fundamental level it is misleading and an avoidance of responsibility.

Ignoring Victims of Wrongdoing

The case for attention and acknowledgement becomes clearer, and the likely harmfulness of denial more apparent, if we shift from individualistic contexts and consider social and political situations in which what we are tempted to deny and ignore is *damage to other people—wounded others, in our own society*. In calling as they do for acknowledgement, the TRC Report and the 1996 Aboriginal Peoples Report assume that nations and societies should not ignore the suffering and pain of their members; nor should they deny that this suffering and pain is the result of wrongful actions and policies undertaken by governments and calls for a response in terms of apologies or redress. Yet acknowledging and reflecting on the pain and suffering of others is not pleasant, especially not in case where we share responsibility for it. We may ignore the protestations of those who suffer in the aftermath of wrongs. We may fail to listen and thus fail to hear and understand. We may become so oblivious to cries and protestations that we treat people as if they barely existed at all. If so, we are by our denial negating them as persons whose needs and interests matter and who deserve our concern.

In these respects, many white South Africans denied the humanity of the black people who were their workers and servants. Many Canadians have similarly denied the humanity of Aboriginal peoples in Canada. We have chosen to ignore many facts, problems, and cries of pain. As a result of our ignoring we know little. Then, if we are charged with responsibility, we are apt to protest that we did not know. But we did know something—enough to ignore the situation in the first place, to avoid paying attention to it. We knew enough to know we did not want to know more. We did not know because we did not want to know. We did not want to know because the truths we would face would be unpleasant and incompatible with our favoured pictures of ourselves, and they imply a need for restitution and redress, threatening our rather comfortable way of life.

Without any pretense to offer a general theory of what one should attend to (and would culpably ignore) and what one may permissibly ignore, it seems entirely reasonable to assert that we should pay attention to the suffering and marginalization of persons in our own society whose interests and well-being have been seriously affected by past action and policy. I would like to echo the presumption of the South African TRC and the Canadian 1996 Report, and agree that we should acknowledge past wrongs. In the case of Canada, this is to say, in effect, that as individuals and as an organized society we should acknowledge our collective responsibility for such wrongs as stolen land, broken treaties, forced assimilation, forced relocations, and abuse in compulsory residential schools.

Why should we offer such acknowledgement? Because these are human beings in pain and in need—human beings in our society and nation. Because, through patterns of colonization, land use, racism, disregard for treaties, and the residential school system, we are linked significantly to the institutions that are responsible for their pain and need; as members of the society and citizens of the state, we share responsibility for these things. Because we are in many significant ways beneficiaries of the injustices done against these people. Because collectively, we have the power to improve their situation. Collective acknowledgement is especially important because strategies such as the construction of museums and memorials and the amending of educational policy are more available to collectives than to individuals. In circumstances where groups and individuals have been significantly wronged, we should *acknowledge* the relevant facts, the feelings of native peoples, and our own complicity in what has gone on. We should share in responsibility for situations of oppression and injustice. We cannot help but *notice* injured peoples, poverty, imprisonment, and court cases about treaties, land claims, and residential schools. Having noticed such phenomena, many of us go on to *ignore* them, and that is something we should not do. Reasons against denial come both from prudence and from morality. To ignore and deny their suffering would be imprudent, since unacknowledged and unaddressed anger and frustration are likely to worsen and may culminate in violence. To do so would be immoral, since we have morally significant bonds with all other human beings and especially with these, our injured and unjustly deprived compatriots.

In cases of past wrongs, there is much to be acknowledged. That those wronged are human beings with human dignity and moral worth. That these things did happen and were wrong. That the people in question deserved better. That their feelings of hurt, anger, or resentment are natural and legitimate. That those who harmed them or who have been complicit in these harms should feel guilt and shame about such things. Significantly, such acknowledgement carries with it an implied commitment that these and similar wrongs should not be perpetrated again.

Granted Acknowledgement and Received Acknowledgement

The 1996 report on Aboriginal issues recommended that Canadian governments and the non-native public grant acknowledgement of past wrongs to native Canadians, who would then receive that acknowledgement. In seeking further to understand acknowledgement, it is useful to distinguish between *granted acknowledgement, self-acknowledgement,* and *received acknowledgement.* Before sincerely granting acknowledgement to others, one must admit or acknowledge the aspect in question to oneself; thus, granting acknowledgement presupposes self-acknowledgement. It is this necessary self-acknowledgement that is missing when there is denial or self-deception. *Received acknowledgement presupposes granted acknowledgement, and granted acknowledgement presupposes self-acknowledgement.* If Aboriginal Canadians are to receive acknowledgement that wrongs were done to them, non-Aboriginal Canadians will have to grant that acknowledgement. And if non-Aboriginal Canadians (as individuals, communities, or through their governments) are going to grant that acknowledgement they will need, first of all, to acknowledge to themselves their shared responsibility for wrongdoing. Self-acknowledgement is often painful and is by no means to be taken for granted. On a personal level, acknowledgement can be difficult and self-deception profoundly tempting. It is hard, and unpleasant, to acknowledge unwelcome aspects of oneself—for instance, that one is an irritable parent, a diabetic, an alcoholic, a domineering boss, or an unsuccessful author. And the same holds on a collective level. It is not pleasant to acknowledge that our country was founded on an unjust and manipulative expropriation of land or that our previous governments were committed to a policy of assimilation founded on a deeply entrenched sense of European superiority. Nor do we want to acknowledge that officials of those governments ignored reports of brutality, malnutrition, and sexual abuse in native residential schools under their jurisdictions because they were racists who deemed native children to be of little value. We would rather deny, avoid, or ignore such unpleasant aspects of our national history, turning our attention away from studies, reports, and the living victims and victims' descendants that point us to them. We would rather think of ourselves as tolerant and moderate, internationally respected as peacekeepers and participants in a successful multicultural society. The facts about Aboriginal Canadians and their history and socio-economic position in Canada tend to depressing, and a suspicion that our country and somehow, we ourselves, have played a substantial role in their tribulations is most unwelcome. We would prefer not to publicize them, not to dwell on them, not to think about them. We would rather ignore these unpleasant facts and not come to know more. We would prefer to deny these realities of our political and ethical life. And generally, we do.

Selective attention and memory amounts to collective self-deception when the motive is to ignore and deny unpleasant facts about the past. Such collective denial and self-deception really do exist, and it is an understatement to claim that they are significant in politics. After the Second World War, Germans were notoriously unwilling to acknowledge having supported Nazism in any way. After the unification of Germany, few of the many thousands of East Germans who had been spies for the secret police were willing to acknowledge any wrongdoing in having done so.[18] After apartheid, most white South Africans were unwilling to acknowledge that they had played some role in supporting a regime that was profoundly and fundamentally unjust and brought great harm to black South Africans. In Canada, relatively few non-Aboriginal Canadians have been willing to acknowledge our complicity in sustaining a society in which most native Canadians are victims of past and present ill-treatment, injustice, and poverty. A crucial objection to such denials is that those who do not recognize such wrongs will not be willing or able to rectify them.

Thus the logical connection between received acknowledgement (on the part of victim groups) and granted acknowledgement and self-acknowledgement (on the part of perpetrator groups) is critically important. Calls for acknowledgement have a certain misleading vagueness and suggestion of passivity which encourage us to gloss over some basic logical facts. *In order for acknowledgement to be received, it must be granted. And in order for it to be granted, those who have been complicit in wrongdoing must acknowledge to themselves their complicity.* Persons significantly affiliated with perpetrator groups—and this may mean *us*—will have to admit and avow past wrongdoing. They, or we, will have to accept some responsibility for it. Doing so is likely to involve and/or entail painful self-analysis. We will have to overcome our refusal to reflect on unpleasant truths. Both as individuals and as a society, we may have to struggle to overcome collective denial, avoidance, ignoring, ignorance, and self-deception.

To grant acknowledgement to Aboriginal Canadians, those of us who are non-Aboriginal will have to admit to ourselves (and publicly) some unwelcome truths contrary to our "official" but superficial understanding of our own past. One example is the absurdity of the still oft-cited idea that Canada has two founding nations, French and English. In the seventeenth, eighteenth, and nineteenth centuries, Canada was not a *terra nullius*, an empty land awaiting settlement by European peoples. Native peoples were already here and at great sacrifice and under some unfair pressure and manipulation, they signed treaties that made available the land on which our present country was built.

Further Clarification

Acknowledgement is knowledge accompanied by a kind of marking or spelling out or admitting as significantly related to oneself something that is known. A person who acknowledges something is articulating something that he or she *sincerely* believes to be *true*.[19] The connection between acknowledgement and truth means that calls for acknowledgement are contestable. The possibility of contestable claims to acknowledgement is by no means trivial in political contexts of past wrongs. A man may call for his acknowledgement as a wounded victim, a *freedom fighter* who was in the course of his *just struggle* against apartheid, cruelly and gratuitously tortured by the state police. At the same time his torturer may insist that he had to interrogate as part of an *authorized state campaign* against *terrorist* forces paid by international *communist* groups.[20] A full defence of the claim that wrongs against one group should be acknowledged by another would include cogent arguments that the acts in question were indeed wrong, and the group in question was responsible for committing them.

Acknowledgement may be complete or partial. One may acknowledge that victims received less than they deserved, but insist that what happened was not wrongdoing, rather an honest error, or well-intended attempt to act under principles of another time. In this case one would partially acknowledge wrongdoing. Many cases of partial acknowledgement are in effect cases of *compromised acknowledgement*. In compromised acknowledgement, the one who offers acknowledgement expresses a mixed message in which there are both elements of acknowledgement and elements of denial. The contradictions and denials of systems such as anti-Semitism, racism, colonialism, and sexism are legendary. In eighteenth-century Europe, women were widely regarded as silly, irresponsible, and irrational; yet they were also the life partners of allegedly rational and responsible men, and the nurturers of children. Slaves were regarded as sub-human—yet some owners took care to convert them to Christianity so that their souls could be saved. South African blacks were supposed to be primitive peoples who did not share the feelings and capacity for education that whites had. Yet they were charged with responsible tasks such as caring for children. Human beings deemed *scum* or *vermin* were used for medical experimentation that presupposed their relevant similarity to those other human beings who had denied them human status. Compromised acknowledgement is common because in many situations of lack of acknowledgement there is, after all, knowledge that will come to the fore. Compromised acknowledgement tends to be hurtful. It is relatively common, a fact that is understandable, since there are disincentives to publicly admitting knowledge that would undercut a discriminatory practice, and yet, contrary evidence, undermining a self-protective ignoring, will tend to present itself. The result is a mixed message, and to the unjustly treated and partially acknowledged person, that mixed message is likely to be confusing and painful.

In cases of compromised acknowledgement, hopes may be raised and then dashed. Speaking of the wounds from historical wrongs, some have alluded to the "second wound of silence." The second wound is the hurt to victims of ignoring what was done to them; to ignore the wrong is to imply that it, and the suffering resulting from it, do not really matter. Truly this is adding the wound of insult to the wound of injury. Acknowledgement by relevant individuals and institutions may help to heal the second wound of silence. Following on the metaphor of the second wound, we may think of the third wound as a kind of insincerity. This is the wound of an insincere or partial apology, or some other form of compromised acknowledgement.

Exploring Claims about Acknowledgement

In the reports of the South African TRC and the 1996 Commission on Aboriginal Peoples, there is a commitment to the idea that acknowledgment has an important role to play in the healing of victims of wrongdoing and in prospects for their peaceful and productive coexistence with perpetrators, perpetrator groups, bystanders, and beneficiaries. Both reports endorse acknowledgement as fundamental for healing and a step towards any significant reconciliation between groups. Given the logical relationships between received acknowledgement, granted acknowledgement, and self-acknowledgement, it is reasonable to interpret both reports as claiming that perpetrators and beneficiaries should grant acknowledgement so that wronged people and peoples can receive it. One form of acknowledging wrongdoing is through moral apologies, in which perpetrators or those institutionally allied to them admit responsibility for doing something wrong.[21]

These reports explore issues primarily from the point of view of victims, and they assume that wrongs of the past should be acknowledged by perpetrators and their affiliates, because *acknowledging those wrongs will assist victims to heal*, will mark a *separation from the wrongdoing of the past and a commitment to reform*, and may *constitute a necessary step towards reconciliation*. The idea is that perpetrators or the state or both will acknowledge to themselves that they have committed wrongs and will, on the basis of this self-acknowledgement, grant public acknowledgement to victims. The victims will then receive acknowledgement, which will articulate a recognition that certain sorts of acts were wrong and a commitment not to do such things again. Acknowledgement may be expressed in various ways: through criminal trials, truth commissions, public inquiries, apologies, reparations, or memorials,[22] and this acknowledgement is of tremendous value—most obviously to victims.

It is most plausible to think of these claims about acknowledgement as having a tacit *ceteris paribus* clause. To say that acknowledgement is important and valuable is not to say that the value of acknowledgement, in this sense of spelling out the truth about wrongs of the past, is so powerful as to outweigh all other values in every context. There are certainly strong moral arguments against applying extreme pressure in attempts to force acknowledgement. And at a social level, a society has to balance requirements for acknowledgement in terms of apologies, compensation, and memorials against competing needs in areas such as health care, housing, and foreign policy.

In considering the value of acknowledgement from the point of view of victims, we may usefully appeal to a view articulated by Jean Hampton, who said that wrongdoing of this sort *expresses a message of lack of moral worth, because the victims are treated as though they simply do not count.*[23] For example, to forcibly evict a community from its land without obtaining its informed consent and making reasonable arrangements for its well-being, so that other people can develop resources there or test their planes there, is to imply that the removed community and its people simply *do not matter*—that their needs and interests and, indeed, their very moral dignity and status as human beings, *need not be taken into account*. It is to treat them as morally and politically negligible. In cases when wrongdoing has implied such radical denial of moral status, *acknowledgement* that what was done was wrong and these people deserved better is powerful and important because it negates that wrongful message of moral insignificance. Instead, the acknowledgement of wrongdoing communicates a recognition of the human dignity and worth of the victim.

Those who have been victims of wrongdoing are likely to know it, to be painfully aware of it, and nevertheless to suffer after-effects.[24] When there is no acknowledgement of the wrongdoing, the initial wound develops into "the second wound of silence," because the lack of acknowledgement indicates that people condone the wrongs and do not care about the baneful results. To receive acknowledgement that these things did happen, that they were wrong and should not have happened, is to receive confirmation, validation, of one's dignity and status as a human being, and a moral being of equal worth. Such recognition was explicitly and implicitly denied—and in the wake of that denial, it needs to be emphatically and publicly articulated. In the context of profound wrongs, that fundamental moral recognition of human status will be the primary and basic reason that acknowledgement is important to victims. It should be *just obvious* that any human being is a human being, that a woman or black or native is a human being just as much as a white, middle-class man, and that whatever grounds rights, responsibilities, and privileges for white men grounds them for other human beings, too. But although such truths are obvious, we have often acted as though they were false. That is why acknowledgement is necessary.

At the TRC victim hearings in South Africa, thousands of people deemed to be of little worth under the apartheid system were respectfully heard as they told their own stories of suffering before a respectful state commission. Their stories were written into the history of the nation that had under apartheid sought to undermine their human dignity and denied their status as citizens. Such acknowledgement matters to victims because it is a recognition of their status as full-fledged persons and citizens, and a rejection of past practice founded on the contrary view. The 1996 Canadian report raised the possibility of a similar commission at which native Canadians could appear and tell their stories so that their full moral status, suffering, and role in Canadian history would be acknowledged. Such acknowledgement offers the hope of ending an awkward separation and alienation between people. It soothes the injured one, ending that person's frustration and putting him or her at greater ease and in a better position to enter an honest, decent relationship.

Are there not counter-examples to the claim that victims need acknowledgement? During his many years in prison, Nelson Mandela never lost his dignity, his capacity for leadership, his style of respectful interaction with others, or his sense of himself as a human being with human rights. When he worked long hours in a quarry, when he had been beaten and had to labour under an uncomfortable sun, he retained the sense that he and his country had a better future. Stories of such courage and conviction show that it is possible to maintain one's sense of self under very severe conditions. Some people can preserve that fundamental of self-worth, self-trust, and self-respect in the face of external denial and obliviousness.[25] But these exceptional cases do not refute the general claim that acknowledgement is valuable to victims. Acknowledgement is important as recognition, as an acceptance of who we are, as we think we are, by others. For most of us, most of the time, it is difficult to preserve a sense of who we are and what we do when those around us deny us dignity and recognition.

At root, receiving acknowledgement is important because of the social nature of the self. It is often said that *the self is socially constructed*. I take this to mean that we do not establish our personal identity and sense of meaning and purpose in life alone, as solitary, isolated individuals. We acquire language, beliefs, knowledge, and skills from other people. We gain much of our knowledge from the testimony of other people, either verbally or in print or other media. Our memories, beliefs, attitudes, interpretations, emotions, motivations, and goals emerge from our experience interacting with other people and are strongly affected by the cultural context in which we live. We speak to and with other people, who may choose whether to listen to us or not, and interpret what we say in various ways, as they will. The roles we occupy in life are social roles that deeply affect us, but are clearly established apart from our own individual efforts. Those roles affect our sense of time and meaning, what we make of our lives, and our capacity to act. Even Mandela was not a leader by himself. Both inside and outside prison, his leadership role was predicated on recognition by others. It is with, and through, other people that we establish our sense of self. If those other people deny or ignore events and harms that have been fundamental in shaping our experience, we will be unable to stand in an honest and constructive relationship with them. Acknowledgement offers soothing, relief, and a basis for open, comfortable, and more trusting relationships. From the point of view of victims, this is why acknowledgement is important.

But this is by no means the end of the story about the value and importance of acknowledgement. There are two other relevant perspectives: those of the perpetrator and the broader society. Clearly, an account of acknowledgement needs development from these points of view as well.[26] The moral significance of acknowledgement to victims is itself a reason for perpetrator groups to grant acknowledgement. If we accept some moral responsibility for the well-being of other people, we should accept an obligation to acknowledge them with regard to their claim to decent moral treatment.

The 1996 Report calls for non-Aboriginal Canadians to *acknowledge* the history and cultures of Aboriginal Canadians and to accept these people and their cultures as part of who we are as a people and a country. Why should we do this? Why would this be important? Because we owe it to these people who are our fellow citizens and from whom we received the land that provides for our country. Because in so doing, we can address and deal with our own feelings of guilt and shame. And fundamentally, because such acknowledgement is a necessary first step in the direction of moral and political reform. If we are not willing to publicly acknowledge the exploitation and injustice that have characterized native-government and native-white relations in this country for the last two centuries, we will have little hope of improving on that bitter past. And that is why acknowledgement is important.

Notes

1 Thomas Scheff, *Bloody Revenge: Emotions, Nationalism, and War* (Boulder, CO: Westview Press, 1994).

2 Joseph Montville in Michael Henderson, *The Forgiveness Factor: Stories of Hope in a World of Conflict* (New York: Penguin, 1996).

3 Michael Ignatieff, *The Warrior's Honour: Ethnic War and the Modern Conscience* (New York: Penguin, 1997).

4 Martha Minow, *Between Vengeance and Forgiveness: Facing History after Genocide and Mass Violence* (Boston: Beacon Press, 1998).

5 Lawrence Weschler, *A Miracle, a Universe: Setting Accounts with Torturers* (New York: Penguin, 1990).

6 Some 7,000 persons appeared at the victim hearings of the TRC. There were over 21,000 statements taken, containing allegations of nearly 38,000 gross violations of human rights. Of these, nearly 10,000 were killings. There were some 7,000 applications for amnesty. Volume I, *Final Report of the Truth and Reconciliation Commission of South Africa* (Government of the Republic of South Africa, 1998).

7 Royal Commission on Aboriginal Peoples, *Final Report*, vol. 1, *Looking Forward, Looking Back* (Ottawa: Ministry of Supply and Services, 1996).

8 Ibid., vol. 1, 7-8.

9 Ibid., 513.

10 Dictionaries tend to interdefine these terms. More than "acknowledgement," "avowal," and "admission," the word "confession" has religious associations and connotations. It suggests that what is acknowledged is the commission of a sin, which is acknowledged to a priest or other authoritative person from whom one is seeking absolution or forgiveness. Wishing to avoid these religious overtones, I have avoided using the word "confession" here. Conceptual issues and the moral wrongness of forcing confession (or acknowledgement) are explored further in Trudy Govier, "Acknowledgement and Forced Confession," *The Acorn: Journal of the Gandhi-King Society* (US) 11, 1 (Fall/Winter 2000-2001): 5-20.

11 Herbert Fingarette, *Self-Deception* (London: Routledge and Kegan Paul, 1969). I also want to allow for the possibility of implicit acknowledgement. An example of implicit acknowledgement would be a case in which a status or achievement or fact is marked (as, for example, by a form of treatment, or by a memorial) and yet there are no words precisely to the effect that "So and So is a person of importance or So and So is a great hero."

12 Fingarette, *Self-Deception*, 71.

13 Herbert Fingarette, "Self-Deception Needs No Explaining," *Philosophical Quarterly* 48: 291.

14 Ibid., 295.

15 As is pointed out by Robert Solomon, "Self, Deception, and Self-Deception in Philosophy," in Roger T. Ames and Wimal Dissanayake, eds., *Self and Deception: A Cross-Cultural Philosophical Inquiry* (Albany, NY: SUNY Press, 1998), 91-122, and Annette Baier, "The Vital but Dangerous Art of Ignoring: Selective Attention and Self-Deception," also in *Self and Deception,* 53-72.

16 Baier, "The Vital but Dangerous Art of Ignoring," 55-56.

17 Culpable ignoring would naturally result in culpable ignorance. When we ignore something, we do not find out about it, and if it is the sort of thing we should have found out about, then we will lack knowledge we could have had and should have had, which will mean we will be culpably ignorant.

18 Often noted, but see in particular Timothy Garton Ash, *The File: A Personal History* (New York: Harper Collins, 1997), and his articles in *The New York Review of Books*, regarding South Africa ("True Confessions," July 17, 1997, and "The Truth about Dictatorship," February 19, 1998).

19 My defence of the claim that acknowledgement is valuable for victims is, in effect, a defence of the claim that sincere, veridical acknowledgement is valuable for victims. It is not a defence of pseudo-acknowledgement, a case in which a person (usually under some form of pressure) "admits" to something that he or she did not do, or that he or she does not believe himself to have done. Arguments given later for the value of acknowledgement are for acknowledgement in this sense, and not for pseudo-acknowledgement. These themes are explored in detail in my essay "Acknowledgement and Forced Confession," in *The Acorn*. Compare note 10.

20 In an apology, the person apologizing acknowledges to the other that he or she did something wrong and is responsible for it. Thus, moral apology presupposes a considerable degree of moral agreement about the original offence (what was done, and the extent to which P was responsible for it.) P can acknowledge W to V only insofar as P and V agree that W did happen and P did W. This means broad agreement as to what W was and how P was responsible for it. If V thinks that W is F, whereas P thinks that W is not F, but is rather G, P may not be able to acknowledge W to V's satisfaction.

21 The notion of apology as an expression of moral acknowledgement is explored more fully in Trudy Govier and Wilhelm Verwoerd, "The Promise and Pitfalls of Apology," *Journal of Social Philosophy* (Spring 2002). See also Trudy Govier and Wilhelm Verwoerd, "Taking Wrongs Seriously: A Qualified Defence of Public Apologies," *Saskatchewan Law Review* 65, 1 (Winter 2002): 139-62.

22 As explained in Minow, *Between Vengeance and Forgiveness*.

23 Jean Hampton in Jefferie G. Murphy and Jean Hampton, *Forgiveness and Mercy* (Cambridge, MA: Cambridge University Press, 1988), 60.

24 Described in considerable detail in Yael Danieli, ed., *International Handbook of Multigenerational Legacies of Trauma* (New York: Plenum Press, 1998).

25 Compare Govier, *Dilemmas of Trust* (Kingston and Montreal: McGill-Queen's University Press, 1988), chapters 5 and 6.

26 Answers are, I think, implied in what has been said earlier, but the issue is complex and considerations of space make it impossible to offer a more complete theory here.

3

Reconciliation for Realists

Susan Dwyer[1]

As the last millennium drew to a close, there appeared to be a global frenzy to balance moral ledgers. Talk of apology, forgiveness, and reconciliation was everywhere. Take, for example, the Canadian government's offer of reconciliation to that country's 1.3 million Aboriginal people, and President Kim Dae-jung's formal acceptance of Japan's written apology for harms caused during its thirty-five-year occupation of South Korea. In academia, so-called forgiveness studies came into their own, most notably with the establishment of the University of Wisconsin's International Forgiveness Institute, and the disbursement of five million dollars from the Templeton Foundation for work on a spectrum of issues from deathbed reconciliations to conciliatory behaviour among non-human primates.[2] But perhaps nothing has done more to subject the concepts of apology, forgiveness, and reconciliation to international attention and critique than South Africa's Truth and Reconciliation Commission.[3]

Of the three concepts of apology, forgiveness, and reconciliation, the latter, can seem the most puzzling. This is not to say that apology and forgiveness do not raise difficult questions in their own right. Aurel Kolnai, for example, points to the paradoxical nature of forgiveness: on the one hand, we think we ought to forgive all—and only—those wrongdoers who deserve to be forgiven; on the other, the more deserving of forgiveness a person is, the less like a wrongdoer he seems, and forgiveness seems to lose its point.[4] Still, most of us have enough experience of apology and

---

forgiveness (at least for minor transgressions) to make these notions appear relatively straightforward.

But what is reconciliation? Is it the end-state toward which practices of apology and forgiveness aim? Is it a process of which apology and forgiveness are merely parts? Or is it something altogether independent of apology and forgiveness? How is reconciliation to be achieved? And under what conditions should it be sought? Curiously, given the frequency with which the term "reconciliation" is used, no one is saying.

The notable lack of any clear account of what reconciliation is, and what it requires, justifiably alerts the cynics among us. Reconciliation is being urged upon people who have been bitter and murderous enemies, upon victims and perpetrators of terrible human rights abuses, upon groups of individuals whose very self-conceptions have been structured in terms of historical and often state-sanctioned relations of dominance and submission. The rhetoric of reconciliation is particularly common in situations where traditional judicial responses to wrongdoing are unavailable because of corruption in the legal system, staggeringly large numbers of offenders, or anxiety about the political consequences of trials and punishment.

Hence, a natural worry, exacerbated by the use of explicitly therapeutic language of healing and recovery, is that talk of reconciliation is merely a ruse to disguise the fact that a "purer" type of justice cannot be realized. This is of moral and practical significance. For example, in being asked to focus on racial reconciliation rather than on punishment, are victims of apartheid having to settle for the morally second best? And, if so, how sanguine can we be about South Africa's long-term social stability? Until we have a clearer idea of what reconciliation is, we cannot know whether it is right—or even morally desirable—to pursue it.

In the next two sections, I progressively mine our pretheoretical understanding of reconciliation to arrive at a core concept that at the same time suggests a way in which reconciliation might be pursued and grounds a response to moral qualms provoked by the use of an unanalyzed conception of reconciliation. First, however, I want to situate my current project in relation to a particular religious conception of reconciliation.

"Reconciliation" has almost exclusively positive connotations, suggesting an end to antagonisms, the graceful acceptance of disappointment or defeat, the healing and repair of valuable friendships, and so on. However, the word also has powerful religious overtones, including intimations of purification and cleansing as well as the restoration of an individual's relationship to God. If one's task is to give content to the concept of reconciliation in a way that displays its political and moral appropriateness, it will be tempting to ignore theological aspects of reconciliation. But this temptation should be resisted, for at least three reasons.

First, it is undeniable that Christian conceptions of reconciliation are deeply implicated in the South African context (under the leadership of Nelson Mandela and Desmond Tutu), in several South and Central American countries recovering from violent pasts, and in the predominantly church-led discourse on racial reconciliation in the US. Second, Christian understandings of reconciliation often conjoin the common idea that "none of us is without sin" with powerful stories of healing and transformation that provide inspiration to many individuals struggling in the aftermath of harms suffered and harms caused. Third, however, I think we must be aware of the ambitious and slightly mysterious picture of reconciliation embodied in Christianity. Ambition and mystery lie in the suggestions that love and faith in God are required for reconciliation. I will eventually concede that a sort of faith—construed in broadly psychological terms—may be needed to undertake the work of reconciliation. But even granting this, the model of reconciliation I will propose is decidedly more modest that the prevailing Christian conception.

Unpacking the Concept: Familiar Cases

As a first step toward understanding what reconciliation might mean, it is helpful to examine some familiar cases in which we are apt to invoke the concept.

We often speak of old friends wanting to be reconciled after a fight, of a person being reconciled to the onset of a chronic illness. Throughout the US, victim-offender reconciliation programs have been developed to bring together criminals and their victims. In still other cases, reconciliation is attempted between groups of people, as in the examples of Canada and South Africa. Thus, we can usefully distinguish between micro-level and macro-level reconciliation, where the former typically involves local, face-to-face interactions—say between two friends—and the latter concerns more global interactions between groups of persons, or nations, or institutions, which are often mediated by proxy.

That we can speak of reconciliation between a range of different things is linked to the further fact that reconciliation has both forward- and backward-looking dimensions. The reconciliation of estranged friends involves their past loyalty to each other as well as a mutual desire to repair their relationship and to maintain it into the future. When Archbishop Tutu advocates racial reconciliation in South Africa, he combines a vivid understanding of that country's history with a sincere commitment to a better tomorrow. An important difference between the South African case and the case of estranged friends is that the idea of reconciliation as restoration of a former state is relevant only in the latter, for in South Africa there is no previous racial harmony to be restored.

Reconciliation can be motivated by a variety of factors. Friends want to continue a desirable relationship in spite of some nastiness between them. National leaders and citizens in South Africa and other places hope for a peaceful and more just future. But consider a woman who longs for a child, yet discovers she cannot become pregnant. The discrepancy between her hopes and her capacities is irresolvable. She wants to become reconciled to this fact, in order to achieve psychological peace. There's no point being miserable about something she cannot help (though regret for lost opportunities may be appropriate). A desire for psychological peace might also be what motivates the victim of a crime to meet the person who stole treasured objects from him. It is not unusual for victims of even minor crimes, such as theft, to be distressed and angry and to lose confidence in their own security. And mediators who facilitate face-to-face meetings between offenders and their victims report that such interactions do serve to assuage such feelings on the part of victims.

As crucial as these psychological motivations are, it is clear that people can also have *moral* reasons for pursuing reconciliation. Sometimes, the source of such reasons is immediate—as in the case of estranged friends, where we might assume that one of the duties of friendship is the willingness to attempt reconciliation in the wake of upset. In other situations, most notably those like South Africa, whatever moral reasons there are for reconciliation will be grounded in a more transcendent and thus more "distant" good, for example, respect for human dignity and human rights, or the value of a yet-to-be-realized civic friendship.

It is not always easy to distinguish moral from non-moral motivations for human action. But when it comes to recommendations for reconciliation, it is vital that we pay close attention to the language in which they are couched. For while features of human psychology bear directly on the desirability of reconciliation, the mere fact that reconciliation would bring psychological peace does not provide a moral justification for attempts to reconcile.

Even more important, facts about human psychology are relevant to the question of whether reconciliation is morally *required*, in that they determine whether reconciliation is even possible in certain circumstances. Suppose that a person is not a victim of theft, but of some more serious crime like kidnapping and torture. It is true that some people appear to have remarkable capacities to put the past behind them and move on. But just how much can we reasonably expect of the average person whose loved ones are either killed or made to disappear by forces of the state? Most recent calls for reconciliation, particularly between nations and their violent pasts and between groups of victims and victimizers, imply that seeking reconciliation is the morally right thing to do. Institutions and individuals would be wrong not to try it. But the obligatoriness of reconciliation—at either the micro- or the macro-level—would appear to be defeated when interpersonal reconciliation is psychologically impossible.

This raises a further matter, namely, that the evaluation of efforts to achieve macro-level reconciliation—such as those taking place in South Africa—must consider the various relations that hold between individual persons and the corporate entities they belong to. Does reconciliation between groups require that all or a majority of members work toward reconciliation? Or, is there some sense to be made of reconciliation between groups, even where micro-level reconciliation is psychologically impossible? (I briefly address these questions below.)

When we focus on commonplace examples of reconciliation, it is easy to be overwhelmed by the heterogeneity of the concept and by the complexities involved in assessing the prospects of its applications. It would be nice to articulate a more basic account of reconciliation that unifies the different cases we have discussed and suggests some ways in which reconciliation might be achieved. This requires stepping outside the socio-moral domain briefly to consider reconciliation in another light.

Unpacking the Concept: A Deeper Account

When confronted with two apparently incompatible but attractive positions or two apparently mutually inconsistent but individually plausible propositions, we often speak of the need to reconcile them. A great deal of intellectual labour involves the description of such tensions and attempts to alleviate them. We see that adopting position A rules out adopting position B, that p and q cannot be true together, etc. Reconciliation can then take a number of forms: maybe proposition p isn't as plausible as it first appeared, and we can reject it without loss; or perhaps a more complete grasp of positions A and B will show them to be compatible after all. Presupposed in all this is a commitment to a normative ideal—usually truth, but sometimes mere logical consistency. If truth and consistency didn't matter, such efforts at reconciliation would be unjustified and unmotivated. Reconciliation is not something we seek for its own sake. And in particular, any imperative to attempt reconciliation depends upon the existence of normative ideals to which we are independently attached.

I suggest that we think of human reconciliation quite generally in terms of tensions—tensions between two or more beliefs; tensions between two or more differing interpretations of events; or tensions between two or more apparently incommensurable sets of values—and our responses to them. Here, the regulative ideals are not exactly truth and logical consistency. Rather, they have to do with understanding, intelligibility, and coherence. These are important features of human lives and we care when they are threatened. My claim is that such considerations serve to ground a comprehensive notion of reconciliation.

Human lives are led narratively. A person's self-conception, along with her conception of the world around her and of her place in it, is usefully understood in terms of the relevant stories she constructs. Her past actions and experiences, her current relationships, her hopes and fears about the future are facts about a person that together make up the story of her life. It is against this cumulative but relatively stable background that her life is rendered intelligible, from the inside as well as from the outside. And we rely heavily on the tacit assumption that the lives of others have narrative unity. Expectations and trust between us could not exist otherwise. You can't depend on, let alone befriend, an individual whose life exhibits no reliable pattern.

But certain things can and do disrupt this coherence. There is betrayal among friends; a person arrives at a painful realization about his future; another becomes the victim of a random crime. Such events and experiences challenge deeply held beliefs, sometimes in profound ways. A woman might think she "really knew" her lover; part of her self-understanding was tied up with being his partner. But his recent treachery throws into doubt the meaning of their past relationship, thus threatening her sense of self. The diagnosis of an illness or disability can rob a person of a particular projected future. Where the anticipation of such a future has guided and shaped his past and present actions, a person may have to engage in a wholesale reevaluation of his life and priorities. Victims of crime are suddenly and sometimes violently forced to reconsider their previous assumptions about physical security and the predictability of others.

We can never undo such disruptions; they are, literally, facts of life. But, especially when they are severe, our continued well-being—perhaps our very existence—depends upon our being able to incorporate them into our personal narratives. For persons, at least, self-understanding, understanding others, being understood by others, and achieving a degree of coherence and stability in our lives matters.[5]

The desires for intra-personal and inter-personal understanding that underpin the construction of a coherent and stable life narrative are quite fundamental. To call them basic human needs would not be an overstatement. And it seems to me that any adequate account of morality must be sensitive to such facts about human psychology. I cannot argue for this claim here, but it is surely plausible that a normative theory must accommodate—it must not be in tension with—basic facts about the type of creatures whose behaviour its principles purport to regulate.[6] Given this assumption, we can understand not only why we are motivated to pursue reconciliation but why reconciliation is of deep moral significance.

At this juncture, it is important to emphasize that the moral significance of reducing tensions in personal narratives does not imply that all such tensions are bad, or that reconciliation aims at the *elimination* of tensions. Some tensions—for example, those that stem from the recognition of our fallibility—help keep us honest, and others might be worth cultivating insofar as they provide the impetus for and sustaining force of creative efforts. The sort of tensions that rightly trigger demands for reconciliation are ones that result from severe identity-threatening disruptions to ongoing narratives. But even in these cases, I am recommending that reconciliation be understood as the incorporation—not as an erasure—of that tension. The tension may need to be kept in view; the objective is to find a way to live with that.

Moreover, the moral significance of reducing tensions in personal narratives does not entail that reconciliation (morally) ought to be pursued no matter what. Despite the fact that human welfare depends upon the ability to maintain (minimally) coherent individual life narratives, reconciliation as incorporation is not morally obligatory. For one thing, it is a familiar moral principal that *ought* implies *can*, and, as I have already noted, individual psychological capacities may render reconciliation impossible for some. Furthermore, not all theories of right action are welfarist.

The construal of reconciliation in terms of incorporation appears to reveal what is common across the wide range of cases in which we are inclined to speak of reconciliation at the micro-level. But how well does the account do at the macro-level?

Let us suppose, not implausibly, that groups, communities, and nations have autobiographies, too. In supposing this, we need not commit ourselves to metaphysically dubious entities; that is, nations need not be thought of as persons or agents. Neither need we assume that they are homogeneous, undifferentiated wholes. In describing the personal case, I said that individual narratives are constructed around self-understanding, hopes and fears, and the like. When it comes to communities and nations, culture, ethnic identity, national spirit and aspirations play analogous roles. And, again paralleling the personal case, these elements form the basis for intergroup relations and expectations.

Larger-scale narratives suffer disruptions as well, although "disruption" seems obscenely inadequate as a description of the events in Bosnia and Rwanda. Nonetheless, the central idea is the same: the continued well-being, or the very survival of a community or nation, depends upon how it manages to incorporate and accommodate these disturbances and challenges to its prevailing narrative of self-understanding.

Dealing with Positive Disruptions

I have yet to describe how reconciliation—understood as narrative incorporation—is to be achieved. But before doing so, I need to acknowledge and rectify a potentially dangerous incompleteness in the account of reconciliation I have offered. The account appears to fare well with respect to the cases so far considered, which all involve a *negative* disruption to an ongoing narrative. But sometimes it seems appropriate to seek reconciliation, when the relevant disruption is actually *positive*.

South Africa appears to be a case in point. While the Truth and Reconciliation Commission is devoted to the investigation of abuses during the apartheid era, the complex event that precipitated its establishment was the *downfall* of apartheid. In contrast to the case of a friend's betrayal, the disrupted narrative here is one of racial separation, radical inequalities, and violence. There are similar (but not strictly analogous) cases at the micro-level. Narratives of long-term drug addiction are disrupted—or at least interrupted—by detoxification, rehabilitation, and genuine resolutions to discontinue the problematic behaviour.

These two examples have elements in common with the others discussed above, insofar as they all involve dealing with past wrongs. But in the case of South Africa and the recovering drug addict, the relevant disruptions apparently require a response more radical than the mere modification of an ongoing narrative. Reconciliation between blacks and whites in South Africa, or between an addict and his family, seems to involve the *dis*continuation of one story in favour of starting another. Indeed, tales of individual recovery are often couched in slightly paradoxical idioms: "I'm a new person"; "That was a former self"; and the like. Given that the very identity (self-conception) of blacks and whites in South Africa has been constructed in terms of oppressed and oppressors, the dissonance between these prior narratives and proposed post-apartheid stories of non-racialism and social equality may preclude the possibility of coherently continuing the prior narratives. If this is right, then either the narrative incorporation conception of reconciliation is incomplete, or it makes no sense to talk of reconciliation in such circumstances.

Conceding the latter option would resolve the difficulty quickly. But it would be an unhelpful concession, especially since so many contemporary pleas for reconciliation arise in contexts marked by deep animosities and justified distrust resulting from terrible human rights abuses. But at the same time, we must not underestimate the challenges of narrative revision. If reconciliation can be hard for friends who share a positive history, and where no one has *died* or been *tortured*, we can only begin to imagine the correspondingly greater difficulties confronting the people of South Africa. Indeed, I suspect that one explanation for the increased rhetoric of reconciliation is that, in contexts like South Africa, forgiveness for past wrongs is simply not possible. Other options—forgetting, trials and punishment, and so on—are ruled out by a constellation of factors. Yet *some* positive-sounding response is called for. Reconciliation might fit the bill. But as I said at the outset, without an account of what reconciliation is and what it requires, proposing reconciliation will seem like a political sop aimed at masking moral defeat. So it is important to see if the model of reconciliation I have sketched is applicable to the difficult cases.

An economical way to accomplish this task is to examine the mechanisms of reconciliation as narrative incorporation, to which I now turn.

The Process of Reconciliation

In my account of reconciliation, the core notion is that of bringing apparently incompatible descriptions of events into narrative equilibrium. Hence the first thing that parties to reconciliation will require is a clear view of those events, where only the barest of facts—who did what to whom and when—are relevant. The second stage will involve the articulation of a range of interpretations of those events. Finally, parties to the reconciliation attempt to choose from this range of interpretations some subset that allows them each to accommodate the disruptive event into their ongoing narratives. It is not required that all parties settle on a single interpretation, only that they are mutually tolerant of a limited set of interpretations. Sometimes this process will require the revision of aspects of the pre-existing narrative; under pressure to make sense of a recent event, a person may come to reinterpret some much earlier experiences. In different situations, different resources will be available for carrying out the task of reconciliation, making some instances relatively easy and others profoundly difficult.

Long-standing friends have, in addition to their individual narratives, a shared story of their life together. Over time friends mutually co-construct a tale about their relationship. This mini-history will include an account of how the relationship began, recountings of shared adventures, slights, injuries, acts of generosity and love, and feelings of joy and security. When a disruption occurs—say, when one friend betrays another—the two are faced with an event that is anomalous with respect to their shared story. If they choose to continue their friendship, they need to make sense of that event. Typically, friends will talk—presenting their respective sides of the story, explaining the motives and intentions behind their actions—and listen. The task is to move beyond the mere statement of agreed-upon facts, about who did what to whom, and toward a mutually acceptable interpretation (or interpretations) of those events.

Arriving at an accommodation need not and perhaps should not involve the excusing of a wrong. It might, but need not, involve an apology and the offer of forgiveness. Whether an apology is called for is precisely one of the topics up for discussion, taking into account how similar disruptions have been handled in the past. Thus, reconciliation and for-giveness are conceptually independent, even if they often go together. With a common language and mutual legitimate expectations of each other, friends have considerable resources at their disposal for engaging in reconciliation. Against a background of reliable behaviour, talk will often be enough to reconcile friends.

Matters are considerably harder in a case like that of the recovering drug addict, who struggles to reconcile with his parents and to the pain he has caused them as a result of his addiction. If they attempt reconciliation, there is probably little or no disagreement between the addict and his mother and father: the addict has lived his life in the grip of a powerful addiction; he has attempted to deny and conceal that fact; he has stolen and lied; and so on. It is typical for long-term drug abusers to make false promises, especially to enter detox and go clean. According to the model of reconciliation I am proposing, the process of reconciling requires that the addict and his parents incorporate into their individual and joint nar-ratives the belief that he *really* intends to give up drugs. But the addict's credibility is near zero. The idea that he is trustworthy and sincere is so radically at odds with each of the participant's existing narratives concern-ing him, that we must wonder whether any coherent incorporation of it is possible. Thus it is an open question whether this shared familial history offers resources for reconciliation, as its analogue in the case of friends does, or whether it presents more of an obstacle. Much will depend on the emotional ties between parents and their children, and on the participants' understanding of their respective filial and parental duties. And there is considerable anecdotal evidence to suggest that some people never give up on their loved ones. Nonetheless, the case illustrates some of the difficul-ties that attend attempts at reconciliation in the aftermath of even positive disruptions, and it alerts us to the potentially more serious problems that emerge in contexts like South Africa and Northern Ireland.

Reconciliation in South Africa

In assessing the applicability of my proposed model of reconciliation to the South African case, it is important to bear in mind the distinction between what I have been calling the micro- and the macro-levels, and ask whether the possibility of reconciliation at the macro-level depends upon the possibility of reconciliation at the micro-level. Moreover, appealing to this distinction will help us respond to skeptical worries about whether reconciliation represents a morally second-best strategy for dealing with past wrongs.

At the macro-level in South Africa, reconciliation is being proposed primarily between races, but people also speak of the nation becoming reconciled to its past. Immediately, there is a tension. For the mention of *a* nation being reconciled to its past presupposes that there is a relatively unified South Africa that can look back on its past. But *that* entity is surely the one that South Africans seek to bring into existence through racial reconciliation. So I want to put aside talk of the reconciliation of a nation with its past and focus instead on the prior question of reconciliation between currently living people. Of course, the past is crucial here too; individual South Africans are inescapably affected by the historical facts of apartheid.

These, then, are our questions: Does racial reconciliation between blacks and whites require that *individual* blacks and whites seek reconciliation with each other? If the obstacles to individual reconciliation are insurmountable, is it still intelligible to talk of national or group reconciliation? Would the pursuit of national reconciliation be purchased at the cost of denying justice to individuals?

The model of reconciliation I have proposed is one of narrative incorporation. Hence reconciliation between blacks and whites would appear to involve the construction of a coherent narrative that encompasses both the atrocities of apartheid *and* the hope for a peaceful, respectful coexistence of political equals. But is this possible? Earlier, we noted that the shared history of friends constitutes a rich resource for reconciliation. It usually provides some motivation and sometimes grounds an imperative to seek it. But the history between blacks and whites in South Africa is not a history of friendship. Rather, it is a tale of mutual hatred, suspicion, and distrust. Far from being a resource, history can hinder attempts at reconciliation.[7]

Further obstacles to reconciliation suggest themselves. As I have already noted, in an all-encompassing oppressive regime like apartheid, individuals' very identities are often constructed in terms of whether they are members of the oppressing or the oppressed class. This has implications for the psychological capacities of persons to engage in reconciliation. Reconciliation may require that people give up fundamental self-conceptions or face some very unwelcome truths about themselves. Consider the black youth whose entire self-understanding has been built around resisting apartheid; or the white businesswoman, who, although not an active oppressor, never objected to apartheid and comforted herself with the thought that the system couldn't really be that unjust. Moreover, the sheer number of people involved, combined with deep-seated and justified distrust on both sides, diminish the possibility of repeated and extended face-to-face encounters between victims and victimizers, of the sort involved in the mechanisms of reconciliation I outlined above.

It does not follow from these considerations, however, that the narrative incorporation view of reconciliation is incomplete. Nor do they show that talk of reconciliation is simply inappropriate in South Africa. To demonstrate why, I need to say something more about the nature of narrative revision.

First, while most fictional narratives have distinct temporal bounds, the stories of our lives are open-ended. Hence, judgements of coherence are sometimes indeterminate. A person's (or a nation's) past is done. Some revision of interpretation is possible, but only so much can be altered without destroying the narrative in question. (One might say that too much revision is tantamount to writing the history of a different person or nation.) Attempts to coherently incorporate new beliefs and attitudes will be limited in this way. Nonetheless, whether some new belief about a person can be coherently incorporated can also be a matter of which futures are imaginable. What might seem anomalous now can make perfect sense later. The attempt by the addict's parents to see him as *having been* a liar and *being* a sincere son is not impossible. Neither is the attempt by black South Africans, to see white South Africans as *having been* oppressors and *being* fellow citizens. In each instance, focusing on just one or the other of the apparently mutually exclusive descriptions involves failing to grasp the whole truth. Here it is useful to recall that reconciliation as incorporation does not require the elimination of the tension that triggers it.

But, of course, when we are hurt and suffering, it can be exceptionally difficult for us to adopt this perspective. As Phylicia Oppelt, a black South African journalist, puts it: "I grew up in a system of apartheid that permeated every aspect of my existence. For most of my life I was taught to expect racial slurs, to accept as a fact of existence that the rights and privileges available to whites were not available to me. I was taught to be less....I have white friends. But all it takes is one racial slur from an unknown person to turn those same friends into representatives of a detested race."[8]

Oppelt reminds us how profoundly arduous the job of reconciliation can be, when one's entire sense of self and one's understanding of others has been structured by a state-sanctioned regime of racial oppression. Trust is extraordinarily fragile. Her words also highlight the fact that effective reconciliation is rarely a solipsistic task.

This leads to a second suggestion (actually a completely familiar point). Sometimes attempts at reconciliation require management or, less contentiously, the facilitative efforts of a third party. Marriage counselors, priests and ministers, conflict mediation specialists, diplomats, and, arguably, truth commissions can and sometimes do perform this role. When we are unable to accommodate a painful event into our narrative without losing coherence, it can help to see that someone else *can* tell such a story. We might not believe it yet, but perhaps we can at least see it as possible.

At this point, we might recall the religious resonances of reconciliation. In particularly difficult situations, reconciliation does require faith. Bono (of U2 fame) recently described David Trimble (the head of the Ulster Unionist Party) and John Hume (the leader of the Social Democratic and Labour party) as men who "had taken a leap of faith out of the past and into the future."[9] But this need not be faith in a divine being. It can be as commonplace as our already implicit belief that the future is nothing if not full of possibility, where the import of this belief is not the old (and false) canard that anything is possible if one puts one's mind to it. Rather, it is expressed in the fact that each of us manages to go on— often quite successfully—despite gross uncertainty about the future. Our experience with unforeseen opportunities and adversities grounds and increasingly contributes to our faith that we have the resources to cope with the twists and turns of our futures.

I do not mean for a moment to suggest that people who were tortured under apartheid or whose loved ones were murdered simply be consoled with the fact that they have survived after all and will probably continue to do so. That would be morally outrageous. Rather I want highlight the fact that our attempts at narrative construction and revision are often fueled by an acquired psychological disposition that might be likened to faith.

It is worth stressing, too, that in difficult cases, a person's word will rarely be enough to secure reconciliation, and reconciliation is unlikely to be instantaneous or even quick. Given his history, the drug addict cannot merely *say* that he's clean, report his intention to remain so, and leave it at that. He must *act* accordingly. An extended, reliable pattern of reformed behaviour can begin to restore a person's credibility where no words can. Similarly in South Africa, we can imagine any number of state-sponsored programs (actions) that might serve to show that the "new" South Africa is genuinely committed to racial equality: education subsidies, health care reform, appointment of blacks to positions of political and social power, and the like.[10]

I began this section by posing three questions: Does racial reconciliation between blacks and whites require that individual blacks and whites seek reconciliation with each other? If the obstacles to individual reconciliation are insurmountable, is it still intelligible to talk of national or group reconciliation? Would the pursuit of national reconciliation be purchased at the cost of denying justice to individuals? I believe that the preceding considerations deliver the following answers to the first two questions; I reserve my response to the third until the next section.

There are real and significant obstacles in the paths of individual South Africans seeking reconciliation. For example, the scope and depth of narrative revision required in the case of the white businesswoman who must now try to see her past self as a passive accomplice in a grossly unjust social and political system may be too great. Similarly, there are obstacles to reconciliation *between* individuals, and not just because some crimes strike us as unforgivable. (Recall, I have stressed that reconciliation does not require apology or forgiveness.) Rather, it might be that individual blacks and whites simply do not feel that, *in their own cases*, there is any tension to be resolved. The disruption of a friendship immediately gives rise to a tension. But the official dismantling of apartheid could not by itself cause the formerly oppressed to suddenly see their former oppressors in a fundamentally different light. Only if an individual wishes so to see another, will she experience a tension of the sort toward which reconciliation is properly directed. Hence, reconciliation between individuals will be possible in some cases: where people have particular desires about their future relationships, where actions manifest the sincerity of these desires, and where people are able to engage in face-to-face encounters that facilitate the negotiation of acceptable interpretations of events.

My claim is only that reconciliation will be *possible* in such conditions, not that it will be inevitable. And often these conditions cannot be met. Nonetheless, it would be precipitous to infer from this that talk of reconciliation between groups makes no sense. Consider, for example, a remark of the late Marius Schoon: "On the whole, I'm in favor of the Truth and Reconciliation Commission. I think it is going to bring about national reconciliation. In my case, it's not going to bring about personal reconciliation."[11] Schoon was speaking in the context of the amnesty hearing for Craig Williamson, who confessed to sending the bomb that killed Schoon's wife, Jeanette, and daughter, Katryn, in 1984. It is as if Schoon, an Afrikaner opponent of apartheid, is able to see how the narrative of his country can be revised in ways that his own personal story cannot be. But, as I have stressed, reconciliation at the macro-level requires the credibility that can be established only by implementation of social and economic programs that concretely address the substantive injustices of apartheid.

Is Reconciliation Morally Second Best?

With a summary of the main features of the proposed account of reconciliation before us, we can render a preliminary judgement on the skeptical worries I mentioned at the beginning of the paper—that reconciliation is a kind of moral "second best," disguised by considerable rhetoric.

I have suggested that reconciliation is fundamentally a process whose aim is to lessen the sting of a tension: to make sense of injuries, new beliefs, and attitudes in the overall narrative context of a personal or national life. Reconciliation is guided by normative ideals of intelligibility, coherence, and understanding; and the mechanisms of reconciliation I have described are, broadly speaking, epistemological, in the sense that they are strategies of narrative revision.

This understanding of reconciliation applies at the micro- and macro-levels. It makes the application of the concept appropriate, even in circumstances where there is no prior positive relationship to be restored. In this sense, reconciliation does not pretentiously masquerade as *wiedergutmachung*—making things good again. Coherent incorporation of an unpleasant fact, or a new belief about an enemy, into the story of one's life might involve the issuance of an apology and an offer of forgiveness. But it need not. Reconciliation, as I have presented it, is conceptually independent of forgiveness. This is a good thing, for it means that reconciliation might be psychologically possible where forgiveness is not. That reconciliation is an epistemological task also makes the involvement of third parties, or some kinds of management or facilitation, both legitimate and potentially fruitful.

A full treatment of the role of third parties, which I cannot provide here, would give a richer account of how group reconciliation can be achieved where individual reconciliation might not be so easy. It would also speak to the concern that the stability of reconciliation might, in some cases, depend upon face-to-face encounters. Expressing skepticism about the work of the Truth and Reconciliation Commission in South Africa, Gertrude Muyana, a victim of random violence during the apartheid era, asks, "How can you reconcile with someone you don't see? You don't know who they are."[12] Archbishop Tutu's commission was highly sensitive to people's need to see each other. But it was not always possible for victims to confront victimizers.

Facts like this are precisely the sorts of things that provoke deep moral concerns about reconciliation. It is very tempting to think that Ms. Muyana deserved better, deserved to see the person who left her partially paralyzed brought to trial and duly punished for the harm he or she caused. More so, in cases where victims *have* witnessed their torturers demonstrating to the world the techniques they employed to extract confessions, it is natural to recoil at the idea that such people may be granted amnesty. Yes, it is good to know the truth. But how, in all good conscience, can victims be asked to bear the further burden of undertaking the hard work of reconciliation? And what about justice?

If a case could be made for the obligatoriness of reconciliation, then the questions above would have an answer. But I have argued that, while reconciliation is morally significant, facts about human psychology undermine any general claim to the effect that reconciliation is morally obligatory for individuals. But it does not follow from this that fixing on reconciliation as the macro-level preferred response to past wrongs amounts to settling for the morally second best.

To see why, consider what makes something a morally second-best option. Grant that there is some action I ought to perform, perhaps volunteer at the local homeless shelter. But I know myself well enough to know that were I to agree to do so, I would not show up. Now I am asked to help out at Thanksgiving. Ideally, I ought to volunteer *and* show up. But since I know I won't show up, I ought not volunteer, since it is morally worse to agree and not show up. In this case, what I opt for, failing to volunteer is the morally second best. I *could* show up; I just know that it is highly unlikely that I will.

Reconciliation, then, will be a morally second-best option only if there is some other strategy a nation *could* undertake that would be better. For example, if justice, in the sense of fair and comprehensive trials and punishment, could be effected, reconciliation will rightly be judged morally inferior. But the availability of realistic alternatives is precisely what is in question in most of the situations in which reconciliation is being recommended. Whether the establishment of truth commissions and efforts at reconciliation are morally inferior responses to violent pasts depends on the availability of other morally acceptable options. Where no such options exist, calls for reconciliation need not be impugned.[13]

Two points must be stressed, however. First, reconciliation should not be touted as aiming at the happy and harmonious coexistence of former enemies. It's one thing to achieve some measure of narrative coherence in the face of atrocity; it's quite another to come to love one's torturer. Although my model of reconciliation does not rule out the operation of a sort of faith in the process of reconciliation, and to that extent resonates with Christian understandings, it paints a decidedly modest picture of reconciliation. Complexities are, of course, involved in attempting reconciliation, but it is not a grand or mysterious undertaking. It seems to me that any conception of reconciliation—at either the micro- or macro-level—that makes reconciliation dependent on forgiveness, or that emphasizes interpersonal harmony and positive fellow-feeling, will fail to be a realistic model of reconciliation for most creatures like us. If we care about reconciliation, let us advocate it in terms that make it credible to the relevant parties. (This is one reason I have scrupulously avoided the language of healing in this essay.)

Second, when calls for reconciliation issue from national or international political leaders, they must be backed up by concrete plans for a variety of supporting measures—for example, economic, health, and educational initiatives—where these initiatives are *not* developed as compensation for past wrongs but rather as explicit demonstrations of the new government's commitment to the processes of racial and social reconciliation. Nevertheless, reconciliation conscientiously pursued and faithfully supported is no guarantee of justice, unless we distort our conception of justice to conform to contingent practical limitations. Reconciliation may often fall short of justice. This point bears emphasis. Political leaders should not pretend that reconciliation is the same as justice. But, again, this does not mean that reconciliation is a second-best option. Justice is not the only thing we value. And in many cases, reconciliation may be our sole morally significant option.

Of course, nothing I have said rules out the misappropriation of the concept of reconciliation by politicians and others. Governments will always be tempted to hide their inactivity behind positive-sounding therapeutic language. But I hope to have shown that reconciliation need not be a mere consolation prize for individuals and nations in the aftermath of violence and oppression. If this is less than some advocates of reconciliation would like, perhaps that is because of their tendency to talk of reconciliation in abstraction from the kind of reconciliation we humans can and do engage in.

Notes

1 I am especially grateful to Arthur Evenchik for our many valuable conversations about reconciliation and for his astute and penetrating comments and questions on earlier drafts of this paper. Thanks are also due to David A. Crocker, Robert Fullinwider, Xiaorong Li, and Paul Pietroski.

2 Scott Heller, "Emerging Field of Forgiveness Studies Explores How We Let Go of Grudges," *The Chronicle of Higher Education*, July 17, 1998, A18-20.

3 For a powerful first-hand account of the operation of the Truth and Reconciliation Commission, see Antjie Krog and Charlayne Hunter-Gault, *Country of My Skull: Guilt, Sorrow, and the Limits of Forgiveness in the New South Africa* (New York: Times Books, 1999).

4 Aurel Kolnai, "Forgiveness," *Proceedings of the Aristotelian Society* 74 (1973-74): 91-106.

5 See Gay Becker's *Disrupted Lives: How People Create Meaning in a Chaotic World* (Berkeley, CA: University of California Press, 1997). Written from an anthropological perspective, the book contains a wealth of case studies that bears out the central point here: people experience trauma in terms of disruption and respond to it by telling new stories about themselves.

6 See, for example, Owen Flanagan, *Varieties of Moral Personality: Ethics and Psychological Realism* (Cambridge, MA: Harvard University Press, 1993).

7 Wole Soyinka argues that the entire history of the African continent, including the spiritual resources of African traditional societies and the practices and enduring legacies of colonialism and slavery, condition the possibilities for reconciliation in South Africa and other African countries. I cannot here do justice to that history, but Soyinka is surely right to remind us that talk of truth and reconciliation never takes place in an historical vacuum. See Wole Soyinka, *The Burden of Memory, The Muse of Forgiveness* (New York: Oxford University Press, 1999), chap. 1.

8 Phylicia Oppelt, "Irreconcilable: The Healing Work of My Country's Truth Commission Has Opened New Wounds for Me," *Washington Post*, September 13, 1998, C1, C4.

9 Kelly Candaele, "Irish Ayes Are Smiling: Ireland Votes for Peace," *In These Times* 22 (1998), 11.

10 Similar considerations are advanced in the advocacy of racial reconciliation in the US. Spencer Perkins, a prominent reconciliation activist put it this way:

"If white Christians...are not willing to back up their reconciliation talk with sacrificial acts, then the majority of blacks and Native Americans are going to continue in their skepticism about all the reconciliation talk." Quoted in Aaron McCarroll Gallegos, "Following the Path of Grace," *Sojourners* (November-December 1998): 24-28.

11 Donald J. McNeil, Jr., "Marius Schoon, 61, Is Dead; Foe of Apartheid Lost Family, *New York Times*, February 9, 1999. Schoon was speaking in the context of the amnesty hearing of Craig Williamson, who admitted to sending the bomb that killed Schoon's wife and daughter in 1984.

12 Lynne Duke, "After Apartheid, a Need to Heal," *Washington Post*, November 15, 1998, A41, A45.

13 Martha Minow, *Between Vengeance and Forgiveness* (Boston: Beacon Press, 1998) hints at this line of thought.

4

Crime as Interpersonal Conflict: Reconciliation between Victim and Offender

Marc Forget

Introduction

In modern Western society, crime is defined as an act in violation of public law. Because the state creates and enforces the laws, it is perceived as the victim when a law is broken. The state's typical response to lawbreaking is to determine guilt and impose punishment. Unfortunately, this approach denies the actual victims of crime the opportunity to confront the offender(s), express their emotions, and gain a better understanding of a sometimes severely traumatic event in their lives. For offenders, the state's criminal justice system offers no opportunity to express remorse, apologize to the victim(s), or offer any form of compensation. This approach, however, is not the only possible response to crime. In ancient understandings of crime, as well as in those of many surviving Aboriginal societies, the victim and the offender are the central focus in society's response to wrongdoing. The goal is to make things right between victim and offender in order to allow both to live peacefully in the same community without fear of revictimizing or revenge. The community's interest is in ensuring that the needs of those involved are met. This approach is conducive to achieving a certain measure of reconciliation, which can play a pivotal role in both the victim's healing from the pain and trauma of the crime and the community's acceptance of the offender.

The importance of reconciliation in the healing process a victim goes through in the aftermath of crime cannot be overstated. After a brief cor-

---

Notes to chapter 4 are on pp. 132-35.

respondence with the man who had attacked and raped her eighteen years earlier, Diane M. was able to end her nightmare. She says it's as if a ceiling had been lifted, "the fear and anger are gone....There's not a bit of hate left."[1] For offenders, facing the human suffering they have caused may be the most powerful way to experience accountability. Stan Rosenthal is serving a long sentence in prison. After years of incarceration he met his victim's family in a mediated encounter. All along he had felt a strong desire to apologize, but the criminal justice system allowed him no contact with his victim's family. For Stan, the encounter was the most valuable experience he's had in prison. He said that no program had a greater impact on him.[2] These are only two of many compelling examples of the tremendous benefits that even simple attempts at reconciliation can offer victims, offenders, and the community at large.

Not only can reconciliation between individuals have a positive effect on whole communities but the principles utilized in reconciliation between victim and offender provide a framework that can be effectively used as part of reconciliation efforts in the wake of wider social conflicts such as civil war and racial segregation.[3]

In order to examine the question of reconciliation between victim and offender, wrongdoing itself must be understood in a dramatically different manner. Crime is much more than just lawbreaking; it usually involves actions that hurt people, and there are lasting, sometimes painful, human consequences.[4] Over the past twenty-five years a number of new approaches, some inspired by ancient or Aboriginal practices, have been offered as alternatives to the state's criminal justice system. Most begin with an understanding of crime as harm caused to people, and their processes involve the victim, the offender, and the community in an effort to make things right.

These approaches are collectively known as restorative justice, and it is restorative justice philosophy, theory, and practice that provide the most effective framework for exploring the potential for reconciliation between victim and offender.

The purpose of this paper is to look at what our society calls crime, define a way to respond to it that provides opportunities for reconciliation between victim and offender, examine the mechanisms of reconciliation, and identify ways in which the justice process can support and enhance the potential for reconciliation.

To begin with, it is important to look at some alternatives to the current perception of crime.

Ancient and Aboriginal Responses to Crime

In *Restoring Justice*, authors Daniel Van Ness and Karen Heetderks Strong use a passage from the *Iliad* to illustrate the importance of the encounter between victim and offender in ancient Greece.[5] "The early legal systems forming the foundation of Western criminal law emphasized the need for offenders and their families to settle with victims and their families."[6] In those early systems an offence was not considered a crime against the state but rather a transgression against the victim and the victim's family. Ancient Hebrew justice aimed to restore wholeness to those affected, and restitution was the norm in Middle Eastern legal codes going as far back as the Sumerian Code of Ur-Nammu (c. 2050 BCE).[7] In the Roman world most of what we call crime today was treated as a civil matter. The word *crimen* (the Latin origin of the word "crime") described a private complaint of one citizen against another. Crime demanded compensation, and the state had an interest only in seeing that a settlement was reached and its terms were adhered to.[8] Punishment was the exception and compensation was the rule.[9]

A central theme in biblical justice, in both the Old and the New Testaments, is *shalom*.[10] Old Testament scholar Perry Yoder found that shalom, as used in the Bible, has three dimensions of meaning: physical well-being, living in right relationship with one another, and a condition of honesty and moral integrity.[11] Shalom describes life lived in a condition of "all rightness." Not only does this state of "all rightness" imply reconciliation between offender and victim but it also has material and physical dimensions that suggest restitution to the victim.

The response to crime that defines it as a conflict between victim and offender, and focuses primarily on making things right between them, is not confined to the distant past. Many pre-colonial African societies used compensatory rather than punitive sanctions,[12] and modern Japanese practice emphasizes compensation to the victim and restoration of community peace.[13] In recent years many groups within the Aboriginal populations of North America, New Zealand, and Australia have begun exploring their traditional responses to crime. Among pre-contact Cree, offences such as theft and damage to property were treated as matters between offender and victim (and their respective families), and the emphasis was on compensating the victim.[14] In Ojibway and Cree communities, elders sometimes undertook to reconcile offenders with their victims. A few years ago in Manitoba, the Hollow Water First Nation established the

Community Holistic Circle Healing Program to work with offenders and victims involved in cases of abuse. The Program's statement on justice reflects the North American Aboriginal understanding of crime:

> People who offend against another are to be viewed and related to as people who are out of balance—with themselves, their family, their community, and their Creator. A return to balance can best be accomplished through a process of accountability that includes support from the community through teaching and healing. The use of judgment and punishment actually works against the healing process. An already unbalanced person is moved further out of balance.[15]

In spite of its historical roots in compensatory processes, and the revival of Aboriginal models that espouse healing and reconciliation, the modern Western criminal justice system remains exclusively focused on establishing guilt and administering punishment. Even though crime was viewed primarily as an interpersonal conflict until only a few hundred years ago,[16] it is now perceived exclusively as a violation of the state, defined by lawbreaking and guilt.[17]

The state-centred system excludes the victim and the community from significant participation in the justice process. Although it is described as offender-centred, our justice system hardly pays more attention to the offender's needs than it does to those of the victim. In the process that takes place between arrest and sentencing, the state's role is overwhelming, and it is the state that defines what justice is and how it will be served.

Before a different view of justice can be adopted, the reasons for the failures and shortcomings of the current approach must be examined. By looking at the modern justice system's origins and the decisive factors in its development, the reasons for its major failures can easily be understood. Most of the deficiencies in today's system take root in the fact that the state has become the victim, and it has taken over the responsibility for the resolution of the interpersonal conflict we call crime.

Evolution of the Modern Criminal Justice

Even though compensation and reconciliation have held an important place in criminal justice in many different societies through the ages, it cannot be denied that feelings of anger and thoughts of revenge have had an influence on the way crime is approached. Some passages in the Old Testament emphasize retribution,[18] the Roman state often applied cruel and barbaric punishment to its enemies and political opponents,[19] and banishment, physical punishment, and even execution are known to have been used by Aboriginal societies in North America.[20]

Nevertheless, as Dutch historian and jurist Herman Bianchi notes, we find compensation and penitence to be the normal solutions to criminal conflicts in ancient societies; revenge and retaliation are a deviance from the norm.[21]

The focus on compensation prevailed in Europe until the twelfth century. Until then the basic law was not a body of rules imposed by authority but rather an integral part of the common consciousness of the community. The people themselves legislated and judged. Law was not an instrument to separate people from one another on the basis of a set of principles but rather a matter of holding people together, a matter of reconciliation.[22] According to legal historian Harold J. Berman, this style of law began to change during the eleventh century, with the Gregorian Reform, or Papal Revolution.[23] The aim of the Gregorian Reform was to establish the church as a distinct legal entity standing over "the world." The church became an independent, hierarchical public authority that executed its own laws through its own administrative apparatus.[24] Canon law was completely systematized, and began to acquire the properties of the modern legal institution. The doctrine of purgatory also emerged around the time of the Papal Revolution, and a new conception of sin was adopted, in which the church not only assigned purgatorial suffering but also had the power to stay it.[25] The use of purgatory required a system of classification for the various sins. This system determined a precise number of days in purgatory for every type of sin. However, by certain actions and prayers one could reduce the amount of time to be spent in purgatory. According to Dutch jurist Louk Hulsman, modern criminal justice practice is entirely modeled on the doctrine of purgatory.[26]

Another seminal event in the move toward state-run criminal justice was the Norman invasion of Britain in the year 1066. As part of a political struggle to entrench his power, William the Conqueror took control of the process of handling crime. His son and successor, Henry I, consolidated his power by defining crime as an offense "against the king's peace" instead of one against a specific victim.[27] Thus the king became the primary victim of crime. The actual victim was pushed out of the justice process, and any amounts that would have been paid as reparation to the victim under the old Anglo-Saxon code were redirected to the king in the form of fines. This new model of crime identified the government and the offender as the sole parties.[28]

As criminal law became the business of the state, it was disembedded from society. Crime came to be seen as something other than a wrong requiring compensation; it became "a defiance of the law itself."[29] The new criminal justice system's function was to uphold the authority of the state, and it did so by instilling in the public a deep fear of the consequences of defying the law. Punishment had to be brutal and vicious, and it had to be administered publicly.[30]

As the use of corporal punishment and the death penalty increased (there were 78,000 hangings in England during the reign of Henry VIII),[31] their effectiveness diminished, and they came to be seen as barbarous. In the age of Enlightenment, philosophers sought "to perfect the proportion between punishments and offences."[32] These concerns with brutality and proportionality of punishment eventually led to the adoption of incarceration as a form of punishment. Until the 1770s imprisonment as a sentence was almost unheard of; prisons were used mainly to hold the accused until trial.[33]

Incarceration solidified the state's control of criminal justice. By the late nineteenth century, prison terms had become the normal sanction, and an offender was considered "a slave of the state" for the duration of his sentence.[34] Government control and ownership of the justice system was now total.

Today it is hard to think of crime as anything more than "breaking a law." The person responsible is charged with an action prohibited by a criminal code or other penal statute, then tried by a prosecutor representing the state, and, if found guilty, is punished according to prescribed standards.[35] However, a closer look at crime reveals that it is much more complex than the one act that contravened the one law. Unfortunately, by focusing exclusively on the legal aspect, the justice system not only ignores such important and complex issues as the victim's suffering, the offender's life circumstances, and the overall impact of the event on the community but it also overlooks the potential for healing and finding constructive solutions, and it obliterates any opportunity for reconciliation between victim and offender.

The modern trial consists of a contest between the prosecutor and the defence attorney; the offender remains passive, while the victim may be asked to testify only as a witness for the state. This adversarial approach denies any opportunity for contact between victim and offender, making any attempt at reconciliation an impossibility.

Norwegian criminologist Nils Christie says that the criminal justice system steals the conflict from victims and offenders, making it the property of the state and of defence lawyers. This robs the community of its ability to face trouble and restore peace. Christie argues that the responsibility for how to deal with crime should be returned to victims, offenders, and their communities.[36]

The restorative justice approach looks for answers in the victim, the offender and the community. Where the state-centred system's orientation is toward the past (determining guilt, and punishing for past actions), the restorative models look to the future, to finding solutions, healing (recovering from trauma, conquering fears, gaining understanding of the events), and to the extent possible, achieving reconciliation.

The Restorative Approach

"Problem-solving for the future is seen as more important than establishing blame for past behaviour. Instead of ignoring victims and placing offenders in a passive role, restorative justice principles place both the victim and the offender in active and interpersonal problem-solving roles."[37]

What is known today as restorative justice began in the small town of Elmira, Ontario, one night in 1974, when two young men got drunk and vandalized twenty-two different properties. They were caught and convicted, and probation officer Mark Yantzi was responsible for preparing a pre-sentence report. In searching for an innovative and meaningful sentencing suggestion, Yantzi presented the case to an informal group of local criminal justice volunteers and professionals that occasionally met to discuss questions of justice. In presenting the case he expressed his belief that the best thing for the community would be to have the offenders meet their victims. Dave Worth, who was involved in these meetings, enthusiastically supported Yantzi's suggestion and encouraged him to present it to the judge. Judge McConnell eventually ordered the two young men to go along with Yantzi and Worth to meet their victims and negotiate compensation, and to come back with a report on the damage the victims suffered.[38] This was the first experiment with what came to be known as victim-offender reconciliation programs (VORP).

VORP, now more commonly known as Victim Offender Mediation, is one of the three main streams of restorative justice currently practised in North America. The other two are Group Conferencing, and Community Circles (Sentencing Circles, Peacemaking Circles, Healing Circles). In a later section each approach will be described, and the potential for reconciliation in each model will be explored. First, restorative justice will be defined; then the possibilities it offers for reconciliation will be considered.

Restorative justice provides an entirely different theoretical framework for responding to crime; its approach is fundamentally different from retributive justice (our current punishment-based approach). Restorative justice focuses on what needs to be healed, what needs to be repaid, and what needs to be learned in the wake of crime.[39] David Moore, a leading restorative justice practitioner in Australia, indicates that social regulation usually falls to one of two extremes. It either punishes an offender in order to convey that certain behaviour is unacceptable (in our retributive system), or it looks past unacceptable behaviour in order to support the offender (in counseling or treatment programs). A third, and more effective approach is to send a clear message that a particular behaviour is unacceptable, while at the same time supporting the offender. This "strikes a balance between an ethic of justice and an ethic of care."[40] According to mediator and author Susan Sharpe, that balance is at the heart of restorative justice.

Rather than defining the state as the victim, restorative justice theory postulates that criminal behaviour is first and foremost a conflict between individuals.[41] This is the most fundamental difference between the restorative and retributive approaches to justice, but there are also many other significant distinctions. In his book *Changing Lenses*, Howard Zehr uses the camera as a metaphor for society's view of crime; depending on the lens used, restorative or retributive, the viewer gets a very different outlook on reality. Just as wide-angle and telephoto lenses offer the photographer dramatically different perspectives, through the retributive lens Zehr says "Crime is a violation of the state, defined by lawbreaking and guilt. Justice determines blame and administers pain in a contest between the offender and the state, directed by systematic rules."[42] Through the restorative lens, by contrast, "Crime is a violation of people and relationships. It creates obligations to make things right. Justice involves the victim, the offender, and the community in a search for solutions that promote repair, reconciliation, and reassurance."[43]

The restorative approach rests on three essential propositions. First, crime causes multiple injuries to victims, the community, and even the offender. Second, the justice process should help repair (or heal) those injuries. Third, victims, offenders, and their communities must be involved at the earliest point and to the fullest extent possible.[44]

Regardless of the particular model used, the restorative approach endeavours to achieve the following five goals:[45]

1. Invite full participation and consensus.
2. Heal what has been broken.
3. Seek full and direct accountability.
4. Reunite what has been divided.
5. Strengthen the community, to prevent further harm.

In a restorative process the victim, the offender, and at times the community share the responsibility for deciding what needs to be done. The restorative justice approach puts much more emphasis on the quality of the process itself than it does on any specific outcome. Its goals of healing and reconciliation depend on the following criteria being met:[46]

- The victim is involved in the process and comes out of it satisfied.
- The offender understands how his/her action has affected other people, and takes responsibility for those effects.
- Outcomes help to repair the harms done and address the reasons for the offense; specific plans are tailored to the victim's and the offender's needs.
- Victim and offender both gain a sense of closure, and both are reintegrated into the community.

Restorative justice theory is best understood through its principles of participation, meeting the needs of victim, offender, and community, and restoration. These principles are reflected in the requirements set for restorative programs:[47]

- *The program must pursue the goal of restoration.* It must promote the restoration of all parties. Its social controls must interfere as little as possible with the restoration of the victim and the offender.
- *The program must meet the needs of victims.* It must help make right the harm to victims. It must enable the victim to participate fully.

It must protect the victims who are less powerful. It must provide standing and dignity to victims.

- *The program must meet the needs of offenders.* It must enable and encourage offenders to accept responsibility for their actions. It must enable the offender to participate fully. It must avoid dehumanizing offenders. It must protect the less powerful offenders. It must help make right the harm to offenders.
- *The program must meet the needs of the community.* It must enable the community to participate fully. It must make right the harm to the community. It must address the community's need for safety.

For justice to be healing it must begin by identifying the human needs created by crime. The victim's needs are most important, and of those the most pressing are usually the needs for support and safety. Victims also need someone to listen to them; they need to tell their story and vent their feelings, and they need others to suffer with them. Victims need to know that what happened to them was wrong, and that something has been done to correct the wrong. They need to have their pain acknowledged and their experience validated by others.[48]

The needs of the offender must also be addressed. Very often there are past injuries in the offender's life that contribute to crime (physical or sexual abuse as a child, substance abuse or addiction, etc.), and there may be physical, emotional, or moral and spiritual injuries suffered as a result of the crime. Any attempt to bring healing to the parties touched by crime must address the needs created by these injuries.[49] The offender's needs may include specific treatment, emotional support, learning interpersonal skills, developing a healthy self-image, and help in dealing with guilt.[50]

In the context of crime, needs cannot be discussed without also addressing responsibility and liability. Violations create obligations. Of course the primary obligation is for the offender to make things right. This is what justice is about. The offender has an obligation to acknowledge and assume responsibility, make reparation (to the extent possible), and apologize. There are needs that the victim, the offender, and the community may have as a result of the crime, which are beyond the means of any individual to make right. Meeting these needs is the community's responsibility.[51]

Restorative justice is dramatically different from the current mainstream approach to crime. Its outcomes bear little resemblance to incarceration and other forms of punishment. Its outlook is positive and future-oriented. Restorative justice offers a process that encourages the parties to search for healing and constructive solutions. Because of its attention to the needs of victims and offenders, and its focus on solutions that heal and restore a sense of wholeness, the restorative approach can bring both victim and offender to feel safe enough to begin exploring the difficult issues of compassion, forgiveness, and reconciliation.

Restorative justice clearly offers potential for reconciliation, but in many cases reconciliation between victim and offender still fails to take place. The next section explores the mechanisms that can lead to reconciliation in a restorative approach.

The Opportunity for Transformation

> The ending both of suffering and of crime, which is the establishing of justice, can come only out of peace, out of a peace that is spiritually grounded in our very being. To eliminate crime—to end the construction and perpetuation of an existence that makes crime possible—requires a transformation of our human being....When our hearts are filled with love and our minds with willingness to serve, we will know what has to be done and how it is to be done.[52]

In the modern legal system a lot of emphasis is put on "due process," the use of procedures, terminology, and sequence that follow well-established and often complex rules. This attention to process is very technical, and does not focus on how the participants (victim, offender, prosecutor, defence attorney, judge) are affected by the proceedings. In contrast, the restorative justice emphasis on process focuses on what the participants (victim, offender, community) are experiencing, how they are feeling, and what they are learning. Attention is paid to the progression the participants are making in their journey through the process of searching for solutions and ways to understand the sometimes terrible events that created the deep conflict between them (often referred to as closure, this doesn't undo the pain or make the offence acceptable, but it allows both victim and offender to see the other as a human being they can at least begin to understand. Closure is also the process by which the fears, shadows, nightmares, and monsters fade away, and a sense of safety and order is reestablished).[53]

Both victim and offender need to be healed, and this healing requires opportunities for confession, repentance, forgiveness, and reconciliation.[54]

What the parties require for their healing is different in every case, but it is crucial for *opportunities* to be apprehended by the victim and the offender. Forgiveness, confession, repentance, and reconciliation cannot be willed or forced by the victim or the offender; neither should they be suggested by a mediator, convenor, or any participant other than the victim or the offender. In fact, through his research at the University of Minnesota's Center for Restorative Justice and Mediation, Mark Umbreit has found that the more the concepts of forgiveness and reconciliation are mentioned to the parties prior to meditation, the less likely it is that the victims are going to participate in the process:[55] "While forgiveness and reconciliation represent a powerful outcome of the process of mediator assisted dialogue and mutual aid between crime victims and offenders, they must emerge in a natural and genuine manner that has meaning to the involved parties."[56]

If reconciliation cannot be willed or forced, and it must emerge in a natural and genuine manner, then what aspects of the restorative justice process should be focused on in order to encourage the emergence of opportunities for reconciliation? It is in the study of mediation that some key answers are found to the dilemmas of reconciliation between victim and offender. In the introduction to their groundbreaking work *The Promise of Mediation*, Bush and Folger write:

> the mediation process contains within it a unique potential for transforming people—engendering moral growth—by helping them wrestle with difficult circumstances and bridge human differences, in the very midst of conflict. This transformative potential stems from mediation's capacity to generate two important effects, empowerment and recognition. In simplest terms, *empowerment* means the restoration to individuals of a sense of their own value and strength and their own capacity to handle life's problems. *Recognition* means the evocation in individuals of acknowledgment and empathy for the situation and problems of others. When both of these processes are held central in the practice of mediation, parties are helped to use conflicts as opportunities for moral growth, and the transformative potential of mediation is realized.[57]

In the context of victim-offender mediation, the transformation or moral growth that Bush and Folger describe is what creates the opportunities for reconciliation. Empowerment and recognition, the prerequisites for transformation, will be explored further, but first the particular approach to mediation which best opens the door to transformation must be identified.

There are two principal trends in mediation today: the settlement driven approach, in which the mediator focuses on helping the parties produce a solution to their "problem," and the transformative approach, in which conflict is seen not as a problem but as an opportunity for growth. Transformative (also referred to as humanistic) mediation is non-directive and "dialogue driven"; it aims to make the parties feel safe enough to have an opportunity to engage in a genuine dialogue about their conflict.[58] This approach allows the participants to experience their own empowerment, which can help them feel empathy for the other party in the conflict.

Humanistic mediation requires a reframing of the mediator's role. Instead of actively guiding the parties toward a settlement, the mediator initiates a process in which the parties enter a dialogue with each other, experience each other as people, share their feelings, and seek ways to help each other find peace.[59] "Through a process of dialogue and mutual aid between the involved parties, the humanistic mediation model facilitates the achievement of outer peace through resolution of the presenting conflict, while also facilitating a journey of the heart to find inner peace, which brings forth the true goal of humanistic mediation—real peace."[60]

The capacity of a restorative approach to offer opportunities for reconciliation between victim and offender is commensurate with its ability to transform the parties involved. Because most restorative models are informal and consensual, they allow the parties to define the conflict in their own terms. The victim and the offender define not only the problems and potential solutions; they also define their very own goals for the restorative process. This self-determination can help the parties mobilize their own resources to achieve their goals. Participants thus gain a greater sense of self-respect, self-reliance, and self-confidence.[61]

The objective of empowerment can be defined by pointing to what takes place in the participants when empowerment is achieved. A participant is empowered when:

- He reaches a clear realization of what matters to him and why.
- He realizes that he can choose whether to stay in or leave the mediation, accept or reject legal or other advice, accept or reject a possible solution, and so forth.

- He gains a new awareness of resources already in his possession to achieve his goals and objectives. He realizes that his resources are sufficient to implement a solution.
- He reflects, deliberates, and makes conscious decisions for himself about what he wants to do.
- He assesses fully the advantages and disadvantages of possible solutions and of non-settlement options, and makes decisions in light of his assessments.[62]

In a restorative process empowerment brings the parties a sense of security, self-determination, and autonomy.[63] However important and beneficial to the process, empowerment is independent of any particular outcome of that process.

As they achieve empowerment, the parties gain enough of a sense of self-worth and security to allow themselves to look beyond their own needs. Recognition is achieved when the parties voluntarily choose to become more open, sympathetic, and responsive to the situation of the other party. Whereas the process of empowerment can be assisted by the mediator, recognition must flow from a desire within the parties; it cannot be forced, and it cannot be encouraged by the mediator or convener.

It is possible to define recognition by pointing to what takes place in the participants when it is achieved:[64]

- She realizes that she feels secure enough to stop thinking exclusively about her own situation and to focus to some degree on what the other party is going through.
- She consciously lets go of her own viewpoint and tries to see things from the other party's perspective. She consciously moves to a more sympathetic view.
- She openly expresses her changed understanding of the other. She admits that she now sees what happened differently, and apologizes in some way.
- She decides to make some concrete accommodation to the other party in terms of how the central issues in the conflict are handled.

In this context recognition is the experience of moving beyond a focus on self that a party experiences from *giving* recognition to another.[65] A sincere offer of recognition is a peace offering. The party receiving the recognition may experience a sense of caring or concern for the other, just as the one offering recognition has.

The transformation that takes place when empowerment of the parties is achieved and recognition is offered does not in itself bring about the reconciliation of the victim and the offender. Even a small measure of reconciliation is a loftier goal than the transformation of the parties.

Reconciliation can be viewed as one pole on a continuum that has hostility as its other pole. The crime itself puts the parties near the hostility pole, while empowerment moves them closer to reconciliation. Recognition can take them even closer to reconciliation, but it is only when the needs of both the victim and the offender are fully addressed that reconciliation becomes a possibility.[66] In "Beyond Retribution" New Testament scholar Christopher D. Marshall proposes that reconciliation is the fulfillment of forgiveness: "Forgiveness is what happens when the victim of some hurtful action freely chooses to release the perpetrator of that action from the bondage of guilt, gives up his or her own feelings of ill will, and surrenders any attempt to hurt or damage the perpetrator in return, thus clearing the way for reconciliation and restoration of relationship."[67] In the restorative justice context, reconciliation is described as "an opening of the heart," and rather than a one time all or nothing event, it is viewed as "a journey involving numerous elements and steps."[68] The process of reconciliation is often described as a spiritual awakening by those who have experienced it.

However, even after meeting all the requirements outlined in this section, a restorative process may still not produce reconciliation. In some cases it is just not possible to reach reconciliation within the time frame of the actual restorative justice process, and that fact does not invalidate any of the other benefits provided by the restorative approach.

Although this section has focused mainly on the mediation model, the concept of transformation through empowerment and recognition applies just as well to the other two major restorative models. The next section gives a brief overview of each of the three approaches, and it offers an assessment of the potential strengths and weaknesses of each model in providing opportunities for reconciliation. (This assessment is based on the author's personal experience and observations as well as on discussions with colleagues.)

The Restorative Justice Models

In North America there are currently three major streams in restorative justice practice: victim-offender mediation; group conferencing; and community circles.

All three processes share a common approach to crime and justice; they give decision-making power to those most affected by the crime, and they make the following specific requirements: that there be an identifiable victim; that the victim participate voluntarily; and that there be an admission of responsibility on the part of the offender. It is important to note that from the outset the number of cases where a restorative process can be used is limited by these requirements. There are variations between specific programs within each of the three models, but the principal difference between the three restorative streams is in who participates in the process, and who shares responsibility for making decisions.[69]

Victim-Offender Mediation

This approach brings victim and offender to meet face to face in the presence of a trained mediator who only guides the process without taking part in the content. Prior to the encounter, the mediator meets privately with each party to answer questions and address concerns about the process; it is important to ensure that everyone involved understands the process and feels safe.

In the mediation session the victim speaks first about her experience of the crime. Then comes the offender's description of how she experienced the event. The parties are encouraged to fully express their feelings surrounding the incident and its aftermath. The mediator then asks the victim and the offender to explore their needs and their interests in the matter. This prepares the parties to begin focusing on how to make things right. As various choices are discussed, the parties consider how well each option would meet their needs. The mediator emphasizes the need for solutions to be both satisfying and feasible. The parties continue exploring possibilities until they agree on a solution, and specific terms and a timeline for completion have been worked out (if appropriate).

The major strength of the victim-offender mediation process is its ability to foster deep and meaningful dialogue. Because only a few people are involved (often only one victim, one offender, and a mediator), there's opportunity for great emotional intensity, which can create openness and promote in the parties a recognition of each other's humanity. The need for preparation of the parties prior to the mediation is crucial; the victim often needs recognition to be expressed by people close to her, not just by the offender. With mediation's exclusive focus on the victim and the offender, transformation can happen within a relatively short time. Once both parties feel their needs have been met, an opportunity exists for reconciliation, although the parties may often need time to first "digest" the content and outcome of the mediation session.

Group Conferencing

Originally called "family group conferencing," this practice originated in New Zealand, and is based on the tradition of the Maori, New Zealand's indigenous people. The process involves the victim, along with members of his family and other supporters, the offender, with her family and supporters, and may also include the police officer called to the incident, school counselor, social worker, etc. As many as thirty participants can be involved in a conference. In addition, a facilitator, or convenor, guides the discussion and helps keep the group focused. As with mediation, the facilitator meets individually with each participant prior to the conference, and in the actual process guides the discussion without being involved in its content. The facilitators ensure that the ground rules are observed, but the process is not rigidly controlled.

A conference usually begins with the offender's account of the incident and his thoughts on who was affected in what ways. The victim then describes his experience of the event, and what the consequences were. The families and supporters of both the victim and the offender have a chance to speak, and once these participants have said what they needed to say the group begins focusing on what needs to be done to make things right. Recognition can be offered by any participant. Everyone can have input in the solution. The conference ends when the group agrees on a solution and all the necessary details have been worked out.

The large number of participants in this process can make it difficult for the offender and the victim to explore their deepest feelings; on the other hand the presence of loved ones can also enhance the sense of support and safety that fosters the expression of deep feelings. Ideally, transformation would be sought for the whole group; in reality it may only take place in the primary parties (victim and offender) and their closest supporters. Having so many participants providing ideas and options, a set of solutions that meet the needs of victim, offender, and community may be agreed to relatively quickly. Because a conference is fairly lengthy and does not focus exclusively on the victim and the offender, there is time for the parties to process what is taking place as the conferencing procedure unfolds. This often helps bring the possibility of reconciliation within reach.

Community Circles

Community circles have their origins in the traditions of the Aboriginal peoples of western Canada. Interestingly, the use of circles in the practice of modern justice was pioneered and promoted by a small group of judges working in the formal criminal justice system.[70] According to circle philosophy, the responsibility for resolving crime is shared by the whole community, not just by the victim, the offender, and those directly affected by the event.

Circles must involve the offender, and every effort is made to have the victim also take part. Supporters (including family members) for both victim and offender are present, as are justice system officials. Some health and social services professionals may also be involved. Anyone from the community may also participate.

As the name implies, the participants in this process form a circle. Although there are characteristics common to most circles, there are no rigid rules directing the process; variations evolve in each community according to local needs and culture. A "keeper of the circle" ensures the guidelines are followed and the use of the "talking device" is respected (an object, sometimes a feather or stick, is passed around the circle; only the person holding the object is allowed to speak). The circle usually opens with a prayer or spiritual ceremony (often described as a "cleansing" or "purifying" ritual), and there is usually a sacred or spiritual dimension to the whole event. The process starts with the offender describing the incident, then everyone around the circle, in turn, has a chance to speak. Everyone who wishes to speak has a chance to do so. This creates empowerment and prepares the parties for the possibility of recognition. The discussion will often concentrate on the incident in its broadest possible context, including its underlying causes and the prevention of similar offences. When the initial exchange around the circle is over (three to four hours), the focus shifts to what must be done to help heal the victim, the offender, the families, and the community. Agreements often contain plans for treatment of the offender, and sometimes also for treatment of the victim or other parties affected.

Having the process open to the entire community can result in a very large number of participants. This may slow the process considerably, but it also brings a greater richness of thought and experience to the circle; this can contribute greatly to the achievement of transformation. Because this approach is mostly used in Aboriginal communities where justice is perceived as the restoration of balance and harmony, a great emphasis is sometimes put on reconciliation. It is important that the victim and the offender be able to live in the same small, close-knit community. However, this prominent focus on harmony can preclude opportunities for true reconciliation when the victim and the offender feel pressured to reconcile.

It is important to keep in mind that the three processes outlined here are evolving, and that the practitioners in each one are constantly learning. There is much cross-fertilization taking place between the various approaches, and the very nature of the restorative environment is fluid. Restorative justice can be understood as a transformation of relationships, rather than as a prescription to follow.[71] In the early years of modern restorative justice it was commonly believed that restorative models were only appropriate for nonviolent minor offences, especially those involving young offenders. The experience of programs applying restorative models to serious crimes (such as sexual assault and murder) in British Columbia and Texas[72] has shown that with proper preparation, sometimes taking years, the benefits offered by the restorative approach can be tremendous in these difficult and painful cases. More recently there have been many concerns expressed by women's groups about the use of restorative models in cases of domestic violence. Again, the experience of programs that have been developed slowly and with much diligence show us that when the participants are well prepared a restorative approach can be highly successful in carefully selected cases.[73] It must be noted that in whichever context it is used a restorative approach can fail not only to foster reconciliation but also to provide recognition and empowerment, and even to produce a workable solution. Some of the common causes of failure include conflicting values, power relations that exist outside the process, and participants who come to the process with a desire to manipulate the outcome. Nevertheless, as is demonstrated in the majority of cases,[74] with proper care and preparation, the three approaches highlighted here make possible the personal transformation that opens the way to reconciliation in a manner not allowed by our current court/prison system.

Real Life Reconciliation

The potential offered by restorative justice for reconciliation between victim and offender is most powerfully demonstrated through real life examples. The following true story is based on the account of mediator Marty Price.[75]

In April 1993, Elaine Serrell Myers was driving home from doing her daily radio show when she was killed by a drunk driver. Suzana Cooper, the drunk driver, was at the time a twenty-five-year-old single mother of two young children. Shortly after Elaine's funeral, her elderly father, Peter Serrell, contacted Marty Price to inquire about the possibility of mediation. Eventually, seven members of Elaine's family, including her widower, got involved in the process. A few months after Elaine's death her family had a meeting with the mediator, during which they shared their pain and discussed the impact of their loss. They also came up with requests they might make of Suzana that could meaningfully address their loss. Their goals fell within two main themes. First they wanted Suzana to make some changes in her life, and to use her experience to help keep drunk drivers off the road. Second, they wanted to ensure that her children would do better in the world than their mother had.

For many months David, Elaine's widower, had believed that he would be unable to contain his anger in the presence of the woman who had killed his wife of twenty-seven years. The family meeting with the mediator convinced David to participate in the mediation. Demonstrating an early move from hate to compassion, David observed that with so many of Elaine's family members taking part in the mediation, the offender would need to have someone there for her support.

Suzana had suffered devastating injuries in the collision that killed Elaine. After three months of hospitalization and recovery in a nursing home, Suzana was arraigned and charged with vehicular homicide. An attorney was appointed by the court to represent her.

Although he was unsure about the idea at first, once Suzana entered a guilty plea her attorney became an active supporter of the mediation process. With her attorney and her best friend as support people, Suzana met with the mediator a number of times to discuss her preparation for the actual mediation session. Reading victim impact statements from Elaine's family members opened her heart and broke through her defensiveness and self-pity. She was overwhelmed by the enormity of the loss and pain she had caused. At that time Suzana was diagnosed as an alcoholic. She decided that she would try to find a way to have her experience make a difference for others, and perhaps save lives.

The mediation lasted four and a half hours. Many tears were shed, many eloquent words were said, and the victims and offender each became allies in the healing of the other. The mediation resulted in an agreement in which Suzana committed to attend Alcoholics Anonymous (AA) meetings and victim impact panels while in prison. She agreed to find ways to work against drunk driving in her community after her release. The agreement also included commitments by Suzana to complete her G.E.D. (General Education Degree—twelfth-grade equivalency), write at least once a week to each of her children, attend church each week, improve her parenting skills, and give 10 percent of her income to charity. She also agreed to write a quarterly letter to Elaine's father to report on her progress on each of the items above.

Following the mediation, Suzana had to appear in court for sentencing. The judge was given a copy of the mediation agreement, and one of Elaine's sisters read her victim impact statement in court. Suzana was sentenced to a thirty-four-month prison term. Her prior drunk driving conviction had increased the mandatory minimum sentence. While in prison, Suzana kept up every one of her commitments.

After the mediation, the members of Elaine's family reported a wonderful new freedom to focus on the present and the future instead of continuing to dwell in the painful past. On the anniversary of Elaine's death the family gathered by her grave. They focused not on how Elaine had died, but on how she lived and how they could carry her legacy forward. They petitioned the governor for a pardon and early parole for Suzana. It was denied.

Suzana was paroled after serving twenty-one months (two-thirds) of her sentence. In the last three months of her sentence, under temporary release, she spoke on Mothers Against Drunk Driving panels, telling drunk-driving offenders how she had killed someone. She also told her story to a number of high school driver-education classes, and worked as a cashier in a no-alcohol night club.

Suzana and Elaine's family keep in regular contact, in a unique healing alliance between victims and offender. Suzana has remained clean and sober and is attending community college classes, with Elaine's family providing her tuition and books. Suzana continues to tell her story to drunk-driving offenders and high school driving students.

Conclusion

The preceding case leaves no doubt that reconciliation between victim and offender has the potential not only to transform individual lives but also to improve whole communities. Crime is more than just an unfortunate, painful, and sometimes tragic event; when perceived as interpersonal conflict, crime offers opportunities for personal and social transformation. A constructive approach to conflict strengthens individuals and builds community, and once a place of support, strength, and compassion has been reached, reconciliation may be achieved. This points the way to greater social harmony and peace.

The effects that restorative justice can have on wider society should not be overlooked, and neither should the opportunities that exist for a restorative justice approach to be effectively applied to a broader social context, especially in cases of violent ethnic or political conflict. There is a striking similarity in the pain, the fears, and the needs experienced by those affected by serious crime and those involved in violent public conflict, and the path to peace and reconciliation can be surprisingly similar in both groups. It is no coincidence that the South African Truth and Reconciliation Commission was founded in restorative justice principles: ubuntu,[76] understanding, focusing on the future, reparation, and reconciliation.[77]

Reconciliation is a difficult but tremendously powerful process that has the ability to transform individuals, communities, and whole societies. Retribution is the predetermined, "natural" response to an offence; reconciliation is the creative alternative. It is the highest form of creativity, and as such it "possesses a capacity to reveal the original face of God."[78]

Notes

1 *Restorative Justice: Making Things Right* (videotape). Cheryl Zehr-Walker, producer. (Akron, PA: Mennonite Central Committee/MCC Communications, 1994.)

2 Ibid.

3 From the author's personal experience, using restorative justice principles and processes working with groups of ex-Sandinistas and ex-Contras in post-war Nicaragua, and working with blacks, coloureds and whites in post-apartheid South Africa.

4 Susan Sharpe, *Restorative Justice: A Vision for Healing and Change* (Edmonton: Edmonton Victim Offender Mediation Society, 1998), 3.

5 Daniel Van Ness and Karen Heetderks Strong, *Restoring Justice* (Cincinnati, OH: Anderson, 1997), 67-68.

6 Ibid., 7.

7 Ibid., 8.

8 David Cayley, *The Expanding Prison: The Crisis in Crime and Punishment and the Search for Alternatives* (Toronto: House of Anansi, 1998), 124.

9 Herman Bianchi, *Justice as Sanctuary* (Bloomington: Indiana University Press, 1994), 9.

10 Howard Zehr, *Changing Lenses: A New Focus for Crime and Justice* (Scottdale, PA: Herald Press, 1990), 130.

11 Perry B. Yoder, *Shalom: The Bible's Word for Salvation, Justice, and Peace* (Newton, KS: Faith and Life Press, 1987).

12 Daniel D.N. Nsereko, "Compensating Victims of Crime in Botswana," paper presented at the Society for the Reform of Criminal Law Conference, on "Reform of Sentencing, Parole, and Early Release" (Ottawa, ON, August 1-4, 1988).

13 Daniel H. Foote, "The Benevolent Paternalism of Japanese Criminal Justice," *California Law Review* 80 (1992): 317.

14 Ross Gordon Green, *Justice in Aboriginal Communities: Sentencing Alternatives* (Saskatoon: Purich, 1998), 30-31.

15 The Church Council on Justice and Corrections, *Satisfying Justice* (Ottawa: 1996), xxiii.

16 Zehr, *Changing Lenses*, 99.

17 Ibid., 181.

18 Ibid., 128.

19 Cayley, *Expanding Prison*, 124.

20 Green, *Justice in Aboriginal Communities*, 31.

21 Bianchi, *Justice as Sanctuary*, 12-13.

22 Harold J. Berman, *Law and Revolution* (Cambridge: Harvard University Press, 1983), 54-55.

23 Ibid.

24 Cayley, *Expanding Prison*, 126.

25 Ibid., 129.

26 Louk Hulsman, *Prison and Its Alternatives*, from the Canadian Broadcasting Corporation radio series *Ideas*, June 17-28, 1996.

27 Adam Starchild, *Friends Journal*, July, 1990.

28 Van Ness and Heetderks Strong, *Restoring Justice*, 10.

29 Berman, *Law and Revolution*, 183.

30 Van Ness and Heetderks Strong, *Restoring Justice*, 10-11.

31 Cayley, *Expanding Prison*, 140.

32 Ibid., 141.

33 Michael Ignatieff, *A Just Measure of Pain: The Penitentiary in the Industrial Revolution, 1750-1850* (New York: Columbia University Press, 1978), 15.

34 Cayley, *Expanding Prison*, 150.

35 Sharpe, *Restorative Justice*, 3.
36 Nils Christie, "Conflicts as Property," *British Journal of Criminology* 17, 1 (1977): 1.
37 Mark Umbreit, cited in *Satisfying Justice* (Ottawa: The Church Council on Justice and Corrections, 1996), xix.
38 Cayley, *Expanding Prison*, 215-17; Sharpe, *Restorative Justice*, 24-25; Church Council, *Satisfying Justice*, 39.
39 Sharpe, *Restorative Justice*, 7.
40 David Moore with Lubica Forsythe, *A New Approach to Juvenile Justice: An Evaluation of Family Conferencing in Wagga Wagga* (Wagga Wagga, NSW, Australia: Centre for Rural Social Research, Charles Stuart University, 1995), 257; as cited in Sharpe, 1998, 7.
41 Mark S. Umbreit, *Victim Meets Offender: The Impact of Restorative Justice and Mediation* (Monsey, NY: Criminal Justice Press/Willow Tree Press, 1994), 3.
42 Zehr, *Changing Lenses*, 181.
43 Ibid.
44 Van Ness and Heetderks Strong, *Restoring Justice*, 31.
45 Sharpe, *Restorative Justice*, 7.
46 Ibid., 20.
47 Van Ness and Heetderks Strong, *Restoring Justice*, 163-64; Zehr, *Changing Lenses*, 230-31.
48 Zehr, *Changing Lenses*, 191.
49 Van Ness and Heetderks Strong, *Restoring Justice*, 33-34.
50 Zehr, *Changing Lenses*, 200.
51 Ibid., 199.
52 Harold E. Pepinski and Richard Quinney, eds., *Criminology as Peacemaking* (Bloomington: Indiana University Press, 1991), 172-80; as cited in Van Ness and Heetderks Strong, *Restoring Justice*, 176.
53 Ruth Morris, *Stories of Transformative Justice* (Toronto: Canadian Scholars' Press, 2000), 4.
54 Zehr, *Changing Lenses*, 51.
55 Mark S. Umbreit, "A Journey of the Heart," *Interaction* (Winter 1995): 10.
56 Ibid.
57 Robert A. Baruch Bush and Joseph P. Folger, *The Promise of Mediation: Responding to Conflict through Empowerment and Recognition* (San Francisco: Jossey-Bass, 1994), 2.
58 Mark S. Umbreit, "Beyond Settlement Driven Mediation: A Humanistic Model of Peacemaking," *Interaction* (Spring 1997): 16.
59 Ibid.
60 Ibid., 17.
61 Bush and Folger, *Promise of Mediation*, 20.
62 Ibid., 85-87.
63 Ibid., 87.
64 Ibid., 89-91.

65 Ibid., 92.

66 Ron Classen and Howard Zehr, *VORP Organizing: A Foundation in the Church* (Elkhart, IN: Mennonite Central Committee U.S. Office of Criminal Justice, 1989), 5.

67 Christopher D. Marshall, *Beyond Retribution: A New Testament Vision for Justice, Crime, and Punishment,* (Auckland, NZ: Lime Grove House, 2001), 26.

68 Umbreit, "A Journey," 10.

69 Sharpe, *Restorative Justice*, 24.

70 Green, *Justice in Aboriginal Communities*, 18-45; Sharpe, *Restorative Justice*, 37-40.

71 Sharpe, *Restorative Justice*, 43.

72 Dave Gustafson is co-director of Fraser Region Community Justice Initiatives Association (CJI) in Langley, British Columbia; David Doerfler is state coordinator for the Victim Offender Mediation/Dialogue, Texas Department of Criminal Justice, Victim Services Division, Austin, Texas. For information on these programs, contact International Victim Offender Mediation Association, c/o Center for Policy, Planning and Performance, 2344 Nicolet Ave. South, Suite 330, Minneapolis, MN 55404 USA.

73 For more information on using restorative models in cases of domestic violence, contact Mediation and Restorative Justice Centre (MRJC), #201, 11205-107 Avenue, Edmonton, AB T5H 0Y2 Canada.

74 Umbreit, *Victim Meets Offender*.

75 Marty Price, "The Mediation of a Drunk Driving Death: A Case Development Study," paper presented at the International Conference of the Victim Offender Mediation Association, Winnipeg, MB, Canada.

76 Ubuntu is a philosophy of humanism, emphasizing the link between the individual and the collective. Restorative justice practice strengthens the link between the acts (crime) and feelings (victimization) of individuals and the well-being of the community as a whole.

77 Johnny de Lange, "The Historical Context, Legal Origins and Philosophical Foundation of the South African Truth and Reconciliation Commission," in *Looking Back Reaching Forward: Reflections on the Truth and Reconciliation Commission of South Africa*, Charles Villa-Vicencio and Wilhelm Verwoerd, eds., (Cape Town, RSA: University of Cape Town Press, 2000), 23-24.

78 C. Duquoc, "The Forgiveness of God," in *Forgiveness, Concilium* 177, C. Floristán and C. Duquoc, eds., (Edinburgh: T.&T. Clark, 1986): 35-44; as quoted in Marshall, 2001.

5

Mass Rape and the Concept of International Crime

Larry May

International criminal law is currently faced with a defining moment: how to understand the truly international character of certain kinds of crime while providing an expanded forum for the prosecution of egregious harms in the world. I offer a resolution of this problem by arguing that unless there has been a complete breakdown of the rule of law in a particular country, international tribunals should only be concerned with prosecuting individuals for crimes that are group-based, in that the harms are directed against individuals because of their group memberships or where there is some kind of state (or state-like) involvement, and typically only where both of these factors are present. Isolated acts of rape should not normally be subject to international prosecution, but examples like the "comfort women" of the Second World War would be properly prosecuted internationally. Given that international criminal trials often intensify conflict among peoples, such trials should only be conducted in the most extreme of cases, and only when there is a very clear reason to prosecute internationally rather than domestically. Reconciliation often will dictate that some forum for remedy other than international criminal prosecutions be pursued.

How should international crimes be distinguished from domestic crimes? If the Rome Treaty creating an International Criminal Court (ICC) is adopted, will the ICC usurp domestic courts? In statements, such as those made by U.S. State Department officials and Senate Foreign Relations Committee members, the argument was advanced that the ICC had dangerously broad jurisdictional powers.[1] One strategy for addressing this worry is to mark out clearly the extent and rationale of prosecutions by international tribunals concerning crimes that historically have been the exclusive purview of domestic tribunals. Rape and other forms of sexual violence provide a good test case of how to draw such a distinction.

In the first part of this discussion, I examine various strategies for understanding the nature of international crimes. Many theorists of international law have recognized that there is a need for some kind of codification of international crimes. But most have also said that it is not possible to have a set of theoretical criteria for what counts as an international crime. In this section I challenge that view. I argue against those who have urged that we give up on finding a theoretical rationale for international crimes.

In the second part of the discussion, I consider the example of rape, and ask why this crime, which is normally prosecuted under domestic law, should also be prosecuted as an international crime. I discuss three examples of rape, each drawn from different areas of the international law of sexual violence. First, I begin by briefly addressing sexual violence in war. Second, I examine the conceptualization of rape as a crime against humanity, with specific attention to a recent case from the Yugoslav tribunal. Third, I turn to an example of sexual persecution from asylum law, the intersection of international human rights law and domestic immigration law. For all three cases, conceptual difficulties are identified with the use of international law to remedy these harms.

In the third part of the discussion, the idea of *jus cogens* norms will be applied to the idea of sexual violence directed at groups. By examining in detail the interests of humanity and the status of perpetrators, an argument is advanced that group-based sexual violence, perpetrated against an individual because of group membership or as part of a state plan, is just the sort of thing that should be prosecuted in international tribunals.

In the fourth and concluding section, I argue that individually oriented crimes should not generally be included as international crimes. I argue against those who defend a more expansive domain of international crime. I take an explicitly defendant-oriented approach to this topic, noting that it is not a good argument to urge a more expansive approach to international crimes merely because victims' rights are at stake. Offsetting considerations of defendants' rights argue for restraint in our approach to the concept, and the prosecution, of international crime.

International Crimes and Moral Legitimacy

International crime, like international law itself, is at best an ambiguous concept. It can refer to crimes that domestic states will enforce due to treaty obligations that those states have incurred. Or it can refer to what is customarily accepted as criminal by the community of nations. It can also refer to the acts that are clearly proscribed by so-called *jus cogens* norms, norms of such transparent bindingness that no individual can fail to understand that he is bound by them, and no state can fail to see that it should either prosecute such acts or turn the perpetrator over to another institution that will prosecute.[2] These differing conceptions of international crime are due to the differing sources of international criminal law. In this section I will argue that, especially with the institution of a new International Criminal Court, we need a clear basis for identifying international crimes, distinguishing them from domestic crimes, and explaining why the prosecution of these international crimes has moral legitimacy.

In 1995, M. Cherif Bassiouni pointed out that the "term 'international crime' or its equivalent had never been specifically used in international conventions."[3] Yet, in 1997 a multilateral convention established an International Criminal Court, where the name of the court signifies that the term "international crime" has now come into use. It is thus of pressing concern that the idea of international crime be explored explicitly. In one sense "international crime" is easy to define. International crimes are simply those crimes recognized in international law. As Bassiouni puts it, "the criminal aspect of international law consists of a body of international proscriptions containing penal characteristics evidencing the criminalization of certain types of conduct."[4] But beyond this simple point, it is not so easy to see what should evidence international criminalization.

Let us begin by considering domestic criminal law. John Stuart Mill asked the salient question: what are "the nature and limits of the power which can be legitimately exercised by society over the individual."[5] His answer was that more was needed than merely showing that a valid law was in place. From standard liberal principles, where liberty is one of the highest values, it is obvious that when the law seeks to incarcerate a person, thereby taking away that person's liberty, a very strong rationale is needed. It is always legitimate to ask not only whether a criminal law exists but also whether it is morally legitimate. A similar question can be asked at the international level, but now the question is not about the legitimate exercise of the power of a particular state but the legitimate exercise of the collective power of all states. Since Nuremberg there has been a healthy debate about what would legitimate the international community's punishment of a person or state.

My focus in this section is on the moral legitimacy of the exercise of the collective, coercive power of states in international criminal trials. The idea of legitimacy, writes Joel Feinberg, "is not an invention of arcane philosophy. It is part of the conceptual equipment of every man and woman on the street."[6] Domestic criminal statutes are legitimated by moral principles and those moral principles are least controversial when they are ones that nearly any person would find reasonable. Moral legitimacy is crucial for any type of law, since the law's effectiveness is so closely linked with the sense of obligation that people feel. Without this sense of the binding effect of the law, there is nothing of moral importance that motivates people to obey the law in the first place.[7] Law's effectiveness is dependent on the moral legitimacy of the law.[8]

I will take a moderate legal positivist position on the legitimacy of law. I believe that there is a minimum moral or natural law content that laws must display to be legitimate. This is what I am calling the moral legitimacy of the law. The morality of law does not need to be robust for law to be legitimate. Here there are a set of moral principles, recognized in virtually every legal system, that make a law worthy of being enforced. Such moral principles ultimately protect the inner normative core of law by guaranteeing that the law is in some rudimentary way fair.[9]

One moral principle that seems crucial to the legitimacy of international (or any other) criminal law is that a person should not be prosecuted for something that either wasn't a crime or couldn't be known to be a crime at the time the defendant acted. This principle of fair dealing has been well known since Roman times, and is often cited by the Latin phrase: *nullum crimen sine lege*. This moral principle seemingly requires that international crimes have a well-recognized and easily accessed source that will allow individuals to figure out what is required of them. In this respect, international law's traditional emphasis on custom is especially problematical. It is for this reason that many theorists of international criminal law have urged that the legitimate sources of international crimes be restricted to only special kinds of customary law, namely that which is uncontested.[10] Customs that are based on *opinio juris* provide the best evidence of *jus cogens* norms.

Rather than require such a theoretical core, some have argued that it is sufficient that there be a codification of crimes in international law.[11] Such a view misses the point behind the call for moral legitimacy. Again, consider the analogy with domestic criminal law. Just because a state has statutorily required that people act a certain way does not mean that the statutory law is legitimate. It is always an open question whether a duly passed law is itself morally legitimate. This is readily seen in the debates about whether statutes prohibiting pornography or other so-called "victimless crimes" have sufficient legitimacy so that the state can punish those who do not conform.[12]

It is not enough that what is criminal is known or knowable; it also must somehow make sense why only these acts are proscribed. Without such a requirement, the actual or hypothetical consent of the citizens cannot be reasonably inferred. If there is no rationale to the laws, then they appear as potentially arbitrary exercises of state power. And here we need a second moral principle, namely that the restrictions on individual liberty required by conformity to criminal law achieve some highly valuable purpose. Merely codifying laws does not guarantee that the laws are morally legitimate.

Many philosophers have settled on the idea that society has an interest in preventing harm, and that only those acts should be criminalized that are aimed at the prevention of harm.[13] Indeed, I would argue that all criminal laws are legitimate only if they are addressed to the prevention of harm, or something of equal importance. If something as significant as harm is not involved then, as is true in the debates about the nature of domestic crime, there would not be sufficient justification for the serious interference with liberty that is involved in criminal punishment. If, for instance, people risk imprisonment for calling each other derogatory names, something has gone seriously awry.[14] The harm potentially inflicted by the defendant is greatly disproportionate to the harm that the defendant will be made to suffer by imprisonment. And here we also need to comment that this is yet another moral principle of legitimacy well recognized in all legal systems, namely that the punishment must somehow fit the crime.

Harm can be understood in terms of interests, in that a harm is a "setback to interests" which is also somehow a denial of rights.[15] For international criminal law, the difficult question concerns whose interests are to be taken into account. If we say that it is the interest of any person, the setback of which constitutes a sufficient harm for criminal punishment, then we have no basis for distinguishing domestic crimes from international ones. But before we get to that issue (which is the subject of a later section of this paper), it is of course legitimate to ask whether "setback to interest" is the best way to understand harm. Why not, for instance, make international crime depend on preventing a person from getting what he or she wants. My response is that wants are generally not significant enough to justify infringement of liberty, for each of us also wants to be free from punishment, and this want is often more important than the wants of another person concerning the disposition of their luxury goods for instance. We look to interest setback as the threshold for legitimate punishment because interests are conceived as non-trivial. It is not legitimate to punish someone for trivial acts, given that punishment itself is not a trivial matter, even if those trivial acts are clearly proscribed in a code of crimes.

Why shouldn't codification be all we can expect, especially in our morally pluralistic and fractious world? As I said above, many theorists of international criminal law bemoan the attempts to give an underlying rationale to the list of crimes that count as international crimes. In many respects these theorists are taking a postmodern approach to international criminal law. They think that it is misguided even to attempt to provide a theoretical structure, because it will somehow do violence to the very origins of specific acts that have come to be listed as international crimes. Specific contexts have given rise to the international community directing its attention in various ways toward perceived wrongs and creating crimes so as to capture the insights of those historical moments. Think of piracy, for instance. Piracy is one of the oldest recognized international crimes. And yet, so it would be claimed, it does grave injustice to such a crime to strip it from its historical context and to try to find an underlying principle that will capture this act, piracy, as well as other acts such as apartheid, genocide, and torture, which have also been proscribed in other historical contexts.[16]

I agree that the reason why societies criminalized acts of piracy may be very different from the reason societies criminalized acts of apartheid, genocide, and torture. But if people are still today to be punished for committing these acts, now long after the time has passed during which these acts were first condemned as criminal, then we need a current account of what makes these acts legitimately punishable now. And more importantly, we need some basis from which people can see that such acts are indeed worthy of criminal sanction at the international level, and not merely anachronistic manifestations of bygone prejudices. Unless we give up on the search for moral legitimacy of criminal punishment and argue the international community is right to prosecute any crimes that it can, it is not sufficient merely to codify international crimes. We must also explain why each of these things listed in the code are non-trivial matters, the violation of which merits the serious loss of liberty involved in punishment.

I believe that one reasonable strategy is to restrict international crimes to those that involve a violation of *jus cogens* norms understood as a violation of the international harm principle, that is, as involving a serious setback to the interests of humanity. Bassiouni has commented that linking international crime to *jus cogens* norms has the advantage of setting the stage for the new ICC, which will presume universal jurisdiction and application to all humans, not just to those in a particular region or particular historical time.[17] In order better to understand what is at stake in the debate I have just rehearsed, and also in my proposal, it will be instructive to look at a crime that has only recently been recognized as an international crime. For this purpose I will explore in some detail the international crime of rape. This crime is only recently and sporadically recognized as an international crime, and it is often not clearly distinguishable from the domestic crime of rape. It is thus a rich example for beginning to comprehend what might be the distinguishing characteristics of truly international crimes.

Rape as an International Crime

Until very recently, most theorists of international law ignored the possibility that international tribunals could be used to prosecute rape. Perhaps because of critical reaction to this omission, some of these same theorists now consider rape a proper subject of international prosecution.[18] But the possibility that international tribunals could be used as an alternative forum to domestic tribunals for rape prosecution has raised the spectre of sovereignty usurpation once again, contributing to the difficulty, at least temporarily, of ratifying the ICC.

One reason that rape was ignored in international criminal law was because it seemed to be merely an "ancillary crime" incident to war. Rape was not seen as itself a violation of international peace the way that genocide, apartheid, and colonialist aggression were. Rather rape was seen as merely something that soldiers did, on their own, thus making it no different from the countless rapes committed by non-soldiers in cities and villages every day across the globe. International tribunals concerned themselves with harms that violated international peace and shocked the conscience of humanity. Rape seemed too ordinary to shock the conscience of humanity.[19] For a crime to be international, it was thought that it had to be more than a garden-variety domestic crime. Yet, recently we have seen rape elevated to become a clear strategy of war, seemingly justifying several high profile international prosecutions for rape,[20] but also raising again the question of why and whether rape should be seen as an international crime.

Over the past decade, issues of sexual violence have begun to take centre stage in international law. Mass rape has been the subject of a few trials before international and domestic criminal tribunals.[21] Along with the new international interest in combating sexual violence has come a renewed discussion of the sources of norms that could justify such intervention in international law.[22] Throughout this section I will focus on conceptual difficulties that have arisen in justifying international action against sexual violence, with special attention to the question of whether it is group-based or individual acts of sexual violence that should be the focus of international tribunals.

Rape as a War Crime

The first conceptual question to be investigated is why rape should ever be seen as anything other than a personal, domestic crime. I begin with the most plausible basis for answering that question, namely where rape occurs during wartime, and may constitute a war crime, not merely a domestic crime. Indeed, it has been common to see rape as merely a domestic crime in two senses of that term: both a domestic (or private, household) crime as opposed to a public crime, as well as a domestic (or municipal, state) crime as opposed to an international crime. For centuries, rape has been considered one of the spoils of war, something that male soldiers expected as partial payment for their courage and bravery on the battlefield. The attempt to characterize rape as an international war crime, on the same level as the murder or torture of innocent civilians, is not new. In 1646, Hugo Grotius said that rape "should not go unpunished in war any more than in peace."[23] Today this seems uncontroversial, although it took 350 years before international tribunals recognized the wisdom of Grotius's remarks. Rape is no longer one of the spoils of war, regardless of how brave or courageous the soldiers have been on the battlefield.

A male soldier who rapes a civilian woman in a town just captured by the male soldier's army engages in an individual act somewhat similar to, but importantly different from, a male assailant who rapes a woman he follows home from work. Arguably, the male soldier's act of rape is different from more "normal" cases of rape in that it is perpetrated in conformity with an organized use of force against a whole civilian population; whereas the "normal" rapist acts in a way that is opposed by the organized use of force of the larger society. The soldier's act of rape is made easier by the existence of the war, especially by the way war tends to disrupt the power of the police and army that would normally protect civilians from such acts of violence. The soldier's act of rape is raised to the level of a war crime, not merely a crime of an isolated individual for two reasons. First, wartime conditions cause rape not to be prosecuted in domestic courts. Indeed, war is often so damaging to the internal legal institutions of a country that it is many years before that country's institutions can be said to embody the rule of law.

Second, rape can be seen as a crime in need of international prosecution because of some international interest affected, rather than merely prosecuted, at the international level, because no domestic tribunal is likely to prosecute it. Rape has not only been perpetrated in an indiscriminate way by victorious marauding troops who do not fear the rule of law but has also been used in quite a discriminate way either as a means to terrorize civilian populations, or to perpetrate some form of genocide or ethnic cleansing.[24] The question arises whether rape and other forms of sexual violence should be seen as true war crimes. Since Grotius's time, war crimes have been treated as violations of international law in the sense that the security of peoples is adversely affected when inhumane acts are committed against vulnerable people. Here the international interest is rather simply explained. On the assumption that wars are inevitable, the international community has a strong interest in minimizing harm to civilian populations during war. The rape of civilians during wartime is clearly one such harm that should be the subject of international prosecution.

While rape is criminalized in nearly every society, it has not been viewed in a similar way to other violent crimes, the crime of torture for instance. Torture is seen as a war crime because of its utterly disruptive effects on the peace and stability of a society. Rape during war was not thought to have a similarly disruptive effect, supposedly because of the "privacy" in which it is conducted.[25] Because of the "private" nature of the act, primarily thought to be one involving sex between a man and a woman, the crime was not thought to have the kind of wider implications and consequences that would jeopardize the peace and stability of the international community. In the next section I begin to explain the somewhat unusual way that rape does disrupt the peace and hence affect the interests of the world community, and of humanity itself.

Rape as a Crime against Humanity

The second conceptual question to be investigated is why one would think that rape could be the kind of crime that adversely affects the international community and hence is to be prosecuted as an international crime. To answer this question I turn to examples where rape has been alleged to be a crime against humanity. The designation of crimes against humanity is supposed to pick out the most heinous forms of crime, a crime that shocks "the public conscience" of the world community or that violates "the laws of humanity."[26] International prosecutions are conducted not because domestic prosecutions are unlikely but in order to signify the importance or magnitude of the offences for all of humanity. Thus, just as in the case of US federal crimes, crimes against humanity signal that a larger constituency has been assaulted because of the way that the victims have been treated.

The most recent definitions of crimes against humanity (in the Rwanda Tribunal Statute and the ICC Statute) include rape and other forms of sexual violence,[27] in large part due to the recognition that ethnic and racial persecutions have increasingly employed sexual violence as part of a plan of intimidation and terror. Indeed, according to the most recent definitions of crimes against humanity, the act of rape, or any other of the listed acts, must be conducted as part of a systematic and widespread plan directed against a civilian population. This is the significant backdrop of this chapter. When rape and other forms of sexual violence are treated as crimes against humanity they are treated very similarly to murder and torture, that is, they are prosecuted not as individualized crimes but because of the racial, ethnic, political, national, or religious character of the crime. Yet, little attention is paid to the rationale for insisting that rape be linked to such group memberships for it to be an international crime.

In a very recent case before the Yugoslav tribunal, sensitivity is shown to the plight of women in the ethnic cleansing campaign in the Balkans. The ICTY Trial Chamber decided the case of Prosecutor v. Anto Furundzija in December of 1998.[28] The accused, Furundzija, was the local commander of the Jokers, a special unit of the military police of the Bosnian Serb regime. A Muslim woman was arrested and brought to the Jokers' headquarters for questioning. Furundzija forced the woman to undress, and threatened her by rubbing a knife along her inner thigh and stomach. The woman was moved to another room where she was beaten and forced to have oral and vaginal sex with a soldier while Furundzija stood by doing nothing to prevent these acts.[29]

The court concluded that there has evolved "universally accepted norms of international law prohibiting rape as well as serious sexual assault. These norms are applicable in any armed conflict."[30] Interestingly, though, the court did not go further to call these norms *jus cogens* norms, as it had done concerning torture, for which the accused was also charged.[31] We will return to this issue in later sections, and I will argue that rape can be seen as quite similar to torture. Now one should only note that the accused was tried for both rape and torture, and the charges of torture were considered to be conceptually different and somehow more serious than the sexual violence charges.

Kelly Dawn Askin has argued that many rapes should be seen as violations of *jus cogens* norms on the same level of seriousness as torture. She urges that rape and other forms of sexual violence be considered crimes against humanity if they are part of a systematic attack on gender grounds, not merely on racial, ethnic, political, national, or religious grounds.[32] I agree with Askin that rape is just as serious as torture, and that if it is directed at women as a group then it could be subject to international prosecution. But there is a problem in characterizing many cases of mass rape as being directed at women as a group.

Consider the case of the so-called comfort women. These women were captured by the Japanese army during the Second World War and forced into a kind of sexual slavery to provide "comfort" for the Japanese troops. The enslavement and rape of these women was so heinous that it called out for international prosecution. The question, though, was what the rationale for the prosecution should be. Various theorists, such as Askin, argue that this is a case where there should be international prosecution due to the harm to women as a group.

The comfort women were chosen because they were women, but it is hard to argue that the Japanese army, or any particular member thereof, intended to enslave these women as a way of harming women as a distinct group.[33] The comfort women were drawn from Korea, China, the Philippines, and Indonesia. The women were not restricted to any particular ethnic group. Nonetheless, it is important to note that Japanese women were not selected to be comfort women, and this was largely true of European women as well. So it is hard to characterize the sexual violence involved in the treatment of the comfort women as directed at women as a group, rather than a particular subset of women. They were sexually exploited because they were non-Japanese Asians, but not merely because they were women, and not clearly so as to harm the group women.[34] It is instead rather clear that these women were persecuted in order to send a message to their ethnic communities, rather than to send a message to all women.

There is often a parallel problem in characterizing rape or sexual violence today as based on membership in the group women. In the Balkans, Serb paramilitary forces raped Muslim and Croat women; these Serbs did not generally rape Serbian women. I do not wish to rule out the possibility that a state or state-like entity could order mass rapes to harm women as a group. My point is that the recent cases illustrate that the ethnicity is normally more important than "gender" from the standpoint of the perpetrators of mass rape and sexual violence. Krishna Patel points out that even where state-sponsored forced impregnation occurred, the harm is directed at "Bosnian women" yet "non-Bosnian women are not systematically and repeatedly raped by Serbian forces." For this reason Patel says that the case is a difficult one conceptually since these women "share two immutable characteristics: their gender and their ethnicity as Muslims."[35] In this case, I am sympathetic to Patel's point that these women can make two related group-based harm claims.[36]

There is yet a third group-based claim that these women can make, and it is this claim that is the most persuasive. If there is state involvement in rapes and other forms of sexual violence, then there is also a group-based claim for international prosecution. In a later section of this chapter, we will explore in some detail the way that state involvement transforms a crime of sexual violence into an international crime. At the moment we need merely to note that even if cases like the comfort women or mass rapes of Bosnian women do not fit under the rubric of group-based crimes against women, the involvement of the state will nonetheless make it possible to see these as international crimes deserving of international prosecution.

If the Serb militia did attack women of all ethnicities, or if the attacks were aimed at degrading the women as women, then I would agree with Askin that the rapes could count as gender-based violations of *jus cogens* norms. But if they are more ambiguous, more aimed at degrading the ethnic community than at degrading the women, then it is less clear that it should count as a gender-based violation of *jus cogens* norms. I remain sympathetic to the movement that seeks to add gender to the group-based characteristics that can trigger international action, even as I remain somewhat skeptical that there will be many cases of this sort. The most important issue here is why group-based harm is indeed the key to justified international prosecutions. To confront this problem, we need a more nuanced understanding of international crimes and their relation to *jus cogens* norms than international courts have provided so far. In this context it is instructive to examine another area of international law where rape counts as sufficiently of interest to the international community to call for an internationally sanctioned remedy.

Rape as Persecution

The third conceptual question concerns why only types of rape that are group-based, and why not individual rapes, should be sufficiently of interest to the international community to count as international crimes. To answer this question I will examine a case outside of international criminal law, but where the group-based nature of harms is key, namely the intersection of domestic immigration law and international human rights law. When recent rape victims have brought asylum claims in US immigration law, rape, like torture or genocide, must be linked to membership in a social group (or sufficiently based on a kind of political opinion) if it is to count as persecution. For asylum to be granted, a person needs to be a refugee, and a refugee is a person fleeing persecution in her home country. The relevant form of persecution for asylum is that "on account of race, religion, nationality, membership in a particular social group, or political opinion."[37] But why should this be the only basis for establishing an asylum claim in such cases?

If one has been subjected to individual isolated acts of persecution, asylum will generally not be granted in the United States, or in many other countries. One likely reason for this is that the proper recourse is through the domestic courts of one's home country. If persecution is group-based, then it is thought to be pervasive and not merely directed at an individual. As with crimes against humanity, the basis of persecution in asylum cases has to be something beyond what is harmful to discrete individuals, unless there is also state involvement.

Consider the case of Olimpia Lazo-Majano, an El Salvadoran woman who sought asylum in the United States. She had been the victim of long-term abuse at the hands of her former employer, Rene Zuniga. Zuniga was a sergeant in the Salvadoran military. He had used his gun, as a well as grenades held against her head, in forcing Lazo-Majano to submit to intercourse. Zuniga also threatened to bomb her home if she did not submit to him. According to the court, "Zuniga told Olimpia that it was his job to kill subversives."[38] In the court's estimation, this involved "a cynical imputation" of a political opinion to Lazo-Majano. Nonetheless, the court held that "Zuniga is asserting the political opinion that a man has a right to dominate [a woman] and he has persecuted Olimpia to force her to accept his opinion without rebellion."[39] The court concluded that "even if she had no political opinion and was innocent of a single reflection on the government or her country, the cynical imputation of political opinion to her is what counts…one must continue to look at the person from the perspective of the persecutor. If the persecutor thinks the person guilty of a political opinion, then the person is at risk."[40]

The key difficulty in Lazo-Majano is to see how persecutions by males of females could be more than individually based. From the perspective of her attacker, this case had all of the appearance of a personal problem—Zuniga seemingly did these things to her because he wanted to get her to have sex with him. If, though, there is a pattern of such behaviour directed against members of an ethnic group in a given country, then it is no longer merely personal. And the international community steps in, represented by the country granting asylum, because the persecution is more serious for being group-based. But why should group-based sexual violence and not individualized sexual violence be seen as important to the international community? Part of the answer is that this form of sexual violence is seen as sufficiently similar to genocide and apartheid to demand international attention. But why are genocide and apartheid given this status?

To answer this question, and the questions from the previous other two sections, I will, in the next section, turn to the concept of *jus cogens* norms.

We have seen three conceptual problems illustrated in these three areas of international law. First, why think that any form of rape should be seen as anything other than a personal (domestic) crime? Second, why think that certain types of rape harm the interests of the international community and hence should count as an international crime? Third, why think only group-based types of rape, like genocide and apartheid, are sufficiently of interest to the international community to count as international crimes? And why think that genocide and apartheid should be of special interest to the international community?

It is the main practical thesis of this chapter that when rape and sexual violence are targeted at a group or are part of a state policy, then these forms of sexual exploitation are also clearly violations of *jus cogens* norms, and for this reason legitimately prosecuted by international tribunals. Mass rape and sexual violence clearly violate moderate legal positivism's ethical or natural minimum, since they are clear assaults against the bodily security of the women who are assaulted. When the assault is either directed at a group or involves a state or state-like actor, then it is of sufficient interest to the international community to call for international prosecutions.[41] In the next section we explore in more detail the group-based model of international crime.

Harming Humanity

The international community takes a special interest in certain categories of acts because these acts victimize humanity. Cherif Bassiouni has said that the only way to make sense of *jus cogens* norms is to recognize that "certain crimes affect the interests of the world community as a whole because they threaten the peace and security of humankind and they shock the conscience of humanity."[42] Bassiouni, though, devoted only one sentence to rape in the first edition of his book on crimes against humanity.[43] Let us begin by looking more closely at Bassiouni's idea, taken from the Hague Convention's Martens Clause, that *jus cogens* norms are grounded in the laws of humanity, and the dictates of public conscience.[44] We will separate this issue into two parts: first we will investigate the group-based nature of the harmful act and then turn to the group-based nature of the actor/perpetrator.

The Interests of Humanity

Let us begin with the status of the harmful act. On first sight there appears to be a difference between the rationale for prosecution based on the peace and security of humankind (which derives from moderate legal positivism) and the rationale based on shocking the public conscience (which derives from natural law theory). It could be argued that an especially vicious act of rape could shock the conscience of the international community, even if it did not threaten the peace and security of humankind. There are, of course, pragmatic reasons why states would be uncomfortable thinking about international crimes in this way, since then state sovereignty about internal criminal matters would be potentially threatened. The possibility that an individualized crime could rise to the level of an international crime merely by shocking the conscience of humanity does not seem to be countenanced in any of the definitions of crimes against humanity that have been formulated in recent years.[45]

Theoretically though, a "shocking the conscience of humanity" test may very well apply to individualized crimes that have no collective nature and are not part of a "state plan." To assess this possibility we need to think harder than we have about how "humanity" can have its conscience shocked in the first place. Since humanity is not the sort of entity that is generally thought to have a conscience, humanity's conscience must be either a shorthand or metaphorical expression.[46] "Conscience of humanity" could be shorthand for what would shock many persons. But if an international crime is one that shocks the conscience of many humans, then that crime is merely a crime that shocks the conscience of humans, not humanity, and we do not have a basis for distinguishing international from domestic crimes.

A traditional natural law approach might allow for a non-metaphorical use of the term "conscience of humanity," but such a usage merely points out again the philosophically problematical nature of traditional natural law theory. If each person's conscience somehow has access to the divine commands of God, and if each person's conscience therefore has a common element with each other person's conscience, we might be able to talk about the conscience of humanity in a non-metaphorical way. But such an account of the relationship between God's commands and the consciences of discrete humans runs up against both empirical and metaphysical problems. Empirically, it is simply contentious at best to think that each person will have the same conscientious judgement about anything. There is such a diversity of moral perspectives in the world, seemingly held by each person's conscience, that it is not obvious or even plausible to think that we all have a similar conscience. Metaphysically, if there is a similarity of conscience at all it seems much more plausible that it concerns the way that conscience works, rather than the substantive judgements of different people's consciences. The discreteness of persons does not seem compatible with such a common core of conscience.[47]

So, rather than thinking of "shocking the conscience of humanity" as a literal phrase, we should think of it as meant to imply that any person, as a human, regardless of state affiliation, is shocked when certain harms are seemingly directed at humanity. Kant sometimes talked as though an immoral act by one individual against another could be understood as directed against humanity. In *Grounding for the Metaphysics of Morals*, Kant's second formulation of the categorical imperative calls for all people to "Act in such a way that you treat humanity, whether in your own person or in the person of another, always at the same time as an end and never simply as a means."[48] Humanity exists "in our own person, as an end in itself," and when one person treats another person not as an end-in-itself, then humanity is also not treated as an end-in-itself.[49] Here humanity is not a common substantive set of beliefs but simply what all humans share in common that makes them all of the same species, disregarding whatever it is that makes individual persons unique. Kant argues that humanity exists in each person and can be harmed when someone disregards the humanity of a person by treating that person as a means to some other end rather than treating that person as a fellow human deserving of respect as such.

Kant's treatment of humans as containing humanity within them can surely be linked to the idea that certain kinds of behaviour shock all of humanity.[50] Think of torture in this context. When an individual person is subjected to excruciatingly painful and demeaning treatment, so as to extract information or a confession, any human would be shocked by the very affront to humanity of which the torture victim is a representative member. This is what, at least on a Kantian view, makes the act of torture immoral. But we do not yet have a basis for distinguishing those immoral acts that are domestic crimes from those immoral acts that rise to the level of international crimes.

One way to draw the distinction between acts that are international crimes and acts that are domestic crimes has to do with whether the act is clearly directed at the humanity of the individual person, instead of being aimed at the unique features of the person. In both cases, the act in question may be thought to be immoral because the individual is being treated as a means rather than as an end in itself, and hence treated in a way that fails to show respect for that person's dignity. It is my contention that for truly international crimes something more than disrespect of the individual victim is required. There must be a clear sense in which humanity, for which an international tribunal stands in, is the victim of the crime.

We have three distinct ways of thinking of "harm to humanity." First, a member of humanity is harmed and thereby the larger whole of which the individual is a part is harmed along with that individual. Second, some characteristic of humanity is harmed, perhaps by harming it within each member of humanity. Third, all of humanity is harmed, say by a nuclear holocaust that destroys humanity. The first approach fails to be a basis for international crime unless there is some reason to think that the harm to the individual does, in some non-trivial way, harm the whole of humanity. The third is useless, except in the most extreme of cases where humanity is truly harmed directly. The second approach is the most promising. What is it that humans have in common? One of the most important things is their ability to act autonomously and to be treated with respect according to what they have autonomously chosen to do.

If an individual person is treated according to that person's characteristics that are out of that person's control, there is a straightforward assault on that person's autonomy. It is as if the individuality of the person is being ignored, and the person is being treated as a mere representative of a group that the person has not chosen to join.[51] The civil rights movement in the US has been premised on the idea that such treatment, concerning racial groups, is a clear violation of a person's autonomy. All of humanity is affected when such acts occur since, in some sense, it doesn't matter that the acts are taken against named, discrete individuals. It may as well be that the acts were taken against anonymous individuals, since their individuality plays so little a role in the treatment. When harm occurs in the way I have just described it can be called group-based, not merely individualized.[52]

In my view, humanity is seen as a victim when the act is committed against individuals because of their group affiliations, that is, according to things that are beyond their autonomous agency. Humanity is a victim when the intentions of individual perpetrators or the harms of individual victims are based on group characteristics rather than individual characteristics. Humanity is clearly implicated, and in a sense victimized, when the sufferer merely stands in for larger segments of the population who are not treated according to individual differences among fellow humans but only according to group characteristics. When acts have this structure then it is clear that truly arbitrary treatment of the sort proscribed by *jus cogens* norms has occurred. The international community thus enters in, so as to vindicate humanity through its international legal tribunals.[53]

One of the most salient norms in this context is that individual persons should not be harmed because of their group memberships. A recent international court opinion states this point quite succinctly when it says that acts rise to the level of the international crime of persecution when "the emphasis is not on the individual victim but rather on the collective, the individual being victimized not because of his individual attributes but rather because of his membership in a targeted civilian population."[54] The point of this analysis is that international *jus cogens* norms protect individuals from a certain form of arbitrary treatment that is group-based.

Consider the short list of practices thought to violate international *jus cogens* norms or obligations *erga omnes*:[55] namely, genocide, apartheid, colonialist aggression, and torture. At the top of that list is genocide, where clearly the emphasis is on the group, the destruction of a people, not the individual. Apartheid can be easily seen in the same light, as clearly directed against a racial group. Colonialism is the mistreatment of a people, including the denial of a people's right to self-determination. Torture is the only practice condemned by *jus cogens* norms that does not readily have a group orientation, as is true for most human rights abuses. But the form of torture condemned by *jus cogens* norms is that practised by the state, or a state-like actor, and it is this element of state action that makes torture also group-based when it is prosecuted at the international level.[56]

When acts are committed against individuals because of their group characteristics, then there is harm to humanity in both senses identified by Bassiouni. As just explained, the conscience of humanity is offended by such actions because they fail to show respect for the autonomy of individual humans and instead treat individuals as mere members of groups of which those individuals have no control over being members. Humanity is offended when any individual is so treated. In addition, the peace and security of humanity is assaulted by such practices, since the group-based harms could just as easily have been perpetrated against any one of a large number of humans. Since the attacks are not based on the unique characteristics of the victims, the rest of humanity's security is also attacked and the peace of humanity is disrupted. Hence, even though these two senses of harming humanity may diverge, there is at least one clear sense in which they converge, namely when harms are group-based. There is also a high plausibility to such a view because it is supported by different traditions, indeed perhaps indicating what is of common ground in those different philosophical views.

Jus Cogens Norms and State-Sanctioned Rape

Let us now turn to the second basis for international prosecutions, namely, when the actor or perpetrator is also somehow group-based. This basis for internationally proscribing certain forms of rape and sexual violence appeals to the special state involvement in certain instances of rape or sexual violence. As the Yugoslav Trial Chamber recognized, implicit in some of the *jus cogens* justifications of crimes "is the fact that the conduct in question is the product of state-action or state-favoring action."[57] If rapes are part of a state-sponsored plan to eliminate an ethnic group within that state's borders, or as a state-accepted way for some individuals to intimidate a sub-group of women in a given community, then that individual crime most clearly rises to the level of an international crime because of its arbitrary nature. The actions of states, or state-like actors, have given the international community its clearest rationale for entry into what would otherwise be a domestic matter. And this is true in two senses of the term domestic: the actions are not merely between two individuals but involve the larger society, and the actions are no longer merely appropriately prosecuted at the domestic level since the domestic state is itself a party to the violence.

In various discussions of *jus cogens* norms, the conceptual basis for these norms was identified to be the demand for security and dignity that can be lodged against states. When it is the state that is assaulting the person, either through an official representative of the state (such as, a member of the army or the police), or because of some state-sponsored plan, then there is a very clear violation of a *jus cogens* norm since security and dignity of the individual is so clearly assaulted. In addition, when it is the state that is the victimizer, then it normally makes little sense to argue that a domestic tribunal should prosecute the crime, since it is so unlikely that the state could impartially prosecute itself.

I wish now to focus our attention on why certain kinds of state action can mark a crime as international. A state's "plan" can be understood as involving omissions as well as commissions. We could treat the notion of a government plan of rape the way that we treat a corporation or university in terms of its plan of sexual harassment. Here the chief question is whether there is knowledge of the illicit practice and whether any efforts have been made to stop it. Failure to make efforts to stop the practice will then be seen as effectively having a policy to condone the practice. The international community then would have a legitimate basis for intervention so as to protect the individual from arbitrary group-based treatment.[58]

When an isolated incident of rape occurs in a given country, it is virtually impossible to prove that the rape is group-based. When there is mass rape in a given country, especially directed at a subsection of the female population of that country, then it is easier to show that the acts of rape are group-based. If there is widespread rape, seemingly directed at certain types of women, then one can infer at the very least that there is some kind of collective negative plan to allow such rapes, even if there is no clear affirmative plan to incite or encourage such rapes.

In the most egregious examples of mass rape and sexual violence, something very much like a plan or policy is afoot. As Catherine MacKinnon has put it, the difficulty is that "rape has so often been treated as extracurricular, as just something men do, as a product rather than a policy of war."[59] While it may be very difficult to show that there was an affirmative governmental plan or policy to use rape as a means of persecution of non-Bosnian women by Serb forces, it is considerably easier to show that there was a negative policy to allow it to occur. All that needs to be shown is that the relevant governmental units were aware of the widespread practice and they did nothing to prevent it.[60]

I do not wish to rule out international prosecutions of rape or sexual violence that lack governmental complicity, but merely to suggest that these will be considerably harder to justify as condemnable by *jus cogens* norms and subject to prosecution by international tribunals. Individuals who are not part of the state structure can engage in group-based harm that could rise to the level of international concern. But in such cases there would need to be something, provable through direct evidence, that linked the individual perpetrator to the larger society. I have previously argued that discriminatory intent on the part of the perpetrator may be sufficient to link a non-state actor to the larger community's plan of group-based harm.[61] But the clearest cases of international prosecution will remain those in which the perpetrator has a role in the state structure, as was true in all of the cases discussed earlier in this paper.[62]

Do the acts need to be widespread in order for the acts to rise to the level of international crimes?[63] Not necessarily. But if we are talking about a single incident of rape, even by a state official, it will be hard to show that such an act is to be imputed to the state rather than merely to the individual perpetrator. For the officials have two persona, their truly official persona and also their personal persona. In order to show that the member of the police was indeed acting in his or her official capacity, it is often necessary to show that there was a pattern of such behaviour and no one in authority over the police officer did anything to stop it, and often in addition that other police were acting in a similar manner. Even better would be the showing that there was an explicit policy, as there appeared to have been in Bosnia, of having the Serbian police use sexual assault as a means of intimidating ethnic Muslims.

I wish now to modify my proposal that if either the act or actor is group-based, then international prosecution is appropriate. In most cases, both of these factors should be present. I will call this the "standard model." The standard model of international crime will best secure the rights of the defendants, the importance of which we will next explore. In some cases, though, it may be justifiable for prosecutions to go forward with only one of these two factors present. For example, if the group-based harm is very widespread, then it may be sufficient for international prosecution even without state involvement. But as I have argued, there is often state involvement here nonetheless, since the state's lack of action to stop the widespread group-based harm is normally an indication of at least a negative plan to allow it.

In international law, acts are inhumane and humanity is implicated when the intentions of individual perpetrators or the harms of individual victims are due to group-based characteristics rather than due to the unique characteristics of the individual perpetrators and victims. Humanity is implicated when the individual actor or sufferer merely stands in for larger segments of the population who attempt to deny individual differences among fellow humans, and look only at group characteristics. This is the specific purview of international criminal law and where prosecutions by international tribunals can be most easily justified. International tribunals, like the ICC, should prosecute mass rape and sexual violence because humanity is harmed or when the harm is state-based.

Why Not Individualized International Crimes?

One of the most serious objections to my view of the nature of international crime is that it regressively turns the clock back. International human rights activists have fought for several generations to get international courts to focus on individuals rather than groups as victims, and to focus on individuals as perpetrators rather than states and other international organizations. The idea is that meaningful human rights change can occur only when individuals are front and centre, such that we cannot ignore who is the victim and where perpetrators cannot hide behind their states or other groups and are forced to become individually accountable for their heinous deeds. The ICC is similarly inspired by the push toward individual accountability and away from merely state-based and other forms of group accountability.[64]

My response takes two prongs. First, as I stated at the beginning, if we fail to distinguish international crimes from domestic crimes, the ICC and similar international tribunals will continue to experience difficulties with those who fear usurpation of domestic tribunals and hence of state sovereignty.[65] This is a pragmatic point, but it is very important. If international criminal law is to progress, multilateral agreements like the ICC treaty must have widespread support. Such support will not be forthcoming if courts like the ICC are seen as potentially usurping the sovereignty of domestic states. And if the multilateral agreements do not gain sufficient support then these international criminal tribunals will fail. So even if one thinks that international criminal law should have a wider purview than what I have proposed, extending that purview will actually make it less likely that there will be efficacious international criminal courts at all.

This first response is practical. The critics of the ICC, like Jesse Helms, are worried about just such a conflation of international and domestic legal norms, and as a result have blocked various states from implementing major human rights treaties. Without some basis for distinguishing among these types of legal norm, the critics will continue to have a powerful argument against participation in these treaties. But if a very clear, in-principle distinction between domestic and international crimes can be maintained, then the encroachments on state sovereignty caused by these treaties will not appear to be so great. And the world will stand to gain by being able to hold all states accountable for some especially egregious and widespread human rights abuses.

There is an interesting analogy with hate crimes. In one sense it is true that it is hard to distinguish in principle between what is outlawed by local and federal jurisdictions. It is, after all, the very same act of racist speaking that is outlawed by both types of law. But at the federal level, it is thought to be necessary to prove an additional element, namely that the speech act was intended to harm a whole group, not just the individual to whom the speech was immediately addressed. When directed at the group a greater potential for widespread harm occurs, thereby bringing in a larger community as the entity on behalf of whom the prosecution is undertaken.

My second response is theoretical and has been rehearsed in some detail in the preceding pages. For the international community to prosecute certain crimes, those crimes must be shown to involve harms to humanity or harms that violate some security interest of the world community. Here the task of defining just what is involved in truly international crimes takes on an urgency. If international crimes are not cast in group-based terms, it will be very difficult to draw a distinction between international and domestic crime.

Why is it important for international law to be premised on group-based rather than individualized norms? The main reason that I adopt a group-based approach is to be able to distinguish clearly between international legal norms and domestic ones. One could challenge this idea by arguing that in an ideal world there would not need to be such a distinction between international and domestic legal norms. Indeed, it could be argued, there is no in-principle basis for distinguishing rights at either level, and much harm can be done by maintaining the distinction in terms of further entrenching unjustified notions of sovereignty when human rights abuses occur.

It is important to continue to maintain a distinction between international and domestic legal norms. I agree that ideally there is no need to draw this distinction. In one sense, all rapes harm humanity in the sense that the individual is a part of humanity. But in another sense, individualized rapes, where the harm is not group-based or not perpetrated by a state or state-like actor, do not directly affect the security of humanity. Only when these acts are based on more than individual characteristics is there a strong threat to the peace and security of humanity that would warrant international concern. As long as there are functioning domestic courts, we should leave to these courts the prosecution of most rapes. The international courts should be used only in highly unusual circumstances, not as a replacement for what domestic states are able to prosecute.

I urge my readers to consider this issue not from a victim-oriented approach but from a defendant-oriented approach. If defendants, who have no state-involvement, are going to be tried in international courts for normally highly individualized crimes such as rape, rather than for clearly group-based crimes such as genocide, it seems that these defendants should have been able to see, at the time they acted, that what they were doing was a violation of international law. As explained earlier, conformity with main moral principles is necessary for law to have moral legitimacy. Moral legitimacy is not achieved merely by making sure that individual actors do not have impunity for their actions. For if this were all that was needed for moral legitimacy, then there would be no basis for a right to a trial, or the right against self-incrimination, etc. All that would be needed would be for the supposed perpetrators to be captured and punished.

Some would argue that it is enough that there exists a list somewhere of what crimes are indeed international ones. The ICC statute provides such a list. Perhaps one could follow H.L.A. Hart's suggestion that international law encompasses just those rules that the world community accepts as legitimate.[66] Statutes like the ICC set out a list of crimes that are to be recognized as international crimes. Once the ICC statute has been ratified, then it will be possible easily to pick out which crimes are considered to be international ones. Such a view has an obvious simplicity to it. And there is no need to have complex philosophical justifications for each item on the list. But such a list would not necessarily constitute a system of international criminal law deserving of respect as a fair system that defendants can legitimately be prosecuted under.

The simplicity of a "list of international crimes" proposal belies its chief drawback. For those states that do not sign on to the ICC statute, or who later change their minds, there is no clear reason for regarding those crimes as anything other than what some states and interest groups managed to insert into the ICC statute.[67] There will be no in-principle basis for seeing these crimes as "deserving" of international prosecution. This problem can be illustrated by the plight of Bosnian Serbs now in jail in The Hague who had no hint that their acts, as unspeakable as they may be, were even remotely likely to land them in jail and awaiting trial before an international tribunal.[68] The ICC will resolve some of this difficulty by supplying the list of international crimes and hence putting future perpetrators of these crimes on notice that they risk international prosecution. But the ICC statute will not solve the problem discussed at the beginning of this chapter of showing that a given list of crimes contains those crimes morally deserving of international prosecution and punishment.

From a victim's-rights orientation, it makes sense to have an expansive domain of international crimes, so that no victimizer can get away with impunity from his responsibility. But from a defendant's-rights approach we must exercise more caution. Most importantly, there must be some underlying rationale for the claim that a certain crime is an international crime. As is true in domestic criminal law, if crimes are merely a random collection of prescriptions, then defendants will not know what they are supposed to do, or, more importantly, why it is considered important to avoid certain kinds of conduct. Such an understanding is important for the general sense of moral legitimacy of the law and for a proper attribution of responsibility to those who commit egregious acts in the world. For it is moral legitimacy that is the true hallmark of the rule of law, not the mere retribution garnered on behalf of the victims of horrendous crimes. We will not gain respect for the international rule of law until international crimes are conceptualized as more than mere random lists of acts that some states and interest groups once thought to be criminalizable.

We should not let our zealousness in seeking to avenge harms to the victims blind us into setting the elements of international crimes too low to do justice to these defendants, whose rights also must be protected. This discussion has tried to show that a variety of conceptual problems arise if one tries to prosecute individuals for international crimes without establishing one or both of the group-based factors outlined above. If it is true that it is too difficult to establish these factors in a court, then perhaps the international reaction to such crimes as ethnic cleansing should not be to have an international criminal trial at all. Perhaps truth commissions linked with amnesty programs are a better response to these group-based crimes. Reconciliation between groups certainly seems to be more easily achieved outside of the adversarial domain of criminal trials.[69]

I have tried here to present a defensible, in-principle basis for distinguishing between international and domestic crimes. I have stressed that such crimes must be group-based, either in terms of the status of the perpetrators or the character of the harm. Even those who disagree can regard my efforts as at least providing a preliminary way of sorting, where a basis for deciding which are international crimes is established in a way that meshes with the uncontroversial international crimes. My critics might choose to use this model as a basis for deciding which additional crimes are to be added to the current lists codified in international instruments, where other putative international crimes can be added on the basis of special justification, by analogizing from the core crimes. And even if this much is rejected, I hope, at the very least, to have spurred a philosophical debate about the concept of international crime. The defendants who will be subject to serious risk of liberty are owed a clear answer to the various conceptual questions I have posed in this discussion.[70]

Notes

1 See Anthony Lewis, "U.S. Denied Its Heritage in Failing to Embrace World Court," *St. Louis Post-Dispatch*, B1, July 21, 1998. See also James Podgers, "War Crimes Court Under Fire," *ABA Journal* (September 1998): 64-69.

2 See M. Cherif Bassiouni and Edward M. Wise, *Aut Dedere Aut Judicare: The Duty to Prosecute or Extradite in International Law* (The Hague: Martinus Nijhoff, 1995).

3 M. Cherif Bassiouni, "The Sources and Content of International Criminal Law: A Theoretical Framework," *International Criminal Law*, 2nd ed. vol. 1, *Crimes*, ed. M. Cherif Bassiouni.

4 Ibid., 31.

5 John Stuart Mill, *On Liberty*, 1 (1859), ed. Elizabeth Rapaport (Indianapolis, IN: Hackett, 1978).

6 Joel Feinberg, *The Moral Limits of the Criminal Law: Volume 1: Harm to Others*, 6 (Oxford: Oxford University Press, 1984).

7 See Tony Honoré, *Making Law Bind*, 12-16 (Oxford: Oxford University Press,1987) arguing that fear of sanctions must remain at least a background concern for law to have a binding force. But Honoré recognizes that fear of sanctions is only a partial basis for binding law in the international arena. If international laws are pointless or tyrannical then there is no moral bindingness, and then the laws are not properly binding at all.

8 See Lon Fuller, *The Morality of Law* (New Haven: Yale University Press, 1964, 1969).

9 Ibid., 184-86, where Fuller presents a similar argument but does not connect the "internal morality of law" to the concept of fairness. Fuller also points out that one can be a natural law theorist, at least a procedural one, and support just this idea that I am attributing to moderate legal positivism.

10 Hart argues against seeing international law as a system of laws because it lacks a rule of recognition, although he also thinks that international laws are no less binding for lacking this dimension. See H.L.A. Hart, *The Concept of Law* (Oxford: Oxford University Press, 1961, 1994), 214 and 231.

11 Bassiouni, "The Sources and Content of International Criminal Law," 44.

12 See Joel Feinberg, *The Moral Limits of the Criminal Law, Volume 4: Harmless Wrongdoing* (Oxford: Oxford University Press, 1988).

13 See H.L.A. Hart, *Law, Liberty, and Morality* (Stanford, CA: Stanford University Press, 1962).

14 An exception to this may occur when racial or ethnic hatred is expressed by one's words. See Mari J. Matsuda, Charles R. Lawrence III, Richard DeLegadu, and Kimberle Williams Crenshaw, *Words That Wound* (Boulder, CO: Westview Press, 1993).

15 Feinberg, *The Moral Limits*, 105-106.

16 James Crawford made this point to me in private conversation, Saturday, October 21, 2000, at a conference at St. Louis University's Law School.

17 Bassiouni, "The Sources and Content of International Criminal Law," 39.

18 M. Cherif Bassiouni, for instance, began his very influential 1992 book on crimes against humanity by pointing out the incongruity of international criminal law which must use "technical legal terms" to criticize that which conscience already so eloquently condemns. And yet even so sensitive a theorist as Bassiouni had only one sentence about rape in the 820 pages of the first edition of his book on crimes against humanity. See M. Cherif Bassiouni, *Crimes against Humanity* (Dordrecht, NL: Kluwer Law, 1992), x. When Bassiouni published the second edition of his book in 1999, he came down squarely in favour of the use of international tribunals like the ICC to prosecute rape. But here Bassiouni does not provide any basis for limiting the international prosecution of rape and other forms of sexual violence. See M. Cherif Bassiouni, *Crimes against Humanity in International Criminal Law*, 2nd ed. (Dordrecht, NL: Kluwer Law, 1999), 361-62.

19 See Kelly Dawn Askin, *War Crimes against Women* (The Hague: M. Nijhoff, 1997).

20 Most recently, the high profile "Foca case" has been prosecuted by the Yugoslav Tribunal. See Jerome Socolovsky, "Landmark Rape Case Opens Today at Yugoslav Tribunal on War Crimes," *St. Louis Post-Dispatch*, March 20, 2000, A1, A7.

21 Prosecutor v. Dusko Tadic, Case No. IT-94-1-T (May 7, 1997) International Criminal Tribunal for the Former Yugoslavia [hereinafter ICTY] Trial Chamber; Prosecutor v. Anto Furundzija, Case No. IT-9517/1-T (December 1998) ICTY Trial Chamber.

22 See Margaret E. Galey, "International Enforcement of Women's Rights," *Human Rights Quarterly* 6 (1984): 463; Hilary Charlesworth and Christine Chinkin, "The Gender of Jus Cogens," *Human Rights Quarterly* 15 (1993): 63; and Theodor Meron, "Rape as a Crime under International Humanitarian Law," *American Journal of International Law* 87 (1993): 424.

23 Hugo Grotius, *De Jurebelli Ac Pacis Libri Tres*, Vol. 2, trans. Francis W. Kelsey (1646; reprint, Oxford: Oxford University Press, 1995), 656-57.

24 See Aryeh Neier, *War Crimes* (New York: Random House, 1998), especially chap. 11.

25 In 1993 a UN sponsored conference on human rights said that violence against women, in both public and private life, violates women's human rights. See *U.N. World Conference on Human Rights: Vienna Declaration and Programme of Action*, U.N. Doc. A/Conf. 157/24 (Part 1) (1993) reprinted in *I.L.M.* 1661, 1678-80 (1993).

26 These are the words of the famous Martens Clause of the Hague Convention of 1907 that Justice Jackson employed as a source of international law for the Nuremberg prosecutions. See Report of Robert H. Jackson, United States Representative to the International Conference on Military Trials 50 (1945) *quoting* Convention (No. V) Respecting the Laws and Customs of War on Land, With Annex and Regulations, Oct. 18, 1907, Preamble, 36 Stat. 2277, T.S. No. 539, 1 Bevans 631.

27 "Statute for the International Tribunal for the Prosecution of Persons Responsible for Genocide and Other Serious Violations of International Humanitarian Law Committed in the Territory of Rwanda," S.C. Res. 955, art. 3(g) (Nov. 8, 1994), reprinted in 33 *I.L.M.* 1598 (1994); *Rome Statute for the International Criminal Court*, A/Conf. July 17, 1998, art. 7.

28 Prosecutor v. Anto Furundsija, Case No. IT-9517/1-T (December 1998), ICTY Trial Chamber.

29 Ibid., 39-41.

30 Ibid., 168.

31 Ibid., 153-57.

32 Askin, *War Crimes against Women*, 93.

33 I have argued that discriminatory intent is the key consideration that must be proved for morally justifiable international criminal prosecutions against individual persons. See my paper "Crimes against Humanity," presented at the APA Eastern Division meetings in Boston in 1999. The matter is also explored in my unpublished book-length manuscript, "Crime and Humanity."

34 See Larry May and Marilyn Friedman, "Harming Women as a Group," *Social Theory and Practice* 11 (1985): 207 for an argument showing how a charge of group-based harm could be made out for women in a particular society.

35 See Krishna R. Patel, "Recognizing the Rape of Bosnian Women as Gender-Based Persecution," 60, *Brooklyn Law Review*, 929, 948 for an argument on how to understand mass rape as indeed a group-based crime against women.

36 See Keith Burgess-Jackson, "A Crime against Women: Calhoun on the Wrongness of Rape," *Journal of Social Philosophy* 31(2000): 286-93, for a similar argument.

37 INA sec 101(a)(42) [8 U.S.C.A. sec. 1101].

38 Lazo-Majano v. INS, 813 F.2d 1432, 1433 (9th Cir. 1987).

39 Ibid., 1435.

40 Ibid.

41 Mass rape and sexual violence are also condemnable by natural law theory's dictates of public conscience since the group-based nature of the assaults fails to treat these women as unique individuals. It is even less controversial that this characterization is in line with the anti-colonialist's view of *jus cogens* norms as protecting colonial and disadvantaged populations from aggression by the more powerful.

42 M. Cherif Bassiouni, "International Crimes: *Jus Cogens* and *Obligatio Erga Omnes*," *Law and Contemporary Problems*, 63, 69 (1996).

43 Bassiouni, *Crimes against Humanity*.

44 Bassiouni, "The Sources and Content of International Law."

45 See especially the Rome Treaty, (Hart, *The Concept of Law*) ("when committed as part of a widespread or systematic attack"). The ICTY Statute has also been interpreted by the Tadic Trial Chamber to require that rape or murder must be part of widespread or systematic attack. In contrast, the first definition of crimes against humanity in the Nuremberg tribunal did not require a group connection, but it also did not recognize rape as a crime against humanity. See *Agreement for the Prosecution and Punishment of the Major War Criminals of the European Axis Powers and Charter of the International Military Tribunal*, Aug. 8, 1945, art. 6(c) (requiring only that the act be committed "before or during the war").

46 See Larry May, "On Conscience," *American Philosophy Quarterly* (1984): 57-67 for a general discussion of the nature of conscience.

47 In this context it is instructive to consult the work of psychologists who work in the field of moral development. Lawrence Kohlberg has argued that what is universally true cross-culturally is that people develop through stages of moral reasoning, not that they have particular substantive conscientious judgements. See Lawrence Kohlberg, *The Philosophy of Moral Development* (San Francisco: Harper and Row, 1981).

48 Immanuel Kant, *Grounding for the Metaphysics of Morals*, trans. James Ellington (1785; reprint, Indianapolis, IN: Hackett, 1981), 36.

49 Ibid., 37.

50 See Laurie Calhoun, "On Rape: A Crime against Humanity," *Journal of Social Philosophy* (1997): 101, 107-108 for a discussion of how a Kantian might view rape as a crime against humanity. See also Keith Burgess-Jackson, "A Crime against Women: Calhoun on the Wrongness of Rape," *Journal of Social Philosophy* 31 (2000): 286-93 for a response to Calhoun.

51 See Bernard Boxill, *Blacks and Social Justice* (Lanham, MD: Rowman and Littlefield, 1984), where he argues that treating people on the basis of characteristics they did not choose to acquire is a serious injustice.

52 See Larry May, *The Morality of Groups*, 116-19 (Notre Dame, IN: University of Notre Dame Press, 1987) for an analysis of the idea of a group-based harm.

53 We might think of the parallel with the United States government entering into what would otherwise be a state matter when there is a "federal issue," that is, a matter that affects the whole of the United States. In a sense, the whole nation enters into the state matter so as to vindicate the national community.

54 Prosecutor v. Dusko Tadic, Case No. IT-94-1-T (May 7, 1997), para. 644.

55 See Ragazzi, n. 4, 72, for a discussion of the similarities between *jus cogens* norms and obligations *erga omnes*.

56 M. Cherif Bassiouni, "International Crimes: *Jus Cogens* and *Obligatio Erga Omnes*," *Law and Contemporary Problems* 59, 69, here Bassiouni says that *jus cogens* crimes are "characterized explicitly or implicitly by state policy or conduct."

57 Tadic Trial Chamber, n. 21, 697.

58 On this point see the parallel analysis of sexual harassment in Marilyn Friedman and Larry May, "Harming Women as a Group," n. 34.

59 Catherine MacKinnon, "Crimes of War, Crimes of Peace," in *On Human Rights*, ed. Stephen Shute and Susan Hurley (New York: Basic Books, 1993), 108.

60 See Larry May, *Sharing Responsibility* (Chicago: University of Chicago Press, 1992), 36-55, for an argument that omissions can implicate an institution in harms such as those associated with racism.

61 May, *The Morality of Groups*.

62 The comfort women were raped by Japanese soldiers. Furundzija was a commander of a local Bosnian Serb police force. Zuniga was a sergeant in the Salvadoran army.

63 In "Crime and Humanity," an unpublished book-length manuscript, I discuss this matter in more detail.

64 See Steven R. Ratner and Jason S. Abrams, *Accountability for Human Rights Atrocities in International Law* (Oxford, Oxford University Press, 1997).

65 Lewis, "U.S. Denied Its Heritage."

66 Hart, *The Concept of Law*, 228-30.

67 There is a serious worry, raised by some, that the ICC list of international crimes reflects the disproportionate influence of certain interest groups. Indeed, the Rome Conference gave extraordinary and unprecedented powers to non-governmental organizations. While most NGOs are engaged in good works at the international level, they are not representative of the peoples of the world, and they often are blinded by the zealousness with which they pursue their often single-agenda interests.

68 Patricia Wald speech at Washington University's School of Law on November 17, 2000.

69 See Martha Minow, *Between Vengeance and Forgiveness* (Boston, MA: Beacon Press, 1998), (exploring the advantages and disadvantages of international criminal tribunals and truth commissions).

70 I am grateful to Marcia Baron, Peter Mutharika, Trudy Govier, Lukas Meyer, James Bohman, Matthew Cashen, and Jack Knight for useful comments on earlier versions of this paper. This paper is excerpted from my book-length manuscript, "Humanitarian Crimes."

6

What Can Others Do?[1] Foreign Governments and the Politics of Peacebuilding

Tom Keating

Introduction

Since the end of the Cold War in 1989, international politics has been marked by two somewhat contradictory trends. First, violent conflict has persisted in many parts of the world. Most of this violent conflict has occurred within countries, and many of the victims of this violent conflict have been civilians. For example, at one point in the mid-1990s, all of the major conflicts in the world were civil or intrastate in nature. While the exact toll in human life and suffering is unknown, it is evident that millions of people have lost their lives in conflicts in Rwanda, Bosnia, Sierra Leone, Somalia, Kosovo, Angola, and Haiti, among others. Countless more have been maimed or displaced, and the number of refugees generated by these conflicts has been unprecedented. Clearly, the end of the Cold War has brought little relief and less security to many people around the globe. This was not, of course, as it was supposed to be. The end of the Cold War was to have introduced a new era of peace and an emphasis on the rights and privileges of human beings. Indeed, the second prominent feature of international politics in the 1990s has been the emphasis given to individual human rights and human security. In addition to various declarations and charters, numerous national reconciliation commissions, and an agreement to establish an International Criminal Court, there has also been a noteworthy increase in the number, variety, scope, and prominence of outside interventions for allegedly

---

humanitarian purposes. In each of the conflicts mentioned above, and in other situations, a variety of international organizations—both governmental and nongovernmental—have intervened, at some point in the conflict, in an effort to put an end to violence and to restore a more permanent condition of peace and reconciliation in these divided societies. Motivated, it seems, by a concern for individual human rights, and a sense of urgency in the face of the scope of humanitarian and political disasters in all regions of the world, a variety of individuals, groups, governments, and organizations have intervened in the affairs of other countries in the hope of contributing to a more stable, peaceful, and just world. It is in this context that peacebuilding through different forms of intervention has become a centrepiece for what the rest of the world has to offer to divided societies.

This essay sets out, among other objectives, to review the factors that have encouraged foreign governments, and the international institutions they operate, to intervene in an effort to contribute to the process of resolving civil wars and reconciling divided societies. It also seeks to examine critically the role of outside agents in this process and to reflect on the ethical and practical considerations involved in intervention. The essay provides a skeptical view of the role outsiders can play and offers a strong caution to advocates of intervention based principally on a concern for the inability of outsiders to avoid exacerbating these politically volatile situations.

Peacebuilding and the Process of Reconciliation

For many years, the response of outsiders to situations of violent conflict focused on the cessation of hostilities and was drawn from the United Nations (UN) experience in peacekeeping. As the complexities and societal repercussions of civil conflicts became evident, these peacekeeping operations took on a wider range of tasks, a phenomenon commonly described as second-generation peacekeeping. Alongside the increased frequency and violence of civil conflicts in the 1990s, there has emerged a vibrant field of research, advocacy, and policy development around peacekeeping, peacemaking, conflict prevention, peacebuilding, and reconciliation. These responses represent the potential range of action at different stages of a conflict. Since the mid-1990s, some governments, international and regional intergovernmental organizations (IGOs), and many non-governmental organizations (NGOs) as well, have adopted a more comprehensive view of civil conflict and have identified the need for a multifaceted approach that supports a sustainable peace in a post-conflict situation to avoid the recurrence of violent conflict in the future. Commonly referred to as peacebuilding, the idea was raised by former UN Secretary General Boutros Boutros-Ghali in his *An Agenda for Peace*, released in 1992. In this document Boutros-Ghali identified peacebuilding as "action to identify and solidify peace in order to avoid a relapse into conflict."[2] The emphasis here was on the prevention of future conflict, or more specifically the prevention of a recurrence of violent conflict with close attention given to addressing the post-conflict situation. In *An Agenda for Peace*, a number of specific measures were advanced, including: "disarming previously warring parties and the restoration of order, the custody and possible destruction of weapons, repatriating refugees, advisory and training support for security personnel, monitoring elections, advancing efforts to promote human rights, reforming or strengthening governmental institutions and promoting formal and informal processes of political participation."[3]

In addition to an Agenda for Peace, national governments also responded. The Canadian peacebuilding initiative was formally launched by the minister of Foreign Affairs, Lloyd Axworthy, in October 1996 and was designed as "a package of measures to strengthen and solidify peace by building a sustainable infrastructure of human security."[4] The initiative suggested a concern for the multidimensional and integrated causes of civil war and thus acknowledged the need to address the economic, social, and political aspects of reconstruction and reconciliation. Rooted in a concern for human security, the initiative also identified the need to address these issues at the level of individuals and groups within what is now commonly called civil society. The peacebuilding initiative has focused on providing direct assistance to countries at various stages of civil conflict. It has also been designed to support the capacity of the Canadian government and of individual Canadians to participate effectively in peacebuilding initiatives. The Canadian approach to peacebuilding has been designed to coordinate the work of various government departments (DFAIT, CIDA, Justice Canada, Elections Canada, and the RCMP) that had become involved in conflict resolution activities at the international level as part of second-generation peacekeeping operations. The Canadian approach has also been designed to support work on a bilateral basis or in cooperation with international and regional IGOs and Canadian and local

NGOs. The overriding objective of Canada's peacebuilding policy is to "support the emergence of participatory and pluralistic societies, with a well-functioning and responsible government administration acting under the rule of law and respect for human rights."[5] In more specific terms Canadian activities have included such things as: humanitarian relief; demining and demobilization; repatriation and reintegration of refugees; police and justice training; support for an independent media; election and human rights monitoring; and reconstruction of schools and health centres, among many others.

Observers, however, are quick to acknowledge that the most desirable solution is to prevent the recurrence of violent conflict through policies aimed at the reconciliation of divided societies. Bush, for example, describes peacebuilding as: essentially crisis intervention, either to prevent armed conflict or, in the wake of armed conflict, to consolidate peace and promote reconciliation.[6] Regardless of the definition, there seems to be consensus on the difficulty of the task. "Rebuilding social capital and livelihood systems in such circumstances is therefore more complex and difficult than restoring physical infrastructure in natural disasters. It involves, among other things, 'redefining and reorienting relationships between political authority and the citizenry, revisiting relationships between different ethnic and social groups, creating a civil society in its broadest sense, promoting psychosocial healing and reconciliation, and reforming economic policies and institutions.'"[7] A report of the International Peace Academy identifies the pertinent questions involved in peacebuilding operations: "What concrete measures must be instituted, and in what order, to prevent the political settlement from fraying and resulting in a new round of violence? What are the roles of various actors, national and international, in the process?"[8]

A more critical view has been offered by Paris who argues that: "A single paradigm—liberal internationalism—appears to guide the work of most international agencies engaged in peacebuilding. The central tenet of this paradigm is the assumption that the surest foundation for peace, both within and between states, is market democracy, that is, a liberal democratic polity and a market economy. Peacebuilding is in effect an enormous experiment in social engineering—an experiment that involves transplanting Western models of social, political, and economic organization into war-shattered states in order to control civil conflict: in other words, pacification through political and economic liberalization."[9] From this perspective, peacebuilding becomes an instrument for constructing a more stable domestic and international political order by widening the network of liberal democratic societies.

Peacebuilding has thus emerged as a prominent feature in the foreign policies of national governments such as Canada's, and in the work of international and regional IGOs and NGOs, all seeking to find ways to contribute to the amelioration of recurring conflict in divided societies. In assessing these efforts, primarily through a review of the practices of outside governments and institutions in Haiti, it becomes clear that peacebuilding is no panacea. It is a practice, or more appropriately a set of practices, burdened with a number of problems and limitations. At the very least, the record suggests the need for a closer examination of the practicality and suitability of outside intervention in support of peacebuilding in divided societies. It also suggests that outside parties have had, at best, limited success in such ventures, and have often contributed to the problems experienced by these societies. The essay suggests that while any intervention is fraught with potentially adverse consequences, outsiders would be best to consider the adage "do no harm" when deliberating on the need for intervening in response to conflicts in other countries. Often this is easier to state than to implement. It is also evident from some situations that refusing to help can bring greater costs than getting involved. It is evident that intervention in support of peacebuilding and reconciliation is not a simple matter. It raises a number of complicated questions. When for example, are elections likely to entrench the divisions within society and when are they most likely to overcome such divisions? When does organizing civil society groups provide a viable mechanism for fostering effective participation in the reconciliation process and when does it merely serve to intensify frustrations before it is abruptly stopped? When are outsiders' solutions appropriate and when must locals devise their own? Making a commitment to the political process of reconciliation should require governments and their agents to address the full complexity of the postwar environment and to comprehend fully the long-term commitment that they are undertaking. Leaving before the job is done or failing to recognize the repercussions of actions undertaken can often become a source of future conflict rather than an appropriate and effective contribution to a lasting peace.

174 · TOM KEATING

Intervention in Divided Societies: Motivations and Pressures

One of the first matters worthy of consideration in such an examination is to understand why foreign governments, IGOs, and NGOs have developed such a keen interest in intervening in other societies to support a process of peacebuilding and reconciliation. Debates over intervention have received a great deal more attention since the end of the Cold War. The increased dominance of Western political and economic practices, and the absence of the threat of a major war resulting from overt interventions, have fuelled the debate. In addition, support for humanitarian intervention has been encouraged by the increased influence of human rights and human security discourse in national governments and in regional and international organizations. When combined with the prevalence of serious civil conflict, humanitarian intervention has gained a great deal of credibility and political support from significant actors in the international system.[10] There are, in my view at least, three background conditions that have supported such initiatives and some combination of three additional specific pressures that have provided the necessary political will for outsiders to intervene in societies divided by civil conflict.

First, one can cite the unfortunate availability of opportunities for such involvement or, to put it another way, the crying need for action to limit the prevalence and recurrence of civil violence in our age. The 1990s were marked by major civil conflicts in all corners of the world. While civil wars are not an exceptional phenomenon and indeed have been a part of the history of most political communities, their prevalence and the level of violence have been a matter of wide attention. Civil wars are arguably more brutal than interstate wars and more likely to violate the sorts of practices that govern wars between sovereign states in the international system, for example, in the extent to which they involve civilians or attacks on civilian property. As a result, civil wars present an especially difficult set of problems for the international community in general and outside governments in particular. At the very least, these conflicts, their intensity, and their presentation by the media have, in selected instances, created considerable pressure on outside governments to respond.

A second factor that has fostered an interest in intervention and peacebuilding is the growing concern about, and promotion of, individual human rights, and the influence of rights discourse among NGOs, within the foreign policy communities of Western governments, and within selected international and regional IGOs. This is partly a reflection of the growing number and activism of NGOs and their extensive involvement in many of the societies that have experienced civil discord. These rights-based declarations have given governments and institutions a rationale for intervening in the domestic affairs of other states and for ignoring the traditional principles of state sovereignty, territorial integrity, and non-intervention. While human rights principles have been a part of international charters for some time, they have now acquired a higher profile and have become the basis for governments and organizations to challenge the sovereignty of states. They have also created expectations and demands that rights matter, and that governments and institutions have a responsibility to protect individual rights and provide for human security in other societies.

A third background condition that appears related to the increased attention to peacebuilding is the end of the Cold War and the strengthening of Western hegemony in the international system. The end of the Cold War was in part both a source and a reflection of a broader trend towards democratization in many parts of the world. This has had the effect of privileging the value attached to liberal democracy and free markets, or market democracy, as guiding principles of governance. The interest in democracy and markets reflected the prevailing view that such practices would foster both domestic and international peace, stability, and prosperity. This position has been reinforced by academics and publicists who support this view. It was also an opportunity for Western governments to assert their values and practices unencumbered by competitors. It was therefore both morally and politically important to do what one could to foster the spread of democracy and economic liberalism throughout the world. Governments began to view the promotion of market democracy as legitimate and significant foreign policy objectives. Nowhere did the need appear to be as great or the benefits as promising as in societies riddled with domestic conflict.

In addition to these general conditions, outside governments and organizations have faced a variety of economic, political, emotional, and ethical pressures when confronted with violent conflict in other societies. These pressures are often manifested as demands for "something to be done," and, as a result, outside governments frequently find themselves in the position of having to take action in response to these demands. Pressures on governments and organizations to intervene in civil conflicts arise from at least three sources. First, and in most instances, pressures emanate from the emotional reactions of citizens, who when confronted with images of suffering in the media turn to their governments and demand that some action be taken to help those suffering, and to remove these horrific images from their television screens and newspapers. These pressures, while arguably based on emotional and superficial sentiments of the population, do nonetheless act as a powerful, though likely short-term, pressure on governments, forcing them to take action, primarily of a more overt and publicly acknowledged kind, to satisfy this emotional outburst. In responding to this sort of pressure, governments may be uncertain about the strength of popular commitment and, in turn, the willingness of the populace to bear the costs of effective action.

A second source of pressure arises from citizens and governments acting in response to moral and humanitarian principles. These sorts of pressures are more than simply an emotional tap turned on and off by media images. They represent instead a phenomenon that appears to be growing throughout the world, the emergence of a caring global community, which, while relatively small in numbers, is nonetheless motivated by sentiments of empathy and moral obligation to respond to human suffering wherever and whenever it may occur. It is this sort of pressure that is most commonly found within non-governmental organizations and the many volunteers that support them. It is also a sentiment that has been cited by some politicians and government officials and by publicists, academics, and others. Though small, the intensity of the views and the willingness to sustain pressure on governments make this group a potentially effective influence on government policy. Moreover, as many of these individuals and groups are themselves acting in the field, their operations and expertise may be important to governments and organizations, forcing the latter to consult with, and to some extent be guided by, their views.

Finally, there remains a third source of pressure for government action in response to violent conflicts in other societies, that being the national and geopolitical interests that realist writers have persistently identified as lying at the core of the actions of governments, regardless of the moral rhetoric that surrounds policy deliberations. Here the simple argument is that governments will get involved when decision makers consider it to be in the national interest. Realists would argue that contributions to peace-building reflect an interest on the part of governments to maintain stabil-

WHAT CAN OTHERS DO? • 177

ity, or to gain influence in particular countries, in order to protect or advance the interests of the intervening government. Similarly, powerful governments might use their influence to direct the IGOs to launch peacebuilding operations in certain divided societies, as a way of legitimizing or obscuring the national interests of these powerful governments.

Outsiders and Peacebuilding in Haiti

Events in Haiti in the 1990s present a rather different but no less telling case study in peacebuilding and reconciliation than the more prominent cases in Bosnia, Rwanda, and elsewhere. Unlike many other countries, Haiti did not experience a civil war, nor was the conflict primarily ethnic in character, though some have noted ethnic overtones to the violence. Instead, Haitian society has been wrecked by years of persistent violence led by the wealthy elite and their paramilitary forces operating both outside of, and at times through, the country's police force. Repeated attempts to establish a more sustainable, democratic peace in the country have proved futile. The violence in Haiti became even more debilitating than usual in the run-up to and aftermath of the country's first democratic presidential elections in 1991. It continued unabated until President Jean-Bertrand Aristide was returned to power with the aid of outsiders' assistance in 1994. Since then peacebuilding efforts have met with limited success.[11] Such efforts also demonstrate some of the underlying problems that confront the peacebuilding process—problems that are often even more evident in other situations.

The response of outsiders to the ongoing civil conflict and democratic crisis in Haiti in the 1990s has, in turn, been driven by a mix of state and institutional interests. Foremost among the players in this response have been Canada, the United States, the Organization of American States, and the United Nations. The Canadian government, for its part, repeatedly emphasized the need for regional and international institutions to take the lead. In part, this was seen as a way to legitimize the international response to the crisis and prevent it from being viewed as an act inspired and conducted by the Americans. Foreign Affairs Minister Axworthy reiterated the important role that Haiti played for the United Nations. "Haiti has been a critical test for the United Nations in promoting democratization as an integral part of enhancing security. It has shown the need for concerted international co-operation in support of democracy, not merely for one leader or even one election, but in the ongoing process of building the institutional and social structures upon which democracy rests. This is where the UN can play a special role, as the builder of peace. We must recognize this, and make the commitments necessary for the UN to work effectively for long-term peace and stability in Haiti."12

The UN has operated four peacekeeping/peacebuilding operations in Haiti since the first outside effort to intervene in the troubled country in 1993. The first, the UN Mission in Haiti (UNMIH) was established in September 1993 as part of the Governor's Island agreement that was intended to restore the democratically elected government of Jean-Bertrand Aristide to power in October of the same year. The operation was abandoned one month later when outside forces failed to secure the cooperation of the military coup for a transfer in power and remained in abeyance until it was eventually resurrected following the establishment of a more secure environment in March 1995. The following year, newly elected President Preval requested that the UN remain in the country and assume primary responsibility for sustaining a secure environment and retraining and professionalizing the police. A second UN operation, the UN Support Mission in Haiti (UNSMIH) assumed responsibility for these tasks in May 1996. As the deadline for this operation neared, it was clear that Haiti remained a very fragile and potentially explosive environment, so a third UN mission was set up with a specified mandate of four months. The UN Transition Mission in Haiti (UNTMIH) ended in November 1997, long before Haiti's needs ended, and so a fourth operation was established. The UN Police Mission in Haiti (MIPONUH) began its work on December 1, 1997, and its original one-year mandate has since been extended. This operation comprises about 300 police officers whose principal task is to train and professionalize the recently established Haitian National Police so as to reduce the number of human rights violations committed by official authorities in Haiti.

In addition to its work as a member of the various UN operations in Haiti, the Canadian government also undertook a number of related tasks in support of a more stable peace in Haiti. Much of this work has focused on establishing sound institutions in support of the rule of law and effective democratic mechanisms for encouraging wider participation and accountability in the political process. Working in conjunction with NGOs, the government has also supported activities designed to develop civil society organizations and to encourage reconciliation and peaceful methods of conflict resolution. The government, through CIDA, has also been involved in programs designed to alleviate poverty and foster economic development.

This brief review of UN operations points to one of the underlying practical problems experienced by outside interventions of this sort. The limited time frames and tenuous resource commitments that govern these operations represent, at best, an ad hoc approach to peacebuilding. Political and material support for each one of these operations had to be cobbled together through a time-consuming and uncertain diplomatic process. These operations have also experienced other problems, including the persistent opposition of China as a result of Haiti's recognition of Taiwan. There have also been problems originating in the conflictual policy which the US Congress has taken towards the UN, a policy that has had repercussions for the UN operation in Haiti, affecting areas such as financing, mandate, and personnel questions. Additionally, and arguably more importantly, there have been differences in opinion over the direction peacebuilding should take in Haiti. Finally, and perhaps most fundamentally, there is a lack of expertise and knowledge about the situation, most importantly about what measures would be most effective in securing a sustainable peace in Haiti. The response to events in Haiti, while typical of the operations of international and regional organizations, and indeed of national governments, demonstrates the inherent difficulty underlying the process of peacebuilding and reconciliation. As has been suggested, peacebuilding is a long-term operation. Short-term measures or commitments undertaken with uncertain futures can, often, do more harm than good. They raise expectations, suggest that outsiders are going to assume responsibility for addressing problems, and encourage locals to look to outsiders to settle their problems. A telling example is provided by the first UN operation in Haiti where UN and OAS observers moved into the country to begin monitoring human rights violations in September 1995. Less than two months later they were quickly withdrawn from the country, leaving at greater risk local Haitians who had become involved in their work. (Similar concerns were expressed for Kosovars who were assisting outside human rights monitors prior to their removal at the time that NATO bombing in the region began.)

Outside pressures finally secured the return of Aristide to power, but it was a power that was severely circumscribed. The price was a commitment on Aristide's part to refrain from political activities after his term ended and the acceptance of an IMF plan that undermined Aristide's more radical economic reforms. This solution led Richard Falk to ask: "What kind of democracy is taking place if the program and orientation of the elected leader is being scrapped as a condition for the support of his return?"[13] After the return of Aristide to power on October 15, 1994, a presidential election was held in 1995, resulting in the selection of a new president, Rene Preval, a candidate more amenable to American views of democracy. Aristide, whose return to power had been delayed until 1994, and who was, as a result of constitutional limitations, prevented from running in the election, ended up serving little more than one year of his five-year term. Aristide's return to power in February 2001 came amidst considerable controversy and violence. The election itself was far from an indicator of Haiti's political health. "Haiti's opposition…boycotted the vote. The United States and the European Union refused to fund it. The Organization of American States (OAS) declined to send election monitors. And United Nations Secretary General Kofi Annan recommended that the UN mission in Haiti should end when its current mandate expires."[14] As the UN operation winds down and Haiti approaches another presidential election, the prospects for a durable and just peace in the country are very uncertain. The end result of more than four years of peacebuilding in Haiti suggests some modest degree of progress. Yet as Amnesty International reports, the outcome is a decidedly mixed one. "Little progress was made in bringing those responsible for human rights violations, past or present, to justice. The ongoing failure of the government to take prompt and effective steps to address serious deficiencies in the justice system remained the greatest obstacle to overcoming impunity."[15] For these and other reasons, the Haitian experience raises many questions about the desirability and practicality of peacebuilding.

Effective peacebuilding requires a sincere and objective commitment on the part of outsiders. In practice, however, it is extremely difficult to identify circumstances where foreign governments would be able to meet these criteria. Peacebuilding has tended to be something that the strong—militarily, economically—do *for or to* the weak. One of the obvious features of the peacebuilding operations that have been conducted to date is that they have been employed against the weakest of states in the international community by the strongest of states. Perhaps this is as it must be, but it would seem to say as much about the inability of the weak states to say no as it does about the superior cause of the intervening party. It also increases the likelihood that other interests will influence peacebuilding practices, not only those conducted by governments but by IGOs (and possibly NGOs) as well. The problems of national interests infecting multilateral processes are not widely acknowledged, but are very real. The UN, working through the Security Council, operates on the basis of political choices made by its member governments and is subjected to the political interests of the permanent members of the Security Council. Many governments and outside observers have complained about the extent to which certain states dominate the UN Security Council. For example, one Ghanian representative to the UN, Mohammed Ibn Chambas complained that: "The creeping tendency on the part of certain nations to see themselves as policy makers and executors on behalf of the entire United Nations membership through their predominance in the Security Council does not send out welcome signals to the rest of us as equal parties in world affairs."[16]

The Haitian experience (alongside others) demonstrates the difficulties that outsiders encounter in responding to such crises in the absence of competing material interests. This is not to argue that humanitarian or similar altruistic motives are not involved in such decisions. It is to suggest, in part, that given the political and material resources that need to be deployed in support of such initiatives, such motives may be insufficient to sustain the government's commitment and the public's support. Moreover, even if this could be overcome it is difficult to conceive of circumstances where humanitarian motives could be cleanly separated from other interests. As one press report noted: "A national interest must also be determined by the degree to which it has an impact on the Canadian way of life. How does an event affect the Canadian economy? How does it challenge the ethical and moral values that lie at the heart of our liberal democracy? How does it threaten those international systems of trade and communication that we are a part of, and which nurture our rights-driven democracy? All these ought to be key considerations."[17] The Canadian government was, no doubt, genuinely concerned about the plight of Haitians, but there were other considerations at play. For example, the government was responding to concerns emanating from the Haitian community in Montreal and the perceived need to address these "francophone" interests in the government's foreign policy. In addition, the government's response was also influenced by its ongoing concern with the credibility of its own peacebuilding policy and with the continued relevance of the UN and the OAS. Finally, the financial press took note of

Canada's economic interests in the region. "Canadians have a vital interest in helping to initiate and sustain democracy and stability in the Caribbean. That is because Canadians have billions of dollars invested in the Caribbean basin, because many Canadians are of Caribbean and specifically Haitian origin, and because the Caribbean is in our neighbourhood, and it is not in our interests to allow those who oppose our interests to take hold there."[18] While these interests are not necessarily incompatible with peacebuilding and reconciliation, they can be expected to influence the methods and substance of policy. Promotion of democracy and political rights can become a useful facade for securing economic rights in the contemporary climate. As Falk has argued, "the belief that military or dictatorial rule is not a receptive setting for foreign investment and economic growth is not acknowledged by pro-interventionists, but underpins their thinking."[19]

Even if one were to assume that Canadian interests were more purely humanitarian than those of other states or did not otherwise interfere with locally defined needs and objectives, the Canadian government must, most often, work in concert with other governments if its activities are to have any influence. This was certainly the case in Haiti, where the Canadian government has been cooperating with the United States and other OAS and UN members in the intervention. In some circumstances such collaboration might not be problematic, but in the more politically sensitive areas, such as constructing civil society and supporting democratic reforms, it becomes more difficult to divorce oneself from the political interests of other intervening states and the implications of these connections. The problem is twofold. First, there is the possibility of guilt by association in that their actions may simply be seen as extensions of one's own. A second concern is that the interests and actions of other governments may clash with or undermine your more humanitarian objectives. Both problems were apparent in Haiti.

The American intervention in Haiti had been tainted by a number of factors. For one, it was not the first time that the United States had intervened in the country. Writing in 1990 of America's first intervention in Haiti, Truillot said: "The 1915-1934 U.S. occupation of Haiti left the country with two poisoned gifts: a weaker civil society and a solidified state apparatus."[20] Chomsky, in a review of American actions in Haiti, noted the problems that resulted from this earlier intervention, including: "the acceleration of Haiti's economic, military and political centralization;

its economic dependence and sharp class divisions; the vicious exploitation of the peasantry; the internal racial conflicts much intensified by the
extreme racism of the occupying forces; and perhaps worst of all, the
establishment of an army to fight the people."[21] For Canadians to assist
the Americans in retraining police officers from a paramilitary group that
the latter helped to create raised obvious problems with the perceived
objectivity of the operation. A second concern was the American government's involvement in the coup that toppled Aristide in the first instance.
"Suspicions of U.S. involvement in the coup range from the deliberate
turning of a blind eye, to the active encouragement and abetting of Aristide's ouster. Even the *New York Times* has reported on U.S. support for
Haiti's corrupt military rulers over the years. Throughout the negotiating
process, the U.S. government has forced Aristide into deeper and deeper
compromises—essentially eviscerating his power—while demanding little
of the military."[22] American concerns also may be undermining the
process of reconciliation as the US government has prevented the depor-
tation of the paramilitary FRAPH leader Emmanuel Constant. While arguing that Constant's return to Haiti might cause instability in the country
and in the judicial system, it is also alleged that Constant was on the pay-
roll of the CIA. As Chomsky concludes, "These lessons (of the past) should
be remembered as Washington moves to construct a: 'civil society' and
'democratic political order' for this 'failed state' with its degenerate culture
and people, quite incapable of governing themselves."[23] It also presents
concerns for Canadians and others working alongside the United States.
This was also apparent in other areas of peacebuilding. Canadian officials
had pressed the Americans to disarm the Haitian military as part of the
original occupation of the country in October 1994, but the Americans
refused. Similar differences have arisen in the training objectives of the
Haitian National Police force. According to one RCMP Sergeant, Canadian
Mounties sought "to train civil police officers, while Americans are training a military style force."[24] Peacebuilding operations that tend to support
the status quo in one area cannot always create the necessary space for
change in other areas.

One of the primary objectives in Canada's peacebuilding policy has
been to construct or reconstruct "civil society" in divided societies. Assum-
ing one can get past the competing and sometimes conflicting interests,
what, if any, are the repercussions of outsiders playing a prominent role in
the development of civil society structures and agents? What effect does

outside intervention have on the process of self-determination? Are outsiders better equipped to determine the necessary types of institutions and procedures required to meet the aspirations of the local population? In deeply divided societies, are outsiders equipped to identify the conditions that are necessary to reconcile these differences? Or in more specific terms, which parties, groups, and processes do you support? These are all hotly contested political issues and the choices have potentially profound implications for the balance of political forces in society. While it is perhaps too early to reach definitive conclusions regarding the effects which such actions might have on Haitians, there is no doubt that this was a matter of concern. In an interview, Camille Chalmers, the director of President Aristide's staff from 1993-94, addressed these concerns. "The military coup that overthrew Aristide and 'beheaded' the popular movement forced Haitian democrats, says Chalmers, to 'gamble on US military intervention opening up the political space necessary to re-establish the networks of popular organization. Unfortunately this hasn't happened'."[25] Some of the concerns that have been expressed about outside intervention reflect an opposition to the paternalistic practices of Western states. Isaiah Berlin has been quoted as saying that "Paternalism is despotic. I may, in my bitter longing for status, prefer to be bullied and misgoverned by some member of my own race or social class, by whom I am, nevertheless, recognized as a man and a rival—that is as an equal—to being well and tolerantly treated by someone from some higher and remoter group."[26] Others have expressed concern about the priorities defined by intervening states and imposed on others and the failure to recognize the variations that might exist in "good governance." Finally, there is the frequently stated concern about the relative priority to be given to political liberties and practices in the midst of deplorable living conditions.

Developing democracies and supporting civil society is an inherently contested political terrain. For observers such as Michael Walzer, this is reason enough to avoid getting involved. "Humanitarian interventions are not justified for the sake of democracy or free enterprise or economic justice or voluntary associations or any other of the social practices and arrangements that we might hope for or even call for in other people's countries."[27] Given the fact that peacebuilding operations enter a domestic political contest that is still unresolved, it becomes virtually impossible for that operation to be completely indifferent to this ongoing political contest. To be on the side of peace or justice or stability does not remove the intervenors from

the contest. Indeed, it gives them a prominent role in the contest. It is perhaps for this reason that local parties are frequently opposed to such interventions. This has become increasingly evident in Haiti. There were, for
example, some reports that suggested that Haitians were disenchanted with
the assistance provided by outsiders. Canadian Press Newswire reported on
March 26, 1997, that: "a group called Down with the Occupation demonstrated in the capital at that time, reflecting resentment among some
Haitians toward the continued presence of foreign forces." A few months
later similar reports appeared. In August 1997, "grassroots political groups
organized general strikes in Port-au-Prince and the town of Cap-Haitian to
protest the UN presence. Demonstrators, some linked to ambitious former
president Jean-Bertrand Aristide, claimed it was more like an 'occupation'
force. Some Haitians also criticize the rules of engagement, which forbid
peacekeepers from intervening in local disputes or violence. 'There is so
much insecurity and they do nothing to stop it,' said a woman selling cig-
arettes last week. 'What are they doing for the country?'"[28] Such sentiments
reflect at the same time elements of frustration at the lack of results, concern that decisions about one's own future are being taken by others, and
fear that outside forces are helping one's opponents.

A more practical consideration involved in peacebuilding is the widely
recognized fact that such actions require political and public support for
sustained involvement. If you are not willing to stay the course, you and
others might be better off not getting involved at all. This was a caution
raised by Pratt and Matthews in their discussion of Canada's human rights
policy. "If intervening powers apply sufficient force, it may be easy to
overturn an oppressive regime or to secure a return to law and order. It is
far less easy, however, to ensure the emergence of indigenous political
forces able to rule more justly and more effectively."[29] Once again the
experience in Haiti is telling in this area. While a Canadian official was
quoted as saying that "We're in for the long haul,"[30] the commitment may
be longer term than either governments or publics are willing to support,
or in the case of Haiti, longer than international organizations or local
authorities are willing to allow. As one officer described nearly three years
of police training in Haiti: "It's advancing, but it is still inch by inch....If
we're not here at least a decade, it won't change much. It's a question of
changing the whole mentality."[31] The necessity of being actively engaged
in the reconciliation process demands a political commitment that often
extends beyond the mandate of elected governments and definitely

beyond the attention of the media. It thus becomes imperative for governments and their public to be willing to see the project through to its completion. This demands a long-term relationship and one that must be sustained with material and human resources. A failure to maintain such commitments not only undermines the influence of intervenors but also poses great risks to individuals and groups within embattled states who have come to rely on the support of outsiders. When outsiders go home, the locals often suffer the consequences.

Commitments require a willingness to bear the costs of these operations. Assessing the costs of peacebuilding is an uncertain exercise at best. Part of the difficulty in assessing the costs results from the need to compare it with a failure to act. Thus, while one might lament the hundreds of millions of dollars spent on a particular operation, others might counter that the amount pales in comparison with how much a larger war or some other disaster would cost. At the same time, it is important to note that such programs are not insignificant in their financial burdens. By the end of 1997 the Haiti mission will have cost Ottawa nearly $450 million out of DND's budget alone. Add to this the costs for RCMP officers, judicial reform, and other projects, as well as funds from other federal departments including the DFAIT and CIDA. At a time when all of these departments have experienced significant budget reductions, the viability of long-term commitments involving sizeable expenditures becomes uncertain at best. The costs have not been in dollars alone. At various times there have been approximately one thousand members of the Armed Forces and in excess of one hundred RCMP and personnel from other police forces, and numerous Canadians working with NGOs in Haiti. RCMP "officers and commanders are frustrated at being left short-staffed at home....Departing members were too often the recipient of snide remarks to the effect they were leaving their duties to others, going to the Caribbean, making good money, being treated as heroes and receiving a medal."[32] The most serious concern is, of course, the safety of personnel. As the RCMP is left to oversee the long-term project of rebuilding a "democratic" police force in Haiti, concern shifts to the protection that these Mounties will receive. In the words of an RCMP assistant commissioner: "As far as the Canadian police are concerned, we are prepared to stay beyond July 31 (1997) if the government so wishes. But can I have a reasonable guarantee of officer safety? There is a risk in police work, and I don't want to lose an officer."[33]

One final consideration that needs to be addressed is the effect of interventions in support of democratic reforms on the credibility, legitimacy, and capacity of the governments and institutions involved. A commitment to support democratic reform in places such as Haiti is by no means a simple task. The prospects for success are often quite remote, given local conditions and the limitations of outside parties. Yet the commitment implies the capacity to deliver the goods. When one fails to do so, despite one's best intentions and efforts, there may be a political price to pay. Future commitments may not be greeted with the same enthusiasm in light of past failures. This might be a recommendation for caution over avoidance, but it would seem to be a necessary consideration. It is an equally important one for international institutions. The UN's "freedom to interfere depends on its multilateralsim, and its impartiality, being taken seriously by one and all."[34] Analysis of the role of the UN's experiences in Central America and Cambodia suggests that the reason for the UN's success owed much to its neutrality, and to the ability of UN personnel to remain impartial. This allowed the UN to play a role where other actors could not. Indeed, in many instances the main contribution of international institutions has been their impartiality. This could very well be placed at risk the closer the institutions move to imposing specific solutions on divided societies. A related problem is the difficulty that outsiders have in maintaining consistency in their approach to such situations. In the midst of the crisis in Kosovo, an MP returned from Sierra Leone to report on the equally if not more serious conflict in that country, yet not a single person attended his press conference. Why Kosovo and not Sierra Leone? Why Haiti and not Burma? As Justin Morris has argued: "It is crucial therefore that those states wishing to participate in a UN which actively promotes human and political rights proceed in a manner which is sensitive to the views and concerns of others."[35] In an analysis of UN involvement in Haiti and the degree of opposition within the organization, Morris goes on to write that: "Irrespective of the existence of Security Council authorization, intervention in circumstances such as these does little to allay the fears of less powerful members of the international community that talk of a new international order and an agenda promoting human and political rights is little more than a sham."[36] A related critique has also been offered by Paris in a comparative analysis of peacebuilding operations. He argues that peacebuilding in the form of market democracy is an inherently flawed instrument for stabilizing societies in conflict. In his view, market democracy encourages competition and conflict, which while perhaps healthy and productive in societies with a well-developed democratic political culture can actually exacerbate tensions in more tenuous circumstances. "The point is not that democracy is inherently violent...but that the adversarial politics of democracy can sharpen confrontations and conflicts in divided societies, rather than fostering greater tolerance for different interests and opinions."[37] Not only has the prevalence of market democracy values and practices in the peacebuilding programs of governments, international organizations, and non-governmental organizations given the impression that there is but one path to a stable and just peace but it may also be a most difficult path for vulnerable societies to travel. For some the difficulties are worth the effort, but Duffield has offered a note of caution. "For conventional wisdom this divisive trend is a temporary phase in the process of development and transition toward liberal democracy. If this is wrong, however, and instability represents the emergence of new types of sociopolitical formation adapted to exist on the margins of the global economy, then the implications are profound. Policy makers would not even be asking the right questions, let alone providing the answers."[38]

Assessing the Interventionist Option

One of the problems that confronts any attempt to reconcile societies divided by years of bitter conflict is that the institutional and procedural devices for addressing social problems are often destroyed or so severely corrupted that they are effectively inoperable. "They involve fundamental questions not only about what to reconstruct but also about how to do so in order not to recreate the unsustainable institutions and structures that originally contributed to the conflict. Even more crucial is rehabilitation of governmental legitimacy and ability to deliver basic services, including user friendly law and order."[39] Reconstructing the institutional and procedural capacities of divided societies has become one of the major tasks pursued by outsiders in their attempt to contribute to the politics of reconciliation. One of the more prominent devices has been elections, but other activities include reforms to the civil service, to the justice systems, and to police forces. The contested nature of the state and state institutions, however, renders each of these problematic. It is further complicated by virtue of the fact that outsiders almost inevitably bring with them the procedures and institutions they have successfully adopted at home. At times, these may not be appropriate for the setting that exists in divided societies. Elections serve as one prominent example of this tendency. Elections are prized in liberal democratic societies as the ultimate test of a government's commitment to respond to the voice of the people and are used to convey a sense of popular participation in the political process and legitimacy for governments. Yet elections also have a tendency to divide by exacerbating differences and encouraging political parties to form around the most easily identifiable differences in the society. These differences may very well be the source of conflict in the first instance, and may serve to further reinforce such differences throughout the society. Moreover, to the extent that elections become the measure of democratic reform by outside parties, and especially by outside funding agencies, it encourages elites to look outwards, to satisfy external legitimizers rather than to seek the support of the people. This only tends to reinforce one of the underlying weaknesses of many weaker states in the international system that have tended to derive much of their legitimacy from outside governments and institutions rather than become firmly established within the society of which they are supposedly a part.[40]

A second criticism that has been directed at peacebuilding activities as they have been practised to date underscores the influence of ideological, and especially economic influences, on the activities of outside governments. Lipschutz has criticized what he labels the neo-liberal peace for its failure to address the underlying justice issues present in most contemporary conflicts. He argues that too often the role of outside governments has been to support the formal institutions of democracy in an effort to restore political stability and, not coincidentally, viable economic activity. Agreements are signed, constitutions are drafted, elections are held, and a deeply divided society appears restored to a level of civility. Yet in almost all important respects, the underlying fissures that have divided the society remain intact and are merely papered over through these cosmetic changes. Underlying issues are not addressed and unjust structures and practices continue and, in some cases, are exacerbated. Once again, Haiti provides an illustration of such problems. Evidence suggests that the only economic activity that has flourished since the return to civility has been the drug trade. As a result, the gap, already criminally great, continues to expand, and the pressing social and economic needs of the people remain unattended.[41]

A third concern surrounding the practice of peacebuilding and reconciliation as it involves outsiders is the central significance of local
involvement. This is a common refrain. "Resolution and reconciliation
are ultimately processes that must be designed, implemented, and sustained by and through the local participants in conflicts."[42] In reviewing
Canadian peacebuilding efforts in Africa, Lucie Edwards stated that:
"We may be able to offer some help, in the form of financial aid, or
advice, or training, or even the temporary stationing of peacekeepers,
but in the end, it will be up to Africans to find their own solutions to
their conflicts."[43] This has long been a concern among those who have
considered the wisdom of foreign intervention in the domestic affairs of
other states. John Stuart Mill, and more recently Michael Walzer, have
maintained that outside intervention should generally be avoided
because it interferes with the desirability and necessity for conflicting
parties to settle their own disputes. This argument is rooted in the view
that a viable political community can only be established by the members of that community. Outsiders, however well-intentioned, will by
their mere presence upset the balance of the community and distort
whatever settlement takes place. If people are to live in harmony with
one another for the long term, they must reconcile their differences
without outside intervention. As J.S. Mill put it in his essay "A Few
Words on Non-Intervention," "there can seldom be anything approaching to assurance that intervention, even if successful, would be for the
good of the people themselves. The only test possessing any real value,
of a people's having become fit for popular institutions, is that they, or
a sufficient portion of them to prevail in the contest, are willing to brave
labour and danger for their liberation."[44] Mill is quick to qualify this
admonition against intervention for cases where governments have been
aided in their oppression by outside elements. Mill's caution against
intervention reminds us that the process by which political communities
are created for a sustainable future are uncertain, prone to violence, and
long term. Or as one observer put it: "the 'creation' of states is an
extraordinarily uncivil process."[45]

Finally, and as many observers have noted, reconciliation is most
often not a short-term affair. It requires a long time for the reconciliation process to bear fruit. It also requires coordinated action in a number of areas. There are few outside actors that have either the resources,
the patience, or the commitment to see this process through to com-

pletion. This is as much a problem for NGOs and IGOs as it is for national governments. Green and Ahmed have argued that: "International nongovernmental organisations (INGOs) and local NGOs (LNGOs), while relatively successful in rehabilitation initiatives in the aftermath of natural disasters, are less so in post-conflict rehabilitation because of their limited conceptual grasp of the situation, legitimacy and efforts to promote sustainability."[46] It has also been argued that: "Rehabilitation initiatives have often focused on specific operations that lacked the kind of coherent, integrated framework needed for realistic sustainable macroeconomic and household livelihood rehabilitation." Part of the problem is "the absence of mechanisms to link donors with a national policy framework, combined with the high degree of donor dependence on NGOs for project design and implementation, [which] tends to reinforce the inclination of rehabilitation programmes to adopt the highly decentralised, unintegrated approaches of relief rather than those of development."[47]

As the experience in Haiti demonstrates, building a stable and just peace in divided societies is a inherently problematic task. As the Canadian government seeks to develop an effective strategy for peacebuilding, it will confront these problems repeatedly. Public and government pressures may encourage the government to act initially, but will publics and governments support the longer-term commitments that are necessary to ensure that peace takes hold. According to Ken Booth, "Outsiders must be patient, and accept their limitations."[48] Goodhand and Hulme offer a similar caution. "Those who seek to intervene will need to be truly humble and avoid making exaggerated claims about 'saving lives' and 'bringing peace' that the logframes of their financial sponsors often encourage."[49] More importantly will peaceful practices become an integral part of indigenous political activity if they are imposed by foreign powers and sustained only with the support of foreign police/armies? If not, it may be in the words of Walzer "better to stay home than to intervene in a way that is sure to fail."[50] Yet to turn our backs provides a decidedly unsatisfactory answer.

The immense problems faced by divided societies in the aftermath of bitter civil wars are not always or inevitably made any easier by the presence of outside governments and their agents. Wilmer, in a discussion of the peacebuilding process in Bosnia, has identified some of the concerns. "The problem is...that we know little about what to do once an intervention has stopped the shooting…we need to know how to go beyond interventions aimed at stopping violence and toward intervention and facilitation aimed at the resolution and reconciliation of conflicts and the reconstruction (or in many cases the construction) of civil society."[51] He goes on to argue that "The problem of moving from intervention meant to deescalate violence to resolution and reconciliation will require both a change in thinking about the relationship between intervention and conflict resolution, and the appropriation of resources to practitioners of the latter."[52] Finally, Kumar adds a note of caution about the entire enterprise. "Those charged with designing and implementing political rehabilitation interventions lack appropriate conceptual frameworks, intervention models, concepts, policy instruments, and methodologies for assistance programmes to rebuild civil society, establish and nurture democratic institutions, promote a culture favourable to the protection of human rights, reconstruct law enforcement systems, or facilitate ethnic reconciliation in a highly unstable political and social environment."[53] Indeed, outsiders, be they governments, international or regional organizations, or non-governmental organizations can, as many authors have noted, become part of the problem rather than the solution. It should therefore be imperative that outsiders adopt a simple but significant guiding principle when considering intervention in support of peacebuilding or reconciliation. That principle is "do no harm." Often this is easier to state than to implement. It is also evident from some situations that refusing to help can bring greater costs than getting involved. It is evident that intervention in support of peacebuilding and reconciliation is not a simple matter. It raises a number of complicated questions. When for example, are elections likely to entrench the divisions within society and when are they most likely to overcome such divisions? When does organizing civil society groups provide a viable mechanism for fostering effective participation in the reconciliation process and when does it merely serve to intensify frustrations before it is abruptly stopped? When are outsiders' solutions appropriate and when must locals devise their own? Making a commitment to the political process of reconciliation should require governments and their agents to address the full complexity of the post-war environment and to comprehend fully the long-term commitment that they are undertaking. Leaving before the job is done or failing to recognize the repercussions of actions undertaken can often become a source of future conflict rather than an appropriate and effective contribution to a lasting peace. Perhaps most important is the need to recognize that there are many things that outsiders simply cannot do and we must avoid the hubris that often surrounds such ventures. In the words of a Cree medicine woman, Ruby Plenty Chiefs, "Great evil has been done on earth by people who think they have all the answers."[54]

Notes

1 This essay was originally prepared for Dilemmas of Reconciliation, A Research Network and Conference, Calgary Institute for the Humanities, University of Calgary, Calgary, Alberta, June 1999. Research for this essay has been supported by a grant from the Social Sciences and Humanities Research Council of Canada (Grant # 410-971628). The author would like to thank Francis Kofi Abiew, Natasja Treiberg, Bill Bewick, and Dennis Westergaard for their assistance in the completion of this essay.

2 Boutros Boutros-Ghali, *An Agenda for Peace* (New York: United Nations, 1992), 11.

3 Ibid., 32.

4 Lloyd Axworthy, "Urgent Tasks Demand Stronger UN Support," *Canadian Speeches* 10 (1996): 36-43.

5 CIDA, "Canadian Peacekeeping Experience," Ottawa, November 6, 1998.

6 Ken Bush, *A Measure of Peace: Peace and Conflict Impact Assessment of Development Projects in Conflict Zones* (Ottawa: IDRC, 1998).

7 Reginald H. Green and Ismail I. Ahmed, "Rehabilitation, Sustainable Peace and Development: Towards Reconceptualization," *Third World Quarterly* 20 (1999): 189-207.

8 Kenneth Bush, quoted in Ernie Regehr, "The Challenge of Peacekeeping," *Ploughshares Monitor* (December, 1995): 2.

9 Roland Paris, "Peacekeeping and the Limits of Liberal Internationalism," *International Security* 22 (1997): 54-90.

10 Francis Kofi Abiew, *The Evolution of the Doctrine and Practice of Humanitarian Intervention* (The Hague: Kluwer Law International, 1999).

11 Amnesty International, "Annual Report, 2001: Haiti," at <www.amnesty.org>.

12 Axworthy, "Urgent Tasks."

13 Richard Falk, "The Haiti Intervention: A Dangerous World Order Precedent for the United States," *Harvard International Law Journal* 36 (1995): 353.

14 Catherine Orenstein, "Aristide Again," *The Progressive*, January 22, 2001.

15 Amnesty International, "Haiti Still Crying Out for Justice" (1998) at <www.amnesty.org>.

16 Mohammed Ibn Chambas, cited in UN *Chronicle* (March 1993): 39.

17 "RIP: The Great Canadian Refugee Rescue Mission," *Financial Post*, December 14-16, 1996, 57.

18 Ibid., 57.

19 Falk, "The Haiti Intervention," 345.
20 Truillot, cited in Noam Chomsky, "Democracy Enhancement, Part 2: The Case of Haiti," *Z Magazine*, July/August 1994.
21 Ibid.
22 "Dangerous Crossroads," North American Congress on Latin America, NACLA Report on the Americas 27 (January/February 1994): 15.
23 Chomsky, "Democracy Enhancement."
24 Linda Diebel, "Haiti: Canada's Mission Impossible," *Ottawa Citizen*, February 23, 1997.
25 Richard Swift, "Camille Chambers," *New Internationalist* 285 (1996): 31.
26 Isaiah Berlin, cited in the *New York Times*, November 7, 1997, A14.
27 Michael Walzer, "The Politics of Rescue," *Dissent* (Winter 1996): 37.
28 *Macleans*, August 11, 1997, 24.
29 Robert Matthews and Cranford Pratt, *Human Rights in Canadian Foreign Policy* (Kingston and Montreal: McGill-Queen's University Press, 1988), 310-11.
30 Diebel, "Canada Is Pushing to Extend Mission in Haiti," *Ottawa Citizen*, February 23, 1997.
31 *Macleans*, August 11, 1997, 24.
32 Ibid.
33 Diebel, "Canada Is Pushing to Extend Mission in Haiti."
34 *The Economist*, September 25, 1993.
35 Justin Morris, "Force and Democracy: UN/US Intervention in Haiti," *International Peacekeeping* 2, 3 (Autumn 1995): 391-412.
36 Ibid., 406.
37 Paris, "Peacekeeping and the Limits," 75-76.
38 Mark Duffield, "NGO Relief in War Zones: Towards an Analysis of the New Aid Paradigm," *Third World Quarterly* 18 (1997): 527.
39 Green and Ahmed, "Rehabilitation, Sustainable Peace and Development," 190.
40 Robert Jackson, *Quasi-states: Sovereignty, International Relations and the Third World* (Cambridge: Cambridge University Press, 1990).
41 Ronnie D. Lipschutz, "Beyond the Neoliberal Peace: From Conflict Resolution to Social Reconciliation," *Social Justice* 25 (1999): 5-39.
42 Franke Wilmer, "The Social Construction of Conflict and Reconciliation in the Former Yugoslavia," *Social Justice* 25 (1999): 109.
43 Lucie Edwards, "Conflict Prevention and Conflict Resolution in Afric," presentation to the Canadian Institute of International Affairs, March 13, 1996.
44 John Stuart Mill, *Dissertations and Discussions*, vol. 3 (London: Longmans, Green, Reader, and Dyer, 1859), 173.
45 Wilmer, "The Social Construction," 109-10.
46 Green and Ahmed, "Rehabilitation, Sustainable Peace and Development," 192.
47 J. Macrae, "Dilemmas of Legitimacy, Sustainability and Coherence: Rehabilitating the Health Sector," *Relief and Rehabilitation Network* Paper no. 12: 197.

48 Ken Booth, "Human Wrongs and International Relations," *International Affairs* 71 (1995): 120.

49 Jonathan Goodhand and David Hulme "From Wars to Complex Political Emergencies: Understanding Conflict and Peacebuilding in the New World Disorder," *Third World Quarterly* 20 (1999): 13-27.

50 Walzer "The Politics of Rescue," 37.

51 Wilmer, "The Social Construction," 109.

52 Ibid.

53 K. Kumar, ed., *Rebuilding Societies after Civil War* (Boulder, CO: Lynne Rienner, 1997).

54 Cited in Martha Minow, *Between Vengeance and Forgiveness* (Boston: Beacon Press, 1998), 8.

7

Aspects of Understanding and Judging Massive Human Rights Abuses

Carol A.L. Prager

"He that increaseth knowledge increaseth sorrow."
—Ecclesiastes 1: 18

Introduction

One cannot say very much about the prospects of reconciliation without first reflecting on exactly what it is that gives rise to demands for it. What are the wellsprings of the collective perpetration of harm? Where does responsibility for it lie? What is its impact on victims and perpetrators? Under all the circumstances, can the gaps in the opposing perceptions of both groups ever be bridged? These are questions that can be explored in the context of concrete historical examples, as some of the contributors to this volume have done, or more generally, as others have done. It is this latter approach that I take here.

In recent years world leaders have been grappling with repeated atrocities which, after the Holocaust, the international community vowed would never again be tolerated. Again and again, mankind has been faced with the spectacle of as many as tens of thousands average human beings committing mayhem on as many as hundreds of thousands other ordinary human beings, including neighbours and acquaintances. One might think that by now enough had been learned to comprehend and prevent such catastrophes. But fresh outbreaks of mass violence underscore their banality while the world stands helplessly by.

Notes to chapter 7 are on pp. 216-19.

Meanwhile, controversies in the literature throw up new objections to understanding in general or in particular.

Indeed, it sometimes seems that the more that is written, the more disputes about the causes of, and responsibility for, massive human rights abuses arise. In this writer's view what often explains these controversies is the tendency for commentators to talk past each other, inattentive to the different undertakings that understanding and judging represent. (When I refer to judging, I have in mind both ethical and legal judgements. The two are even more intimately related in the development of international norms than elsewhere.) I argue that in the context of mass violence many issues, especially the prospects for reconciliation, revolve around a more comprehensive appreciation of understanding and judging.

Doubtless there are tensions between the two that will never be resolved. This is a realm characterized by horns of dilemmas, and anyone venturing into it cannot expect to escape unskewered. Nothing written here, moreover, should be construed as excusing the perpetration of evil. No doubt, in a general sense, massive human rights abuses can, in principle, be both explained and judged, and the fact that they can be explained does not lessen the need to judge. Morality categorically demands that individuals refrain from participating in mass human rights abuses. My objective here is to revisit the enduring ethical dilemma of human responsibility in the light of mass atrocities, turning it, as it were, so as to catch the glint of a new facet. One such facet is the question of what we are to make of the ethical situation when the few individuals who do what seems to be ethically required are viewed not simply as good, but as heroic human beings.

In the realms of understanding (or explaining) and judging, an important development is for the impulse of the latter to crowd out the former. This tendency is anomalous today in the context of a broad tendency to explain away crimes committed by individuals by reference, for instance, to dysfunctional backgrounds. No doubt, the enormity and destructiveness of mass human rights abuses explain the overpowering need to condemn, repudiate, and distance oneself from such behaviour. One wants to affirm, *I am not like that. That behaviour is alien to me, and intolerable.* It is by means of articulating a variety of intensely felt, often personal, perspectives that writers have dealt with the anguish and passions triggered by such horrific events. In *Explaining Hitler: The Search for the Origins of His Evil*, Ron Rosenbaum explores the ways such idiosyncratic perspectives have led writers to strikingly different, and sometimes irreconcilable, views even of Hitler's guilt.[1]

Because it provides unwelcome insights into the human condition, the shift from judging to understanding can be anguishing. Many writers insist it is wrong to attempt to explain such events, or even deny that they can be explained at all.[2] For others, especially those closest to atrocities, the two are seen as a piece, judging taking precedence over understanding and configuring the issues surrounding it. (In one sense, we can indeed agree with Clemenceau that, like revolution, genocide and massive human rights abuses are all of a piece.)

On the other hand, although mass cruelty does seem inexplicable, it is reiterated with such frequency that its incomprehensibility is difficult to maintain. Indeed, where evil, which can be defined as the deliberate inflicting of harm,[3] is typical rather than exceptional behaviour, the need to understand is much greater, albeit more threatening. In order to understand, moreover, one must temporarily suspend judgement, an apparent impossibility for many personally involved or other empathic observers. On the other hand, while there clearly can be no disinterested way of approaching the mass perpetration of harm, it is still necessary to point out the limitations of an approach focused exclusively on judging. In what follows, I make frequent reference to the Holocaust literature because so many of the present issues have been raised there. But the analysis presented here applies to every case of mass atrocities. I then turn to the resistance to understanding and then to attempts to explain.[4]

The Refusal to Understand

The very idea that the cruelty apparent in massive human rights abuses can be understood flies in the face of the perspective of victims and survivors. The fact that the horror of their experiences continues to torment the "lucky" ones who escaped with their lives powerfully reinforces the need to judge. As is well known, many Holocaust survivors, for example, were never again able to live ordinary lives; the incidence of emotional and physical illnesses, and suicide, among survivors has been well documented. Apparently, therapies can rarely "cure" the trauma that remains after torture or rape. Jean Amery, who committed suicide in 1978, wrote of his concentration camp experience of torture: "Anyone who has been tortured remains tortured….Anyone who has suffered torture never again will be able to be at ease with the world, the abomination of the annihilation is never extinguished. Faith in humanity, already cracked by the first slap in the face, then demolished by torture, is never acquired again."[5]

In a similar vein, Claude Lanzmann wrote: If there is one thing that is an intellectual scandal it is the attempt to understand *historically*, as if there were a sort of harmonious genesis to death....For me, murder—whether the murder of an individual or mass murder—is an incomprehensible act....There are moments when understanding is pure madness."[6] In short, understanding is not only disorienting but profoundly threatening.

Primo Levi, known for his notion of the "gray zone" of ambiguity in concentration camps, eloquently and perceptively put it this way:

> Perhaps one cannot, what is more, one should not, understand what happened, because to understand is almost to justify. Let me explain: "understanding" a proposal or human behavior means to "contain" it, contain its author, put oneself in his place, identify with him. Now, no normal human being will ever be able to identify with Hitler, Himmler, Goebbels, Eichmann, and endless others. This dismays us, and at the same time gives us a sense of relief, because perhaps it is desirable that their words (and also, unfortunately, their deeds) cannot be comprehensible to us. They are non-human words and deeds, really counter-human, without historic precedents....If understanding is impossible, *knowing* is imperative, because what happened could happen again.[7] [Emphasis supplied.]

Levi's emphasis on the need to "know," echoed by Lawrence L. Langer in *Preempting the Holocaust*,[8] however, is integrally related to judging. It is the insistence that we not overlook or minimize a single unspeakable aspect of an instance of the infliction of evil. Langer argues against "preempting the Holocaust" by "universalizing" it in general categories or by thinking anything positive can be learned from it. "Losses" remain inherently "unredeemed" and "unredeemable." Attempts to generalize constitute a defence against the depression that results from thinking of the Holocaust in "forensic" terms. For him, the only way to get past such horrific events is to go through them by imagining them in their particular literal reality. Langer maintains: "If some forms of human misery do indeed still lie beyond our powers to comprehend, it would be irresponsible to allow our psychological and intellectual hesitation to estrange us from that misery.

The only alternative, a complex and difficult one, is to find ways of making the inconceivable conceivable until it invades our consciousness without meeting protest and dismay."[9]

Indeed, understanding is a devastating experience, not only for survivors but also for others who try to fathom how such extreme cruelty could have been inflicted by so many apparently "normal" human beings on so many others. Primo Levi, who, as much as any witness to the Holocaust, appreciated the moral ambiguity of the camps and the Holocaust, knew if he permitted himself to experience a Nazi in all his human dimensions, he would have been defenceless against the Nazi's determination to kill him. There is a sense in which understanding blunts our indignation. This was apparent in the aftermath of the terrorist attacks on the World Trade Centre and the US Pentagon when Susan Sontag and Bill Maher opined that the terrorists who died in the attacks where not cowards because in the process of murdering thousands they martyred themselves. Commenting on the remarks of Sontag and Maher, William Ian Miller wrote, "I take it as the decline of our virtue that we can somehow see 6,000 of our citizens blown up and start to make excuses for the people who blew us up instead of first defending ourselves, and getting them back so they don't do it again. I don't want to have too much understanding for the guy who rapes my daughter....I think that sometimes we have to not be so rational. Sometimes it's more important for moral purposes to punch back and not worry about whether we are making more of a mess."[10]

Finally, there is the fear among some Holocaust experts that the "deceptive and dangerous promise of understanding [is] [d]angerous perhaps because at the heart of the labyrinth, the forbidden fruit on this particular tree of knowledge, lurks the logic of the aphorism 'To understand all is to forgive all.'"[11] Understanding might make evil seem comprehensible or even rational, diluting its significance and condoning mass murder and inhumanity.

Quantums of Freedom

It is intuitively obvious that degrees of moral responsibility for harming others depend on the degree of freedom individuals actually possess under varying circumstances. Although legal and ethical systems are necessarily predicated on human freedom, and the Western tradition upholds a very high standard of individual accountability, the actual extent of freedom is virtually always qualified; complete moral and legal responsibility are necessary fictions. The less moral freedom a person experiences, the more likely he is to be swept along by weaknesses, circumstance, and external pressures. It is a matter of determining how much of an individual's ambient space is filled with coercive forces, and how much space there is in which an individual can see, feel, and act freely. When the coercive factors have crowded out the empty spaces, resisting such pressures is a mark of exceptional character, or, when one's own life is at risk, heroism. This is apparent, for example, in the recent investigation of an American massacre of Korean civilians during the Korean War at No Gun Ri. It is likely that the men who obeyed orders will be exonerated, but that the few who defied orders will be given special commendations.[12] This state of affairs, however, turns our traditional way of viewing responsibility for harm on its head.

The law reflects an appreciation of varying degrees of responsibility. Crimes of passion may be treated more leniently than comparable crimes committed under other circumstances. "Fighting words" are outlawed because individuals are not expected to show restraint when thus provoked. Group libel and Holocaust denial are often legally proscribed, not only because they deeply wound but also because they might provoke violence. It is understood that abusive and addictive behaviours perpetuate themselves through generations, working to diminish freedom. While human relations are predicated on individual responsibility, and religious, legal, and moral beliefs are unintelligible without it, the notion of moral freedom may become highly attenuated as the individual becomes more enmeshed in the factors that contribute to collective cruelty.

When the International Law Commission codified the principles of the Nuremberg Tribunal, the Commission debated the wording of article eight, which stated that the defence of following orders failed if the individual had a "moral choice." Some Commission members thought that orders of superiors precluded a "moral choice," while others believed that in some cases individuals could find ways to disregard orders.[13] "Moral choice" entailed a meaningful degree of freedom, short of losing one's own life, to behave otherwise.

It is generally conceded that one cannot have a moral obligation to do the impossible. There are, however, degrees of possibility, as well as of despair and optimism through which inferences about human possibilities are filtered. Again and again, what emerges from the analysis of collective cruelty is the inferior morality of the group in contrast with the individual. Holocaust rescuers, for instance, were invariably individuals or couples, while individuals enmeshed in groups were at serious risk of being infected by destructive group dynamics. It is all too human to go along with group pressures.

In a classic study of group behaviour Gustav Le Bon noted that "the isolated individual possesses the capacity of dominating his reflex actions, while a crowd is devoid of that capacity."[14] This is all the more the case, according to Le Bon, when a crowd exercises some degree of public authority. Highly educated crowds behave no differently. Not only does crowd psychology polarize thinking into radically opposed absolutes but it can also unleash cruel impulses that are ordinarily repressed. Moreover, those who have been engaged in appalling group behaviour typically believe they have performed praiseworthy acts.[15] Le Bon concludes that group offences may be crimes in the legal but not psychological sense.[16]

In a similar vein Herbert C. Kelman addresses what he terms "sanctioned massacres," examining factors that reduce restraint in violence. "Sanctioned massacres," Kelman suggests, are best "viewed as outcomes rather than causes of violence," and are used as rationalizations of behaviour.[17] Kelman concludes that what instigates such violence is the "policy process."[18] "Sanctioned massacres" occur where ethical inhibitions have been calculatingly and effectively removed, and victims deprived of their moral significance. Kelman writes:

> Through processes of authorization, the situation becomes so defined that standard moral principles do not apply and the individual is absolved of responsibility to make personal choices. Through processes of routinization, the action becomes so organized that there is no opportunity for raising moral questions and making moral decisions. Through processes of dehumanization, the actor's attitudes toward the victim and himself become *so structured that it is neither necessary nor possible to view the relationship in moral terms.*[19] [Emphasis supplied.]

Concentration camps are instructive because they provide the limiting case of the deprivation of freedom for victims and perpetrators to a lesser extent. In fact, the raison d'être of concentration camps is the obliteration of freedom and the laying bare of an irreducible human nature in both victims and guards. The destruction of their freedom and dignity so demoralized prisoners that most did not rebel, and guards lost inhibitions against abusing and murdering prisoners. There were occasional heroes who seized possibilities that others missed. But they were rare. The more typical experience, according to Varlam Shalamov, who spent twenty-five years in the gulags, was this: " All human emotions—of love, friendship, envy, concern for fellow man, compassion, a longing for fame, honesty—had left us with the flesh that had melted from our bodies during our long fasts....The camp was a great test of our moral strength, of our everyday morality, and ninety-nine per cent failed it....Conditions in camps do not permit men to remain men: that is what the camps were created for."[20] Camp prisoners had been stripped of their humanity and had exhausted their inner resources.

Viktor Frankl, a Holocaust survivor, characterized moral struggles with the following maxim: "act as if for the second time, as if you are not doing what you are about to do," emphasizing that the line of least resistance is to take the less praiseworthy course of action, and that choosing the more admirable course of action requires, under the best of circumstances, considerable struggle. Human characters are so complex, however, that although quantums of freedom powerfully affect the capacity to choose, there is no one-to-one relationship between the two. An individual with diminished freedom can exhibit greater moral courage. Oskar Schindler, a Nazi with obvious human flaws, rescued many Jews.

While the actual extent of moral freedom has to be considered in each case, more generally it is useful to think of genocide and other massive human rights abuses as political, historical wrongs that have such complex causation that responsibility for them transcends and subsumes acts of individuals. Daniel Goldhagen's insistence that it was not "ordinary men," as Christopher R. Browning argued, who were responsible for the Holocaust but "ordinary Germans" implicitly supports this contention.[21] In Goldhagen's account, perpetrating the Holocaust came naturally to Germans of that generation because of their virulent anti-Semitism, and the Holocaust became, after a certain point, predictable.[22] Indeed, Goldhagen, unlike other writers on the Holocaust, maintains it can be explained. At the same time, events that can be predicted and explained are propelled by powerful engines of history in contrast to the relative freer acts of individuals, which are less predictable. Such overdetermining causation is taken into account by truth and reconciliation commissions, which offer the possibility of amnesty provided that the crimes in question have been committed for a political cause and do not include gratuitous violence.

In their attempts to explain, some writers[23] have argued it is necessary to move beyond human-scale motivations, with which in introspective moments we can sometimes identify, to more general and terrifying abstract levels of explanation for systematic violence. According to this perspective, instances of collective violence are not generally cases of ideologically shaped murderous rage, but rather of calculated state policies to achieve specific ends, such as the creation of a preferred world or the determination of membership in groups and their purposes.[24]

A television interview with the Marxist scholar Eric Hobsbawm by Michael Ignatieff reveals how Hobsbawm justified the destruction of tens of millions of Russians by reference to Stalin's Marxist project. Ignatieff first asked Hobsbawm to explain his long-standing membership in the Communist Party:

> Hobsbawm answered: "You didn't have the option. You see, either there was going to be a future, or there wasn't going to be a future and this was the only thing that offered an acceptable future."
>
> Ignatieff then asked: "In 1934, millions of people are dying in the Soviet experiment. If you had known that, would it have made a difference to you at that time? To your commitment? To being a Communist?"
>
> Hobsbawm answered: "This is a sort of academic question to which an answer is simply not possible. Erm...I don't actually know that it has any bearing on the history I have written. If I were to give you a retrospective answer which is not the answer of a historian, I would have said, 'Probably not.'"
>
> Ignatieff asked: "Why?"
>
> Hobsbawm explained: "Because in a period in which, as you might say, mass murder and mass suffering are absolutely universal, the chance of a new world being born in great suffering would still have been worth backing. Now the point is, looking back as an historian, I would say that the sacrifices made by the Russian people were probably only marginally worth while. The sacrifices were enormous, they were excessive by almost any standard and excessively great. But I'm looking back at it now and I'm saying that because it turns out that the Soviet Union was not the beginning of the world revolution. Had it been, I'm not so sure."

> Ignatieff then said: "What that comes down to is saying
> that had the radiant tomorrow actually been created, the loss
> of fifteen, twenty million people might have been justified?"
> Hobsbawm immediately said: "Yes."[25]

The listener is left wondering in what sense a world can possibly be "better" or "radiant," if it entails the destruction of tens of millions of human beings.

Thus it is simplistic to insist on a strict individual moral responsibility once the dam has broken, and torrents of history are engulfing ordinary people. Just as points of no return are reached in the lives of individuals, they are also reached in histories of states.[26] When necessary and sufficient conditions for genocide, including malevolent leadership, are present, it becomes clear that tidal waves of history can help shatter existing moral categories.

The Qualities of Heroes

Another direction from which to approach the matter of moral responsibility for gross human rights abuses is the qualities of those who defied pressures to "go along." In general we lack information about how extensive this kind of heroism has been. No doubt, many such heroes are unsung. A group that has been studied, however, consists of those who rescued Jews during the Holocaust, and those who protected Chinese civilians from Japanese soldiers in Nanking, often at tragic personal costs.[27]

The moral dilemmas faced by rescuers are not, however, four-square with those faced by individuals who followed orders. Rescuers were not generally parts of chains of command and could carry out their compassionate work in secrecy. On the other hand, the potential penalty for rescuing was greater than it was for those who refused to do what they were told, at least during the Holocaust, where perpetrators often could choose not to participate, although social pressures not to opt out were heavy.

While cruelty can be reinforced by group dynamics, it seems that altruism is confined to individuals whom we think of as heroes. Although there are some inspiring cases of group courage and sacrifice (such as the Warsaw ghetto uprising, during which Jews of the ghetto fought the onslaught of German SS troops even though they knew they were doomed, and at Masada, where ancient Hebrews killed themselves to avoid being enslaved or killed by advancing Romans), they are not nearly as numerous as individual examples of courage.

The heroism of rescuers is compounded by the fact they themselves often considered their courageous behaviour unremarkable. Researchers interviewing rescuers were repeatedly told that what they did was "nothing special, no big deal."[28] Some rescuers maintained simply that "you should always be aware that every other person is you."[29] What appeared to be natural responses to suffering in their minds were, in fact, under the circumstances, extraordinary deeds. In particular, of those who acted out of compassion, a small percentage, compared with those acting on grounds such as religious belief or personal conviction, were animated by a relatively rare trait in humans, indicative of a high level of psychological development. Compassionate responses presuppose a courageous openness to one's own pain and fear. Beyond the courage to be open to one's suffering, compassionate responses entail a magnanimous extrapolation from one's own experience to others. In this process rescuers underwent a transformation from disorientation based on the fact that their customary behaviour and ethical beliefs no longer made sense, to construction of a stronger and more moral self.[30] Non-rescuers did not undergo this transformation and thus remained psychologically and ethically disoriented.

It is significant that most of the world's religions embrace some version of the categorical imperative, which, from one perspective, can be seen as an attempt to erect out of compassion, which is an "emotional-moral" response,[31] a rational duty. But risking one's life to save another, however praiseworthy, is so extraordinary an act that it cannot be morally required; humanitarian obligations fall short of this. (This consideration helps explain the reluctance of states to involve their own ground troops in humanitarian interventions.) Significantly, researchers have identified in rescuers a high degree of "individuality or separateness." That is, rescuers were more autonomous and, hence, less affected by group perceptions and norms.[32] Rescuers had a keener sense of their own freedom. They contrast with perpetrators who were often less evolved human beings, and more dependent on group approval. Even in today's Germany, opposing racism, according to Chancellor Gerhard Schroeder, takes a special kind of "civil courage."[33]

Baumeister's Magnitude Gap

Many explanations of the inflicting of evil are dismissed by victims who see guilt in black-and-white terms, and subscribe to the "myth of pure evil," which includes the idea that "evil is driven primarily by the wish to inflict harm merely for the pleasure of it."[34] Goldhagen, for example, draws special attention to the sadism of Holocaust perpetrators. The myth, however, overstates the role of sadism in mass violence, which involves relatively little calculated sadism. Stories of drunken perpetrators abound in Algeria, in Bosnia, in Nazi Germany, suggesting that often there are inhibitions to mass killing that have to be overcome for atrocities to occur.[35]

There is, however, another explanation for what Hannah Arendt called "banality of evil." This is the disproportion between the ease with which perpetrators can inflict harm and the life-transforming impact it has on victims. Everyone has seen gangster movies that portray the cavalier ease with which a gangster snuffs out a life, but when it is his turn, becomes a terrified coward groveling for his own. This points to the "magnitude gap" that Roy F. Baumeister identifies in *Evil: Inside Human Violence and Cruelty*. It helps explain why so many ordinary people can be ordered, threatened, or conditioned to do unspeakable things to other human beings. Baumeister's account brings into sharp relief a phenomenon that has not been accorded appropriate significance. It is the fact that perpetrators of evil and their victims experience the same act in sharply different ways. Victims, like Lanzmann, Amery, and many others, stress the annihilating trauma and life-transforming aftermath of cruelty and view their experience in categorical terms of right and wrong. Their cry is "never forget." It would, of course, be heartless to expect them to feel and think otherwise.

For perpetrators, however, cruelty figures in a much smaller way because it is much easier to inflict than endure. Their reaction to reminders of their past cruelty is typically "let bygones be bygones."[36] Understandably victims' accounts dominate our thinking about such events, unless we have strong sympathy with the perpetrators' cause. Indeed the very refusal to understand may well represent a poignant attempt to restore the imbalance between the perspectives of victims and perpetrators. Nevertheless, intriguing research has demonstrated that when there has been aggression on both sides (not, of course, the case in the Holocaust) both the perpetrators' and the victims' accounts involve factual distortions of responsibility.[37] This is seen in Kosovo, where Kosovars were most often victims of Serbian atrocities, but were seen by the Serbs as terrorists. At the same time, terrorists typically see themselves as "freedom fighters."

The human condition abounds with motivations for inflicting cruelty. A potent one is the challenge to one's sense of superiority. If individuals, or social groups, believe that they are superior, but evidence for their superiority is lacking so that others not only fail to recognize their superiority but have contempt for them, as Baumeister contends, they often feel an overpowering desire to lash out. Absolutistic nationalism, which has often underwritten the cruelty of the murderous twentieth century, invariably involves this dynamic.[38] A cognate phenomenon, arguably, can be found in radical Islam, torn between pride and attainment, modernity and tradition.[39]

The Anguish of Primo Levi

The enduring fascination with Holocaust survivor Primo Levi, who may have died by his own hand in 1987, can be explained by the fact that his view of his concentration camp experience was shot through with ambiguity. A humanistic but deeply pessimistic witness of the Holocaust, his reflections on victims and perpetrators were nuanced. Refusing to see his experience in black and white, he envisioned it within a "gray zone" of ambiguity. Levi wrote:

> Here…we are dealing with a paradoxical analogy between victim and oppressor, and we are anxious to be clear: both are in the same trap….The need to divide [history] into "we" and "they" is so strong that this pattern, this bi-partition—friend/enemy—prevails over all others. Popular history, and also the history taught in schools, is influenced by this Manichean tendency, which shuns half-tints and complexities….This *desire* for simplification is justified, but the same does not always apply to simplification itself, which is a working hypothesis, useful as long as it is recognized as such and not mistaken for reality. The greater part of historical and natural phenomena are not simple, or not simple in the way we would like….The network of human relations inside the Lagers were not simple: it could not be reduced to the two blocs of victims and persecutors.[40] [Emphasis in original.]

Levi held that the Holocaust "system" bore much of the responsibility for the evil of the Holocaust, but that gratuitous "unnecessary cruelty" was the moral responsibility of individuals, a view shared by the South African

Truth and Reconciliation Commission and the Nuremberg Tribunal. Levi is an intriguing and controversial figure because, unlike many survivors, he was not concerned to judge or explain his experience, but to bear witness to it. Given the extraordinary person Levi was, he did this with all his humanity. In his later years he experienced a crushing guilt for his survival of the camp on the ground that the morally most admirable did not survive. This, in turn, led him to a profoundly tragic, and ultimately unbearable, sense of the human condition. He wrote:

> Compassion and brutality can coexist in the same individual and in the same moment, despite all logic; and for all that, compassion itself elides logic. There is no proportion between the pity we feel and the extent of the pain by which the pity is aroused: a single Anne Frank excites more emotion than the myriads who suffered as she did but whose image has remained in the shadows. *Perhaps it is necessary that it can be so. If we had to and were able to suffer the sufferings of everyone, we could not live. Perhaps the dreadful gift of pity for the many is granted only to saints.*[41] [Emphasis supplied.]

Some might reject the comparison between camp inmates and the perpetrators of ethnic violence and genocide. But from one point of view, at least, different degrees of dehumanization and corresponding diminution of freedom characterized both.[42] Individual freedom and, thus, responsibility are in short supply in violent ethnic conflict, either because one is subject to the total control and dehumanization of a concentration camp or has been more or less stripped of the opportunity for moral choice by attenuating circumstances such as government control of the media, political culture, demonizing ideologies, bureaucratic structures, and so forth. In other words, an ethic based exclusively on individual responsibility in these circumstances misses the mark.

The Moral Responsibility of Leaders

As noted, the instigator or the most direct cause of "sanctioned massacres" is the "policy process," or as Levi put it the "system." Genocide, at least, cannot occur without official policy and direction. Racial stereotypes may be available and there may be racial incidents, such as the violence against Turks and blacks in Germany today, but leadership (political, intellectual, and/or religious) is essential to transform hatred and contempt into systematic atrocities. (The passivity of leaders such as Pius XII can also be critical.) Governments played essential roles in propagating ideologies that demonized enemies and made heroes of their exterminators in numerous cases, including Israeli-occupied territories, Kenya, Rwanda, and the former Yugoslavia. In this context, genocide and other mass human rights atrocities are seen by their perpetrators as "rational" means to achieve political objectives.

Paradoxically, although international relations can be seen as a realm of relative non-freedom, in this context, at least, it offers the greatest hope for countering ethnic violence through the opportunities open to political leaders.[43] For good or ill, statesmen can make a critical difference. Without Hitler there may well have been no Holocaust. Without Milosevic, there might not have been the brutality of Bosnia and Kosovo. On the other hand, just as the Nazis used bureaucracy to make killing more efficient and remote, Swedish diplomacy during the Holocaust responded to Nazi Germany's demands with "bureaucratic resistance" saving Jewish lives in Hungary and elsewhere in the process.[44] Unlike most other European states, Bulgaria and Denmark never deported Jews. Statesmen not only have the greatest ability and incentives to constructively affect the course of history, they can also act with more impunity than ordinary people. Many world leaders, moreover, are disciplined by their preoccupation with their place in history. Individuals such as F.W. De Klerk, Nelson Mandela, and public figures like contributor Richard Goldstone have made unique and important contributions. At the same time, there may be limits to what leaders of good will can do. One thinks, for example, of Indalecio Prieto, the Spanish minister of Defense who did everything he could to avert the Spanish Civil War and Neville Chamberlain who, however wrong-headedly, did what he thought best to prevent the Second World War.

The Roles of Morality and Law

Legal and moral responsibility defines the world human beings can live in with self-respect and a sense of fairness and justice, and serves as a bulwark against the all-too-human and all-too-easy tendency to inflict cruelty. In this realm to understand is not to condone; individuals cannot evade responsibility and/or guilt for their deeds. Legal and ethical prohibitions provide powerful incentives for self-control, and failing those, for shame and guilt. They work to offset the realities that evil does not have the same significance for the perpetrator that it has for the victim, and that the world abounds with "reasons" to inflict harm on others. It is always appropriate to affirm these standards, and massive human atrocities rightly cry out for this affirmation. Today, increasingly, these standards must be asserted and demanded as many observers see humankind rushing headlong into a new barbarism.[45] The insistence on individual moral responsibility is not only required by existing moral and legal systems but also provides a much needed sense of control over events, however illusory, in the face of catastrophes of the twentieth and the twenty-first centuries.

Generally considered an authority for the proposition that people who participate in genocide are most often "ordinary" individuals, Christopher Browning nevertheless affirms strong individual moral responsibility. He maintains: "The story of ordinary men is not the story of all men. The reserve policemen faced choices, and most of them committed terrible crimes. But those who committed crimes cannot be absolved by the notion that anyone in the same position would have done as they did. For even among them, some refused to kill and others stopped killing. Human responsibility is ultimately an individual matter."[46]

At the same time, it is apparent that massive human rights abuses present us with strikingly novel ethical dilemmas. It is not hard to understand the despair of victims like Primo Levi who understood that the most terrible acts could be hedged about with moral ambiguity. Indeed, the significant question arises whether traditional moral discourse can encompass genocide and gross human rights abuses. There are reasons to wonder. One of the most compelling is that in ordinary interpersonal relations egregious ethical breaches are relatively few, conspicuous, and, hence, reasonably easy to confront. In the case of genocide and other gross human rights violations, on the other hand, abuses may be so endemic, responsibility attenuated, and morally praiseworthy behaviour so exceptional that it is not to be expected of average individuals. Since psychopathology is relatively rare among those who commit such crimes, we are faced with the horrifying phenomenon of hordes of average human beings murdering or inflicting the utmost cruelty on other ordinary human beings.[47] From at least one point of view, mass violence turns traditional moral discourse on its head. On the one hand such crimes are so barbarous and cruel as to seem unfathomable and hence unforgivable. On the other, they are so commonplace that no part of the world is free from them.

Although Lawrence Langer's and the present author's views are by no means four-square, Langer also recognizes the need for new moral language and terms. He writes: "The long list of exempting terms...[including] atonement and expiation, repentance and absolution, confession and forgiveness—reflects a valiant but misguided, ultimately doomed effort to reclaim for a familiar vocabulary an event that has burst the frame of conventional judgmental language."[48]

Reconciliation: Where Understanding and Judging Might Converge

Our notions of understanding and judging bear on beliefs regarding the degree of reconciliation that can be achieved after the killing has ended. Where ethnic violence has been systemic, war crime trials may seem most likely to culminate in as much justice as institutions can provide. But there are limits in principle and in practice to what war crime trials can accomplish. The practical difficulties in finding evidence, the slowness of the judicial process, the fact that there are never enough courts to try all perpetrators—or enough judges, as in the case of Cambodia—mitigate against extensive use of war crime tribunals. Moreover, trials that vividly rehearse the horrifying wrongs that have been perpetrated can prevent or delay the societal healing that may be possible. This was obvious, for example in the French trial of Klaus Barbie. War crime trials are essential, however, for bringing leaders, those with the greatest "moral choice," to justice. In principle, too, they work to satisfy a legitimate demand for retribution.

For the reasons advanced here, war crime trials may have more difficulty dealing with those who followed orders and those who went along, although each case must be decided on its own merits. There can be trade-offs between pursuing every individual who might conceivably be guilty of war crimes, on the one hand, and achieving societal reconciliation,[49] on the other. This dilemma becomes critical when violence has been endemic, where, as in the Holocaust, Rwanda, Cambodia, and Kosovo, as many as a hundred thousand "average" individuals participated in the atrocities. In his controversial *Hitler's Willing Executioners* Daniel Goldhagen, for example, has argued that over 100,000 Germans were implicated in the Holocaust, while the Nuremberg Tribunal ordered the execution of only eleven German war criminals.

The reconciliation commission approach may grow out of practical, forward-looking considerations, but it has much to recommend itself in terms of moral argument as well. The increasing use of reconciliation, notably in South Africa, Guatemala, Argentina, and Brazil, as well as the demand for reconciliation following gross human rights abuses in Rwanda, Cambodia, and Sierra Leone, signify recognition of the need for a more comprehensive approach for dealing with the aftermath of genocide and other mass killing. Truth and reconciliation commissions satisfy many desiderata. Major ones are the need to provide a broad historical narrative of what has occurred[50] and the need to take political and historical considerations into account. It is important that political motivation for abuses has been a ground for the granting of amnesty. Finally, truth and reconciliation commissions may be seen as acknowledging that our own humanity includes degrees of inhumanity. Reconciliation commissions can also be effective, or required, when no side achieved a clear victory and some modus vivendi must be found.

Conclusion

Understanding and judging mass human rights atrocities have sometimes been thought about in ways that obfuscate differences to the detriment of understanding. This is to be expected, because massive human rights abuses mightily challenge our ability to both explain and to judge. As many victims and others have maintained, completely understanding such appalling barbarity is impossible, and to some, attempting to do so is wrong. Victims especially focus on judging, trying to bridge the poignant magnitude gap between the defenceless victim and potent, overpowering perpetrator. This is entirely comprehensible given victims' physically, emotionally, and spiritually annihilating experiences. Victims look for meaning in what typically turns out to be meaningless, banal historical sequences, and often the only meaning available is outrage and memory. Further, many victims are concerned to avoid the implication that understanding might lead to anything approximating exoneration.

Judging raises its own daunting difficulties. Where morally praiseworthy behaviour in mass atrocities is often possible only for heroes, while many average individuals can be expected to be moral "cowards" and "invalids," in the words of Primo Levi, we face a novel and unwelcome moral situation. Ethical analysis discriminates between the ethically required and the ethically praiseworthy, and this entails an appreciation of the fact that human beings are not required to be extraordinarily courageous. The notion of humanitarian work, such as the work of the International Red Cross, bears this out. No one expects humanitarian workers to fight to stop mass violence when they find themselves in the midst of it. To the contrary, we expect humanitarian workers to withdraw to safety. Humanitarian obligations do not extend to the risking of one's life. Indeed, the very notion of humanitarian war is, in this sense, an oxymoron. Even peacekeepers are not ordinarily expected to participate actively in fighting.

The perspective of victims has dominated our thinking about mass violence to such an extent that some commentators have shied away from explaining it, or rejected the idea that it can or ought to be explained. It is clear that our existing ways of explaining and evaluating mass atrocities are inadequate; however, it is wrong to say that massive human rights abuses cannot be explained at all. Although from one perspective, understanding and judging can be seen as qualitatively different modes of perceiving and reckoning with mass atrocities—modes that can never have a seamless interface—this does not mean that understanding is not impossible or not critically important.

Tragically the evidence often demonstrates that ordinary perpetrators perceived limited room for manoeuver. Their societies had vulnerable political cultures and fault lines that can generate conflict whenever new strains appear, as the resurgence of neo-Nazism in Germany today underscores. When there are societal tectonic shifts, "provocations" for abuses will increase. Ultimately, of course, the degree of guilt and/or responsibility of anyone involved in massive human rights abuses must be determined on an individual basis. Meanwhile victims suffer horribly and unjustly no matter how their situation is viewed or what is done to address the harm done to them. Arguments depending on attenuating circumstances are not available to political leaders who unleash mass cruelty for their own purposes, or to sadists and psychopaths.

Langer is right in saying "the Holocaust experience challenged the redemptive value of all moral, community, and religious systems of belief." But he is wrong in believing that the evil of the Holocaust cannot be generalized. The Holocaust is unique in its scale and historical purpose but not in the quality of the evil perpetrated. One has only to reflect on the horrific cruelty of the Japanese in Nanking or Algerian terrorist groups in

Algeria to realize that the evil of the Holocaust, while historically unique, can indeed be generalized.

These considerations help explain the moral and intellectual contortions we find ourselves entangled in when understanding and judging massive human rights abuses. Ultimately nothing—not war crime trials, reparations, apologies, or reconciliation commissions—can be done to bring justice to victims for the atrocities that have been committed against them. Attempts at societal reconciliation do address group aspects, which have great importance, of many human rights abuses. The vast, empty, and terrifying spaces that remain after attempts to understand, judge, and reconcile massive human rights abuses have done their utmost can only be filled with a tragic sense of life. The understandable attempt to ward off this tragic sense of life and its attendant sense of despair, works to perpetuate the chasm between understanding and judging.

Notes

1 Ron Rosenbaum, *Explaining Hitler: The Search for the Origins of His Evil.* (New York: Harper Perennial, 1998).

2 Ibid., *Explaining Hitler*, Introduction and *passim*.

3 Roy F. Baumeister, *Evil: Inside Human Cruelty and Violence* (New York: W.H. Freeman and Company, 1999).

4 This essay was written before September 11, 2001, and as young people might put it, seems "very September 10th." Its argument, nevertheless, does not apply to terrorism, which intuitively one would identify as a different phenomenon, although occupying the same continuum. Similarities and differences between the two need to be worked out, but in general one would say that terrorism is generally a more concerted undertaking entailing greater moral choice. How much moral freedom a sixteen-year-old suicide bomber possesses, however, is worth considering.

5 Cited by Primo Levi in *The Drowned and the Saved* (New York: Summit Books, 1986), 25.

6 Cited by Tzvetan Todorov, *Facing the Extreme: Moral Life in the Concentration Camps*, translated by Arthur Denner and Abigail Pollok (New York: Metropolitan Books/Henry Holt, 1996), 277.

7 Primo Levi, *The Reawakening* (New York: Collier Books, 1965), 213-14.

8 Lawrence L. Langer, *Preempting the Holocaust* (New Haven: Yale University Press, 1998).

9 Ibid., 65.

10 Laura Miller, "Terrorism and Cowardice: Interview with William Ian Miller," *Salon.com News*, 7.

11 Rosenbaum, *Explaining Hitler*, xvii.
12 Charles Lane, "Wounded," *The New Republic*, October 25, 1999, 6.
13 Minutes of the 27th meeting (Wednesday, May 25, 1949) of the International Law Commission, *Yearbook of the International Law Commission*, 1949, (New York: United Nations, 1956), 195-96.
14 Gustave LeBon, *The Crowd: A Study of the Popular Mind*, 2nd ed. (Dunwoody, GA: Norman S. Berg, 1987).
15 Ibid., 163 ff.
16 Ibid., 28.
17 Herbert C. Kelman, "Violence without Moral Restraint: Reflections on the Dehumanization of Victims and Victimizers," *Journal of Social Issues* 29, 4 (1973): 38.
18 Ibid., 38.
19 Ibid., 38.
20 Cited by Todorov, *Facing the Extreme*, 31.
21 Christopher R. Browning, "Ordinary Germans or Ordinary Men? A Reply to the Critics" and Daniel Jonah Goldhagen, "Ordinary Germans or Ordinary Men?" in Michael Berenbaum and Abraham J. Peck, eds., *The Holocaust in History: The Known, the Unknown and the Disputed* (Bloomington, IN: Indiana University Press, 1998), 252-65 and 301-307, respectively.
22 Rosenbaum, *Explaining Hitler*, 345.
23 See Ron Rosenbaum and Roger W. Smith, "Human Destructiveness and Politics: The Twentieth Century as an Age of Genocide," in Isidor Wallimann and Michael N. Dobkowski, eds., *Genocide and the Modern Age: Etiology and Case Studies* (Syracuse, NY: Syracuse University Press, 2000), 21-39; and Zygmunt Bauman, *Modernity and the Holocaust* (Ithaca, NY: Cornell University Press, 1989).
24 The other seven elements in the "myth of pure evil," include "Evil seeks to do harm and does it deliberately....The victim is innocent and good....Evil is the other, the enemy, the outsider, the outgroup....Evil has been that way since time immemorial....Evil represents the antithesis of order, peace, and stability....Evil characters are often marked by egotism....Evil figures have difficulty maintaining control over their feelings, especially rage and anger." Baumeister, *Evil*, 72-75.
25 Interview contained in Robert Conquest, *Reflections on a Ravaged Century* (London: John Murray, 2000), 10-11.
26 Laurent wrote: "There is a profound difference between individuals and nations; the former have their vices and their passions which are continually leading them to do wrong; the others are fictitious beings whose agents are generally the most intelligent and most ethical of their time. And even where intelligence and morality are lacking, public opinion contains them and will increasingly contain them within the limits of duty." Cited by Martin Wight, in Gabriel Wight and Brian Porter, eds., *International Theory: The Three Traditions* (New York: Holmes and Meier, 1992).

27 See Iris Chang's account of their fates in *The Rape of Nanking: The Forgotten Holocaust of World War II* (Toronto: HarperCollins, 1997).

28 Martha C. Nussbaum, "Unlocal Hero," *The New Republic*, October 28, 1996, 38.

29 Ibid., 38.

30 Cited by Eva Fogelman, "The Rescuer Self," in Berenbaum and Peck, eds., *The Holocaust and History*, 663-67.

31 Fogelman, "The Rescuer Self," 668.

32 Nechama Tec, "Reflections on Rescuers," in Berenbaum and Peck, eds., *The Holocaust in History*, 653.

33 John Schmid, "Schroeder Is Urging Germans to Wake Up to Racism," *International Herald Tribune*, Monday, September 4, 2000.

34 Baumeister, *Evil*, 72.

35 Baumeister, *Evil*, 339.

36 Baumeister, *Evil*, 43.

37 Baumeister, *Evil*, 91.

38 John Plamenatz, "Two Kinds of Nationalism," in Eugene Kamenka, ed., *Nationalism: The Nature and Evolution of an Idea* (Canberra: Edward Arnold, 1976).

39 See, for example, Fouad Ajami, "Nowhere Man," *The New York Times* (October 7, 2001) and Bernard Lewis, "The Roots of Muslim Rage," *The Atlantic* (September 1990).

40 Levi, *The Drowned and the Saved*, 36-37. See also, for example, Felicja Karay, *Death Comes in Yellow: Skarzysko-Kamienna Slave Labor Camp*, translated by Sara Kitai (Amsterdam: Harwood Academic Publishers, 1996), and from one generation removed, Tzvetan Todorov's powerful *Facing the Extreme: Moral Life in the Concentration Camps* trans. Arthur Denner and Abigail Pollak (New York: Henry Holt, 1996).

41 Levi, *The Drowned and the Sacred*, 56-57.

42 Cf. Martha Minow, *Between Vengeance and Forgiveness: Facing History after Genocide and Mass Violence* (Boston: Beacon Press, 1998).

43 Cf. Bill Berkeley who writes: "Rwanda's genocide is but the clearest example of a pattern that runs through nearly all of Africa's ruinous civil conflicts, a pattern not of "age-old hatreds" but of calculated tyranny. The forces tearing these countries apart are the same forces that have ravaged other parts of the world throughout history: the forces of despotism, Machiavellian intrigue, 'divide and rule.'" From "Ethnicity and Conflict in Africa," in Belinda Cooper, ed., *War Crimes: The Legacy of Nuremberg* (New York: TV Books, 1999), 185.

44 Paul A. Levine, "Bureaucracy, Resistance, and the Holocaust," in Berenbaum and Peck, eds., *The Holocaust and History*, 518-35.

45 See Robert D. Kaplan, *The Ends of the Earth: A Journey at the Dawn of the 21st Century* (New York: Random House, 1996); John Lukacs, *The End of the Twentieth Century and the End of the Modern Age* (New York: Ticknor & Fields,

1993); and Wiliiam Pfaff, *The Wrath of Nations: Civilization and the Furies of Nations* (New York: Simon & Schuster, 1993).

46 Christopher R. Browning, *Ordinary Men: Reserve Police Battalion 101 and the Final Solution* (New York: HarperCollins, 1992), 188.

47 That mass violence is not new to our century is borne out by Tocqueville's comments on the events of June 6, 1848, in France: "How in those unhappy times a taste for violence and a contempt for human life suddenly spread. The men I was talking to were sober, peaceful artisans whose gentle and slightly soft mores were even farther removed from cruelty than from heroism. But they were dreaming of nothing but destruction and massacre." From "1848, Seed Plot of History 150th Anniversary," *The National Interest*, 52 (Summer 1998): 53.

48 Langer, *Preempting the Holocaust*, 184.

49 See, for example, Martha Minow's excellent, *Between Vengeance and Forgiveness: Facing History after Genocide and Mass Violence passim* and a review of Anne Sa'adah's, *Germany's Second Chance: Truth, Justice and Democratization* (Cambridge: Harvard University Press, 1998) in *Foreign Affairs* 78 (March/April 1999): 146.

50 See Minow chap. 4, for an excellent discussion of truth and reconciliation commissions, but see Langer, 67: "The pragmatic decision to choose 'reconciliation' over justice in places like Argentina, Chile, Haiti, and South Africa (to be followed, perhaps, by Rwanda and Bosnia-Herzegovina) creates a dubious legacy for the worldwide victims of brutality and an even more doubtful precedent for those who would seize and misuse power in the future."

CASE STUDIES

8

We Are All Treaty People: History, Reconciliation, and the "Settler Problem"

Roger Epp

> To have no history is to face only natural obstacles and one's own limitations.
> — Sheldon Wolin, *The Presence of the Past*

I

In an Ottawa stateroom in January 1998, elders and chiefs present, the Canadian government made a "solemn offer of reconciliation" to Aboriginal peoples. The offer was read by the minister of Indian Affairs—not the prime minister, as some noted—as part of long-awaited response to the five-volume report of the Royal Commission on Aboriginal Peoples (RCAP), which had been appointed following the armed standoff between Canadian troops and Mohawk warriors at Oka. The government's offer accepted the Commission's historical outline of the relationship between Aboriginal and non-Aboriginal peoples in what is now Canada: first, separate worlds; then, contact and cooperation; displacement and assimilation; and, finally (hopefully), renewal and respect. "Sadly," it said,

> our history with respect to the treatment of Aboriginal people is not something in which we can take pride. Attitudes of racial and cultural superiority led to a suppression of Aboriginal culture and values. As a country, we are burdened by past actions that resulted in weakening the identity of Aboriginal peoples, suppressing their languages and cultures, and outlawing spiri-

---

Notes to chapter 8 are on pp. 241–44.

tual practices. We must recognize the impact of these actions
on the once self-sustaining nations that were disaggregated,
disrupted, limited or even destroyed by the dispossession of
traditional territory, by the relocation of Aboriginal people,
and by some provisions of the Indian Act.[1]

The minister, Jane Stewart, on behalf of her government, assured those
who had assembled that "we have listened and we have heard," that "the
days of paternalism and disrespect are behind us," and that a commitment
to a new relationship meant "coming to terms with the impact of our past
actions and attitudes....History cannot be changed, but it must be understood in a way that reflects that people today are living out the legacy of
decisions made in a different time."[2] The most tangible expression of reconciliation announced that day was a monetary one: a $350 million fund
for community-based healing projects to deal with the particular legacy of
physical and sexual abuse at residential schools.

The government's statement of regret and its commitment to change
had been encouraged by RCAP. Its report, optimistic and ambitious, with
more than four hundred recommendations, had begun with the assertion
that a "great cleansing of the wounds of the past" was necessary before the
work of reconciliation could begin and before it was possible to "embrace
a shared future," to "complete" the Canadian federation.[3] For the recent
past—roughly the early nineteenth century to the 1960s, with its cultural
triumphalism, its "battering ram" of the Indian Act, and its residential
schools—was filled with "evidence of the capacity of democratic populations to tolerate moral enormities in their midst."[4] It could be forgiven but
not forgotten. Still, the RCAP report held out as a realistic goal a new relationship based on mutual recognition, respect, and sharing, and a "just
accommodation" of Aboriginal political and cultural aspirations within
Canadian institutions. That goal was reiterated in the government's carefully crafted response as a matter of "building a true partnership."

Subsequent events, however, quickly made the solemn offer of reconciliation seem less a beginning than a high-water mark from which Ottawa
has retreated awkwardly. Whether Canadians generally were more than
vaguely aware of the offer at the time it was made, or shared its sentiments,
or can recall it now, is an open question. In any case, backlash has become
the political order of the day. BACKLASH is the word shouted from the
cover of *Report Magazine*, whose inflammatory interpretation of a series of

recent Supreme Court decisions was couched in terms of "public outrage over the reverse racism of the Indian rights industry" and a country "on the edge of anarchy."[5] In the province of British Columbia, which has become the focus of land-claims litigation and treaty negotiations in the absence of any historic "extinguishment" of Aboriginal title, the extremist forecasts of radio talk-show hosts and the inferences of headline writers (e.g., *The Vancouver Sun*: "BC Indian chiefs lay claim to entire province, resources"[6]) strike an all-too-responsive chord. Attuned to the prevailing political winds, the federal government gave virtually no public defence of the Nisga'a treaty to which it was a signatory, through all the public controversy that ensued, and apparently has lost interest in more treaty negotiations; a new BC provincial government, elected by a landslide in 2001, has promised a referendum on the entire treaty process that is sure to be divisive. On the other side of Canada, in New Brunswick, violent confrontations followed judicial decisions about the status of historic treaty rights to fish and cut timber—the courts, as one analyst put it, having been left "by political default" to define the formal relationship between Aboriginal and non-Aboriginal peoples. In the coffee shops, meanwhile, "words of bigotry and fury resonate across a part of the country better known for tranquility and a powerful sense of community."[7] The federal government's role was a reactive and, again, largely a passive one, at least until the conflict had escalated to incendiary wharf-side hostilities. No wonder that an increasing number of Canadians tell pollsters that relations with Aboriginal peoples are deteriorating.[8]

All of this is grist for those skeptics who, at the time of the offer of reconciliation, dismissed it as part of a worldwide fashion for apologies, reflecting both the new advice in crisis management literature that previously would have counselled stonewalling and the "gimme-a-hug political culture of the late 1990s, where empathy and symbolic gestures so often substitute for real action."[9] Limited-liability guilt management on behalf of Canadians is one plausible characterization of federal policy.[10]

But Ottawa's caution also reflects the marked political-ideological shift since the early 1990s, when the federal and all ten provincial governments could still sign on to an omnibus constitutional accord that, while ultimately unsuccessful when put to Canadians, included among its many provisions the recognition of an "inherent right of self-government" for Aboriginal peoples. That constitutional window has closed decisively. By the end of the decade, moreover, those who imagined themselves outside the so-called Aboriginal rights orthodoxy could claim the respectable sponsorship of a major newspaper (*The National Post*), the Official Opposition in the House of Commons, and academics such as Tom Flanagan, a former Reform Party research director, whose book-length response to the RCAP report, *First Nations? Second Thoughts*, was published to widespread acclaim in policy circles. By the logic of his argument, the entire enterprise of reconciliation is not only a misguided and dangerous one, politically and economically, because it encourages the "orthodoxy" that would turn the country into a "multinational state embracing an archipelago of aboriginal nations that own a third of Canada's land mass." More germane to my purposes, it is an unnecessary one. Aboriginal peoples ("Siberian-Canadians") are mere descendants of prior waves of immigrants; they did not constitute sovereign political states, only kinship groupings or "tribes"; European colonization of North America was both inevitable, owing to an advanced technological civilization, and justifiable, owing to the availability of uncultivated lands; "land-surrender treaties" mean no more than what they say; the assimilation of Aboriginal individuals into the mainstream should be encouraged for their own well-being.[11] There is, in short, no ruptured relationship, only a natural succession. There is no enduring cultural difference worth preserving or mediating politically. Certainly there is nothing for which to make amends.

Such is the landscape on which the question of reconciliation is now encountered. Aboriginal peoples, their traditions, and especially their status and rights are the subject of unprecedented attention, if not understanding; and the resulting body of writing is too large to canvas profitably here, but large enough, it is safe to say, to command its own section of any quality bookstore. There are Supreme Court decisions sold inside stylish covers.[12] There are collections of legal essays on complex topics like Aboriginal title. There are manifestos by Aboriginal intellectuals,[13] declarations by political bodies like the Grand Council of the Crees,[14] and biographies of Aboriginal leaders. There are abstract policy studies with their rehearsed menu of identity categories: "First Nations," Indian, Metis, Inuit, "C-31," "non-status," "equal Canadians," "citizens plus."[15] There is fresh scholarship from across the humanities and social sciences. There are guides to native sites and spiritualities, some in German translation for the tourists, bearing out Peter Nabokov's warning about "sentimentalizing and fossilizing" cultures, and his suspicion that "were there not Indians we would have somehow come around to inventing them, as a utopian antithesis to so much that alienated us."[16] There are, in addition, the relentless fragments of daily media coverage of court cases, blockades, corruption allegations, and leadership struggles.

The politics of that landscape are complex and highly charged. Aboriginal assertions cut to the heart of the most basic political questions in this settler country—questions having to do with identities, histories, and imagined communities. They invite strong emotions: anger, fear, confusion, evasion, weariness, even hope of all kinds. They divide real Aboriginal communities along lines of generation and gender, "traditionalist" and "accommodationist," "elites," "grassroots," and "warriors." They transform Aboriginal rights critics into opportunistic, latter-day champions of fisheries conservation or the welfare of reserve residents (whom they will never meet) against alleged band council nepotism and profligacy. They prod a federal government, stung periodically by international human rights publicity while promoting Canada as the best place in the world in which to live, to recycle old policies that would safely contain the meaning of self-government, without seeming to reject it, and to drag its feet where it might instead negotiate, in hopes that the courts will decide an issue first and absorb the political fallout.

There are many dilemmas of reconciliation that might be explored in this context. An obvious one is the role of legal determination and monetary compensation in coming to terms, say, with historical grievances about land or residential school abuses. Beneath this, however, there are subtler, deeper, more elusive reconciliations or cultural divides that are very much at play: between liberal-individual and tribal-communal identities, between venerative and instrumental attitudes to language, between oral and written histories, between covenantal and contractual understandings of treaties. The Supreme Court in its *Delgamuukw* decision saw itself as attempting precisely such a reconciliation. But that raises a second fundamental question: Whose work is reconciliation? Judges? Ministers of Indian Affairs? Aboriginal negotiators? Or does it extend far beyond them?

I have begun with a long introduction because the subject itself is a sprawling and intimidating one, about which it seems hard to say something new. Moreover, the nature of the subject makes it important to position myself inside it. For I will long remember the sharp, protective question asked by a bright Anishinabe student, whose professor had shown her a conference paper I had written about historical and contemporary Aboriginal diplomatic activity, and ultimately about the disciplinary presumptions in the field of international relations that had rendered it invisible.[17] "Why," she asked, "are you writing about this?" The same question could be asked fairly of this paper, and indeed of the entire literature that takes the Aboriginal as its subject. My interest here lies in rethinking the relationship in ways that correct the inevitable, singular focus on the aboriginal side of it, so that instead of posing the question about reconciliation as a matter of what "they" want—recognition, compensation, land—and what "we" can live with, the subject under closest scrutiny becomes "ourselves." In other words, the subject is not the "Indian problem" but the "settler problem." This might be said to be work left mostly untouched by RCAP's five volumes.

In this spirit, I want to explore two related interpretive claims. One is that solemn offers of reconciliation, however sincere, however eloquent, are spoken not into a void but rather into a liberal, settler political culture, fundamentally Lockean still in its philosophical fragments: forward-looking, suspicious of history, or, more likely, indifferent to it, and incorporating into its imagined social contract an almost wilful amnesia about whatever might be divisive. Reconciliation in a liberal society may turn out to mean only the ability of strangers to live together in pursuit of individual projects.

The second claim is more straightforward, and at least as contentious. It is that while an offer may be spoken in Ottawa by a minister of the Crown, on behalf of all Canadians, the burdens, the opportunities, or, more neutrally, the imperatives of reconciliation are not distributed equally. Treaty rights, land claims, or self-government are scarcely abstract issues in places where non-Aboriginal communities, struggling to survive against the decline of traditional economic sectors—fishing, logging, farming—are understandably threatened by negotiations or court judgements that require them to share access to dwindling resources and available livelihoods. This is the reality to which *Report Magazine* and the radio fear-merchants play so skillfully. But it is a reality all the same: in northwestern British Columbia around Nisga'a territory; in Burnt Church, New Brunswick; in prairie towns like Punnichy, Saskatchewan, where it is not uncommon for residents to buy up adjacent lots and tear down the houses to pre-empt the possibility of Indian renters from the nearby reserve moving in next door.[18] In such places, mostly rural, interdependence is a difficult but almost inescapable challenge. The casual racism of everyday speech is shocking to outsiders. Reconciliation, in turn, is a task to be taken up without the cover of scholarship or the luxury of geographical distance. But it is in such places, too, places where not one but two working human cultures—Aboriginal and settler—have been despatched to the dustbin of history by the proponents of the new economy, that words of reconciliation must ring true and people must be enlisted in new relationships. Dauntingly pessimistic as this might sound, there is, I will argue, promise here as well, but it lies in breaking free of Lockean myths and thinking anew about history and inherited obligations.

II

"In the beginning," wrote John Locke, the seventeenth-century English political philosopher, in his *Second Treatise of Government*, "all the world was America."[19] In other words, in what amounted to a political creation myth, embellished with a crude anthropology to suit European imaginations, America was a blank slate—the primordial void out of which the institutions of private property and limited government were established by means of consent, and painted with adjectives such as "wild," "wasted," and "wretched." While Locke had also written a colonial constitution for the Carolinas, he had, of course, never visited the Americas. All the same, he was certain that its peoples lacked real government and the efficient, productive cultivation of land that justified ownership of what had been given to humankind in common for sake of preservation. Like other social contract theorists, beginning with Thomas Hobbes, Locke's political philosophy relied more centrally than is often recognized on the alterity of the Aboriginal. His association of liberty with property and of property, in the first instance, with appropriation from nature— by the mixing of one's labour—was singularly attractive in colonial America. At the very least, it provided intellectual comfort to those who had traversed an ocean for the prospect of freehold title and were determined never to be tenants again.[20] Locke's conception of natural property as an extension of the labouring self allowed even the "wild Indian" ownership of "the fruit or venison which nourishes him." But, he claimed, neglecting all the Aboriginal assistance that settlers received in growing suitable crops, cultivation of the earth was the "chief matter of property." The Lockean standard of "civilization" rested on relative efficiencies in the use of land: "For I ask whether the wild woods and uncultivated waste of America left to Nature, without any improvement, tillage or husbandry, a thousand acres will yield the needy and wretched inhabitants as many conveniences of life as ten acres equally fertile land doe [*sic*] in Devonshire where they are well cultivated."[21]

The practical consequence of Locke's argument was plainly drawn in the eighteenth century by the eminent European diplomatist Emmerich Vattel. His *Law of Nations* began from the familiar contractarian premise that the earth once belonged to all in common, but that at some stage of population growth cultivation was required of every nation as a matter of natural duty, since hunting or herding were no longer sufficient, and for that reason, morally justifiable. "Those who still pursue this idle mode of life occupy more land than they would have need of under a system of honest labour, and they may not complain if other more industrious Nations, too confined at home, should come and occupy part of their lands." Vattel made clear his disapproval of the Spanish "usurpation." By contrast, the colonization of North America—whose "vast tracts of land" were only "roamed over," rather than inhabited, by "small numbers" of "wandering tribes"—could be considered "entirely lawful." Those tribes had "no right" to keep it to themselves: "provided sufficient land were left to the Indians, others might, without injustice to them, settle in certain parts of a region, the whole of which the Indians were unable to occupy." It was not against nature, he concluded, to confine them within narrower bounds.[22]

Vattel is more commonly remembered for his insistence that membership in international society was exclusive to sovereign states on the (emergent) European model. This, too, was a position rooted in contractarian premises and, in particular, in Locke's concern to distinguish political commonwealths from families and political authority from the sort of patriarchal justifications for absolutist kingship that had gained a following in his day. Locke again drew those distinctions through the counter-example of the American tribes. While admitting his ignorance as to the political arrangements of these "little independent societies," the logic of his argument required that they remained in a state of nature, lacking proper government, that is, founded on the consent of individuals for the limited purpose of preserving their lives and property.

These intellectual positions can scarcely be relegated, like museum pieces, to the status of ideological curios. For one thing, they continue to resonate in everyday speech, for example, in the familiar claim that settlement of the Canadian prairies should be insulated from moral and politi-

terra nullius

✳ cal scrutiny on the grounds that "there was nothing here before we came" and "we made something of it." This is the story reflected in countless community and family histories of the homesteading era. Doubtless the same could be said of northern miners and loggers. Indeed, the Lockean myth has been renewed in successive generations of immigrants, who came to this "new" world to escape an impoverished or oppressive past, to live as equals, and to wrest a future from an unforgiving environment through hard work. There is enough experiential truth in all of this to sustain it in what is now an overwhelmingly urban country. In a famous essay, "In Defence of North America," George Grant once called it the "primal" spirit of a society that, uniquely, "has no history (truly its own) from before the age of progress" and that in its "conquering relation to place has left its mark within us."[23] But, as Flanagan's book demonstrates, Locke and Vattel also still constitute the intellectual bedrock for a coherent, and powerful, contrary position on such contemporary subjects as treaties, land claims, and Aboriginal rights in general. As he puts it, they stand on the civilized side of a fundamental divide, which is marked by (1) the extension of rule by "organized states" over "stateless societies," and (2) the displacement of hunter-gatherers by cultivators, such that the European entry into North America and Australia was "the last act of a great drama—the spread of agriculture around the world."[24] So much for what RCAP's *Report* characterizes as the era of dispossession and assimilation.

Flanagan's simple dichotomies are a tempting target in themselves, even if their purpose is acknowledged to be primarily a polemical one. They disregard examples of Aboriginal cultivation and resource management and, ironically, diminish at the same time the status of the cattle ranchers whose "winning of the open range" is so important to the mythology of the North American West. They discount Aboriginal modes of governance, as well as the influence of Aboriginal practices such as federalism on the American colonists. And they misconstrue the centralized state and agrarian communities as partners in progress. The reality of early-modern Europe, much less Stalinist Russia, post-colonial Africa, or even the Canadian West, suggests a much more conflictual relationship over the loss of autonomy and the extraction of wealth.[25] A close reader of Flanagan's book could register other quibbles, for example, at the way he dismisses the idea that historical treaties involving European states and Aboriginal polities could imply meaningful diplomatic relationships among rough equals—on the linguistic conceit and the relatively recent international legal doctrine that only sovereign states could be signatories of such agreements. Even as recent a compendium as the *Consolidated Treaty Series, 1648-1918*, would tell a more complicated story about recognition within international society. So would the US government's commissioning of a report as late as 1918 to answer the "question of the aborigines" in international law—a report whose conclusions Flanagan cites as proof of his position rather than as evidence of contestation. And so would the now-forgotten diplomatic campaign of 1923-24 to prevent Iroquois admittance to the League of Nations, at a point when the matter of membership for Canada and the other so-called white settler dominions of the British Empire had not been settled.[26]

To pursue such a line of criticism, however, is to miss what is most revealing about Flanagan's argument: namely, a mode of reasoning that is conceptual, not historical. In this fundamental sense it mirrors the work of the classic English social-contract theorists. That work betrays little of its own time. It founds its arguments about political authority and the preeminence of the individual on abstract claims about nature. It begins (in the case of Hobbes) from a concern, not unlike Flanagan's, to confine the meaning of language against political dispute. And it resorts (in the case of Locke) to a crude evolutionism of property and government as if to preclude any other arrangements. In this mode of political reasoning, the past is problematic, even dangerous.

In the first place, the past is dangerous as the domain of unavenged grievances and, partly for that reason, of partial solidarities nourished by memory. This is manifestly clear in Hobbes, who invites his readers, not to *remember* the destruction of the English civil war, but to *calculate as a logical possibility* that life would be "nasty, brutish, and short" in the absence of the order provided by strong government. Michael Ignatieff has restated Hobbes's position most forcefully in recent years in the context of extreme nationalism, genocide, and "truth-commission" proceedings. "All nations," he writes, "depend on forgetting: on forging myths of unity and identity that allow a society to forget its founding crimes, its hidden injuries and divisions, its unhealed wounds." What reconciliation requires is for people to "awake from history," to recognize which inherited identities are not fate, and to reject the "nationalist fiction" for the "liberal fiction," in which individuals are recognized as "simple, equal units of one indivisible humanity."[27] When my students read Ignatieff, they have no trouble situating his arguments about Yugoslavia, Rwanda, and South

Africa in a Canadian context. With what seems relief, they seize on and amplify it: the past is past; we could never agree on what happened; worse, appeals to history would "put us into a defensive mode" as the "inheritors of our ancestor's sins," while locking Aboriginal peoples into a victim identity; government policy should not be based on "retribution" for past actions; what's more important is to find practical ways out of the cycle of poverty. And so on. Their reactions are common enough. Alan Cairns has registered a similar warning to steer clear of the "divisive legacy of history" in his recent book, *Citizens Plus*: "The past identities that separated us from each other survive in memory and are reinforced by politics and policies that both feed on and provide sustenance to difference."[28] If the past is problematic as the domain of grievance and partial solidarities, however, and if awaking from it is crucial to reconciliation, it follows—almost perversely—that by far the greatest work falls to Aboriginal peoples. It is up to "them" both *to forget* and *to accept* the loss of historically constituted identities, and, by doing so, to release settlers' descendants from a vague sense of intergenerational guilt. That way "we" will not complain when tax dollars are spent prudently and transitionally on the practical task of improving quality of life.

For polemicists such as Flanagan, the past appears problematic in another more intriguing way as well. Arguably, more troubling than any remembered injustices—which, in the last resort, can be chalked up to the inevitable march of civilization—are historical claims about successful coexistence, which might then bear on the contemporary understanding of treaties or else recommend the recognition of Aboriginal "nations" within a renovated Canadian federation. Even the memory of reciprocity apparently is dangerous. Indeed, the RCAP report's treatment of this side of the historic relationship may be its most valuable contribution, simply because it rehearses a history that Canadians have either forgotten, or, more likely, never been taught. Certainly it flies in the face of the myth of North America as a blank slate, as *terra nullius*, before the Europeans arrived, and the complementary myth of conquest that received such a resounding backhanded boost in 1992 during the denunciations of the Columbus centenary. History tells a more complicated tale. Out of necessity or principle, the British Crown engaged in extensive diplomatic relations with Aboriginal peoples from first contact. As its eighteenth-century conflict with France carried across the Atlantic, it negotiated treaties of peace, alliance, trade, and coexistence with Mikmaq and Iroquois—negotiations conducted in Aboriginal languages, according to elaborate tribal protocols, and, arguably, bearing out confederal relations of "living kinship" (or "many families living in one house") into which the stranger could be adopted.[29] In 1763, the Crown issued a proclamation recognizing Indian nationhood, territory, and rights in land that could only be extinguished with consent—the basis of recent claims in British Columbia and the North. In the 1870s, it made real concessions in treaties signed on the Canadian prairies so that land could be opened quickly for settlement at a fraction of the cost the US was spending on its "Indian wars." In a very real way, most Canadians exercise a treaty right simply by living where they do. On the prairies we are all treaty people.

So why is there no more volcanic an issue in Canadian society than treaty rights? It is not a sufficient answer to point to political and media presentation of aboriginal demands as unreasonable, unending, and likely to bankrupt the country. Canadians are not simply passive recipients. They live in a political culture in which a certain idea of equality has gained a powerful foothold—fed by such different sources as the US civil rights movement, the adoption of a Charter of Rights and Freedoms, and the reaction against the proposed "distinct" constitutional status of Quebec in Canada. Tribal identities are a puzzle, if not anathema, in liberal societies; they make conflicting demands of well-intentioned people who, with reason, understand the struggle for non-discrimination as a significant one. But surely another part of the reason is the mark left by the myth of *terra nullius*. Imbued with that myth, Canadians can live more comfortably, forgetfully, with the dirty little secret that the treaties were a one-time land swindle than with the possibility that they might mean something in perpetuity. They do not want to know that Aboriginal peoples had their own understandings of treaty-making as a form of sharing. Some of them would be outraged by James Tully's claim that "Canada is founded on an act of sharing that is almost unimaginable in its generosity"—not only land, but food, agricultural techniques, practical knowledge, and trade routes.[30] Certainly they would not accept his conclusion that a post-colonial relationship might be built out of the memory of that sharing. Instead, they clamour for "closure," for "final settlements." They want no more surprises. Though they often identify themselves as conservatives, curiously, they recognize no inherited obligations.

This kind of anti- or post-mnemonic society, writes the political theorist Sheldon Wolin, can again be traced back to social-contract theory in ways that are pertinent to my own analysis. Contract theory holds out the possibility of a fresh, voluntary start. Its "sacrament of innocence," he argues, so attractive and culturally formative in North America, offers "absolution from the foolishness of our fathers and mothers" and, in every generation, "soothes us with the knowledge that we were not there." It posits memoryless, dehistoricized—but equal—persons. When set over against the ambiguous legacy of an expansionist history filled with economic opportunity and social mobility for immigrants, "the function of social contract thinking becomes clear: to relieve individuals and societies of the burden of the past by erasing the ambiguities." It understands that for a certain kind of political society to operate, "some things had to be forgotten"—Ignatieff's point precisely—or at least not "publicly recalled." It assumes that "it is possible to talk intelligibly about the most fundamental principles of a political society as though neither the society nor the individuals in it had a history."[31]

Over against the contractarian tradition, Wolin proposes the idea of a birthright, derived from the biblical story of the brothers Esau and Jacob, in which the latter, the younger, disguises himself in order to acquire his father's blessing. A birthright assumes that "we come into the world preceded by an inheritance" that is collective, that extends over time, that we can disavow but do not choose, and that comes with "accumulated burdens" as well as benefits: a name, debts, obligations, quarrels: "When we accept a birthright, we accept what has been done in our name." We also accept an obligation to use that inheritance, "take care of it, pass it on, and, hopefully, improve it." In this way, a birthright is not a fixed entity. Its meaning in any generation—Wolin has in mind the American Constitution, but we might substitute the treaty relationship between Crown and Aboriginal peoples—needs interpretation; as such, it is subject to dispute, revision, and renewal, the work by which we "make it our own."[32]

Significantly, the story of Esau and Jacob ends with a dramatic reconciliation. After a long estrangement, it is the usurper Jacob who takes the initiative and returns, though fearing for his life, to face his brother, with whom he is bound—like it or not—in a common history that cannot be denied except at the expense of one's own identity.[33] Nor can its moral imperatives be resisted indefinitely. There must be a facing-up. The relationship between Aboriginal peoples and settlers, I suggest, constitutes an equally powerful common history, inherited, not chosen, whose birthright we can either disavow, because its burdens seem too great, or else make our own through respectful initiatives.

III

I am a fourth-generation settler on the Canadian prairies, on Treaty Six land, one who wonders what it means to live here and what I must know in order to do so.[34] My father's family homesteaded in 1894 in the rural district trustingly named *Eigenheim*, literally, home of one's own. That same December, my grandfather was born. Not far away, in 1897, Almighty Voice, the Cree who had been arrested for illegally butchering a cow and then escaped the Duck Lake jail, was killed by a barrage of bullets and cannon fire in what the *Canadian Encyclopedia* calls the "last battle between whites and Indians" in North America. In 1918 my mother's family came to the same district and farmed near the corner of Beardy's Reserve. They had left behind a homestead in Oklahoma that had been claimed also in 1894 when Indian Territory was opened up in the great land rush, among the patchwork of allotments chosen by Cheyenne, some of whom had survived the massacre upstream on the Washita River at the hands of General Custer's Seventh Cavalry. I am, in other words, a product of Indian policy on both sides of the border. My story cannot be told apart from those of Cree and Cheyenne. When I was a child, especially in the first years after my maternal grandfather's death, we picnicked and I ran along the reconstructed pallisades at Fort Carlton, due north of Eigenheim, where Treaty Six was first negotiated and signed late in the summer of 1876. Sixty years later, while my great-uncle's family had turned inward in mourning at the death of a wife and mother, still in her thirties, thousands of people, including the governor-general as well as members of the local community, passed by the farm in a cloud of vehicles to the same site to mark the treaty's diamond anniversary. She was buried, meanwhile, at the country-church cemetery where all my ancestors who died in Canada are buried. If there is sacred ground for me anywhere on this earth, ground that signifies sacrifices made and remembered, it is there.

I have lived most of my life on Treaty Six land. I grew up in a small town in the southeast corner of that vast tract of 120,000 square miles, though I would have no significant contact with Aboriginal people before brief stints in young adulthood as a daily newspaper journalist and a government bureaucrat. I now live and teach on the western side of the treaty area. I have driven across it so many times, west to east and back, that its terrain has become familiar.

I have taught introductory politics to Cree students at a cultural college housed in a former residential school, filled with peepholes and bad memories, where I once brought a group of uncomfortable non-Aboriginal students for a joint session on "self-government" that was a spectacular failure, a mismatch of those who had no sense of themselves as historical beings and those who did. I returned to the same building some years later to struggle as the solitary *moniyaw* in a Cree-language class. I have brought my children to a powwow in the community, after which my daughter confessed surprise that "there were so many of them," having received an impression in her elementary school curriculum of the demise of a people. I have attended a wake for a suicide. I have heard horrific accounts of local political intimidation and hopes to bring about change whether through ballot boxes or building occupations. I have sat quietly at a morning meeting—Regis and Kathy Lee on the large-screen TV at one end of the room—while skeptical elders debated a proposal to derive a contemporary watchdog on band government from the traditional concept of "whipman," thereby demonstrating both the richness of Cree as a language of public affairs and, whenever they reverted to an English word such as "rights," its limits. I write beneath an eagle's feather for no other reason than that it was a gift from a friend, an elder in the making, whom I had seen through a degree.

I am not sentimental either about real, existing reserve communities, though they contain much more cultural vitality than is commonly imagined, or else about the prospects of racial harmony "if we could only get to know each other." Even in a self-selected university environment, I am disabused regularly of the latter notion. The class I teach on Aboriginal political issues in alternate years, typically a mix of non-Aboriginal and Aboriginal students, is easily the most difficult on my plate, the most likely to leave me with an unshakable sense of inadequacy, but also, because so much seemingly is at stake, the most likely to produce honest human encounters—the life-changing kind. This is the class I bring to the top of Driedmeat Hill to talk about treaty-making with an eyeful of land in every direction. This is the class from which I learned to venture the unlikely idea that rural and Aboriginal peoples on the Canadian prairies might actually be well placed to understand each other—this after a non-Aboriginal student shattered stereotypes on all sides by describing what was for her an inseparable interconnection of personal identity with the land on which her Ukrainian family had farmed for three generations. She did not have to disavow her own settler-cultivator ancestors in order to understand dispossession. Quite the contrary. It is not too strong to say that she feared such a loss for herself.

IV

For the Canadian government to face up formally to its "past actions and attitudes" is no small thing. Simple acknowledgement is an essential step in any process of reconciliation. This is so even if it is possible to wonder about its commitment to what it began, its careful confession of general but not specific wrongs, its willingness to say what without really asking why, or its tendency to portray the Crown as the sole active agent in the history of dispossession. Moreover, this is so even if most Canadians paid no attention to the offer. The offer remains a significant point of reference. While, as Ignatieff writes, the most gifted political leaders may "give their societies permission to say the unsayable, to think the unthinkable, to give rise to gestures of reconciliation that people, individually, cannot imagine,"[35] the effect of broad-brush government statements should be neither exaggerated nor minimized. Canadians do experience their history as a burden, only selectively available to them. Aboriginal communities live its legacy in brokenness and suspicion, most of it, indeed, directed internally. To offer reconciliation is to state for the record that a relationship has been ruptured and that the resulting estrangement needs to be overcome short of Aboriginal disappearance into mainstream society.

The most meaningful work of reconciliation, however, will lie in small, face-to-face initiatives for which the imperative is greatest where communities exist in close proximity. In a qualified way, I take Alan Cairns's point, though on a local and regional level, not a national one, that "those who share space together must share more than space" and that relations between them must be politically rather than legally mediated.[36] Paul Tennant has proposed something more germane in the land claims hothouse of British Columbia: namely, creative strategies for bilateral local diplomacy between municipalities and First Nations—"the art and practice of neighborliness"—based on mutual respect, "co-equality," common goals, and regularized channels of communication.[37] Such initiatives might readily be extended to schools and relevant community organizations. What they require is yet another kind of historical acknowledgement, not of wrongs, but of the sheer survival of Aboriginal communities with a degree of cultural continuity despite decades of government policy to the contrary. In other words, that means coming to terms with the reality of coexistence and of difference that must somehow be bridged by the practical work of understanding.

For me, the most familiar setting for such imperatives is the rural prairies—not only specific communities but also the province of Saskatchewan, given the estimates that Aboriginal people, Indian and Metis, will account for between one-third and one-half of its population within the next half century. Such a scenario must surely raise doubts for those policy "realists" who are confident that the future is on their side by force of numbers, if nothing else, and who dismiss talk of mutual respect in political relations as belonging to some prior century when rough parity prevailed. In Saskatchewan, rough parity *is* the future. Correspondingly, the dilemmas of reconciliation have as much to do with the future as the past; they are real enough. The province is not a wealthy one. Its economic core, agriculture, is in trouble. Its population is aging. Its tax base is not expanding enough to meet the demands for services, especially in health care, a problem which is exacerbated by the fact that status Indians are exempted from taxation on on-reserve and related income and, until recently, from provincial sales tax on purchases anywhere. Needless to say, taxation is already a political lightning rod for a range of resentments.[38]

Saskatchewan, however, provides only the most politically concentrated setting for what is a wider phenomenon across the rural prairies (and, indeed, rural Australia). I am certain that the position I am venturing will seem incredulous to many of the people who live there. For good reason: across North America, farmers have been the means and justification of colonial expansion, rivals for land, and symbols of a very different, proprietary and instrumental, relation to it. They are, after all, Locke's producers. Agrarian-populist culture, moreover, still ascribes honour and shame in relation to hard work and visible prosperity, and if that culture is hard on its own members, especially during times of financial stress, it is no less forgiving of "lazy" Aboriginal neighbours who appear to disregard the code altogether.[39] Its politics eschew pity and "welfare." It is readily aroused on grounds of equality over issues like Aboriginal hunting rights and, of late, the way in which Indians seem more successful than farm groups at prying money out of Ottawa. As one farmer told a radio talk-show, "we had our own treaty"—the "Crow" statutory grain transport rate—"and we had it taken away."

Not only that, as the rural economy contracts to fewer and fewer serv-ice centres, rural communities are characterized by a dramatically differ-ent demographic trajectory than that of Aboriginal communities. Their populations are declining or, at best, stable, and aging at that. They are threatened by the consolidation of schools and medical care in larger towns (while, on adjacent reserves, new facilities may be under construc-tion) and by the erosion of meaningful local authority (while the talk in Aboriginal circles is about self-government and co-management of resources). These differences are easy to draw. But they represent only part of the picture. And, increasingly, what comes to the fore may be the sim-ilarities, the common challenges, and the interdependencies between them. Rural and reserve-based Aboriginal communities, which are, of course, generally rural as well, are each significantly dependent on gov-ernment transfers—including pensions and a few professional incomes—and on the infusions of money that come with treaty land entitlement deals. Each lives with the fact that their brightest young people will leave for higher education and likely not return. Each is confronted with the limited opportunities of a global economy, where investment concentrates in cities, and where the rural places most desperate for employment bid against each other to absorb in a concentrated form the social and envi-ronmental messes of low-wage manufacturing, garbage dumps, toxic (even nuclear) waste, tire incineration, pulp mills, and massive hog barns. While the romanticized images of the pioneer, the rancher, or the costumed Indian are appropriated for big-city summer fairs and the festivities sur-rounding world-class sporting events, rural and Aboriginal people are now routinely perceived as parasites on the public purse. In the scolding phrase that is heard increasingly, they are unwilling to "move to where the jobs are." Government strategies will ease more farmers off the land; from time to time, though not so explicitly as in the US, that has been a policy goal for Aboriginal people too. In the new political economy, "the good citi-zen...is one who is mobile, who is willing to tear up all roots and follow the promptings of the job market."[40]

To portray rural and Aboriginal communities merely as partners in hardship and grievance—enjoined in a futile fight against some inevitable tide of history—would leave an overly pessimistic impression. There are also cultural correspondences that can be bridges for coexis-tence; without them, there would be no basis of understanding from which to deal with what are now flashpoints. For the most part, that common ground is still unappreciated and unexplored. On occasion, though, it appears in flashes of recognition, as in the classroom incident described above, or in the case of another student from redneck ranching country, who was shocked to discover that of all the essays generated from a conference on a contentious piece of federal conservation legislation, the one that rang truest to his situation was by an Aboriginal speaker. A provisional list of cultural correspondences might well include an understanding of the importance of multigenerational family identity—of inheritance—rooted to land and community, shaping something other than the "portable self" of urban modernity; and a relationship to nature as something other than playground or object. I do not want to make too great a claim for this brief list; it is distilled from conversations, mostly untested, and the risk in suggesting it at all is that it can be translated into another set of stereotypes that substitute for the complexity of real communities. But there is something to it. It constitutes part of the common ground for treaty *peoples* whose inheritance is filled with mixed blessings, and includes obligations of memory and relationship on all sides. It can nourish tentative steps in the "art and practice of neighbourliness," in *miyowicehtowin* (good relations) and *witaskiwin* (living together on the land).[41]

Notes

1 "Notes for an Address," Hon. Jane Stewart, minister of Indian Affairs and Northern Development, Ottawa, January 7, 1998. The government's full response is *Gathering Strength: Canada's Aboriginal Action Plan* (Ottawa: Minister of Supply and Services, 1998).

2 Ibid.

3 Royal Commission on Aboriginal Peoples, *Final Report*, vol. 1, *Looking Forward, Looking Back* (Ottawa: Minister of Supply and Services, 1996), quotations at 7-8, xxiv.

4 Ibid., 602.

5 Paul Bunner, "On the Brink," *Report Magazine*, October 25, 1999, 12-17.

6 *Vancouver Sun*, February 2, 1998, A1.

7 Ken Coates, *The Marshall Decision and Native Rights* (Montreal and Kingston: McGill-Queen's University Press, 2001), 169, 127.

8 "Portraits of Canada 2000," Centre for Research and Information on Canada, 8.

9 Bruce Wallace, "The Politics of Apology," *Maclean's*, January 19, 1998, 33.

10 Menno Boldt, *Surviving as Indians: The Challenge of Self-Government* (Toronto: University of Toronto Press, 1993), 18-21.

11 Tom Flanagan, *First Nations? Second Thoughts* (Montreal and Kingston: McGill-Queen's University Press, 2000). It is no surprise that Flanagan's book amplifies the ideas expressed in various iterations of the Reform Party's policy Blue Book in the 1990s. Indicatively, it makes one passing reference to residential schools.

12 In addition to anthologies of past judgements, see *Delgamuukw: The Supreme Court Decision on Aboriginal Title* (Vancouver: Douglas and McIntyre, 1998).

13 Taiaiake Alfred, *Peace, Power, Righteousness: An Indigenous Manifesto* (Don Mills, Ontario: Oxford University Press, 1999).

14 *Sovereign Injustice: Forcible Inclusion of the James Bay Crees and Cree Territory into a Sovereign Quebec* (Eeyou Astchee/Nemaska, Quebec: Grand Council of the Crees, 1995).

15 Alan Cairns, *Citizens Plus: Aboriginal Peoples and the Canadian State* (Vancouver: University of British Columbia Press, 2000).

16 Peter Nabokov, "Present Memories, Past History," in Calvin Martin, ed., *The American Indian and the Problem of History* (New York: Oxford University Press, 1987), 151.

17 The shorter, published version is Roger Epp, "At the Wood's Edge: Toward a Theoretical Clearing for Indigenous Diplomacies in International Relations," in Robert Crawford and Darryl Jarvis, eds., *International Relations—Still an American Social Science?* (Albany: State University of New York Press, 2001).

18 This story is told in Murray Mandryk, "Uneasy Neighbours: White-Aboriginal Relations and Agricultural Decline," in Roger Epp and Dave Whitson, eds., *Writing Off the Rural West? Globalization, Governments, and the Transformation of Rural Communities* (Edmonton: University of Alberta Press, 2001). See also Ken Coates's chapter on northern British Columbia in the same volume and, on New Brunswick, his *The Marshall Decision and Native Rights* (Montreal and Kingston: McGill-Queens University Press, 2001).

19 John Locke, *The Second Treatise of Government* (Indianapolis: Hackett, 1980), chap. V, para. 49.

20 Catherine McNicol Stock, *Rural Radicals: Righteous Rage in the American Grain* (Ithaca: Cornell University Press, 1996), chap. 1.

21 Locke, *The Second Treatise*, para. 37.

22 Emmerich Vattel, *The Law of Nations, or the Principles of Natural Law*, trans. Charles Fenwick (New York: Oceana Publications, repr. 1964), 7, 81, 207-209.

23 George Grant, *Technology and Empire: Perspectives on North America* (Toronto: House of Anansi, 1969), 17. Locke is a central figure in the essay cited.

24 Flanagan, *First Nations? Second Thoughts*, 39. See also Gordon Gibson, "A Principled Analysis of the Nisga'a Treaty," *Public Policy Sources*, a Fraser Institute Occasional Paper, Number 27 (1999), 12.

25 This point is compellingly made in James C. Scott, *Seeing Like a State* (New Haven: Yale University Press, 1998).

26 Epp, "At the Wood's Edge," 306-11, 313-14; C. Parry, ed., *Consolidated Treaty Series, 1648-1918*, 170 vol. (Dobbs Ferry, NY: Oceana Publications, 1969); Martin Wight, *International Theory: The Three Traditions*, ed. Brian Porter and Gabriele Wight (Leicester: Leicester University Press/Royal Institute of International Affairs, 1991), chap. 4.

27 Michael Ignatieff, *The Warrior's Honour: Ethnic War and the Modern Conscience* (Toronto: Penguin, 1998), quotations at 170, 167, 64.

28 Cairns, 8-9.

29 See, e.g., James (Sakej) Youngblood Henderson, "First Nations Legal Inheritances in Canada: The Mikmaq Model," *Manitoba Law Journal* 23 (1996): 1-31; Francis Jennings, ed., *The History and Culture of Iroquois Diplomacy* (Syracuse: Syracuse University Press, 1985); and Harold Cardinal and Walter Hildebrandt, *Treaty Elders of Saskatchewan* (Calgary: University of Calgary Press, 2000).

30 James Tully, "A Just Relationship between Aboriginal and Non-Aboriginal Peoples of Canada," in Curtis Cook and Juan Lindau, eds., *Aboriginal Rights and Self-Government* (Montreal and Kingston: McGill-Queen's University Press, 2000), 59.

31 Sheldon Wolin, *The Presence of the Past: Essays on the State and the Constitution* (Baltimore: Johns Hopkins University Press, 1989), chap. 2: "Injustice and Collective Memory"; chap. 8: "Contract and Birthright," quotations at 144-45, 37, 139.

32 Ibid., 137, 139, 146. This work is for newcomers too. The ethos I have in mind is expressed well in a different context, by a Welsh writer, anxious to instruct the many English retirees moving into her countryside, buying pastoral scenery at affordable prices: "When you move to an old house in the Welsh countryside, you are taking on more than a nice place to live, in a beautiful landscape. The siting of houses, the materials used to build them, and the people who lived there in the past, are all part of the continuing story of a locality, and a new owner has the responsibility to acknowledge this. One way is to try to understand the way of life, past and present, in these old houses, and their relationship with the broader sweep of history." Noragh Jones, *Living in Rural Wales* (Lnandysul, Wales: Corner Press, 1993), 281.

33 One such position is developed at length in Charles Taylor, *Sources of the Self: The Making of the Modern Identity* (Cambridge, MA: Harvard University Press, 1989), Part I.

34 See my essays, "The Measure of a River," *AlbertaViews*, March 2000, 45-51; and "Oklahoma: Meditations on Home and Homelessness," *Conrad Grebel Review* 16 (Winter 1998): 61-69.

35 Ignatieff, 188; Martha Merritt, "Forgiveness, Despite the Pressures of Sovereignty and Nationalism," in Jean Bethke Elshtain, *New Wine and Old Bottles: International Politics and Ethical Discourse* (Notre Dame: University of Notre Dame Press, 1998).

36 Cairns, 7.

37 Paul Tennant, "Delgamuukw and Diplomacy: First Nations and Municipalities in British Columbia," Paper presented to a conference of the Fraser Institute, Ottawa, 1999, quotation at 9. Tennant does not mean to shrink First Nations to the present status of municipalities ("undignified creatures kept on a rather short leash") but to enhance the political-legal status of each.

38 One optimistic initiative in this context is the Federation of Saskatchewan Indian Nations' report, *Saskatchewan and Aboriginal Peoples in the 21st Century: Social, Economic, and Political Changes and Challenges* (1997).

39 See Mandryk, "Uneasy Neighbours," and Cameron Harder, "Overcoming Cultural and Spiritual Obstacles to Rural Revitalization," both in *Writing Off the Rural West*, ed. Roger Epp and Dave Whitson (Edmonton: University of Alberta Press, 2001), 205-21 and 223-46.

40 Wolin, 45. This is precisely Flanagan's advice in *First Nations*.

41 Cardinal and Hildebrandt, 14, 39.

9

Toward a Response to Criticisms of the South African Truth and Reconciliation Commission

Wilhelm Verwoerd

Introduction

The Promotion of National Unity and Reconciliation Act (no. 34 of 1995) mandated the South African Truth and Reconciliation Commission (TRC) to (a) get as "complete a picture as possible" of the "nature, causes and extent" of the politically motivated gross human rights violations that occurred during the period of March 1, 1960 to May 10, 1994; (b) help restore the human and civil dignity of victims by granting them an opportunity to relate their own accounts of the violations of which they are victims; (c) grant amnesty to those individuals giving "full disclosure" of politically motivated crimes during this period of resistance to/defence of the apartheid system; (d) make recommendations to the president and parliament on reparation and rehabilitation measures to be taken, including measures in order to prevent the future commission of human rights violations. Under the chairpersonship of Archbishop Desmond Tutu, most of these tasks were completed after two-and-a-half years, by the end of June 1998. This included making findings on more than 36,000 alleged gross violations of human rights contained in around 20,300 statements taken from victims or survivors of these violations. A comprehensive, five-volume *Truth and Reconciliation Commission of South Africa Report* was handed to the president on October 28, 1998.[1] Upon completion of the amnesty part of the TRC process, an additional volume or "codicil" will be added to the TRC *Report*.

Notes to chapter 9 are on pp. 275-78.

In this paper I begin by describing the main criticisms encountered by the TRC. These criticisms highlight the difficulties and tensions surrounding a prominent part of the process of reconciliation in post-apartheid South Africa. Given a tendency by many outsiders to be too positive about the TRC, these criticisms are sobering reminders of the *dilemmas* of reconciliation.

The TRC process certainly proved to be a humbling experience. The many controversies, confusions, and criticisms accompanying this incomplete process of public, official acknowledgement highlight how difficult it is and will be to implement the vision contained in the preamble of South Africa's new Constitution, namely to "heal the divisions of the past and establish a society based on democratic values, social justice and fundamental human rights."

Some moral criticisms of the TRC process, however, go beyond the mere illumination of pitfalls on our post-apartheid "road to reconciliation." The "justice-based," "truth-based," and "reconciliation-based" criticisms described here pose deeply troubling, complex questions about the moral foundations of the TRC process. They threaten to overshadow the vital moral value at stake. Given my belief in the positive potential of the TRC process, I want to challenge the above-mentioned criticisms. I do not hereby want to deny the weaknesses of the TRC process. Obviously, the wide-ranging criticisms of a uniquely public and transparent process must be taken seriously—if only to ensure that other countries struggling to heal the divisions of their pasts learn from our mistakes. But here I want to focus, instead, on often-neglected weaknesses of these criticisms.

My response consists, first, of a general remark on the unavoidable messiness of any attempt to deal with large-scale human rights violations. Second, I reflect on a problem underlying most criticisms of the TRC, namely the lack of clarity about the "genre" of this particular process. Third, I focus on a prominent justice-based criticism in which concern is expressed about the TRC's sacrifice of retributive justice. I challenge this criticism from the perspective of restorative justice. Hopefully, I will thus help to make the critics think twice before they throw out the fragile TRC baby with the dirty bathwater of a politicized, imperfect process.

Criticisms of the TRC

A rough distinction can be made between justice-based, truth-based, and reconciliation-based criticisms.[2]

Justice-Based Criticisms

Justice-based criticisms can broadly be divided between those focussing on the *individual* rights of "victims" and/or "perpetrators" of human rights violations and those criticisms expressed in the name of *social* justice.

Individual Legal Justice

Rights of Victims

The following three cartoons clearly convey the widespread concern that justice, specifically "retributive" justice, was being "left out of the picture" by the TRC:

This cartoon was drawn early in the TRC process, at the time when the first round of "victim hearings"[3] took place. These hearings included heartrending testimony by those who suffered gross violations of human rights. These testimonies included references to a number of perpetrators, many of whom have applied for amnesty. Thus, as Tutu and Co. scaled the mountain of victims' skulls, many wanted to know: why are the guilty not being prosecuted and punished? Why are those responsible for these violations given the chance to walk free? Why does justice give the victims a cold shoulder?

One of the most prominent amnesty hearings concerned the application by Jeff Benzien, a former captain in the Western Cape security police. He became notorious for his highly effective "wet bag" "information-gathering" technique in his dealings with anti-apartheid activists. This method of torture involved sitting on top of a prisoner whose hands were tied behind his back, placing a wet bag over the head of the prisoner and smothering him until he "breaks" and begins to talk. Like all amnesty applicants, Benzien was required to make a "full disclosure" and convince the members of the amnesty committee that his actions had a "political objective."[4] At the hearing some of Benzien's victims insisted that he demonstrate—in the full glare of the media—this "wet bag" torture technique. Shortly afterwards the following cartoon appeared in print:

This cartoon paints another disturbing picture of amnesty. The Benzien cartoon takes us beyond a depiction of amnesty as an unjust bystander whose indifferent, disrespectful acts of omission add insult to victims' injuries. Amnesty also involves acts of commission: it strangles justice, it violates victims' rights to seek legal redress, it shocks onlookers by giving centre stage to prominent torturers.

The evil perpetrators in this cartoon are Brigadier Jack Cronje, captains Jaques Hecther and Roelf Venter, Warrant Officer Wouter Mentz, and Sergeant Paul van Vuuren. When their highly publicized amnesty hearings took place in 1996, the public was exposed for week after week to detailed disclosures of the forty-seven killings (amongst other violations) for which these five men from the former Northern Province Security Police Branch claimed responsibility.[5] They were granted amnesty in early February 1999.

In response, Grogan vividly articulates the widespread criticism of amnesty as the deeply problematic protection of perpetrators from punishment. This time the figure of retributive justice clearly does not accept being "left out of the TRC expedition." She is certainly not an unmoved bystander. Given the confidence in her judgement of the guilty, the blindfold is taken off. And, with righteous indignation written all over her face, Tutu can barely prevent her from implementing the harsh punishment Cronje and Co. deserve.

These cartoons capture what might be termed victim-oriented, individual justice-based criticisms. These criticisms arise from the emotional reaction to and moral concern about the fact that amnesty denied victims their right to seek redress through courts and prevented perpetrators from being punished.

Rights of (Alleged) Perpetrators

Natural Justice/Fair Procedures

There is another important set of criticisms deploring the TRC's "lack of justice." From the perspective of those who are accused of involvement in gross human rights violations, there is a troubling contrast between the impartiality and the procedural protection of the justice system and a Commission allowing, for example, untested allegations to be made in public human rights violation hearings. In the words of retired police commissioner General Johan van der Merwe: "We have been quite disappointed, especially with the committee investigating gross violations of human rights. The principles of natural justice are not being adhered to. There is no way we will be able to say afterwards that justice has prevailed."[6] Underlying this criticism is a difficult balancing act constantly faced by the TRC: satisfying the public interest in the exposure of wrongdoing while ensuring fair treatment of those accused of wrongdoing, balancing the victims' right to know who violated them with the fundamental importance of due process.

The next cartoon illustrates the price many victims had to pay in the name of "natural justice." In a number of cases (black) victims were prevented by alleged (white) perpetrators to mention their names at the public hearings in which victims were given a dignified space to at last be heard and acknowledged. Some prominent former members of the security police took the TRC to court, demanding the right to cross-examine, to be notified in advance, etc. What made their successful resort to the courts such a bitter pill to swallow was the fact that some of these perpetrators later applied for amnesty in connection with the same violations they prevented their victims from speaking about.[7]

Accountability

One of the problematic, unintended outcomes of the TRC process is criticized in this cartoon:

The publicity surrounding the TRC's narrow focus on "gross violations of human rights," i.e., on those perpetrators who killed, tortured, abducted, and severely ill-treated political "enemies," made it very tempting to blame the sins of the past on a few exceptionally "bad eggs."[8]

The next cartoon is even more explicit:

The main actors in this cartoon are Colonel Eugene de Kock and former State President P.W. Botha. De Kock, also known as "Prime Evil," was the commander of a very notorious security police hit squad based at a farm called "Vlakplaas." On the sun is written "Total Strategy," which refers to the policy used by the previous government to justify its actions against the "Total Onslaught" by ANC "terrorists" and "communists."

These cartoons, amongst many others, raise the question about the fair allocation of blame/accountability between operatives and politicians, between those who applied policies and those who made policies to deal with political enemies.[9]

Social Justice

Many critics were not only using "justice" in the relatively narrow sense of prosecution and punishment of individual perpetrators through the formal justice system. Take, for example, the following cartoon:

The TRC held hearings on different sectors of South African society, such as the media, the legal system, faith communities, the business sector, and their respective relationships with the system of apartheid (TRC Report, vol. 4). At the time of the business hearing, there was a lot of debate about the desirability of a reparation tax on those who benefited from apartheid. This debate was linked to wider concerns about the lack of emphasis on social justice within the TRC process.

For example, representatives of communities that have been impoverished through forced removals asked the TRC, "why are you excluding us, we are also victims of Apartheid,"[10] or the allocation of very scarce resources to the TRC was challenged—"just think how many houses could've been built with the millions the state is spending on the TRC!" This criticism of the TRC has been eloquently expressed by an old township woman attending a TRC public meeting in the Grahamstown Town Hall, on February 17, 1997. "Your lives have changed," she said, addressing the TRC spokespersons. Pointing to their double-breasted suits, she continued, "it is all right for you to forgive and embrace the perpetrators of heinous crimes for the sake of reconciliation. Indeed it's all right for

Nelson Mandela to forgive since his life has also changed. But our lives have not changed. We still live in the same shacks or matchbox houses....How can we forgive if our lives have not changed?" This question echoes the more academic formulation by Mahmood Mamdani:

> The negotiated settlement began with an attempt to articulate a notion of justice within the broader framework of "reconciliation." It was a programme that highlighted a RDP [Reconstruction and Development Programme], land redistribution, and affirmative action. From this beginning, however, we have moved along a trajectory that has de-emphasised justice in the interest of reconciliation and realism, both local and international. The changing framework increasingly corresponds to the terms of reference of the Truth and Reconciliation Commission, whereby injustice is no longer the injustice of apartheid: forced removals, pass laws, broken families. Instead, the definition of injustice has come to be limited to abuses within the legal framework of apartheid: detention, torture, murder. Victims of apartheid are narrowly defined as those militants victimised as they struggled against apartheid, not those whose lives were mutilated in the day-to-day web of regulations that was apartheid....If reconciliation is to be durable, would it not need to be aimed at society (beneficiaries and victims) and not simply at the fractured political elite (perpetrators and victims)?[11]

These various justice-based criticisms confirm the fact that the concept of justice in ordinary life and language functions mainly as a (passionate) protest against wrongdoing as well as a demand for rectification.[12] For many, the TRC granting amnesty is not the right response; it stands in stark contrast to the punishment, repudiation, protection of society, redress for victims, and due process provided by the formal justice system. For others, neither the TRC nor the justice system goes far enough in dealing with the wrongs, the widespread socio-economic inequalities resulting from an apartheid past.

Truth-Based Criticisms
The "hole" truth?

While there were gaps in all submissions by political parties, this cartoon reflects widespread frustration with the quality, in particular, of the

National Party's submission to the TRC. F.W. de Klerk, as the solitary figure representing the NP, is a true reflection of what actually happened. In
contrast to the ANC's high-level delegation, all of whom participated in the
presentation and answering of questions, the NP brought a smaller delegation and it was only De Klerk that spoke. This made it difficult to distinguish between his role as leader of the "new," post-1994 National Party
and his former roles as state president, cabinet minister under P.W. Botha,
member of the State Security Council, etc. In the absence of those who
should have taken joint responsibility and helped to explain the "motives
and perspectives" of the "old" NP, many expectations were unmet and
questions unanswered. This helps to explain the picture of an insincere
submission with a big hole in the middle.

The problem of "holes" in the truth also characterized many institutional submissions to and individual testimonies before the TRC. This
applied in particular to a number of amnesty applications.

Tip of the Truth

In a number of cases the TRC has been successful in exhuming the bones
of activists, buried in secret graves, often on farms used by the security
police. The Commission not only—literally—uncovered the truth in
these cases but also promoted "reconciliation" in the dictionary sense of
"coming to terms with a painful truth." By facilitating dignified reburials
families were helped, at last, to lay haunting uncertainties about "disappeared" loved ones to rest.

The fact that there are still more than two hundred known cases, excluding those outside South Africa, which the Commission was unable to deal with in its short lifetime, helps to explain Tutu's agonizing response to the TRC investigator's finger: "You mean this is just the tip?!"

The TRC was required to come up with as "complete a picture as possible" about certain categories of violations within a particular period of time. However, in many ways the TRC was unsuccessful in uncovering much of the truth. It was relatively successful in dealing with security police operations, but made limited progress in uncovering many activities of the military, especially outside the borders of South Africa. Even though the Commission made progress as far as a significant group of violations is concerned, it clearly was not very successful in terms of a whole range of other issues. The whole truth has not been told as far as the violations falling within the TRC's mandate is concerned. If one adds to this the many, many deaths and other violations that did not fall within the Commission's narrow mandate—for example, the continuing, slow deaths from enforced poverty under apartheid, or the deaths of vulnerable farm workers in many rural parts of the country where apartheid power relationships are still alive and kicking—then it becomes even more obvious that the TRC has indeed only scratched the surface of the whole truth about past human rights violations in Southern Africa. Indeed, the mere tip of the "apartheid skull" has been exposed.[13]

The previous two cartoons deal primarily with the question of factual, historical truth. They point to the limitations of an institution such as a

Truth Commission to achieve a full picture of the historical truth about past human rights violations. The next cartoon tells a different story. It highlights the criticism that the TRC was basically a handmaiden of the African National Congress, the current governing party, and was biased against the former regime of the National Party.

Partial, Biased "Truth"?

This was a typical representation of the TRC in the prominent NP-aligned Afrikaans newspaper, *Die Burger*. Tutu and Boraine became evil inquisitors of the poor victim, the National Party. Thus a party very much associated with being the main perpetrators of abuses under apartheid found it possible to depict its members as victims of an "ANC-inspired witch hunt." Alex Boraine asks "Are you hurting?" and the man on the rack answers "No, no, only when I laugh." Written on this torture rack is "BIEGBANK," which literally means "Confession Couch." The word "bieg" means "confession," but in a predominantly Protestant community it has a strong Roman Catholic overtone. The picture of the TRC as "enforced confession" became a powerful tool to alienate Afrikaners from this process. Note also how Tutu was depicted. At the beginning of the process he was more or less normal with clean glasses and having quite a normal face, but as the process went on and NP supporters became more and more critical, Tutu was progressively demonized. The glasses became dark, giving a sort of gangster-type image, and if you see his feet in other cartoons he would wear long, witch-like shoes. So they really explicitly demonized the chairperson of the TRC—a person most other people would find it rather difficult to see as a representative of the devil.

Various other cartoons also reflect this perception of a pro-ANC bias on the side of the TRC. This perception, especially within white and coloured communities and supporters of the Inkatha Freedom Party, was confirmed by a number of opinion polls during the lifetime of the TRC. From this perspective the main problem is not the "holes" and half-truths in the submissions of many of those appearing before the TRC, but the TRC's own lack of impartiality.[14]

Moral Truth

An important task, perhaps even the most important task, of the TRC was to contribute to the "restoration of the moral order" in post-apartheid South Africa, to help "recover the soul of the nation," to nurture a fragile culture of respect for human rights and human dignity. This task required the TRC to make a number of difficult moral judgements. Not surprisingly, these judgements became the source of another category of criticisms.[15]

The next cartoon draws attention to the controversy surrounding the TRC's allocation of moral blame between the liberation movements and the previous state.

For some, the TRC's findings on victims of gross human rights violations—as part of its attempt to help "restore the civil and human dignity of victims" and to "promote national unity and reconciliation"—were too "inclusive." By treating all individual victims equally, the TRC allegedly failed to make the necessary moral distinctions between those who fought a "just war" against apartheid and those who upheld a system declared internationally to be a "crime against humanity." It was claimed that the TRC's victim findings and conclusions on culpability threw the net of moral blame too widely and obscured the moral truth about the past. For example, according to prominent ANC representatives, including President Thabo Mbeki, the TRC's findings on ANC accountability for certain gross human rights violations "criminalized the liberation struggle" by "equating the ANC's actions with those of the apartheid regime."[16]

More generally, the TRC was criticized for its apparent overemphasis on moral evil. For example, appearing under the heading "Tutu's Report Tells the Truth but Not the Whole Truth," Jeremy Cronin's review criticizes the report for focusing too much on "the little perpetrator" inside each of us. He is concerned that not enough room was given to celebrate the struggle, the "'little freedom fighter,' the collective self-emancipator that we all could be." He asks, "what about the 'humanist,' ubuntu-filled ways of crossing the bridge" instead of only "recognizing the potential for evil in each one of us"?[17]

On the other hand, it was also felt that the TRC's "spirit of understanding"[18] went too far in its respect for the moral goodness, the essential humanity of perpetrators of gross human rights violations. The next cartoon clearly conveys this sentiment:

Reconciliation-Based Criticisms

Truth AND Reconciliation?

The following cartoon, drawn as the TRC was about to start its work in December 1995, suggests a rather optimistic belief that the TRC's exposure of truth, its "opening up of festering wounds" would promote reconciliation.

Eighteen months later—after hundreds of public testimonies by victims, detailed disclosures by a number of perpetrators, and deep tensions between the TRC and the National Party—this is the much less confident depiction of the link between "Truth" and "Reconciliation":

Some of the reasons for this gap is the perception in the black community that whites don't really care about black victims; a lack of trust in the TRC's commitment to the promotion of reconciliation, primarily within the white Afrikaner community; and confusion between amnesty, forgiveness, and reconciliation. These reasons are illustrated by the following cartoons.

"Where Are the Whites?"

Some reconciliation-based criticisms were mainly directed at the response, or rather the lack of responsiveness, of "white South Africa" to the TRC process. The next two cartoons echo the widespread question from black South Africans: "where are the whites?"

A few months later Zapiro moved from his sharply satirical picture of "white South Africa"—as an isolated, potbellied, beer drinking, middle-aged, male couch potato who hears, but does not listen—to this warning of the detrimental impact of this indifference to TRC revelations on race relationships in South Africa:

The rainbow—with colours all blending together to produce a beautiful whole—has probably become the guiding metaphor to inspire people with a positive sense of different colours and communities working together in post-apartheid South Africa. But the cartoon plays on the separateness of those colours—and in particular the distance between the two ends: white and black.

CURRENT STATE OF

The Rainbow Nation *

Red   Orange Yellow Green Blue   Indigo Violet

*Anyone who knows how to join the dots, write to: Pres. N. Mandela Union Building Pretoria

Black

White

TRC

ZAPIRO

Thus the perceived white response to TRC revelations—sitting back, drinking another beer and watching rugby, i.e., continuing the same comfortable lifestyle—rubbed salt into the wounds of black survivors.

Promoting Reconciliation or Revenge?

The mandate of the TRC was framed by the post-amble to the Interim Constitution (Act 200 of 1993).[19] This epilogue included the following statements, under the heading "National Unity and Reconciliation":

> The adoption of this Constitution lays the secure foundation for the people of South Africa to transcend the divisions and strife of the past, which generated gross violations of human rights, the transgression of humanitarian principles in violent conflicts and a legacy of hatred, fear, guilt and revenge.
>
> These can now be addressed on the basis that there is a need for understanding but not for vengeance, a need for reparation but not for retaliation, a need for ubuntu but not for victimization.

However, from the perspective of many white South Africans, mainly in the Afrikaans-speaking community, the TRC worsened the "legacy of revenge." This perception is reflected in a number of cartoons that appeared mostly in *Die Burger*, including this graphic one:

A devious (demonic?) Tutu, poking a huge sword of "RETRIBU-TION" in the back of a noble-looking figure, an Afrikaner businessman, saying: "Give NOW…before you might have nothing left to give! (After we have taken everything)." Behind Tutu the placard reads: TRC ACT: REC-ONCILIATION NOT REVENGE.[20]

Reconciliation, Forgiveness, Amnesty

Another subset of criticisms highlights the contested and confusing concep-tual and moral links between "reconciliation," "forgiveness," and "amnesty."

Sometimes this kind of criticism was directed at the apparent Christian bias/basis of the TRC's interpretation of its mandate. The prominent role of emeritus Archbishop Tutu—presiding over hearings in full clerical attire, with the Christian cross prominently displayed around his neck, opening proceedings with a (Christian) prayer, often making passionate pleas for victims and other people to forgive—has been a source of criticism.[21]

Many people both inside and outside the TRC warned against expect-ing too much too soon from the reconciliation process at a national level. They were concerned about the imposition of a too-strong notion of rec-onciliation (closely associated with emotional encounters between indi-viduals and Christian notions of confession, contrition, forgiveness and restitution)—on a diverse and divided society trying to consolidate a frag-ile democracy.[22] Accordingly, some argued that the most one can and should hope for, at least in the short term, is "peaceful co-existence." Oth-ers, including most prominently Archbishop Desmond Tutu, cautioned against accepting an unduly limited notion of reconciliation. They believed that apologies by individuals and group representatives, and forgiveness on the part of victimized individuals and groups were vitally important for national reconciliation.[23] A nation attempting to "transcend the divisions and strife of the past" had a "legacy of hatred, fear, guilt and revenge."[24] The need to deal with these attitudes and feelings should not be underestimated.[25]

The tendency to conflate "reconciliation" and "forgiveness" helps to explain a further confusion between amnesty and forgiveness, reflected in the following cartoon:

The punch line of the cartoon is the criticism of the lack of remorse shown by most amnesty applicants. However, this picture also draws attention to a number of confusions that contributed to the perception of a "perpetrator-friendly" process. First, amnesty—granted "in order to advance reconciliation…between the people of South Africa"[26]—is equated with asking for forgiveness. Second, in the cartoon it is Tutu, on behalf of the TRC, who is receiving this plea—despite the fact that requests for amnesty were received by the Amnesty Committee, which was run basically by judges and whose decisions could not be overturned by the rest of the TRC.

Given Tutu's strong association with a Christian notion of reconciliation, in which forgiveness plays a large role, and given the equation of the head of the TRC with the work of one of its committees, many people came to think that by granting amnesty, the TRC was actually forgiving these perpetrators on behalf of the state and the rest of society.

Thus, the troubling perception was created that amnesty not only "obliterated" victims' rights to seek legal redress but also robbed victims of their moral right to forgive or to withhold forgiveness. Or if amnesty did not actually usurp victims' right to forgive, the framing of amnesty by the need to "advance reconciliation," coupled with Tutu's zeal for forgiveness, was perceived as at least putting undue moral pressure on victims to forgive. As Kalukwe Mawila, a young black South African, put it to me:

> What really makes me angry about the TRC and Tutu is that they are putting pressure on us to forgive. For most black South Africans the TRC is about us having to forgive. People I know don't make subtle distinctions between reconciliation and forgiveness. I don't know if I will ever be ready to forgive. I carry this ball of anger inside me and I don't even know where to begin dealing with it. The oppression was bad, but what is much worse, what makes me even more angry is that they are trying to dictate my forgiveness.[27]

Toward a Response

Expect Messiness

When one is dealing with serious wrongdoing on a large scale, when a society is trying to deal with "radical evil,"[28] with widespread gross human rights violations, with mass violence, it is important to remind ourselves of the inadequacy of any response. In her book *Between Vengeance and Forgiveness: Facing History after Genocide and Mass Violence*, which includes a wide-ranging discussion of the strengths and weaknesses of trials, truth commissions, reparation measures, etc., Martha Minow gives a sobering warning to anyone engaged in a process of responding to "collective violence":

> I do not seek precision here; nor do I mean to imply that we can wrap up these issues with analysis or achieve a sense of completion…no response can ever be adequate when your son has been killed by police ordered to shoot at a crowd of children; when you have been dragged out of your home, interrogated, and raped…; or when your brother who struggled against a repressive government has disappeared and left only a secret police file, bearing no clue to his final resting place. Closure is not possible. Even if it were, any closure would insult those whose lives are forever ruptured.[29]

This warning to expect messiness, no matter which institutional response one chooses, is highly relevant to any interpretation of the TRC process. Coming to terms with particular tensions emerging from the TRC process partly involves a more general ability to deal with the unavoidable tensions, the lack of tidiness involved in any response to large scale evil. In other words, some of the trouble many people have with the TRC process is a product of their own, unrealistic expectations. Many critics underestimate the inherent limitations of a process, which Mahomed DP accurately described as follows:

> The granting of amnesty is a difficult, sensitive, perhaps even agonising, balancing act between the need for justice to victims of past abuse and the need for reconciliation and rapid transition to a new future; between encouragement to wrongdoers to help in the discovery of the truth and the need for reparations for the victims of that truth; between a correction in the old and the creation of the new. It is an exercise of immense difficulty interacting in a vast network of political, emotional, ethical and logistical considerations.[30]

Clarifying the Genre of the TRC Process[31]

With the benefit of hindsight it is clear that some of the criticisms of the TRC process could have been avoided by institutional redesign (e.g., giving the TRC more power to implement tangible reparation and resources for therapeutic support, or more resources to explain the complex workings and limitations of the TRC to the general public, or a separate committee on reconciliation). Other problems accompanying the TRC process (e.g., unrealistic reparation expectations of victims appearing before the TRC, the handling of particular amnesty decisions, findings procedures, etc.) should be placed before the commission's own door. I believe, however, that much of the criticism and confusion surrounding the TRC process is a sign of a deeper problem, namely a lack of consensus about what can and cannot reasonably be expected from this bold experiment in responding to (some of) the wrongs of our past.

We are still groping for the language to adequately assess the significance of the TRC.[32] Therefore we struggle to distinguish the TRC process from and link it to other means of recognizing past injustices and "laying the foundations for a democratic and open society," such as the Reconstruction and Development Programme, the Land Claims court, and certain cases handled by the criminal justice system (e.g., the trials of Eugene de Kock and Freddie Barnard). Archbishop Tutu formulated this point in his own inimitable fashion:

> One of the first lessons we learned in dealing with biblical literature was asking "what is its literary type or genre?" because once you knew the answer to that question we would not pose inappropriate questions of the literary piece, expecting it to provide information it was never designed to furnish. So, for instance, if when reading Wordsworth's poem "Daffodils," and encountering the lines "When all at once I saw a crowd,/ A host, of golden daffodils...dancing in the breeze," you were to ask, "by the way, which band was playing?" or, "who were the dancing partners?" you would have missed the bus quite comprehensively.

Tutu went on to claim that many people have made the same sort of mistake about the TRC. For example, expecting the TRC to follow the same procedures as a court of law "They accused the TRC of allowing wild allegations to stand untested and unchallenged. They did not seem to understand when we said, especially of the victim hearings, that the primary purpose was to give people who have been silenced so long the opportunity of telling their story in a sympathetic setting which was victim-friendly, as required by the Act."[33]

I agree with the Archbishop that the standards of procedural justice to protect the rights of the accused within a temporary, investigative institution such as the TRC should not be judged by those applicable to the criminal justice system.[34] And I would add that the limited potential "healing" of victims appearing at a single, public hearing should not be evaluated with an intimate, long-term therapeutic relationship in mind; nor should the promotion of "national unity and reconciliation" be measured by the yardstick of interpersonal reconciliation between particular victims and perpetrators.[35]

But first lessons first. Let me therefore begin to clarify what Archbishop Tutu helpfully termed the "genre" of the TRC process. A useful point of departure is Ricoeur's "simple and transparent" answer to this basic question: why do we remember past injustices? "We must remember because remembering is a *moral duty*. We owe a *debt* to the victims. And the tiniest way of paying our debt is to tell and retell what happened [to them]....We have learned from the Greek storytellers and historians that the admirable deeds of the heroes needed to be remembered and thus called for narration. We learn from a Jewish storyteller like [Elie] Wiesel that the horrible—the inverted image of the admirable—needs to be rescued still more from forgetfulness by the means of memory and narration."[36]

This perhaps too simple answer helps me to focus more clearly on the strengths and inherent limitations of the TRC process. It broadly defines the genre of this process. One might say that the TRC was required to act mostly like a Jewish and not a Greek storyteller. In other words, the partial fulfillment of our moral duty to remember the victims and to rescue the horrible from forgetfulness should be the primary lenses through which we read this complex process. In the words of Antjie Krog: "For me the Truth Commission microphone with its little red light was the ultimate symbol of the whole process: here the marginalized voice speaks to the public ear, the unspeakable is spoken—and translated—the personal story brought from the innermost of the individual to bind us anew to the collective."[37]

Krog is referring to the so-called "victim hearings," where the trauma of survivors of specified categories of gross human rights violations were given centre stage. But her description can to some extent also be applied to the public hearings of the Amnesty Committee, where the little red light is still flickering, perhaps more brightly; where often "the unspeakable is spoken," translated and recorded "so that these horrors will never be forgotten."[38]

Some of the facts and the findings emerging from these "victim" and "perpetrator" hearings are and will be challenged by lawyers and historians. Given the higher standards of evidence they should work with (under fewer time and resource constraints), I would expect some of these criticisms to help us move closer to more reliable factual and historical truth about particular aspects of the period covered by the TRC mandate. But the limitations of the TRC's search for factual truth should not obscure the vital moral truths gathered by this process. Truths about moral *evils*, about past *injustices*, about *gross* human rights *violations*. In other words, the genre of the TRC story is primarily a "morality of the depths," specifying "the line beneath which no one is allowed to sink,"[39] concentrating on minimum protections for human dignity, emphasizing minimum standards of decency.[40] The eyes of the TRC were mostly not on the moral "heights," on our potential to soar highly—doing good, playing and laughing, fighting for freedom and happiness, flourishing as individuals, communities, and a nation. Still, the TRC's limited focus on what happens if human rights are *not* respected is of great potential significance, especially for our children and their children. For this painful process gave us some of the tools to build probably the most effective bulwark against future violations.[41] That is, the TRC window on some grievous wrongs of the past provides us with invaluable raw material for nurturing a culture of human rights.[42] By holding up a painful, powerful mirror the TRC process and *Report* confronted all of us with our frightening potential for evil. In the words of then deputy president Thabo Mbeki: "And because some decided neither to see nor to hear, we can, today, hear the stories told at the Truth and Reconciliation Commission that speak of a level and extent of human depravity that could never have heard the meaning or been moved by the poetry of the words, umntu, ngumntu ngabantu! [people are people through other people]."[43]

Mbeki went on to link the work of the TRC with a call for us to "recover" our "soul" as a nation. "The political order that tore our country apart is now no more. Yet it gave us a bitter heritage, which we must strive to overcome. Above all else we must create the situation in which the soul can sing and louder sing to restore a social morality that says the pursuit of material gain at all costs is not and cannot be what distinguishes us as South Africans; [we must create] a patriotism that is imbued by love and respect for the fellow citizen, regardless of race, colour, gender or age, and a recognition of our common humanity."[44]

His call to enable our national soul "to sing and louder sing" was an extension of the following beautiful imagery in W.B. Yeats's "Sailing to Byzantium":

> An aged man is but a paltry thing
> A tattered coat upon a stick, unless
> Soul clap its hands and sing, and louder sing
> For every tatter in its mortal dress.[45]

Perhaps Yeats's imagery may be even further extended to throw light on the fragile deeper meanings of the TRC process: the public victim hearings provided spaces for singing—where we could sing sad songs for some of the biggest tears in our "mortal dress," where we could lament some of the scars in our body politic. The TRC process gave us opportunities to clap hands, softly, for those who have survived....But it was also a place to refrain from singing. To listen, respectfully, in silence. A place to cover our face in shame for our moral blindness and deafness to the suffering of fellow South Africans, in the past and in the present. In the salutary words of President Mandela from a speech in the National Assembly on April 15, 1997: "All of us, as a nation that has newly found itself, share in the shame at the capacity of human beings of any race or language group to be inhumane to other human beings. We should all share in the commitment to a South Africa in which that will never happen again."

This moral significance of the TRC process might, however, be undermined by too little consensus on the genre of the TRC process. I have referred before to Jeremy Cronin's criticism under the headline "Tutu's Report Tells the Truth but Not the Whole Truth" (*Sunday Independent*, November 15, 1998). Cronin, a prominent leader in the SACP, is of course not the only one asking questions about the place of anti-apartheid heroes and liberation fighters in the TRC process. My sense is that these questions are pointing to very important dimensions of our constitutional commitment to "honour those who suffered for justice and liberation," but they miss the bus, as Archbishop Tutu warned, with regard to the central moral significance of the TRC process. I believe these comments from editorials in the *Mail & Guardian* between November 6 and 12, 1998, are closer to the truth about the TRC:

> The final report could be described as the founding document of the new South Africa....The term "founding document" is more commonly used to describe a country's Constitution. And there are grounds for pride in the South African Constitution....But, for all that, the Constitution is a theoretical exercise, in large part the product of intellectual effort in the

ivory towers of academia. The final report, in a very real and immediate way, defines us. With all its horrors, it is the earthly product of the blood and tears attendant on a difficult birth. It is a testament to the equality of man, if more in the disregard for the tenets of humanity than the observance of them. In a sense it bestows the legitimacy of experience on the Constitution, which might otherwise seem remote to our society.

Sacrificing the Rights of Individual Victims?[46]

The Preamble of the Constitution begins with: "We, the people of South Africa, Recognize the injustices of our past; Honour those who suffered for justice and freedom in our land." How can this place of honour for those "who suffered for justice" be reconciled with the sacrifice of justice via amnesty? More specifically, where does a "perpetrator-friendly" amnesty process fit into a "victim-driven" TRC process? With the right hand of its Human Rights Violations hearings and the Final Report, the TRC has tried to contribute to the healing of wounds, but with the left hand of amnesty it appears to (unintentionally) be rubbing salt into those wounds!

Pragmatic considerations concerning the nature of South Africa's "negotiated revolution" are often emphasized in defense of amnesty. In the words of a key architect of the TRC, Minister Kader Asmal: "We sacrifice justice, because the pains of justice might traumatise our country or effect the transition. We sacrifice justice for truth so as to consolidate democracy, to close the chapter of the past and to avoid confrontation."[47] Dr. Alex Borraine, deputy chairperson of the TRC, seems to agree: "amnesty is the price we had to pay for peace and stability."[48]

This kind of pragmatic defence is morally inadequate given the weighty principles sacrificed through the amnesty process. The justice-based criticism under consideration here does articulate the deeply troubling moral issues raised by the Amnesty provisions in the Act. I. Mahomed, DP, recognized the legitimacy of the moral intuition underlying this criticism as follows: "Every decent human being must feel grave discomfort in living with a consequence which might allow the perpetrators of evil acts to walk the streets of this land with impunity, protected in their freedom by an amnesty from constitutional attack."[49]

He also correctly characterized the focus of the moral concern as the "effective obliteration" of the fundamental human rights of individuals to protection by the State and to seek redress for harms suffered:

> The effect of an amnesty undoubtedly impacts upon very fundamental rights. All persons are entitled to the protection of the law against unlawful invasions of their right to life, their right to respect for and protection of dignity and their right not to be subject to torture of any kind. When those rights are invaded those aggrieved by such invasions have the right to obtain redress in the ordinary courts of law and those guilty of perpetrating such violations are answerable before such courts, both civilly and criminally. An amnesty to the wrongdoer effectively obliterates such rights.[50]

Given these fundamental issues, the ground on which adequate justifications stand should be very firm. Typical consequentialist justifications do not pass this test, neither do appeals to truth or reconciliation as even greater goods. This is not the place to support these claims with detailed arguments. Here I want to focus on a most promising type of response,[51] a response that meets the criticism on its own ground. It is a less defensive response—contained in the TRC Report—that challenges some of the assumptions underlying the justice-based criticism, by claiming a strong connection between "restorative justice" and the TRC.

In the TRC Report "restorative justice" is broadly defined as a process that:

> (a) seeks to redefine crime: it shifts the primary focus of crime from the breaking of laws or offences against a faceless state to a perception of crime as violations against human beings, as injury or wrong done to another person;
> (b) is based on reparation: it aims at the healing and the restoration of all concerned—of victims in the first place, but also of offenders, their families, and the larger community;
> (c) encourages victims, offenders, and the community to be directly involved in resolving conflict, with the state and legal professionals acting as facilitators;
> (d) supports a criminal justice system that aims at offender accountability, full participation of both the victims and offenders, and making good or putting right the wrong.[52]

In contrast to retributive justice—where the first question is "How do we punish this offender?"—restorative justice asks, "How do we restore the well-being of the victim, the community and the offender?" At the heart of this approach to crime and punishment is not the isolated (and isolating) imprisonment of the individual lawbreaker but the future well-being of the society, the *reintegrative* punishment of offenders. A growing number of practitioners and theoreticians are convinced that restorative justice offers better opportunities to meet the needs of victims, offenders, and the community at large than punishment under the current, conventional criminal justice system.[53] Victims become key participants;, they are placed in the centre of the justice process. They are given the opportunity to work constructively through the facts and feelings surrounding the crime against them, rather than becoming spectators or state witnesses with very little if any input into and no control over the prosecution of the offender(s)—who have already (severely) harmed the victims' sense of control over their lives.

Offenders are not necessarily put behind bars. By removing criminals from society and the victims, this form of punishment might bring temporary protection, but it also separates offenders from the effects of their crimes. This isolation tends to harden the "arteries of emotion," it encourages rationalization and the denial of guilt and responsibility resulting in many criminals becoming worse offenders once they leave prison. Reintegrative punishment tries to bring shame and personal and family/community responsibility back into the justice process: instead of just "doing my time," offenders—through negotiated community responses—are given opportunities to understand and acknowledge their crimes, to take responsibility and make things right.

So restorative justice can be seen as a community-based, negotiated, more democratic form of justice, with responsible reconciliation seen as the best prevention. This stands in marked contrast to the typical criminal justice imposed by the state (on behalf of the victim and the community), strong on repudiation but with questionable effectiveness in terms of long-term protection and especially rehabilitation. Conventional criminal justice is also not equipped to deal with situations where the state itself has been involved in criminal activities. This requires a broader conception of rehabilitation and (moral) responsibility. This broader conception forms part of the notion of restorative justice.

At first sight there is clearly a close relationship between a conception of justice that subordinates sanctioning to the goals of healing and reconciliation and a Truth and Reconciliation Commission that shares these aims:

- The TRC has been an attempt to avoid a (short-term, gut-level) retributive punitive response to crime, to laws which have been broken. The work of the TRC, which includes painting "as complete a picture as possible of the causes, nature, and extent of gross human rights violations," provides us with an opportunity to grapple with the shortcomings of a retributive criminal justice philosophy and to think creatively about ways to overcome some of the problems plaguing (preventative) punishment in the form of imprisonment.
- The TRC process gave much more prominence to victims of gross human rights violations than would have been the case in the conventional criminal justice system. More than seventy public human rights violation hearings were held across the length and breadth of South Africa, granting hundreds of people the opportunity to "relate their own accounts of the violations of which they are the victim." Section 11 of the Act also provided explicit guidelines to commissioners to ensure that victims are treated with great respect, thus helping "to restore their human and civil dignity."
- The TRC focused on not only the narrow legal responsibility of individual offenders, but also on the more far-reaching moral responsibility of individual perpetrators, political parties, the previous state, and other key sectors of South African society.
- The TRC tried to involve the community/civil society/citizens to a much larger extent than the conventional justice system—from selection of Commissioners through to public hearings, statement taking, follow-up support after hearings, and the formulation of a Reparations and Rehabilitation policy and recommendations.
- The TRC also took a long-term perspective to the healing of the effects of (gross) human rights violations. It does not promise a quick fix of the damage, but by helping to put a history and a human face on the crimes of our (political) past the TRC aimed to contribute to a process of reconciliation.
- With its focus on "nation-building," on the well-being of the community, and on individual and social reparation, the TRC challenged some of the weaknesses of typical human rights doctrines: too much emphasis on the individual, and too little attention given to the duties and responsibilities accompanying rights claims.[54]

However, the vision of restorative justice also challenges the TRC process, especially as far as the issue of amnesty is concerned. Restorative justice is not a soft option. It is indeed critical of a retributive focus on punishment as a goal in itself, especially when this punishment takes the form of (isolating) imprisonment. However, the fact that restorative justice is primarily concerned with reconciliation does not mean that appropriate penalties and sanctions do not play a very important role, particularly as far as serious offences are concerned. Restorative justice tries to involve the victims, the community, and the formal justice system in the response to wrongdoing; it moves beyond the enforcement of a narrow conception of criminal guilt and legal responsibility and attempts to restore a real sense of shame and responsibility within the perpetrator.

This means that both retributive and restorative conceptions of justice highlight the problematic nature of amnesty, of pardoning instead of (some form of) appropriate punishment. The difference is that whereas retributive justice opts for "just justice" as the alternative to amnesty, restorative justice aims at the goal of responsible reconciliation. What does this mean for the TRC?

The fact that a "different kind of amnesty" is implemented—i.e., no blanket pardoning, publishing of names and offences, etc.—does bring the TRC closer to restorative justice. However, tensions remain. The public shaming can easily become another form of isolating punishment (for perpetrators and their families). To some extent this is addressed by strong recommendations on providing reparation to victims and rehabilitation to perpetrators—for the sake of the victims, the wider society, and the perpetrators (and their families).[55] But TRC legislation did not allow for a process that might lead to some form of negotiated additional sanctions applied to the perpetrators, nor for any mediated and controlled interaction between the parties concerned. The separate functioning of the Human Rights Violation and Amnesty Committees reinforced the distance between victims and perpetrators and perpetrators and the rest of the community. Given the constraints imposed by the legislation, and other practical considerations, the responsibility of community organizations in this regard becomes very important. In the words of the *Report*: "The fact that people are given their freedom without taking responsibility for some form of restitution remains a major problem with the amnesty process. Only if the emerging truth unleashes a social dynamic that includes redressing the suffering of victims will it meet the ideal of restorative justice."[56]

Despite these and other limitations of the TRC process in terms of the ideal of restorative justice, I belief the TRC process embodies more of this ideal than the conventional, retributive criminal justice system. I conclude with the words of Howard Zehr: "The TRC process is flawed, opportunities have been missed, but the importance of this [restorative justice] understanding—not only in South Africa, but for the world—must not be underestimated. It is a bold step on an uncharted path."[57]

Notes

1 These tasks were divided between three statutory committees, the Human Rights Violations-, Amnesty-, and Reparation and Rehabilitation Committees, which, in turn, were supported by an Investigation Unit and a Research Department. Approximately $35 million have so far been spent to achieve these tasks. For more detail on this process see *Truth and Reconciliation Commission of South Africa Report* (1998).

2 I will be drawing on a wide range of political cartoons to illustrate different criticisms. On the strengths and weaknesses of political cartoons as commentary on the TRC process see W.J. Verwoerd and M. Mabizela, eds., *Truths Drawn in Jest: Commentary on the TRC through Cartoons* (Cape Town: David Phillip, 2000).

3 At more than 70 hearings across the length and breadth of SA, over an 18-month period, around 2000 people gave testimony on the violations they or their loved ones suffered. See A. Krog, *Country of My Skull* (Johannesburg: Random House, 1998) for an excellent account of these hearings, and TRC *Report*, vol. 3.

4 See Section 20 of TRC Act.

5 Krog, *Country of My Skull*, 82-100.

6 *Sunday Weekend Argus*, June 29-30, 1996, 3.

7 See TRC *Report*, vol. 1, 174-200.

8 The cartoon appeared at a time when there was a lot of public controversy over the existence of a list of high-ranking ANC members who allegedly worked in the past for the previous state's "National Intelligence Agency."

9 See Mabizela, Dikeni, and Jaffer in W.J. Verwoerd and M. Mabizela.

10 See TRC *Report*, vol. 1, 48-93 for detail on the mandate of the TRC.

11 M. Mamdani, "Justice or Reconciliation," *South Africa Review of Books* (December): 2-5. See W.J. Verwoerd, "Individual and/or Social Justice: Hard Choices Faced by the South African Truth and Reconciliation Commission," *European Journal of Development Research* 11, 2: 115-40 for a response to this criticism.

12 H.P.P. Lötter, *Justice for an Unjust Society* (Amsterdam: Rodolphi, 1993).

13 See TRC *Report*, vol. 2, 42-324.

14 See also A. Jeffery, *The Truth about the Truth Commission* (Johannesburg: SA Institute of Race Relations, 1999), who argues that the TRC was biased against the Inkatha Freedom Party.

15 Compare M. Ignatieff, "Articles of Faith," *Index on Censorship*, vol. 5 (1996): 114. "Agreement on a shared chronology of events might be possible though even this would be contentious; but it is impossible to imagine [Zagreb, Belgrade and Sarajevo] ever agreeing on how to apportion responsibility and moral blame. The truth that matters to people is not factual nor narrative truth but moral truth. And this will always be an object of dispute in the Balkans."

16 See Asmal, Asmal and Roberts and Burton's replies, both in C. Villa-Vicencio and W.J. Verwoerd, *Looking Back, Reaching Forward: Essays on the South African Truth and Reconciliation Commission* (Cape Town: Juta, 2000).

17 J. Cronin, "Tutu's Report Tells the Truth but Not the Whole Truth," *Sunday Independent*, November 15, 1998.

18 See TRC Act, section 3 (1).

19 Also contained in the Preamble of the TRC Act.

20 Background: In February 1998 Archbishop Tutu gave a passionate talk on reconciliation to the Afrikaans Chamber of Commerce. He dealt with the biblical basis for confession and applauded the valuable contributions of many Afrikaners to the reconciliation process. He also emphasized that long-term peace and prosperity for all South Africans demand that we must urgently address the intolerable socio-economic inequalities in South Africa. See Esterhuyse and Jaffer in Verwoerd and Mabizela for a discussion of the complex relationships between the TRC and "the Afrikaner community."

21 See, for example, Meiring and Villa-Vicencio in Villa-Vicencio and Verwoerd; S. Dwyer, "Reconciliation for Realists," *Ethics and International Affairs* 13: 81-98, and in this volume.

22 See contributions by Villa-Vicencio, Hayner, Gerwel, and Meiring in Villa-Vicencio and Verwoerd.

23 See D. Tutu, *No Future without Forgiveness* (London: Rider Books, 1999); D. Shriver, *Forgiveness in Politics: An Ethic for Enemies* (Oxford: Clarendon Press, 1995).

24 See Postamble of Interim Constitution of South Africa (Act no. 200 of 1993).

25 See TRC *Report*, vol. 1, 108; Shriver; T. Govier and J. Verwoerd, "Trust and the Problem of National Reconciliation," *Philosophy of the Social Sciences* 32, 2 (June 2002): 178-205.

26 Epilogue to Interim Constitution, Preamble of Promotion of National Unity and Reconciliation Act.

27 *Sunday Independent*, December 6, 1998.

28 Carlos Nino, *Radical Evil on Trial* (New Haven: Yale University Press, 1995).

29 Martha Minow, *Between Vengeance and Forgiveness: Facing History after Genocide and Mass Violence* (Boston: Beacon Press, 1998).

30 AZAPO at para. 21.

31 In this section I draw on Verwoerd, "Toward a Recognition." See also T. Govier and W. Verwoerd, "Forgiveness: The Victim's Prerogative," *South Africa Journal of Philosophy* 21, 2 (2002): 97-111.

32 Minow, *Between Vengeance and Forgiveness*, 4.

33 C.W. du Toit, ed., *Confession and Reconciliation* (Pretoria: Reasearch Institute for Theology and Religion, 1998).

34 See *TRC Report*, vol. 1, chap. 4.

35 See *TRC Report*, vol. 1, chap. 5; vol. 5, chap. 9; Govier and Verwoerd, "Trust and the Problem of National Reconciliation," 2002.

36 P. Ricoeur, "The Memory of Suffering," in *Figuring the Sacred: Religion, Narrative and Imagination* (Minneapolis, MN: Fortress Press, 1995).

37 Krog, *Country of My Skull*, 237.

38 Ibid.

39 H. Shue, *Basic Rights* (Princeton: Princeton University Press, 1980), 18-19.

40 R. Bhargarva, "The Moral Justifications of Truth Commissions, " in Villa-Vincencio and Verwoerd; A. Margalit, *The Decent Society* (Cambridge: Harvard University Press, 1996).

41 I concur with Susan Mendus's interpretation of human rights as primarily "bulwarks against evil" and not "harbingers of goods," and agree that "the political impetus for human rights comes from the recognition of evil as a permanent threat in the world." S. Mendus, "Human Rights in Political Theory," in D. Beetham, ed., *Politics and Human Rights* (Oxford: Blackwell, 1995).

42 See J. Allen, "Balancing Justice and Social Unity: Political Theory and the Idea of a Truth and Reconciliation Commission," *University of Toronto Law Journal* 49: 315-53. In this article Allen confirms the significance of the TRC's focus on past injustices by referring to Wolgast's important point that "the sense of injustice is prior to any particular conception of justice that we may articulate; a conception of justice is a response to and more or less successful articulation of our sense of injustice" (E. Wolgast, *The Grammar of Justice* [Ithaca: Cornell University Press, 1987]).

43 T. Mbeki, "Culture: The Barrier which Blocks Regress to Beastly Ways," in *Africa: The Time Has Come, Selected Speeches* (Cape Town: Tafelberg, Mafube, 1998), 259.

44 Ibid.

45 W.B. Yeats, *Selected Poetry* (London: Pan Books, 1974).

46 In this section I draw on Verwoerd, "Individual and/or Social Justice."

47 Hansard, May 16-18, 1995.

48 A. Borraine, "Alternatives and Adjuncts to Criminal Prosecutions," unpublished paper delivered in Brussels, July 20-21, 1996.

49 Azanean Peoples Organization (AZAPO) and Others v. President of the Republic of South Africa and Others, 1996. Butterworth Constitutional Law Report (BCLR) 8, 1015-140. I. Mahomed, DP was the Deputy President of the Constitutional Court of South Africa.

50 Ibid., at 1024 G-I.

51 For a response to other aspects of this justice-based criticism see Verwoerd, "Individual and/or Social Justice."

52 *TRC Report*, vol. 1, 126.

53 See J. Braithwaite, *Crime, Shame, and Reintegration* (Cambridge: Cambridge University Press, 1989); H. Branchi, *Justice Sanctuary: Toward a System of Crime Control* (Bloomington: Indiana University Press, 1994); H. Zehr, *Changing Lenses: A New Focus for Crime and Justice* (Waterloo, ON: Herald Press, 1990); J. Consedine, *Restorative Justice: Healing the Effects of Crime* (Lyttelton: Ploughshares, 1995); and J. Llewellyn and R. Howse, "Restorative Justice: A Conceptual Framework," discussion paper, Law Commission of Canada, 1998, 1-107.

54 For more detail on the links between restorative justice and the TRC see *TRC Report*, vol.1, 9, 125-31; Villa-Vicencio, "Restorative Justice"; J. Llewellyn, "Justice for South Africa? – Restorative Justice and the South African Truth and Reconciliation Commission," in C.M. Koggel, ed., *Moral Issues in Global Perspective* (New York: Broadview Press, 1999); and Llewellyn and Howse; E. Kiss, "Moral Ambition within and beyond Political Constraints: Reflections on Restorative Justice," in R. Rotberg and D. Thompson, eds., *Truth v. Justice: The Morality of Truth Commissions* (Princeton: Princeton University Press, 2000).

55 Cf. *TRC Report*, vol. 5, 304-49.

56 *TRC Report*, vol. 1, 131.

57 Zehr, *Changing Lenses*, 20.

10

Reimagining Guatemala: Reconciliation and the Indigenous Accords

Jim Handy

On February 25, 1999, the Guatemalan version of a truth commission, the Commission to Clarify History (*La Comisión para el Escalarecimiento Histórico*), issued its long-awaited report to a huge and expectant audience in a packed National Theatre and a few thousand more people watching the proceedings on closed circuit television in the park outside. In the report, the Commission detailed 658 massacres and 200,000 killings committed during the thirty-four years of civil war, almost all of them occurring in the most brutal period, from 1978 to 1984. Of these 658 massacres, the Commission reported that thirty-two were the responsibility of the guerrillas and the rest, 626, were committed by the army or its dependencies. The coordinator of the Commission, Christian Tomuschat, in his remarks introducing the report, argued the army and other security services of the state arrived at the "complete loss of human morals."[1]

The report of the truth commission went further than many had hoped or feared. Among the many important pronouncements of the Commission, and the one greeted most vociferously by those in the audience, was the determination on the part of the Commission that various acts of the military and its dependencies could be constituted as "genocide." The Commission reported that, of the 200,000 victims, over 83 percent were Maya and argued that in four areas of the country, where Maya constituted close to 98 percent of those affected by the violence, the army engaged in "acts of genocide" in which the army "contemplated the total or partial extermination of the group."[2] Most analysts of the report suggested this

---

was important because the amnesty accord protecting soldiers and guerrillas, which had been signed as part of the peace process, had specifically excluded acts of genocide. The Commission's report seemed to open the door for the prosecution of army officers and presidents. This was clearly the interpretation of many in the audience who, on hearing Tomuschat declare in his opening remarks that the Commission had determined that acts of genocide had occurred, began to chant "First Pinochet, now Ríos Montt," referring to the head of state in Guatemala in 1982 and 1983, during much of the worst of the violence.[3]

However, the commission's determined focus on the violence perpetrated against the Maya majority of Guatemala suggests an even more important aspect of the process of reconciliation and peace in Guatemala. The ethnically focused, genocidal nature of the violence in Guatemala over the last two decades makes it clear that for any real reconciliation to occur, Guatemala must begin to address fundamentally the racist and exclusionary nature of Guatemalan society. For true reconciliation to occur, we have to recognize that violence, even violence at the horrific levels employed in Guatemala, is often a reasoned and sometime effective tool used to maintain inequity and to continue institutional forms of violence. Thus, it is not enough to identify those responsible for crimes and to punish them—as important as that is—but the underlying reasons for the violence must be addressed and mechanisms put in place to eliminate them. For this to happen in Guatemala requires a fundamental rethinking of the concept of Guatemala as a nation state and an elimination of the institutional racism that has long been a prominent feature of Guatemalan society. It requires that the non-Mayan- (*Ladino-*) dominated state recognize levels of community organization and responsibility and permit a degree of regional and ethnically based self-determination that would be a complete reversal of the dominant historical discourse in Guatemala and, to a large extent, in the Americas as a whole. As recent events suggest, this will be an even more difficult task than bringing the military perpetrators of so much violence to justice. Until this happens, however, attempts at reconciliation will only address the symptoms of internal discord (the institutional violence of the last thirty years) and not the cause.

In this discussion, I explore both why this alteration is necessary and suggest why it is so difficult. To do the former, I explore briefly the history of marginalization of the Maya in Guatemala and how that marginalization was central to the non-Maya conception of the Guatemalan nation. I will then turn to a discussion of the ways in which that marginalization was challenged in the latter half of the twentieth century and how that challenge helped precipitate the worst period of violence. This will be followed by a discussion of the ways in which Mayan revitalization after 1985 helped lead to the ending of the civil war and the signing of the Peace Accords in 1996. I will examine the conflicts that have emerged in Guatemala concerning indigenous rights. Finally, I will explore briefly the disappointing history of what has been done since the signing of the accords, focusing on the recent failed attempt at constitutional change.

Bleaching the Blood

Non-Mayan Guatemalans have, historically, been trapped in a conundrum of their own making. Those self-proclaimed descendants of the Spanish, who rather desperately tried to construct a nation out of the remnants of the Spanish empire, the Mexican empire, and the United Provinces of Central America in the middle of the nineteenth century, struggled with an unacceptable reality. They inhabited a country that had a vast Mayan majority, but their conceptions of nationhood demanded that Guatemala be a product of Europe, leavened by the benevolent environment of the Americas.

In the initial years of nationhood, they attempted to ignore the fundamental differences that separated the various elements of the population. A tiny ruling white elite introduced legislation and fostered economic change which they believed to be enlightened, but which in no way took into consideration Guatemalan society outside of Guatemala City and a few other urban centres. The excluded rural society was inhabited by Maya and *mestizos* (*Ladinos*) who, of course, had very different conceptions of their proper role in society and the very nature of that society. As these "enlightened" measures began to be felt in the countryside, Ladino and Maya rural inhabitants made common cause, put one of their own in the presidency, and demanded a Guatemala which less slavishly emulated Europe and North America.[4]

The contradictions inherent during this "conservative" interregnum, in a country that tried to protect Mayan communities as the basic structure of society while building a nation and tying the national economy to international capital and markets, primarily through coffee, eventu-

ally proved too much. The slightly chastened white elite and more pros-
perous Ladinos made common cause and initiated the "liberal revolution," whose policies proved to be the cornerstone of modern
Guatemala. The liberal revolution sought, most of all, to foster the production of coffee. At this it was most successful, and Guatemala—and
this new elite—prospered as it had never done before. The motor force
of this prosperity was the abundant and cheap, if reluctant, labour of the
Mayan majority. As one German/Guatemala planter succinctly
expressed it in the late nineteenth century, "Not the soil but the low
wages of the labourers are the wealth of the Cobán."[5] The institutions of
forced labour and close military control over highland villages to insure
the continued necessary supply of labour put in place during this period
did much to establish the basis for the violence that would erupt one
hundred years later.

The economic underpinnings of the liberal state were established
solidly over the basis of an exploitative regime of export agriculture. The
control necessary for the continued functioning of that regime was provided by the establishment of a professional army and the heightened distinction between Ladinos and Maya in Guatemalan society.[6] However,
Ladino intellectuals and politicians continued to try to understand the
nature of Guatemalan society and to foster a sense of nationhood among
its inhabitants. They were essentially unsuccessful. Guatemalan intellectuals obsessed about the role of the Indian in Guatemala society. But,
they did so primarily as a means for finding a way to effectively eliminate
the Maya as a living presence, not to establish an intellectual basis for the
creation of a new hybrid society, much less one that embraced diversity.
While some of those engaged in this debate in the late nineteenth and
first half of the twentieth centuries expressed some sympathy for the
Maya and attacked policies that led to their material and perceived cultural deprivation, none suggested a future that included a recognizable
Maya component to that society. Perhaps most noteworthy in this regard
because he has been seen as a progressive was the Nobel Prize-winning
author, Miguel Angel Asturias, whose solution for the Maya problem in
the 1920s was determined miscegenation with heavy doses of immigration from Europe, preferably Germany, which would "bleach" the
clogged blood of this mestizo nation.[7]

The Mayan Rebirth: Demography and Social Change

The dynamic between Ladinos and Maya in Guatemala began to change in the second half of the twentieth century. There were many complex reasons for this change, but one of the most important was very simple: the demographic recovery of the Maya. Estimating the historic (or even the current) number of Maya is far from an exact science. There is a substantial literature on the subject and not all of it is in even approximate agreement. I will use what might be considered to be relatively moderate or careful figures from the range available to us. According to these figures, before conquest, which began in 1524, there were perhaps two million Maya in what is now Guatemala. By 1650, through a combination of war, slavery, abuse, and mostly disease, this number was reduced to 120,000—a loss of about 93 percent of the population. That number barely moved for the next one hundred years and only slowly began to increase in the years immediately preceding independence in the 1820s. It was not until the second decade of the twentieth century that the number of Maya reached one-half that of the pre-conquest population, and not until the 1960s that they regained the population lost in the 150 years after conquest.[8] Before the latter part of the twentieth century then, it was easy for most Ladinos to believe that the Maya would disappear as a distinct people and as a set of culturally distinct nations. Easy for non-Maya to believe that they could construct a "nation" along the modern, Europeanized, liberal lines they believed was their future destiny. During this time, it was also difficult for the Maya, struggling with the continued lingering effects of huge population loss, to develop a coherent, powerful, credible, and articulated political and cultural alternative to that vision.

Between 1964 and 1991, the number of Maya in Guatemala increased from two million to between four and six million, as the general population increased from four to ten million.[9] The tremendous increase in the numbers of Maya had a significant impact on the continuing debate about the place of the Maya in national society.

This debate took shape around marked changes in national politics as well. In 1944 members of the urban middle class—students, intellectuals, and young military officers—seized power and embarked on what became known as the "ten years of spring." The revolution—as it was also known—was the political expression of a complex set of often contradictory ideals. During the last three years of the revolution, the political leadership sought to challenge the political and economic control exercised by the land-owning elite and foreign interests. To do so, they fostered a moderate agrarian reform law and, in an attempt to use the rural masses as a bulwark against the expected reaction, a radical program of peasant and rural worker organization.

The leaders of this revolution were assimilationist in their approach to Mayan rural inhabitants, and sought to emulate what they perceived to be the successful Mexican approach to eliminating ethnic differences by ostensibly supporting the economic and class interests of peasants. However, they had only limited control in the countryside, and by the end of the revolution, Mayan groups were able to use what were intended to be assimilationist national organizations to support local, regional, and ethnic struggles. The rebirth of Mayan political and economic organization in Guatemala clearly has important roots in the revolution from 1944 to 1954, but not, as is often argued, because later indigenous organizations found inspiration in the political ideals of the revolution.[10]

The revolution was overthrown by a combination of conservative forces. The most important of these was the Guatemalan military, which acted primarily to end the radical peasant and Mayan organization throughout the country that had accompanied the agrarian reform. Following the revolution, the military, purged of its few reformist tendencies, and the most conservative of landowners set out to replicate an idealized Guatemala—the imagined Guatemala of the past with a quiescent Maya labour force, few challenges to their political power from an urban middle class, an obedient military, and continued profits from expanded export agriculture. They were briefly successful.[11]

This archaic vision of Guatemala began to unravel in the 1960s. In 1962, dissident military officers revolted and, unsuccessful in their attempts at an immediate coup, began a protracted guerrilla war, which is generally considered to be the beginning of Guatemala's thirty-four years of civil war. The guerrilla challenge was not particularly serious through the first two decades and was easily if brutally controlled by the military. The existence of the guerrillas, however, proved to be a ready tool around which the military was able to construct a national security state and to accumulate increasing power over the state and the economy.[12]

Maya had little to do with the guerrilla battles in the 1960s and early 1970s, primarily because the guerrillas were located in areas far removed from the major concentrations of the Mayan population. But significant changes were happening in the Mayan highlands during this period. Faced with increased population pressure, few economic opportunities outside of the village, and fewer political opportunities, Maya began to focus determinedly on local community development, and as part of this process sought to wrest control of local politics from the dominating local Ladino elite. In both of these endeavours they were surprisingly successful. Assisted in the first through local cooperatives promoted by the Catholic Church and, after the earthquake of 1976, by local reconstruction committees, Maya in many communities were able to build surprisingly vibrant local economies. They were assisted in adding local political control to economic change through Catholic Action and the Christian Democratic party that became in many areas of the highlands a party dominated locally by an aggressive new generation of Mayan leaders, no matter its relatively tame national inclinations. These local successes and the growing dynamism of Mayan society soon led to increased, if still relatively limited, involvement in national politics. A small group of the national Mayan leaders emerged, and a nascent Mayan political party was formed. In combination, these local and national initiatives began to foretell of a significant change in national and local politics and to suggest a movement to reshape Guatemala as a nation.[13]

A Nightmare of Violence

The twisted tale of how these political, economic, and social changes were replaced in the period between 1978 and 1984 with the worst period of violence Guatemala had experienced since the initial conquest is long and complex and not really directly of importance here. I will touch only upon the most important points along the way.

The most common starting point for the period of intense violence is the massacre that occurred in Panzos, Alta Verapaz, in April 1978. It is a fitting beginning, as it contains within it many of the elements that would become distressingly familiar in the next half decade. In Panzos, predominantly Q'echi peasants had become increasingly alarmed over what appeared to be attempts to expropriate their land, in an area that seemed to promise future development opportunities in oil and cattle raising. They successfully petitioned locally to have their grievance heard by the national government, and on a day in April they came en masse to the municipal capital, they believed, to present their grievances to a representative of the National Institute for Agrarian Transformation. Instead they were met by the army, who opened fire on the assembled group, killing over twenty and throwing their bodies into mass graves.

To understand the response of the military to this simple petition in Panzos, we must explore briefly the perceived connections between these local development efforts and a reinvigorated guerrilla movement. In the early 1970s, the remnants of the guerrilla movement from the 1960s had moved into the Ixcán area of Guatemala from southern Mexico. There they began a process of slowly trying to win the support of the majority Mayan population, which had been conspicuously absent from the guerrilla struggles in the 1960s.[14] The extent to which they were successful in winning that support has been a subject of much debate, with clearly opposing sides drawn partly at least by ideological considerations.[15]

What is clear is that the prospect of this happening frightened the military command and provided them with the opportunity, at least as some perceived it, to complete the process of nation building by destroying the community basis of Mayan culture. The incredible violence of this attack is not surprising, perhaps, given the extent to which the military had successfully inculcated itself with its obsession about its role as the last bulwark against the external and internal enemy represented, in their minds, by communist aggression. They had as a group, it is clear, over the course of two-and-a-half decades, convinced themselves of the truth of their lies concerning the imminent communist menace. This fear was stoked by the frightening possibility that this menace would take shape in the body of a majority Maya population, a population that was clearly undigested into the nation of Guatemala and which also clearly sought substantial, if as yet mostly unarticulated, alterations to the very framework of the Guatemalan state. There was obviously an element here of the fear of a just retribution; non-Maya understood the discrimination and marginalization that had been visited on Maya in Guatemala and found it hard to believe why they would not revolt in substantial numbers.

Whatever the reasons for the descent into violence in rural Guatemala, the profile of that violence is well-documented. It started with the selective killing of community and peasant leaders, deteriorated into the military participating in and at times being manipulated by local feuds and jealousies, and descended—most notably in the period from 1981-83—into widespread massacres in which whole populations were killed or forced to flee. This latter period was marked by the extension of military control and military terror throughout the highland region through a system of strategic hamlets and civil patrols, a control used, according to the Dutch Catholic Congress, as a means for "destroying in a systematic manner all that sustains the life of the community…as a principal object to disarticulate the social life and cultural inheritance of the Indian people," or in the words of the Army General Staff itself, as a means "to increase the effectiveness of actions taken to create nationalism and maintain it."[16]

The Long Road to Peace

Looking forward from the perspective of the early 1980s, as society in rural Guatemala lay in ruins and more than a million of Guatemala's eight million population huddled in refugee camps outside of the country or swelled the numbers of dispossessed in the major cities, it seemed almost inconceivable that Guatemalans could ever forge a lasting peace. What has been accomplished in the last decade seems at times nothing short of miraculous. But, in retrospect the road to peace has clear signposts.

By 1984, the military had essentially undisputed control over the countryside and powerful elements in the military high command decided that their interests were best served through indirect control. Consequently, they initiated a military guided return to democracy which culminated in the election of a civilian president in 1985. The election of a civilian president meant neither that the military was giving up power nor that there would be a determined movement towards peace, nor even that military repression would end. Indeed, widespread but more selective repression would continue for the next decade, and it would be over a decade before a comprehensive peace accord would be signed.[17]

In a very real sense, two very reluctant suitors, the guerrillas and the army, were forced to the altar by a reinvigorated civil society, with various civilian administrations tagging along, sometimes willingly and sometimes clearly very reluctantly. Despite continued repressions in the 1980s, popular organizations emerged and demanded to have a voice in the construction of a new Guatemala. Labour organizations were the first to emerge from the violence of the early 1980s, and by the latter half of the decade they had forged an alliance with some popular organizations to form the Unidad de Acción Sindical y Popular. Academics and human rights investigators formed a dizzying array of research organizations, the most important of which was the Associación para el

Avance de las Ciencias Sociales (AVANCSO) which from the mid-1980s focused its attention on investigating continuing violence and on analyzing the social conditions that helped produce the violence.[18]

The most important impetus for the halting steps towards peace negotiations came from a determined Catholic Church hierarchy and popular predominantly Mayan organizations created around demands to combat militarization in the countryside. The first civilian president, Vinicio Cerezo, had hosted the signing of the Procedure for Establishing Firm and Lasting Peace in Central America in 1987 in the town of Esquipulas. This accord committed governments throughout the region to establish national reconciliation commissions to promote democracy by means of a national dialogue. Committed by this accord, the government established the National Reconciliation Commission in October 1987, and under the auspices of this commission, a meeting was held in Madrid with representatives from the combined guerrilla forces (the URNG) and the government, with military observers in attendance. Little came of this meeting, but one of the four members of the commission, Bishop Rudolfo Quezada Toruño, spearheaded an offensive by the Catholic Church, demanding that the government hold a "national dialogue" and that this dialogue include a broad consideration of social concerns as a necessary part of the peace process.[19]

The "Grand National Dialogue" began in February 1989. Eighty delegates took part, representing diverse sectors from popular organizations and academics to business associations. The two most important business organizations in the country, the Coordinating Committee of Agricultural, Commercial, Industrial, and Financial Associations (CACIF) and the major farmers' organization, refused to participate. The Grand National Dialogue was essential in the road to peace because through it the demand was articulated, and continuously and consistently reiterated in the coming years, that any peace accord needed to address broad social conditions. No lasting peace accord, it was argued, could simply address the issue of a ceasefire and demobilization of the guerrillas. In early 1989, representatives of the URNG held meetings with the popular organizations in the national dialogue as a means of attempting to insure that these concerns would be addressed at the negotiating table.

After the election of a new administration in 1991, headed by the evangelical protestant Jorge Serrano Elías, the government held its first official talks with the guerrillas and general agreements were signed establishing a framework for the "search for peace through political means." In the midst of a virulent campaign launched by the most conservative business and military sectors opposing them, the negotiations stalled. However, the Grand National Dialogue developed into the Multisectoral Forum, which began a deeper and more widely representative search for a road to peace. The Forum had been forged by a broad cross-section of popular, indigenous, academic, and progressive business sectors that clearly represented the most dynamic and determined sectors in the search for peace.

Of most importance in the consolidation of the Forum was the way in which it had allowed popular Maya sectors a national voice and the opportunity it had provided to allow for cooperation between popular Mayan sectors and Mayan cultural nationalists. From the mid-1980s, perhaps the most impressive and courageous organizations in the country had been a loosely allied number of predominantly Mayan organizations that had been forged around the complimentary tasks of challenging military domination in the countryside and demanding an accounting for the disappearance of family members. The first such group had been the Grupo de Apoyo Mutuo (GAM), formed in 1984 as an organization of the family members of the disappeared. GAM was less effective than it might have been because of the predominantly Ladino and urban basis of the leadership. GAM was joined in 1988 by the National Coordination of Widows of Guatemala (CONAVIGUA) which was organized initially by a Cakchiquel Maya widow, Rosalina Tuyuc. CONAVIGUA spread quickly through the highlands and became an increasingly powerful national organization, with over 12,000 members, 90 percent widows of the violence, by the early 1990s. They soon joined in a loose alliance with other Maya popular organizations, most notably the Comité de Unidad Campesina (CUC) and its more Maya-dominated offspring, CONIC, and the Council for Highland Ethnic Communities (CERJ). These organizations were tremendously important through the early 1990s in focusing public attention on demands for ending militarization in the countryside, disbanding the civil patrols, ending forced recruitment, as well as accounting for the dead and uncovering clandestine cemeteries.[20]

These organizations coalesced around two important points in the early 1990s. The first was the organization of popular resistance to the fifth centenary of Columbus's landing in the Americas and the second was Rigoberta Menchú's winning of the Nobel Prize in 1992. In 1991 the second continental meeting of Indigenous, black, and popular resistance to the celebration of the fifth centenary was held in Quezaltenango,

Guatemala's second largest city. Guatemalan popular Mayan organizations were well-represented at the meeting at which Rigoberta Menchú played an important role. This meeting supported Rigoberta Menchú's nomination for the Nobel Prize and pledged to aggressively demand that the plans for the celebration of the fifth centenary be abandoned throughout the Americas. In Guatemala, the movement was a constant feature in newspaper reports. It focussed its attention on the need to end militarization of Mayan communities and continually made the connections between the original conquest and the current military occupations of their towns.[21] Of particular importance in the debate surrounding the anniversary were the frequent calls in the publications of various progressive institutions concerning the need to redefine Guatemala in "multiethnic, pluricultural" ways. For example, a full-page advertisement taken out by the national university in support of the protests declared, "The last decades have shown us various aspects of the multiethnic and pluricultural essence of Guatemala. The vindication of indigenous peoples, peasants, women, and other organized sectors...has questioned the existing paternalistic and homogenous state." The advertisement went on to question the very existence of a Guatemalan state except as "an image created by intellectuals allied with dominant groups."[22]

When Rigoberta Menchú won the Nobel Prize, in the face of the barely disguised opposition of the government, the popular Maya movement received another significant shot in the arm. The various organizations involved in this movement clearly dominated popular discourse in Guatemala and they did much to publicize the legacy of the violence in the countryside and to denounce the continuing atrocities there.

The Second Continental Congress held in Quezaltenango did more than just invigorate the popular Maya organizations. The debate at the congress also demonstrated quite clearly the split between these popular Mayan groups, with still fairly close connections to the URNG, and those involved in the Mayan cultural movement. During the 1980s, a substantial group of Maya intellectuals began slowly and at first fairly tentatively to search publicly for a coherent alternative to the current conceptualization of Guatemalan society and the Guatemalan state. Many of these intellectuals were trained in doctoral or advanced academic studies outside of Guatemala, many in literature, linguistics, or communications. They naturally focused their attention on language as the most important element of culture. They initially couched their observations and demands in non-threatening terms and were often organized around the semi-official, elite-dominated Academia de Lenguas Mayas. They especially rejected a class-based—or even class-informed—analysis of Guatemala's crisis. Instead they sought to forge a multi-class Mayan alliance that would focus the issues solidly on the ethnic division and the need for a reconceptualization of Guatemala that took into consideration the heterogenous nature of Guatemalan society and of the Guatemalan state. In the meeting in Quezaltenango the distance between this intellectual elite and the more popular organizations became readily apparent, with the cultural group angry at what they perceived to be their exclusion from the discussion and the focus on popular, class-based issues. The meeting ended with the cultural activists angry and excluded.[23]

However, the need for cooperation between the two sectors of Mayan activism was obvious and both tendencies began to meet and to debate points in the Multisectoral Forum after 1991. They were able to put aside their differences, at least temporarily, in the struggle to thwart the Serrano autogolpe (self-coup) in May 1993.

By May 1993 the Serrano administration was falling apart. Popular Mayan and anti-military organizations clearly dominated the media and popular debate in Guatemala. Sectors of the military and business were becoming increasingly uneasy about the inability of the government to control this debate. The Serrano administration itself was beset by charges of corruption and an antagonistic congress seemed set to investigate the president. Serrano, attempting to copy Alberto Fujimori's successful self-coup in Peru, and relying on popular disgust with a corrupt and inefficient congress and confident of military support, declared on May 25 that he would disband congress and rule by decree. This was the most serious challenge yet to the nascent civil society in Guatemala. It met the challenge solidly.

The Multisectoral Forum, led symbolically at least by Rigoberta Menchú who was fortuitously in Guatemala for the first international congress of indigenous people, rallied popular opposition to the coup. Its members entered into a dialogue with the most important progressive private sectors and formed the Instancia Nacional de Consenso which made clear the broad popular and multisectoral opposition to the coup. The Instancia kept up constant pressure on the military and congress and successfully focused international opposition to the coup, sufficient that the military withdrew its support and Serrano was forced to flee the country.

The most important magazine in the country called the defeat of Serrano a "democratic revolution," and the Instancia Nacional del Consenso, after the withdrawal of the most traditional private sector associations, formed the Assembly of Civil Society, which was to have a tremendous impact on the path to the peace accords.[24]

With the momentum gained from the struggle to oust Serrano and the presence of the former Procurador of Human Rights, Ramiro de Leon Carpio, as interim president, propelled along by pressure from the Assembly of Civil Society, the government and the guerrillas signed four substantial peace acccords in 1994 and 1995. The Agreement on the Rights and Identity of Indigenous Peoples (*Acuerdo Sobre Identidad y Derechos de los Pueblos Indigenas*) was signed on March 31, 1995. The momentum was maintained after the election of new president in 1996, and the final two substantive accords were signed early that year. On December 30, 1996, the government and the URNG signed the Peace Accords, ending thirty-four years of armed conflict.[25]

Of course, signing the Peace Accords and putting them into effect are two very different things. There have been immense problems in Guatemala in trying to enforce and abide by the various accords. Despite the pressure from both the Assembly of Civil Society and the Consultative Group of foreign donor nations, few of them have been implemented successfully and many doubt that they can. What interests us most here, however, is primarily the attempts to implement the Accord on the Rights and Identity of Indigenous People and what that tells us about the prospects for reconciliation in Guatemala.

A New Dawn

The signing of the Indigenous Accord in March 1995 was both the culmination of a long process and the beginning of what promises to be an even longer one. To understand this, we need to explore first the often contradictory pressures that led to the signing of the accord and the debate that surrounds it.

By 1992, two very distinct indigenous movements had emerged in Guatemala: a group of popular Maya organizations active in the Assembly of Civil Society and with links to class-based popular organizations and to the URNG; and a group of cultural activists who focused their attention on Mayan culture, often rejected class concerns, and sought to provide the intellectual basis for a Mayan nationalism. While they often disagreed on issues and approaches (indeed, they are divided by some very intense personal disagreements), they were both important in focusing the debate that surrounds the indigenous accords and they have been able to cooperate on a number of issues.

The first was the struggle to have Convention 169 approved in Guatemala. Convention 169, the Convention Concerning Indigenous Peoples and Tribes in Independent Countries, was proposed by the International Labour Organization in 1989, to replace the 1957 convention, after much discussion with indigenous organizations and in consultation with the World Council of Indigenous People. It is a broad-ranging convention that commits signatory countries to respect indigenous rights to resources, to customary justice, to traditional lands, to appropriate political organizations, culturally affirming education, and language rights. The Second Continental Congress of Resistance held in Quezaltenango in 1991 had committed organizations in the various countries to push for the ratification of the convention.[26]

When the Convention was first proposed in Guatemala it provoked little reaction. The Catholic Church immediately supported it, as did some members of congress. Virtually all Maya groups dedicated themselves to pressuring for its passage. However, as the significance, both real and imagined, of the convention began to be discussed, the level of conflict escalated. It is clear that debate over the convention became a starting point for a wider-ranging debate over the nature of Guatemalan society and the Guatemalan state. As such, the various sides that formed around Convention 169 foretold an even more vociferous debate concerning the indigenous accords. Private sector associations, especially CACIF and the large landowners' association (AGA), immediately opposed it, arguing that the accord would threaten private property.[27] Conservative politicians and commentators warned that the convention violated the constitution of 1985 and some publicly wondered where it would end. They suggested that ratification of the convention would lead to acceptance of the projected Universal Declaration of the Rights of Indigenous Peoples being prepared within the United Nations. In one particularly rabid editorial, Mario Antonio Sandoval warned that this declaration would sink Guatemala back into a dark and feudal past. Its provisions respecting religion would be "a tacit approval of idolatry," and the land provisions would not only mean that private property owners in towns in "indigenous" regions could have their property confiscated but that "false hopes" would be raised among indigenous people that Guatemala City, Mexico City, and even Manhattan would be returned to them.[28] Even influential "progressive" journalists opposed the convention. Julio Godoy argued that, "The minds that support it intend…to turn this Maya Land into Yugoslavia," and suggested that, "we cannot support a convention in which we are practically recognizing the existence of two types of citizens in Guatemala."[29] As much as he would hate the comparison, Godoy's words echoed those of the military as that institution came around to oppose the accord. In October 1992, the minister of Defence argued, "Here there is only one nation and we must not talk of indigenas, ladinos, mestizos and the rest, when all together we make up Guatemala."[30] The bill made rapid progress through its first readings in congress, but as opposition mounted, its progress slowed. It was eventually passed by Congress on March 5, 1996, with the proviso that it was accepted only in so far as it did not contradict the Constitution of Guatemala.[31]

By that time, however, events including the signing of the indigenous accord, had made the passage of the convention somewhat anti-climactic. The Accord concerning the Identity and Rights of Indigenous Peoples, signed in March 1995, was in many ways a strange document signed in rather bizarre circumstances. Like all the other peace accords, it was an agreement signed between the combined guerrilla forces, the URNG, and the government. There were no Maya at the table for the discussion of the accord for either side. However, the Assembly of Civil Society in consultation with the Council for Organizations of the Mayan People in Guatemala (COPMAGUA) helped frame the initial draft of the accord. The accord reflects more assuredly the views of the popular Mayan organizations than those of the cultural activists. The accord was also very much a compromise between those intent on insuring there could be no challenge to the territorial integrity of Guatemala through the accord—a view shared by both the government and guerrilla negotiators—and Mayan groups who were intent on both the recognition of a pluricultural state and at least limited autonomy in Mayan regions and Mayan communities.

Nonetheless, the accord is a relatively far-reaching document. It commits the government to recognize constitutionally the pluricultural, multilinguistic nature of Guatemala. It demands that the government approve both Convention 169 and the UN Declaration of the Rights of Indigenous Peoples, and commit itself to introduce culturally reinforcing education in

Mayan languages with curriculum controlled by the community. It also focuses strongly on the role of community, recognizing the importance of community and on consensual decision making, supports communal ownership of land, and dedicates the government to both protect community land and compensate communities for land already taken from them. What is perhaps most interesting about the accord is what was left out of it; issues such as regional or even community autonomy and historic land rights were dropped as they were considered to be too contentious.[32] As a document on which to base the most important elements of reconciliation in Guatemala, the indigenous accord is a flawed tool; but it is a tool, nonetheless.

Nation State and Mayan Communities

The indigenous accord, more than any other element of the peace accord, envisions what has been called a "new national project."[33] As such, it has added fire to an ongoing and often vehement debate about the nature of Guatemalan society. This debate is far-reaching, and touches on almost all aspects of life in Guatemala. For example, the National Indigenous and Peasant Council (CONIC) has argued that there needs to be a new understanding of the relationship of peasants to the land which takes into consideration Mayan relationship to nature. Accepting such a change, they argue requires fundamental alterations in both the economic and legal regulations concerning land use and control. For the purposes of our discussion, however, we will concentrate on those aspects of this new national project that focus on the definition of nation and the role of the state.

In the early years of the transition to peace, popular Mayan organizations concentrated their attention on specific and practical demands such as the need to demilitarize communities and discover clandestine grave sites. The cultural activists, on the other hand, focused on broader, less concrete issues, such as the need for cultural rights, respect for language, and a legal redefinition of nation. Eventually, by the mid-1990s, these interests would find some elements of common ground. Initially, however, it was the ideas of the cultural activists that prompted the most vehement response.

Two of the most influential cultural activists, Demetrio Cojtí Cuxil and Luis Enrique Sam Colop, are able to air their views not only through the vibrant academic community in Guatemala but in a regular column each writes in major Guatemala City newspapers. A third, Estuardo

Zepeda, who also has a column, is more erratic, more confrontational, and concentrates much of his venom on the Mayan left. Their columns allow a group of Ladino academics and journalists to support or challenge their views through the medium of the national newspapers as well. Any regular reader of the various national newspapers is well aware of the ideas and opinions of the regular columnists on these points. But the result is rarely sterile; rather there is a lively debate about the future of Guatemala that both attracts widespread attention and contributes to the ability of Guatemalan society to reconceptualize itself.

The argument of the cultural nationalists is complex and varied, but it can be boiled down to its essence. Guatemala is not, nor will it ever be, a homogenous national state as most Ladinos have wished for and pretended since independence. All attempts at assimilation have and will fail. In the words of Demetrio Cojtí, the Maya will "frustrate the dreams of those who look to 'construct a nation' over the bodies of the Mayan nations."[34] Rather, they argue that Guatemala needs to recognize the multinational, pluricultural, and multilinguistic nature of Guatemalan society and construct a state which reflects that. They focus primarily on the role of language in preserving and transmitting culture, and argue for a recognition of a regionalized, decentralized Guatemala organized around the major Mayan languages.

The focus on language goes beyond arguments about the need for government recognition. Clearly familiar with national theorists who have pointed to the importance of primary languages in constructing nationhood, Mayan cultural activists have worked hard at expanding the scope of the major Mayan languages, especially Quiché, Cakchiquel, Ketchí, and Mam, introducing language classes for adults, demanding instruction for children in Mayan languages, and fostering a growing and dynamic publishing industry in Mayan languages.

They have been able to turn the arguments of the Ladino elite concerning the degradation of Mayan society on their head, arguing that it is Ladinos that have no "national culture." Consequently, they argue, Ladinos seek to create an identity through emulating Europe and humiliating the Maya. Cotjí points to the confusion apparent in Ladino national symbols, in which the day of nationality is the commemoration of the defeat of the Quiché hero, Tecun Unám, and the Day of the Race is the commemoration of Columbus's first landing. The result, they argue, is an insecure identity that seeks to find existence through the humiliation of the Maya.[35]

The Ladino response to these arguments have been surprisingly defensive. The most prolific defenders of the Ladino nation in the Guatemalan press were the troika of Karin Escaler, Mario Roberto Morales, and Mario Alberta Carrera, all columnists in national newspapers; they span the political spectrum from the far right to the supporters of the left. Mario Alberto Carrera is the most thoughtful of the three and the least inflammatory. However, he has taken exception to many of the arguments presented by the Mayan activists. He was particularly incensed when a Mayan commentator attacked the writings of that great hero of the intellectual left in Guatemala, Miguel Angel Asturias.[36] On another occasion, he adopted another argument favoured by the intellectual left when he argued that the "Indian didn't exist before 12 October 1492." The idea of an Indian emerged with conquest. Thus, he argued, it was impossible to determine who was or was not an Indian in Guatemala. Given that it was impossible to differentiate Mayan from Ladinos, he argued, "Wouldn't it be simpler and more logical for us all to call ourselves Guatemalans?"[37]

This theme, that the new Guatemala needed to treat everyone equally, enunciated by Mario Roberto Morales, was echoed by Karin Escaler. Escaler, well-known as a constant supporter of the military, not surprisingly echoed the Defence minister's (and neo-liberal) arguments about the need to treat all in Guatemala equally. In a series of editorials she argued that the common good demands the rejection of all special privileges for any one in Guatemala, including those "privileges" offered the Maya in the indigenous accords.[38] This argument was echoed by a many other Ladino columnists.[39]

The most vehement opponent of the accords was Mario Roberto Morales and it is also in his columns in which the concern about Ladino identity is most clearly shown. He argues that he does not oppose Mayan attempts to organize; rather, in inflammatory language, he exhorts Ladinos to organize themselves and defend their rights. He predicts the coming of an ideological and legal "ethnic war," and he argues, "We need to engage in it, brother ladinos, or else we will have lost our identity before we have begun to defend it."[40] On another occasion, he argued that if the Mayan activists were correct in asserting that they were, indeed, the majority in Guatemala, then Ladinos were an ethnic minority. As such, he argued, he wished to proclaim his pride in being an ethnic minority that did not deny either its Spanish or Mesoamerican roots and thus he and other Ladinos needed to reclaim the recognition and respect appropriate for an ethnic minority.[41] On another occasion he argued that Ladinos had every right to appropriate aspects of the Mayan culture. "My ethnic group and I," he argued, " will defend our right to the indigenous culture with the same fervour that we defend our right to European culture." I will applaud the indigenous movement, he said, "when they stop using us as the negative counterpoint for a positive alternative."[42]

The public debate in the years following the signing of the indigenous accords did not instill confidence in the ability of Guatemala to overcome the opposition to the measures in the accord and to implement them. Nonetheless, the Arzú government, with the eventual collaboration of most of the political parties represented in congress, began to make plans for constitutional change that would allow the government to implement many aspects of the peace accords, including the indigenous accord. After much delay the political parties agreed to a set of constitutional reforms on October 16, 1998. The reforms were to be put before the population in a popular referendum on May 15, 1999. The reforms reinvigorated the debate concerning the indigenous accords.

Some thirty reforms to specific articles in the 1985 constitution were proposed. For the purposes of the referendum, they were divided into four distinct questions, dealing with "the nation and social rights," the Legislative Assembly, the executive, and justice. Each of these sections was assembled on a different-coloured ballot and voters were asked to vote yes or no for each section. There were important aspects to each of these sections, perhaps most notably the section on the executive, which dealt with the military. However, it was the first question on the nation and social rights that attracted most attention.

This section sought to alter the existing constitution to abide by the indigenous accord. It started by declaring that, "The Guatemalan nation was a solidarity, within its unity and the integrity of its territory, it is pluri-cultural, multiethnic, and multilingual." In further revisions, it sought to alter article 66 of the existing constitution to promise that the state would respect the identity of Mayan *pueblos*, their ways of life, social organization, customs and traditions, languages, and traditional authorities, "privileging the integrity of the territory and the indivisibility of the Guatemalan state." It also established distinct Mayan languages as official languages in various regions of the country.[43]

As can be easily seen, these reforms were limited and cautious, insuring before any reforms were to be considered the integrity of the existing state. Despite this caution, the proposals provoked a storm of protest. In the weeks running up to the vote, virtually every public figure was asked their opinion of the vote and all the columnists in Guatemalan newspapers expressed their opinion. Those in favour of the reforms seemed to have the upper hand; the government party, the popular Front for a New Guatemala, and the guerrillas supported the reforms. The rightist FRG initially opposed the reforms and then withdrew its opposition. It was clear, however, that despite the support of some of the leadership of the party, most of the congressional members were less than enthusiastic about the reforms and the party never worked to insure its members would vote. A small right-wing party, ARDE, led by a pastor from the evangelical El Verbo church, spearheaded the political opposition to the reforms. He and a group of supporters, many of them members of the Guatemala City elite, formed the Fatherland League (*Liga Pro-Patria*) to oppose the reforms. While there was some discussion about many of the reforms, debate focused on the changes designed to reflect the indigenous accords.

Virtually all the Mayan public figures and the Mayan cultural activists supported the reforms, with the noteworthy exception of Estuardo Zepeda. In contrast to much of the earlier debate around the indigenous accords, they were supported by a large number of Ladino columnists. For example, Dina Fernández Garcia argued that the constant refrain used to oppose the reforms, that all must be equal before the law, was nothing but trickery. "Everyone knows," she said, "that some are more equal than others and that the indigenous population occupies the basement in the construction of our country."[44] Many other popular journalists supported the reforms. The concentration of forces in favour of the reforms led analysts to suggest that the reforms would pass by a measure of at least 2 to 1.[45]

Not everything pointed to a yes victory. Representatives of the most powerful private sector interests opposed the reform, as the president of CACIF argued, because "to give special privileges to indigenous groups would generate divisions" in Guatemalan society.[46] This was the constant theme reiterated time and again by those opposing the reforms. The *Liga Pro-Patria* argued constantly that the proposed reforms "violate the principle of equality, dignity, and rights for all Guatemalans and give privileges to the Mayan, Xinca, and Garifuna ethnicities." They also argued that the recognition of indigenous languages would destroy the "common sentiment" necessary for unity and promoted by a common language.[47] The *Liga* frequently introduced court challenges against various sectors, including the government and the United Nations Mission in Guatemala, to prevent them from openly supporting the yes side. Two days before the vote, two well-known proponents of the yes side were assassinated as they campaigned for the vote.[48]

In the final analysis, the yes vote lost soundly, 366,000 votes to 328,000. An analysis of the vote makes it clear that the very nature of the vote marginalized the Maya yet again. Over four million people were eligible to vote; only 18 percent of those voted. In every department with a Mayan majority, the yes vote won on all four questions, except Totonicapán, in which the yes vote won on the indigenous accords but the no side prevailed on two of the questions. However, absenteesm was even higher in the departments than in the capital. This fits a common pattern in Guatemala. Voting stations are located in the municipal capital; close to 80 percent of the indigenous population lives in smaller centres outside of the municipal capitals. For many of these people the trip to the voting tables for the Sunday vote would take hours of walking or travelling on rare public transport, and so few of them were able to vote. Almost one quarter of the total votes tallied were in the capital city, which voted overwhelmingly in opposition to the reforms. The votes of the largely Ladino capital city tipped the scales in favour of those opposed to the reforms.[49]

What does the failure of the reforms mean for Guatemala? Many commentators tried to put the defeat in the best light, arguing that the rejection was primarily the result of disillusionment with political leaders or with the process that brought the reforms forward. The more honest commentators made it clear that the vote was primarily a rejection of constitutional change recognizing Mayan demands. As Luis Morales Chún argued in an editorial on the day of the vote, before the results were known, "In the final hours of the campaign against the vote, it was left completely clear that on the part of some political groups there is a permanent attitude against the indigenous people, against the peace accords, against the right of Guatemalans to live in a legal system that can end racism and discrimination."[50]

Guatemala's major newspaper defended the no vote but did so in an argument that suggests the problems Guatemala still has to face. The paper's editorial argued that those proposing reforms had lost sight of the forest for the trees, suggesting reforms without understanding what those reforms would do to "the total national project." It went on to argue that the political leaders had to champion "serious national projects," in contrast one supposes to the frivolous ideas expressed by the Mayan nationalists.[51]

Reconciliation and the National Project in Guatemala

Attempts at reconciliation in Guatemala a decade and a half after the military permitted the return to a civilian president do not look particularly promising. There have been advances—most notably in the success of the efforts of local groups in demilitarizing rural communities. Two powerful condemnations of the military have been produced by the Catholic Church and the Truth Commission, designed primarily as a step towards healing the wounds of the violence that engulfed the Maya in Guatemala. But even as mass graves continue to be uncovered in the countryside and many in the country become increasingly aware of how horribly terrible, how widespread, and how devastating that violence was, few of the necessary steps required to address the causes of that violence have been taken.

A half a decade after the signing of the peace accords, few senior military officers have been found responsible for crimes during the violence. In 2001, more than three years after his killing, the murderers of Bishop Gerardi (the head of the Catholic Church's own investigation into the violence) were finally brought to trial. Colonel Lima Estrada, his son, Captain Lima Oliva, a private security guard, and a priest were convicted in relation to the killing. While Colonel Lima is the highest-ranking military officer convicted of human rights abuses and the successful completion of this trial was considered to be a major accomplishment for the Guatemalan judicial system, this case was peculiar in the level of internal and international pressure brought to bear on the government, judicial system, and military. Even with this intense international pressure, the case used up almost a dozen judges and many of the witnesses were forced to give depositions and flee the country for their own protection.

Most tellingly, the military officer most people think was primarily responsible for the much of the violence—some suggest he needs to be held accountable for more than 100,000 killings—former General Efraín Ríos Montt, seems to be as secure from prosecution as he ever was. Currently president of Congress and head of the ruling party, he remains a popular political figure in Guatemala. The only thing for which he has been successfully brought to trial was a relatively minor infraction involving changing liquor prices after congress had voted on liquor duties; he was absolved of any wrongdoing in this case. Attempts to indict him for war crimes in Spain have failed; there seems to be no chance he will be indicted for these crimes in Guatemala. If his party can change the law preventing him from running, he may well be Guatemala's next president.

The frustration, the continued rancour, that the inability to prosecute those responsible for these crimes generates was perhaps best expressed by Luis Enrique Sam Colop in an editorial in October 2000. Here he compared the genocide perpetrated against the Maya to the Holocaust against the Jews during the Second World War. The difference, he emphasized, was that the Nazis lost and were subject to trial for their actions. In Guatemala, in contrast, he argues those responsible for the Guatemalan holocaust have never been held responsible and augment their power everyday. It is a continual insult to the memory of all those Maya who lost their lives in that holocaust that Ríos Montt and others hold power and attempt to assert their legitimacy and that of the state they represent.[52] At the local level this frustration is felt on a daily basis. One resident of San Martin Jilotepeque, a small town in the highlands badly hit by the violence, talked about how difficult it was for him. He lost most of his family in the violence; he expects their remains are buried in the "clandestine" grave on the edge of town that has yet to be exhumed. The former military commissioner he knows was responsible for ordering their deaths is a neighbour; he needs to deal with him constantly as a member of the community. No accounting has been made; none seems possible.

Thus, repression continues, impunity remains unchallenged, social and economic inequality gets worse, and the military remains in the streets. Most seriously, the failed referendum shows that a large sector of the population remains staunchly opposed to a reconstruction of the Guatemalan nation which realistically addresses its actual composition rather than an idealized vision of what Guatemalan nationalism might possibly be.

Still, those who have watched what has happened in the last two decades in Guatemala must be amazed at what Guatemalans have been able to achieve. In the most moving and graphic description of the violence in the devastated Ixcán, Ricardo Falla argued that the story needed to be told not to seek vengeance but rather to affirm in a glorious burst of thanksgiving and celebration that those who had survived the violence could say, "We are alive, despite it all, against all odds, we are alive."[53] Perhaps the clearest lesson of the last two decades is that it would be a serious mistake to underestimate what the Maya who had survived such violence and their supporters are capable of accomplishing.

Notes

1 *Guatemala: Memoria del Silencio*, Resumen del Informe de la Comisión para el Esclarecimiento Histórico, 16, 20; for a summary of Tomuschat's speech see *el Periódico*, 26 de feb. 1999, 4.

2 *Guatemala: Memoria*, 17, 21.

3 *el Periódico*, 26 de feb. 1999, 4.

4 This, of course, is a shameless simplification of a complex and convoluted period of Guatemalan history. For a more complete discussion see R.L. Woodward, *Rafael Carrera and the Emergence of the Republic of Guatemala, 1821-1871* (Athens: University of Georgia Press, 1993); Julio Pinto Soria, *Raíces históricas del estado en Centroamérica*, 2nd ed., (Guatemala: Editorial Universitaria, 1983); and Arturo Taracena Arriola, *Invención Criolla, Sueño Ladino, Pesadilla Indígena* (Antigua, Guatemala: CIRMA, 1996).

5 Cited in E. Higbee, "The Agricultural Regions of Guatemala," *Geographical Review* 37, 2 (1947): 177-201. See also D. McCreery, *Rural Guatemala, 1760-1940* (Stanford: Stanford University Press, 1994); Julio Castellano Cambranes, *Coffee and Peasants in Guatemala* (Stockholm: Plumsock Foundation, 1985); and Jim Handy, *Gift of the Devil: A History of Guatemala* (Boston: South End, 1984).

6 Carol Smith, "Origins of the National Question in Guatemala: A Hypothesis," in Carol Smith, ed., *Guatemalan Indians and the State* (Austin: University of Texas Press, 1990); Jim Handy, "Anxiety and Dread: State and Community in Modern Guatemala," *Canadian Journal of History* 25, 1 (1991): 43-65.

7 Miguel Angel Asturias, *El Problema Social y otros textos* (Paris: Centre de Recherches de l'Institut d'Etudes Hispaniques, 1971); Steven Palmer, "A Liberal Discipline: Inventing Nations in Guatemala and Costa Rica, 1880-1900," PhD dissertation, Columbia University, 1990.

8 George Lovell and Chris Lutz, "Conquest and Population: Maya Demography in Historical Perspective," paper presented at the Latin American Studies Association, Los Angeles, 1994.

9 The importance of the "Indian question" in Guatemala is illustrated by the inability (or unwillingness) to agree on the current number of Maya. Government figures suggest the Maya are around 40% of the population. A recent work by the International Fund for Agricultural Development, using what they call the most conservative estimates, puts the percentage of Mayan population at 43.8%, whereas a recent paper by George Lovell and Chris Lutz estimates that population at 60%. Mayan groups generally argue that the

Mayan population is between 60 and 65% of the population. See *Censos Nacionales de 1981, IX Censo de población*, vol. 1, 37; Mauricio Gnere, *Indigenous Peoples of Latin America*, Working Paper No. 30, IAFD, 1990; and Lovell and Lutz, 1994.

10 Jim Handy, *Revolution in the Countryside: Rural Conflict and Agrarian Reform in Guatemala, 1944-54* (Chapel Hill: University of North Carolina Press, 1994).

11 Handy, *Revolution in the Countryside*; Susanne Jonas, *The Battle for Guatemala* (Boulder: Westview Press, 1991).

12 Jonas, *The Battle for Guatemala*; Handy, *Revolution in the Countryside*; Michael McClintock, *The American Connection, Vol. 2: State Terror and Popular Resistance in Guatemala* (London: Zed Press, 1985).

13 Arturio Arias, "Changing Indian Identity: Guatemala's Violent Transition to Modernity," in C. Smith, ed., *Guatemalan Indians and the State*, 1990; Kay Warren, *The Symbolism of Subordination* (Austin: University of Texas Press, 1989); Douglas Brintnall, *Revolt against the Dead* (New York: Gordon and Breach, 1976); Handy, *Revolution in the Countryside*; Ricardo Falla, *Quiché Rebelde* (Guatemala: Editorial Universitaria, 1978).

14 Mario Payeras, *Los Dias de la selva* (Mexico City: Siglo xxi, 1980).

15 Smith, "Origins of the National Question in Guatemala"; Jonas, *The Battle for Guatemala*; David Stoll, *Between Two Armies in the Ixil Towns of Guatemala* (New York: Columbia University Press, 1993); and Mario Payeras, *Los Pueblos Indígenas y la Revolución Guatemalteca* (Guatemala: Editores Madre Tierra, 1997).

16 Cited in *Noticias de Guatemala*, October 15, 1982, and Comité Pro Justicia y Paz de Guatemala, *Human Rights in Guatemala*, 1984, 10-11. See also Robert Carmack, ed., *Harvest of Violence* (Norman, OK: University of Oklahoma Press, 1988).

17 Centro de Estudios, *La Democracia de las Armas* (Guatemala: Nueva Imagen Guatemala, 1994); and Angela Delli Sante, *Nightmare or Reality: Guatemala in the 1980s* (Amsterdam: Thela, 1996).

18 James Goldston, *Shattered Hope: Guatemalan Workers and the Promise of Democracy* (Boulder: Westview Press, 1991); and Tania Palencio Prada, *Peace in the Making* (London: Catholic Institute for International Relations, 1996).

19 Tania Palencio Prada and David Holiday, *Hacia un nuevo rol ciudadaño para democratizar Guatemala* (Montreal: Centro Internacional de Derechos Humanos y Desarollo Democrático, 1996).

20 Jim Handy, "Demilitarizing Community in Guatemala," *Canadian Journal of Latin American and Caribbean Studies* 19, 37-38: 35-60; Santiago Bastos and Manuela Camus, *Abriendo Caminos* (Guatemala: FLACSO, 1995); Bastos and Camus, *Quebrando el Silencio* (Guatemala, FLACSO, 1996); and Alex Taylor del Cid, "Morning Comes for the Dawn," MA thesis, University of Saskatchewan, 1994. Rosalina Tuyuc and the birth of CONAVIGUA are well-celebrated in Guatemala and there is significant literature on both. For two of

the many interviews with Rosalina Tuyuc see *La Hora*, March 6, 1993, 7; and *Polémica* 15: 34-36. For a summary of her life in English see Emilie Smith-Ayala (comp.), *The Granddaughters of Ixmucamé* (Toronto: Women's Press, 1991), 34-36.

21 Kay Warren, *Indigenous Movements and Their Critics* (Princeton: Princeton University Press, 1998). For examples of the newspaper coverage of the movement see *Prensa Libre*, October 4, 1992, 6; and *Prensa Libre, Domingo*, October 11, 1992, 6-7; *La Hora*, 12 de October 1992, 3.

22 *Siglo Veintiuno*, October 12, 1992, 49 and 79.

23 For the most important writings of this group see Demetrio Cojtí Cuxil, *Configuración el Pensamiento Político del Pueblo Maya* (Quetzaltenango, Guatemala: Association de Escritores Mayanese, 1991); Demetrio Rodríquez Guaján, ed., *Cultura Maya y Políticas del Desarrollo* (Chimaltenango: Editores Cocadi, 1989). For analysis of these arguments see Edward Fischer and R. McKenna Brown, eds., *Maya Cultural Activism in Guatemala* (Austin: University of Texas Press, 1996) and Warren, *Indigenous Movements*.

24 Rene Poitevin, *Guatemala: La Crisis de la Democracia* (Guatemala: FLACSO, 1993); Palencio Prado and Holiday, esp. 41-42; Tinamit, June 3, 1993; and Centro de Estudios, 118-24; Handy, *Revolution in the Countryside*.

25 *Prensa Libre*, December 30, 1996, 2, 4; see also *el Periódico*, December 27, 1996, 16-17; and *Siglo Veintiuno*, December 5, 1996, 4.

26 See "Convenio 169: Documento Especial," *Inforpress Centroamericana*, 5 de November 1992; also, "Declaration of Xelaju." The Declaration of Xelaju was the declaration of a meeting of the Committee of 500 years of indigenous resistance. This group met in Quezaltenango in 1991. The Declaration has not been published.

27 *La Hora*, October 29, 1992, 12.

28 *Prensa Libre*, November 2, 1992, 10; November 4, 1992, 10.

29 *Siglo Veintiuno*, November 4, 1992, 11.

30 *La Hora*, October 5, 1992, 2.

31 There is an immense literature concerning the progress of Convention 169 in Guatemala. See *Ruitzijol* (September 1996): 7-8; *Noticias de Guatemala*, "Crónica del 169" (March 1996): 3-4; and editorials in *Siglo Veintiuno*, 16 de November 1992, 20; 31 de October 1992, 12-13; 20 de September 1992, 6-7; and *Prensa Libre*, 5 de November 1992, 12; 11 de October 1992, 8-9.

32 *Ruitzijol*, March 16-31, 1995, 1; Warren, 1998, 56-57; and Demetrio Cojtí Cuxil, "Estudio Evaluativo del Cumplimiento del Acuerdo Sobre Identidad y Derechos de Los Pueblos Indígenas," in *Los Acuerdos de Paz* (Guatemala: FLACSO, 1996), 53-90.

33 Victor Gálvez Borrell et al., *Qué sociedad queremos?* (Guatemala: FLACSO, 1997), 7.

34 Cojtí Cuxil, 1995, 40-47.

35 For examples of various Mayan writings about nationalism see Associación de Escritores Mayanses, *Configuración del Pensamiento Político del Pueblo Maya*

(Guatemala: Cholsamaj, 1995); and V. Gálvez Borrell et al.; Luis Enrique Sam Colop, "The Discourse of Concealment and 1992" in *Maya Cultural Activism* (Austin: University of Texas Press, 1996).

36 *Siglo Veintiuno*, Februrary 28, 1997, 13.

37 Ibid., January 24, 1997, 13.

38 Ibid., *Domingo*, May 4, 1997, 15.

39 See, for example, Alfred Kaltschmitt, Ibid., April 5, 1997, 13.

40 Ibid., February 10, 1997, 13.

41 Ibid., February 24, 1997, 13.

42 Ibid., April 7, 1997, 13.

43 *Reformas a la Constitución Política de la República de Guatemala*, 1999.

44 *Prensa Libre*, May 12, 1999.

45 See, for example, Lucy Barrios, "Si y No en recta final" *Prensa Libre*, May 10, 1999.

46 Ibid.

47 Danilio Valladares, "Indigenas Entre el Si o No," *Prensa Libre*, May 12, 1999.

48 "Matan a Secretario General adjunto del FDNG" *Siglo Veintiuno*, May 14, 1999.

49 "No se modifican la Constitución" *Prensa Libre*, May 18, 1999.

50 "Tiempo y destino," Ibid., May 16, 1999.

51 Ibid., May 18, 1999.

52 *Prensa Libre*, October 25, 2000, 15.

53 Ricardo Falla, *Masacres en la Selva* (Guatemala: FLACSO, 1992).

11

Coming to Terms with the Terror and History of Pol Pot's Cambodia (1975-79)

David Chandler[1]

The wheel of history turns ceaselessly.
Don't put your hand or your foot into it or it will certainly cut them off.

— Khmer Rouge saying.

In this essay, I will be dealing with a key institution of Democratic Kampuchea (DK) which encapsulated the terror that suffused the regime and was intimately connected with DK's triumphalist notions of history. I'll also discuss the ways in which recent Cambodian history has been imagined and altered by successive regimes. I'll examine how induced memories, followed by induced amnesia, can play havoc with attempts to assemble and interpret historic data, to say nothing of efforts to achieve reconciliation or closure. These manipulations of history, which form a part of Cambodian political culture, impede the search for justice that continues to elude millions of survivors of the Pol Pot era.

The key facility that I will discuss was known in the DK era by its code name, S-21, the subject of my most recent book.[2] The "S" stood for *santebal*, a neologism translatable as "security police"; the meaning of "21" is unclear. The role of workers at the secret facility was to interrogate, document, and " smash" people suspected of plotting against the regime. From May 1976 onward, S-21 occupied the site of a former high school in a southern suburb of Phnom Penh.

Between late 1975 (when S-21 occupied another site) and January 1979, when the so-called Khmer Rouge regime was overthrown by a Vietnamese

---

invasion, over 14,000 men, women, and children were dealt with at the facility by the security police. Thousands of these prisoners were interrogated, often at great length. Most of them were tortured. All but half a dozen survivors were eventually killed. Over the years, a voluminous archive was maintained at S-21 that provides vivid and detailed documentary evidence of the crimes against humanity committed by the Khmer Rouge during their years in power.

In the early 1980s, when Cambodia was effectively a Vietnamese protectorate, S-21 was transformed into a museum of genocidal crimes, modeled to an extent on facilities in Eastern Europe that commemorate the Nazi Holocaust against the Jews. Cambodia's Vietnamese mentors, led by a colonel named Mai Lam, were eager to demonstrate that DK had been a "fascist" regime that had engaged in "genocide," rather than a recognizably Communist one obsessed with smashing its political opponents.

Whether or not what happened under the Khmer Rouge constituted genocide under the UN Convention has inspired heated debate among scholars and human rights activists. There is no doubt that massive crimes against humanity occurred in DK. The Khmer Rouge leadership must be held responsible for them. Arguments over whether what occurred was genocide or not are bolstered or break down when the regime's intentions are discussed or when it is noted that the vast majority of the regime's victims were ethnic Cambodians, or Khmer.[3]

What happened under DK? Between April 1975 and January 1979 close to two million people died of malnutrition, overwork, misdiagnosed diseases, and executions. At least 200,000 of them were executed summarily as enemies of the state. Over half a million Cambodians subsequently left the country and took up residence overseas. Under these circumstances, the word "genocide" has a certain explanatory power, even if the UN convention might not be easily brought into play. The phrase "crimes against humanity" is even more descriptive.

S-21 was a crucial instrument of DK's political will. It was also a secret institution embedded within a secretive regime. Outside of the people who worked there and the prisoners, only a handful of high-ranking officials knew of its existence or what went on inside its walls. According to the former head of the prison, interviewed by an enterprising journalist in 1999 (after managing to keep out of sight for twenty years), confession texts of important prisoners went directly to the so-called "upper brothers," led by Pol Pot, "Brother Number 1," who ran the country. His deputy, Nuon Chea, who was responsible for Party matters, followed the operations of the prison with special attention, and so did "Brother Number 3," Son Sen, who was charged with Cambodian national security at the time.[4]

When I embarked on my research on S-21 I hoped to use the prison's voluminous archive, which consists largely of the prisoners' forced confessions, to write a narrative history of DK. However, I soon discovered that the confessions and the "memories" that they contained were often phantasmagoric and had always been induced through terror. Because many of the prisoners (but which ones?) were clearly innocent of the crimes to which they confessed, the archive was a rat's nest of uncorroborated truth, half-truth, and falsehood that was impossible for me to unravel.

The confessions were important to the rulers of DK, just as similar documents had been to Stalin in the 1930s and for East European politicians later on—to say nothing of confessions extracted under torture by non-Communist regimes in power in the 1970s in Greece, Chile, and Argentina. The confessions provided all these leaders with tangible evidence of the guilt of the enemies that they believed surrounded them. They were induced historical texts, linked to the ruling party's triumphal notions of its history and to what the psychiatrist Donald Spence has referred to as "narrative truth." As we shall see, they also had psychological uses and importance.[5]

Reading the confessions from S-21 is like revisiting Franz Kafka's novel *The Trial,* in which Joseph K is not accused because he is guilty, but is guilty because he has been accused. Many new arrivals at S-21 were asked, bewilderingly, "Why were you arrested?" to which many of them replied, truthfully, that they didn't know. In one such case, the interrogator said, "The Organization isn't stupid. It never catches people who aren't guilty." Linguistically, the interrogator was correct. After all, the Cambodian phrase, which we translate as "prisoner" (*neak thos*), literally means "guilty person."[6]

In what follows I will be drawing on documents from the S-21 archive to illuminate the themes of history and terror as produced and practised in DK. I also want to suggest why coming to terms with that history in recent times has been so difficult, not only for the current Cambodian government but also for surviving victims of DK. In this regard, I will discuss Cambodian popular memory and the ways in which the Museum of Genocidal Crimes, along with other factors, may have helped to shape Cambodians' understanding of their recent history by providing a standardized "explanation" for an unnerving era. Finally, I will be examining the current regime's efforts to alter, override, or expunge these memories, and to "move on," largely via imposed forgetfulness and legalistic legerdemain toward an ersatz form of national reconciliation. I will be placing the government's efforts in the context of the impending trials of certain Khmer Rouge leaders. These trials, many hope, will provide the closure that is necessary for genuine justice and reconciliation. Others, myself included, doubt that meaningful trials will ever take place.[7]

Like several of the governments in recent years, the Cambodian government has decided to deal, albeit obliquely, with the horrors of the past. Unlike most of the other governments, however, the Cambodians have decided not to confront the horrors by means of a far-reaching tribunal, a truth commission, or any extended judicial inquiries. Instead, they have suggested that it is time that the horrors were forgotten. Cambodia's prime minister, Hun Sen, in the course of offering amnesties to some high-ranking Khmer Rouge leaders in December 1999, enjoined Cambodians, succinctly, to "dig a hole and bury the past."

His statement, delivered off the cuff, represented a serious change in policy. Whereas Cambodian schoolbooks published in the 1980s had stressed the evils of the Khmer Rouge era, schoolbooks today hardly mention the period at all. Similarly, in the 1980s, with Vietnamese encouragement, a national consensus was built around remembering, demonizing, and opposing the Khmer Rouge. Nowadays a new consensus is being built around induced amnesia and mandated reconciliation. The same authorities have proposed both scenarios, suggesting that in Cambodia "history" (like the "history" produced by confessions at S-21) there is an induced phenomenon that is also a tactical weapon available to those in power.

In fairness, the earlier consensus played on and reflected widespread fears that the Khmer Rouge might return to power. As long as the Khmer Rouge (and their non-Communist allies) posed a genuine military threat, authorities believed that the country needed to be united to oppose them. One form this opposition took was the wholesale demonization of DK.

When the threat slowly evaporated in 1996-98, the second scenario began to come into play. DK's former foreign minister Ieng Sary (condemned to death alongside Pol Pot in absentia in 1979) accepted an amnesty from Phnom Penh in 1996. Some time later, after "Brother Number 3," Son Sen, was murdered by his colleagues, Pol Pot " Brother Number 1," was tried by a "peoples' court" and sequestered by a Khmer Rouge faction led by the movement's military commander, Ta Mok. Pol Pot died in 1998. In the following year, Nuon Chea, "Brother Number 2," and another Khmer Rouge leader, Khieu Samphan, were granted amnesties by Hun Sen. The trial of Ta Mok, who was arrested in 1999, is in the offing. Other trials of lesser Khmer Rouge figures may follow. The Phnom Penh government, however, is reluctant to prosecute the people it has amnestied, and has been slow to proceed with trials for the ones it holds in prison. As this is written (March 2003) the possibility has become less remote than before that the Khmer Rouge leaders will be brought fully to account, but it still seems unlikely that the DK era will ever be examined systematically in a judicial context.

Many observers of Cambodia, and many Cambodians, find this situation abhorrent. After all, they assert, horrendous crimes against humanity were committed under DK. Some of the known criminals are free, and so are several people who shared command of the country. What the "Cambodian people" want, however, and how many of them want it, is easy for outsiders to speculate about but impossible to determine. Polling is in its infancy in Cambodia, and most Khmer are unaccustomed to thinking about issues on a national scale. Their political culture, like most others in the world, is roomy enough to contain overlapping traditions of revenge, forgiveness, forgetting, indifference, and rehabilitation. There is no national consensus on the issue of a trial for the Khmer Rouge, just as there is nothing like the widespread support for the death penalty that apparently exists in the United States.[8]

As outsiders, we are entitled to ask if opening old wounds, on a national basis, is more beneficial for at least some of the wounded than covering them over and hoping they will heal. Comparing psychic wounds to physical ones, to be sure, is not very helpful; after all, some physical wounds heal if they are bandaged up, others heal if they are exposed to the air. Moreover, to complicate matters, as Steve Heder pointed out at a conference in Madison, Wisconsin, in 1998, there is no sure way of knowing whether the Germans or the Japanese, the excavators or the buriers of their respective pasts, are, en masse, psychically better off.

In the earlier consensus, the "S-21" museum played a prominent role. The exhibits that were set up there in 1979-80, and at the prison's killing field of Choeung Ek outside Phnom Penh, made the point that an evil regime had preyed upon its people in a ruthless, "fascist" fashion. The annually celebrated "days of hate" throughout the 1980s made a similar point. Every May 20, memories of the Pol Pot period were systematically aired in public, so as to demonize "Pol Pot" and his "genocidal clique" and to justify the confrontation with Khmer Rouge guerrillas on the Thai-Cambodian border. Survivors of S-21 were called upon, year after year, to talk about the cruelties that they had endured.

Although the word "fascist" has passed out of favour, the sites of S-21 and Choeung Ek are still presented to the foreign tourists, who now make up the majority of people visiting them, as horrors dropped onto the Cambodian people from elsewhere. Signage at the sites makes no mention of the Communist Party of Kampuchea (CPK), or of Vietnamese involvement in establishing the exhibits.[9]

One effect of these efforts has been to produce a "standard narrative" of the DK period in which the perpetrators seemed to come from somewhere else and in which nearly everyone was an innocent victim. This narrative resonated with many others over the years, in which many Cambodians have come to see themselves as more sinned against than sinning, and as the helpless victims of outside forces. The theme recurs in several survivors' accounts, particularly those written by people who were adolescents or children in the DK era, and in no position to understand the ideas behind the revolution, or the international context in which DK occurred.[10]

Judy Ledgerwood's essay about memory and S-21 links this governing narrative to what Michael Vickery, writing in the early 1980s, has critically referred to as the Standard Total View of Democratic Kampuchea, convenient for demonization and consistent with many survivors' memories, but of limited use for serious historians.[11]

In fact, while some kind of standardized narrative suited the needs of journalists and of those in power, and probably satisfied many survivors as well, few Cambodians were brought to judgement under the Vietnamese for their activities in the DK era. Instead, the Vietnamese consistently granted informal amnesties to ex-Khmer Rouge who "repented" and chose to live under their jurisdiction. In the process hundreds of former DK cadre were quietly absorbed into the successor regime, which was led to a large extent by men like Hun Sen and Chea Sim, who had defected from the movement in 1977-78. The regime reserved its enmity for those who took up arms against them and, of course, for the two-man "genocidal clique" of Pol Pot and Ieng Sary, respectively the prime minister and foreign minister of DK. The pair was condemned to death in absentia by a tribunal hastily assembled in Phnom Penh in August 1979, and closure of a kind, if not reconciliation was hurriedly achieved.[12]

The decade-long demonization of the Khmer Rouge, however, has allowed Western journalists, for example, to write that Pol Pot "murdered" over two million people, a telling example of oversimplification. Many others in the West, to put it mildly, could not care less. Lindsay French's recent paper about an exhibit of photographs from S-21 at the Museum of Modern Art suggests, indeed, that the pleasure of looking at victims (from anywhere) can easily outweigh our interest in who the people are or in their historical context. Similarly, it may be more in the interests of some outsiders that the Cambodians deal "appropriately" with their suffering than that they try their best to overcome and sublimate a wide range of traumatic memories.[13]

Turning back to S-21, which so hauntingly exemplifies the regime: people have often asked me why people who were so secretive and technophobic maintained such a massive, well-organized archive. I've also been asked why so many confessions were extracted, filed, and maintained when the existence of S-21 was a secret and when all but a handful of the prisoners were killed. Why was everyone photographed if everyone who was photographed was killed? Finally, there's the question of what value so many induced, uncorroborated confessions, so many spurious (or genuine but ineffectual) conspiracies, and so many versions of the "truth" might have had for the Khmer Rouge leaders who read the documents at the time.

One answer is that workers at S-21 wanted to avoid the wrath and gain the approval of their concealed and terrifying superiors. Playing it safe, they processed as many documents as fully as they could.

Moreover, the former schoolteachers running the prison led by a former mathematics teacher named Kang Kech Ieu (Duch) wanted to administer a modern, well-documented security operation, worthy of a Communist regime, consonant with the flow of history, and pleasing to themselves.

A more intriguing rationale for the archive, suggested to me by Steve Heder, is that the confession texts, and to a lesser extent the mug shots of "guilty people," were intended to serve as an ongoing, dialectical history of the Communist Party of Kampuchea (CPK), then governing the country. The confessions and mug shots were materials for a counterhistory, evidence of the multitudinous enemies that the Party had uncovered and smashed on its way to liberating the country from centuries of oppression. Because enemies were everywhere, the revolution, as Mao Zedong had often argued, had to be continuous. "Bourgeois" tendencies existed inside individuals long after bourgeois institutions had been smashed.

The archive showed DK's leaders that the party's therapeutic machinery, "sweeping clean" the entire country, was working well. In a sense, the interrogators at S-21 were therapists and the prisoners' confessions were the objectified fantasies of the interrogators' all-powerful patrons or "patients," i.e., Pol Pot and his associates. Like Stalin in the 1930s or Mao Zedong a decade later in Ya'nan, the men and women in Cambodia's Party Center needed to know that those whom they considered to be their enemies were in the process of being caught, exposed, "rectified" and "smashed" and that their often baseless fantasies were being objectified and put to rest.[14]

In pre-revolutionary Cambodia, as in many other countries, centralized power, control over historical documents and the production of history went hand in hand. From medieval times until the 1950s, historical chronicles were prepared at the Cambodian court to legitimize the genealogy of a given ruler and to chart his accession to power. These crowded, heroic, and often fictive documents were held in the palace and became parts of a king's regalia. Very few historical texts were composed elsewhere. In other words, what the rulers considered to be "history" was what was written down on their behalf. The process is not unique to Cambodia, of course, but it has implications for the way that the history of the Pol Pot era is being handled today, and how this handling (or mishandling) of history, as we shall see, impedes reconciliation. More linear, verifiable, "neutral" notions of history were introduced in Cambodia by the French in the colonial era, but these "new" histories in spite or perhaps because of their exactitude, seldom caught fire among the Khmer.[15]

Historiography became even simpler under Pol Pot. There were no schools in DK, and no history textbooks. Instead, small-scale and national histories, centred on the Communist Party, were composed, controlled, and held by what was known as the "ruling apparatus" (*kbal masin*). Texts prepared for study sessions, like those in the past, praised the Party and described how its enemies had been defeated. At the same time, history writing as a genre became different. Whereas Khmer Rouge history texts, like pre-revolutionary ones, reflected favourably on the ruler, Marxist-Leninist history, in theory, was teleological, dialectical, and collective, supposedly in tune with scientific laws. By mastering these laws, it was thought, the Communist Party of Kampuchea had seized power and would maintain itself thereafter.

Several Party histories from the early 1970s that follow this line of thinking have survived. With what Timothy Carney has called its "unexpected victory" in April 1975, the CPK achieved the closure it desired. Cambodia's "2,000 year" history became, at that moment, coterminous with the Party's rise to power. In much the same way, millennia of Vietnamese history, displayed in the National Museum in Hanoi, come to their apotheosis in exhibits on the top floor depicting the triumph of the Indochina Communist Party, led by Ho Chi Minh, in September 1945. For the Pol Pot regime at least, alternative or plural readings of the past were both irrelevant and untrue. They could be discarded, buried, or whited out. In this sense, Party histories, despite their surface modernity, conformed to earlier models and foreshadowed the attitudes taken by the subsequent regime.

I would argue that the prisoners at S-21 and their confessions provided a shadow-history of the Party and a challenge, unsuccessful to be sure, to its ideas and its power. To allow the shadow-history a life of its own would have opened up Democratic Kampuchea in unpredictable and potentially ruinous ways. While the revolution itself was thought of as continuous, the notion of history ending with the defeat or disappearance of the Party was unthinkable. Similarly, in 2000, DK's successor regime seems to believe that an open, internationally monitored trial of its former enemies might threaten those in power or at least rekindle notions and interpretations of history that might destabilize the ruling party and lessen its leaders' ability to control events.

In May 1976, Pol Pot, speaking to some of his colleagues, gave them a clear idea of how history might be written from then on. Pol Pot noted that "Our history must be compiled in a brief, accessible form. We must compile the history of struggle, including short narratives of our peoples' and army's revolution, which we can broadcast on the radio or publish in periodicals so that the people may study it further, *change their perceptions of history and absorb the new narrative* (ruong raav)"[16] [emphasis added].

History under DK had hardly any heroes. There are several reasons for this. To begin with, the energies of the revolution were thought to be collective, impersonal ones, overriding the individualism that Party documents criticized in pre-revolutionary culture. The leadership of DK was collective at the centre and, in theory at least, throughout the country. More importantly, the leaders of the CPK believed that they owed much of their success and perhaps their intrinsic strength to secrecy. Even in victory, they concealed themselves from view and clung to revolutionary pseudonyms. They withheld biographical data about themselves. They seldom appeared in public. By sticking to these methods, which imitated what they believed to be the behaviour of Communist leaders in other countries, the men and women who comprised the Party Center believed that they had defeated "the United States." Their war against other enemies continued. Politics, indeed, became the continuation of war by other means. From concealed positions, the leaders retained their freedom of manoeuvre.

Some of the secrecy dissipated when the CPK came into the open in October 1977, and Pol Pot made a state visit to China, but until the closing months of the regime there was very little evidence that Pol Pot had succumbed to a cult of personality. The tentative steps in this direction taken at that time were reversed as soon as DK was overthrown, suggesting that the leaders felt more comfortable in hiding.[17]

This hero-deprived history, dominated by the faceless and supposedly clairvoyant "revolutionary organization" (*angkar padevat*), came equipped with a series of easily recognizable villains: Japanese fascists, French colonialists, American imperialists, foreign intelligence agencies, Vietnamese "consumers of territory," compradors, princes, landlords, "hidden enemies burrowing from within," and so on. In a speech in December 1976, Pol Pot compared the revolution's enemies to "germs." The confessions at S-21 teem with the names of enemies while mentioning the Party's heroic, hidden leaders elliptically if at all. This may be because individuals are seen by definition to cause harm while collectivities, acting on behalf of history, and attuned to it, protect the people.

The continual search for enemies in DK was a crucial ingredient of practice. Because Cambodia's leaders subscribed to the Maoist doctrine of continuous revolution, "enemies" were perennially created and purges (the Cambodian compound verb, *boh somat*, translates as "sweep [and] clean") were continuously needed to assure the safety of the "upper brothers" and to maintain the revolution's purity and momentum. "Sweeping and cleaning" could never stop. Building and defending the country were permanently linked, and they went hand in hand. At another level, because struggle was a permanent feature of politics, national reconciliation was never considered.

Because the revolution was continuous, its enemies could never be permanently removed. Put another way, because enemies would always be everywhere, revolutionary vigilance and terror could never stop. Moreover, even if external and internal enemies disappeared, counterrevolutionary *attitudes* were still embedded within everyone's personality. The extirpation of enemies and standpoints were neverending. The enemies altered on a daily basis like the daily specials on a restaurant menu. A 1976 handbook for interrogators at S-21 made the point succinctly "the Party changes frequently. The Party changes the prisoner being interrogated in no fixed pattern. The Party goes from one group to another and sometimes changes our duties. The Party also changes its methods for making documents, for interrogation, for doing politics, for propaganda, for torture. We must adjust ourselves to the situation, leaping along with the movement of 3 [metric] tons per hectare."[18]

My exposure to the S-21 archive and other DK documents has convinced me that the handful of men and women running Cambodia in the 1970s, led by Pol Pot and Nuon Chea, saw themselves as the custodians of Cambodian history and as the heirs and beneficiaries of Marx, Lenin, Stalin, and Mao. They were interested in power for themselves, to be sure, but Pol Pot in particular strikes me as having been imprisoned or swept along by strongly held, contradictory beliefs that transcended his personal ambition. Nuon Chea, trained as a member of the Thai Communist Party in the 1940s, seems never to have questioned the rightness of the cause. The same convictions impelled the director of S-21, Kang Kech Ieu (Duch) as he went about the Party's business, guided the conduct of interrogators at the prison, and ushered over 14,000 men, women, and children to their deaths.[19]

> The most dangerous of Pol Pot's ideas, perhaps, was that he had grasped the wheel of history (kong *pravatt'sas* a favorite Khmer Rouge expression, drawn from the *Communist Manifesto*.) To maintain his grip, control the future, mimic the success of Stalin and Mao and to produce a pleasing "narrative truth," Pol Pot and his colleagues felt obliged to set in motion an unstoppable reign of terror. They could never look back. It was impossible (as well as immoral) to reverse the wheel. Compromise and delay were out of the question. Enemies were everywhere. Victory, while supposedly inevitable, was always out of sight. In the meantime, as a former engineer who survived DK has recalled, CPK cadre frequently told their audiences that, "We prefer to kill ten friends rather than keep one enemy alive."[20]

Ironically, the ratio of innocent to guilty victims at S-21 may have been close to this.

The hubris and paranoia of the Party leadership, as far as hidden enemies were concerned, come to life in a passage from a 1978 speech by Pol Pot to the Party cadre. As he spoke, DK and Vietnam had been at war for several months. DK's headstrong, poorly conceived economic programs had led to tens of thousands of deaths from malnutrition and overwork. Tens of thousands of "class enemies" had been imprisoned in provincial "education halls" (the word "prison" was not used in DK), where thousands of them had already died of starvation, mistreatment, and executions. The upper reaches of the Party had been savagely purged. The national administration was in tatters. Hidden enemies, the leadership insisted, continued their subversion. Against these odds, Pol Pot was feverishly optimistic, and it is worth asking, though we will never know the answer, if he believed what he was saying. Whether he suspected that the end was near is impossible to say. Here is what he said:

> [Hidden enemies] were able to carry the signboard (*plaque*) "Revolution" temporarily, masquerade as revolutionaries, burrow away, build up their treasonous forces inside our revolutionary ranks and damage our revolution at a time when our revolution wasn't strong, hot or battle hardened, when it still took the form of a secret network or when it was cut off from the masses. But at the moment when the revolutionary mass movement sprang out seethingly, resplendent with power, when the secret networks awoke, at that point the buried enemies boring from within no longer had a place to hide, no matter how important they were. Every single one of their silent, shielded, masked activities aimed at destroying the revolution could be seen clearly by the revolutionary masses and could be smashed at once.[21]

The entanglement of friends and enemies in this Manichaean passage begins with the word "masquerade," for in the pre-1975 period being discussed, some of the Party's enemies who had received "false" training in Vietnam were pretending to be Communists while the "real" Communists were pretending to belong to a non-Communist united front, led by Prince Sihanouk. Both factions were "secretly building up their forces," and when the revolution resplendently "sprang out" at an unspecified date, giving the enemies no "place to hide," the Party's resplendent leaders remained concealed. Similarly, the Party's enemies could only be "seen clearly by the revolutionary masses and smashed at once" after they had been secretly arrested, intensively interrogated, and put to death in a secret prison. What was "seen clearly" by the masses was whatever the Party Center served up to limited numbers of them, ostensibly on their behalf. In effect, Pol Pot was sharing his clairvoyance with a selected group of true believers who needed encouragement and who knew that many of their colleagues had already been crushed by the wheel of history, for reasons it was impossible for them to understand.

The passage opposes an open, enlightened, wakeful, resplendent, and liberating CPK, to the closed, dark, dormant, burrowing, and enslaving forces arrayed against it. The sun, as it were, is being compared to germs and mice. To those listening to it, the passage might have suggested the Buddha's battle with the forces of evil assembled by Mara.[22] When the article appeared, moreover, "enemies burrowing from within" had become synonymous with the Vietnamese "consumers of Cambodian territory" who were "burrowing into" the country from the East and posing a threat to the "Cambodian race."

The passage also suggests that the Party Center needed to control the way the past was read. Any indications that the leadership had miscalculated the future or misjudged subordinates had to be erased. As in Stalin's Russia, "enemies " had to be found who could be exposed to the sunlight of the Party and could be accused of everything that went wrong. Since the leaders could not be guilty any more than the people on whose behalf the revolution was being waged, guilt had to be assigned to the tissue connecting the leaders and the people, namely errant members of the CPK.

"Swept clean" and "smashed" by terror, these "CIA agents," "Vietnamese," "germs," and "national traitors" were periodically snuffed out, only to have another ring of them come into view, popping up like targets to be shot down.

It should be clear by now that the history embodied in the confessions from S-21, or in speeches like this, is not a narrative political history, or even a valuable primary source for such a history. Instead it is a history that narrates and objectifies the regime's triumphs and its darkest fears.

Because the CPK was small, young, and relatively tightly knit, and because its fears were so pervasive, open-ended attacks on "strings of traitors" within its ranks were bound to have devastating effects. There were no mechanisms at S-21 or elsewhere in DK that could decelerate the destructive process. As the men running S-21 did as they were told, or imagined would be pleasing, they helped to destroy the Party, dismantle the administrative structure of the country, and undermine Cambodia's military effectiveness. The killing machine, like the wheel of history again, had no braking system. The hubris and paranoia of the Party Center had no limits. At a semantic level, the all-consuming purges made macabre sense. After all, how could anyone ever be sure that the last concealed enemy, the one who could be blamed for everything, had been found?

Only when removed from power and forced into exile did the Party Center stop devouring its own. The destruction of enemies, which had been one of the its core activities, seems to have been anesthetized for almost twenty years. When it reasserted itself in 1997 and 1998 with the murder of Son Sen and members of his family and the subsequent "trials" of Pol Pot by his colleagues, what seems to have been the Party's destiny—to tear itself to bits—was fulfilled. The Party dug a hole and buried the past. It imploded on itself and most of its surviving members soon defected en masse to the authorities in Phnom Penh.[23]

Most Cambodians today, when they talk about the Khmer Rouge regime, present themselves as victims. They have been conditioned to do so not only by their own memories and experiences but also by the propaganda efforts of the regime that replaced DK in 1979 and which has held the balance of power in Cambodia (except for a brief UN protectorate) ever since. A similar process of standardizing readings of the past is taking place in China, vis à vis the Cultural Revolution.

In the process, as we have argued, a total narrative of life under DK has emerged that satisfies peoples' needs for innocence and demonization and allows some of the survivors (whether they had been victims, perpetrators, or bystanders) to become reconciled with what they want to remember of the past. In this way, the lucky ones may find it easier to continue living. Others will continue to find it painful or impossible to confront or to escape the past. To those of us concerned systemically with justice, the ambiguous mixture fails to please. The clear-cut certainties of Nuremberg, even when confronting a regime as horrific as DK, have lost a great deal their power.

At the same time, the horrors of the DK era cannot be minimized or overlooked. The phrase "crimes against humanity" are still descriptive. The names of the collective leadership are known. The leaders who survive can bear responsibility for the horrors that occurred.

Within this context, blaming Pol Pot, who is dead, and comparing him to Hitler, makes more sense to many survivors of DK than being told by Hun Seen that then was then and now is now, or that nothing much happened in DK. Such oversimplifications are nonetheless unsatisfying to historians and also to those who would like to bring the perpetrators of the crimes to justice or simply to bear witness to the horrors inflicted on the country by the Khmer Rouge, however out of date this testimony may appear to others.[24]

It is as inane to blame the horrors of DK on a single man or on "genocidal clique" as it is to blame the horrors of the Cultural Revolution in China on "the Gang of Four." But doing so satisfies our craving for labels and for "personal" explanations. At the same time, it seems almost as wrong-headed to exhibit DK terror at the Museum of Genocidal Crimes (or at the Museum of Modern Art, where twenty-three mug shots from S-21 went on display, as art, in 1997) without providing any background, suggesting comparisons, or explaining DK's intentions. Calling the DK era a typhoon and Cambodians its helpless victims trivializes history, excuses the perpetrators, and infantilizes the victims and the survivors. On balance, deciding by fiat that what happened is no longer interesting because remembering what happened no longer serves the interests of those in power may be even more bizarre. In the meantime, some of the leading perpetrators are free to take the sun, talk guardedly to reporters, and cultivate their gardens.

Over the last fifty years, several governments have chosen, courageously or not, to come to grips with their recent traumatic or criminal experiences. Other countries have not. Germany, El Salvador, Chile, and South Africa fall into the first category, while Japan and China fall into the second, where it seems Cambodia also belongs, at least for the moment. All six countries, of course, have developed judicial systems, and, except for China, more familiarity with elements of democratic rule than has ever been the case in Cambodia.

The only hope for a tribunal or a truth commission to be convened in Cambodia, I believe, lies in the willingness of those in power to agree that in doing so they would enhance their prosperity and prestige. There have been few indications that this is the case or that the leaders are in a rush to change their minds. National reconciliation on their own terms is high on their agenda. They believe that when one's enemies have become one's friends, or are forgotten, Cambodia can be permanently at peace. The regime has imposed a view of history onto the people, and that is that. Popular pressure, such as it is in Cambodia, is insufficient to alter this decision. Popular views, insofar as they can be determined, seem split between the conflicting pressures of justice (which means re-entering the past) and peace, which may come more easily with forgetfulness. Like several other regimes over the last decade or so that are confronting horrors in the past, Cambodians are face to face with the dilemmas of reconciliation.[25]

At the same time, Cambodia is changing so rapidly in so many ways that even before the year is over the prospects for a responsible tribunal may have improved. The long-postponed trials of Ta Mok and Duch may open up areas of investigation that will be impossible for the regime to avoid. The prisoners may name names. Continuing international pressure for a tribunal, which is unlikely to let up, is also a crucial factor that may produce results.

It should be clear that I favour plural approaches and plural explanations for the patterns of recent Cambodian history and that I am more at ease pointing to dilemmas of reconciliation than I am at resolving them. This does not mean that crimes against humanity, of the sort that were committed on a daily basis at S-21, can be ignored, buried, or approached in a relativistic fashion. It is immoral to let Nuon Chea, Ta Mok, and Duch—to name only three—off the hook. Moreover, I believe that some sort of tribunal, even one that is stage-managed by those in power, will produce elements of reconciliation and closure merely by opening (and then shutting) a gruesome chapter in Cambodia's past.

Cambodia has had a long, continuous, and often tragic history. The current regime's control of the historical narrative, which resembles what earlier regimes have done, is an obstacle to full-scale reconciliation, and to the objective examination of the Khmer Rouge era. Reconciliation always comes with heightened awareness and a shared sense of responsibility. It will only be possible if the government agrees to open its eyes, not only to the tyranny of DK but to the smaller tyrannies inflicted on Cambodians throughout their past and on a daily basis. Reconciliation is also a matter of allowing a range of alternate voices to be heard. As some outsiders (like DK's former patron, China) plead for amnesia, others (like the United States) seek a full-scale international tribunal, ventilating Cambodia's "bad" history (but not America's). What matters most is what is most unlikely, namely that Cambodians be allowed to decide what to do about their history and how they can take possession of it.

The current regime's reluctance to confront the recent past, its suppression of plural explanations and alternate voices, its contempt for legal processes and its scorn for the human rights issues involved in a tribunal contain many elements of continuity with Cambodia's past. The terror of

DK has subsided, but history is still largely the property of those in charge, to be used as they see fit, against their real and imagined enemies. For the time being at least, for anyone else to put their hand or foot inside the wheel of history would be a serious mistake.

Notes

1 I am grateful to Trudy Govier, David A. Crocker, Tom Scheff, and two anonymous reviewers for comments on earlier versions of this paper.

2 David Chandler, *Voices from S-21: Terror and History in Pol Pot's Secret Prison* (Berkeley and Los Angeles: University of California Press, 1999).

3 For contrasting views on this issue, see Ben Kiernan, ed., *Genocide and Democracy in Cambodia* (New Haven: Yale University Southeast Asian Series, 1993) and Steve Heder, "Racism, Marxism, Labeling and Genocide in Ben Kiernan's *The Pol Pot Regime*," *Southeast Asia Research* 5, 2 (1997): 101-53.

4 See Nic Dunlop and Nate Thayer, "Duch Confesses," *Far Eastern Economic Review,* May 6, 1999, and Nic Dunlop, "KR Torture Chief Admits to Mass Murder," *Phnom Penh Post* April 30-May 13, 1999. According to Thayer (personal communication, June 2001) Duch considered himself to be a "technician of the revolution."

5 See Donald P. Spence, *Narrative Truth and Historical Truth* (New York: Norton, 1982).

6 Franz Kafka, *The Trial,* translated by Edwin and Willa Muir (New York: Schocken Books, 1937; and Vann Nath, *A Cambodian Prison Portrait: One Year on the Khmer Rouge's S-21* (Bangkok: 1998), 32. Similar exchanges occurred between captors and prisoners in the Soviet Union in the 1930s and in the purges that swept through China later on. For examples, see Chandler, *Voices from S-21,* 77 and 182, n. 2.

7 For a discussion of this issue, see David Chandler, "Will There Be a Trial for the Khmer Rouge?" *Ethics and International Affairs* 14 (2000): 67-82. The article owes much to my discussions with David A. Crocker. Since the article appeared, international pressure has been applied on the Hun Sen government to proceed expeditiously with a tribunal, but these efforts have been thwarted by the regime's go-slow tactics. See Stephen R. Heder, "Dealing with Crimes against Humanity: Progress or Illusion?" *Southeast Asian Affairs 2001* (forthcoming). As this is written (June 2001) the prospects for a trial seemed to have improved, but by September 2002, no trial had occurred. See Matt Reed and Kay Kinsong, "PM: KR Trial Could Begin in December," *Cambodia Daily* June 15, 2001.

8 For a stimulating discussion of the death penalty issue, see Gary Wills, "The Dramaturgy of Death," *New York Review of Books*, June 21, 2001.

9 Similarly, the mug shots on display at Tuol Sleng are heavily weighted toward photographs of women and children, who made up a small minority of the

people confined in the prison. To be fair, of course, an exhibit of all 6,000 surviving mug shots would be hard to mount and impossible to view. See Doug Niven and Chris Riley, eds., *Killing Fields* (Santa Fe, NM: New Mexico Twin Palms Press, 1996). For a vivid description of Choeung Ek as a tourist site in the 1990s, see Robert Kaplan, *The Ends of the Earth* (Boston: Boston North End Press, 1996), 403-404.

10 On the process that was involved in the creation of this victimized notion of "Khmer-ness" in the colonial era, see Penny Edwards, *Cambodge: The Cultivation of a Nation, 1860-1945* (Ann Arbor: University of Michigan Press, 2002). For survivors' accounts, see, among others, Chanritty Him, *When Broken Glass Floats* (New York: W.W. Norton, 2000); Someth May, *Cambodian Witness* (New York: Random House, 1986); and Molyda Szymusiak, *The Stones Cry Out* (New York: Hill and Wang, 1986). Harder-headed views of the DK era, written by men who were adults at the time, are Haing Ngor, *A Cambodian Odyssey* (Ithaca, NY: Cornell University Press, 1987) and Pin Yathay, *Stay Alive, My Son*, 2nd ed., (Ithaca, NY: Cornell University Press, 2000).

11 See Michael Vickery, *Cambodia 1975-1982* (Boston: South End Press, 1983), 64-188. In his analysis, Vickery argued that there were important temporal and spatial variations to the behaviour of DKL and to the responses of people living under it. When he conducted extensive interviews with survivors along the Thai-Cambodian border in 1980-81, he found that these variations often overshadowed the simplified, totalistic narratives recited by some survivors and relayed by many outsiders, especially Western journalists.

12 On the formation and policies of the post 1979 government, see Evan Gottesman, *Survivors' Theater: Cambodia after the Khmer Rouge*, forthcoming.

13 Judy Ledgerwood, "The Cambodian Toul Sleng Museum of Genocidal Crimes: National Narrative," *Museum Anthropology* 21, 1 (Spring-Summer 1997): 83-98; Lindsay French, "Exhibiting Terror," paper read at 1998 Annual Meeting of the Association for Asian Studies, Washington DC; and Rubie Watson, ed., *Memory, History and Opposition: Under State Socialism* (Santa Fe, NM: Santa Fe New Mexico School of American Research Inc., 1994). See also Maurice Bloch, "Time, Narratives and the Multiplicity of Representations of the Past," in Bloch, *How We Think They Think* (Boulder, CO: Westview Press, 1998), 100-13.

14 For an expansion of this argument, see Chandler, 49-51. On post mortem photographs at the prison, author's interviews with Nhem En, a photographer at S-21, May 1997 and December 1998.

15 Interestingly, no complete version of the Cambodian chronicles was published in Cambodia until 1969. To be sure, the French resuscitation of "Angkor" (the medieval temple complex in northwestern Cambodia), replete with reign dates and kings' names, inspired Khmer nationalists in the 1940s and later; in 1977, Pol Pot declared that "Slaves like us built Angkor under...exploiting classes, so that these royal people could be

happy. If our people can make Angkor, they can make anything." U.S. Foreign Broadcast Information Service (FBIS) October 4, 1977. An image of Angkor has appeared on every Cambodian flag since independence. But the wholesale identification of Cambodia's "history" with "Angkor" can be misleading: see Claude Jacques's seminal article, "Nouvelles orientations pour l'etude de l'histoire du pays khmer," *Asie du sud-est et monde insulindien* 14 (1982): 39-57.

16 Minutes of DK ministerial meeting number 2, May 13, 1976, document 705, Cambodia Documentation Center archive, Phnom Penh. See also S-21 document, Cornell Microfilm reel (hereafter CMR) 96.4, 6: "In the matter of struggle, our people are the ones that do it. Our people are the ones who make history."

17 For evidence of a cult of personality under DK, see Chandler, *Voices from S-21*, 40 and David Chandler, *Brother Number One: A Political Biography of Pol Pot*, 2nd ed. (Boulder, CO: Westview Press, 1999) 148-53.

18 Untitled interrogators' notebook from S-21, 1976, CMR 99.7, 73. "Three [metric] tons per hectare" was the utopian goal set for paddy harvests in Cambodia's Four Year Plan, launched in 1976. For the text of the plan, see David Chandler and Ben Kiernan, eds., *Pol Pot Plans the Future* (New Haven: Yale University Southeast Asian Series, 1988), 36-118.

19 For a distressing exposure of Nuon Chea's thinking, expressed to sympathetic Danish visitors in 1978 with no thought of publication, see Laura Summers, "The CPK: Secret Vanguard of Pol Pot's Revolution," *Journal of Communist Studies* 3 (1987): 8-30.

20 Henri Locard, *Le "petit livre rouge" de Pol Pot ou les paroles d'Angkar* (Paris: L'Harmnattan, 1996), 175.

21 "Pay Attention to Sweeping Out the Internal Enemies," *Tung Padevat* (Revolutionary Flags), July 1978, 9-10.

22 Intriguingly, the gateway to Wat Promruot in Siem Reap, erected in the 1990s, depicts the Buddha assailed by these "forces," who are dressed in Khmer Rouge costume. See also Eleanor Mannika, *Angkor Wat: Time, Space and Kingship* (Honolulu: University of Hawaii Press, 1996), 155-60, where she discusses bas-reliefs dealing with this subject.

23 For a narrative of events in 1997-1998 affecting the CPK, see David Chandler, *Brother Number One: A Political Biography of Pol Pot*, 180-83. The peoples' tribunal that condemned Pol Pot was re-enacted for the benefit of the journalist Nate Thayer and his TV cameraman, proving to outsiders that Pol Pot was alive but out of favour.

24 The marvelous work being carried out by the Documentation Center-Cambodia (DC-Cam) in Phnom Penh, under the leadership of Youk Chhang, needs to be cited in this context. The Center gathers, maintains, and publishes materials from its voluminous archive of the DK era. It conducts and publishes its own research, and encourages outside scholars to consult the archive.

25 For a sustained treatment of these issues, emphasizing the differences between the German and Japanese responses to their experiences in World War II, see Ivan Buruma, *The Wages of Guilt* (New York: Vintage, 1997). See also Martha Minow, *Between Vengeance and Forgiveness: Facing History after Genocide and Mass Violence* (Boston: Beacon Press, 1998), 118-20. On Cambodia, see David Ashley, "The Failure of Conflict Resolution in Cambodia: Causes and Lessons" in Frederick Z. Brown and David G. Timberman, eds., *Cambodia and the International Community: The Quest for Peace, Development and Democracy* (Singapore: The Institute of Southeast Asian Studies, 1998), 49-78 and also Alexander Laban Hinton, "Why Did You Kill? The Cambodian Genocide and the Dark Side of Face and Honor" *Journal of Asian Studies* 57 (February 1998): 93-122.

12

National Reconciliation in Russia?

Janet Keeping[1]

Introduction

Does the notion of "reconciliation" apply to the events taking place in contemporary Russia? Is national reconciliation occurring in Russia? These are the questions I will address in subsequent sections of this essay, but before doing that, it is necessary to say something about what constitutes reconciliation, and especially about what constitutes "national reconciliation."

Concept of Reconciliation

Reconciliation seems to require for its application some kind of relationship that has suffered a rupture. That relationship is repaired, at least to some degree, when the participants in this relationship reconcile. Where there has been no previous, shared history or relationship, there can be no reconciliation. Complete strangers do not reconcile: they establish a relationship where there was not one before. The interpersonal context for reconciliation is the most easily understood, because it is the most common. We all understand the notion of reconciliation after family disputes or marital troubles. Even if the injury sustained by the relationship is never completely healed, we are ready to say that reconciliation has occurred when sufficient repair has been achieved to allow the relationship to go on—the family to function as a family, even if not as well as before the rupture, or the marriage to continue as more than an empty facade (at least that would

---

Notes to chapter 12 are on pp. 339-40.

be the requirement of many of us). Many of us are also getting used to hearing about reconciliation having occurred within larger social groups, and even about "national reconciliation." Some careful thought has been given to the philosophical underpinnings of reconciliation at the level of broad social institutions. For example, Trudy Govier and Wilhelm Verwoerd[2] have argued for the need to look at reconciliation from both "quantitative" and "content" perspectives in order to overcome some of the difficulties in applying the concept of reconciliation in contexts other than the usual interpersonal ones. We would not, they suggest, expect to find the same qualities in national reconciliation as we would require at the personal level. And surely this is true: a national reconciliation, whether in Russia or elsewhere, would presumably not be the same thing as reconciliation between a previously warring husband and wife because the relationship or relationships to be restored would be so different.

> Quantity issues concern the level at which reconciliation is sought—whether it is national, community, small group, or interpersonal. Content issues concern the kind of "reconciliation" involved—whether one is seeking merely nonviolent coexistence, or decent neighborly relations, or the restoration of a close friendship or an intimate love affair....We argue that both quantity and content can vary in degrees, and that appreciating this fact exposes new and highly relevant possibilities.[3]

Govier and Verwoerd argue against Susan Dwyer's idea that reconciliation is "the reconciling of narratives," on the grounds that most fundamentally it is people and not narrative accounts that are alienated and may be brought together. While I agree with them on this point,[4] I think that the process of reconciling narratives can also be integral to the reaching of reconciliation. It would seem quite natural to expect that people who need to reconcile with one another could do so through an exchange of "accounts" of the events and interpretations of those events that divide them. This would seem especially likely where the issue that divides them lies in the public realm. Such a process would often not suffice to achieve reconciliation, whether that is understood as an end state or a stage on the way to it, but it could significantly contribute to reconciliation. And where a mutually acceptable narrative was found, this narrative would form the basis for the reconciliation that would allow the parties to go forward together in a mutually beneficial way.

Govier and Verwoerd argue for an understanding of reconciliation that "may be understood as involving centrally the building or rebuilding of trust." I suggest a slightly different conception. If a relationship can be re-established that allows progress to be made towards a sustainably more decent society (or whatever other social institution we are concerned with in the context at hand), then I think I would be content to say that some degree of reconciliation had occurred. Probably a degree of trust is necessary in order that my criterion be met; whether this is the case I leave for others to debate. In the case of Russia, it would seem to me that where progress towards achieving a sustainably more decent society is being made, it is characterized by some modicum of trust, at least to the extent that key players know where they can expect others to cooperate and where they have to be prepared for obstruction and other forms of non-cooperation. At a minimum, one might say, the boundaries of mistrust amongst the participants have been somewhat clarified.

A concept of reconciliation will "work for me" in the context of Russian issues if it fits with what I take to be the central question in this context. That is the question of whether Russia is going forward, that is, whether the present so-called "transition period" in Russia will result in meaningful progress for the citizens and residents of the country. To reflect on this question, one needs a notion of what constitutes "progress." Progress, it would seem to me, would be achievement of a better life for those for whom that country is home, where "better" is cashed out in terms of substantial movement towards greater respect and protection for the dignity of the individual. Since we know that progress in this sense cannot be achieved without robust legal protection for human rights, the sense of national progress I use here is consistent with concepts of reconciliation that are "informed by basic commitments to constitutional democracy and human rights."[5]

I am ready, then, to say that reconciliation has taken place when members of a particular social institution have overcome some kind of alienation from one another which has allowed, is allowing, or will allow them to work together to make mutually advantageous advances towards a better life. Is this happening at a national level in Russia? In order to answer this, we have first to think a bit about the kind of society contemporary Russia is.

Russia Today

When the Soviet Union was dissolved in 1991, the Russian Federation emerged as a separate country. The more than seventy years of Communist dictatorship were preceded by hundreds of years of absolute rule by a series of non-Communist dictators. With the considerable lessening of controls on speech that marked the end of the Communist regime, a lid was partially removed from a boiling cauldron of overlapping and intersecting injustices. At the same time, an empire had been largely lost. For hundreds of years, the priorities of successive Russian governments had been devoted to empire building and maintenance, at the cost of nurturing a sense of nationhood. In *Russia, People and Empire*, Geoffrey Hosking quotes Sergei Witte, one of the ministers of Finance near the time of the Revolution, who complained about the economic destruction wrought by empire building. Witte says, "the mistake we have been making for many decades is that we have still not admitted to ourselves that since the time of Peter the Great and Catherine the Great there has been no such thing as Russia: there has been only the Russian Empire."[6] In Hosking's view, it is only just now that Russians are beginning to form a country. He says, "Russians are closer today to nationhood than they have ever been, but the question still remains open whether they can decide who should belong to that nation and what its boundaries should be, and whether a political system can be created that gives all or most of them a feeling of having some stake in it."[7] Russians have not ever lived within such a political system. And, as Richard Rose observes in "Getting By Without Government," "Russian expectations about government are also low. Past experience and the absence of an effective alternative [to the Communist Party] justify these low expectations. This need not disrupt everyday life, however, for Russians learned long ago how to get by without, or in spite of, government."[8]

The most serious and best informed of commentators on contemporary Russia seem more or less united in the view that Russians need first to find, and define, themselves. For example, in February 2001, the American "National Intelligence Council" held a conference on "Russia in the International System." Consider these remarks by Blair Ruble of The Woodrow Wilson Center:

> The present moment is marked by continuing confusion over what it means to be Russian. Russians are searching for a national mission and identity that will help place them into

the twenty-first century international system. Like Italy and Germany in the nineteenth century, the Russian world and the Russian state are not coterminous. Like Italy and Germany over a century and a half ago, Russia is only now becoming a nation state. Such comparisons should give pause as both Italy and Germany found national form together with surface stability through pursuit of an expansionist authoritarian impulse that eventually brought both states to ruin. A similar authoritarian impulse resonates in a contemporary Russia torn by instability, even though excessive rule from above may only compound the country's long-term economic and social difficulties. More profoundly, a search for cultural identity and meaning appears to animate Russian life more than either economic or geopolitical forces. This is so, in part, as a consequence of the Russian Federation's expansive diversity, which makes any definition of Russian identity problematic....*Russia is presently divided by as many factors as can divide human beings.*[9] [Emphasis added.]

Reconciliation in Russia?

Probably the biggest stumbling block to application of the concept of reconciliation at a broad level in Russia is the difficulty in pinpointing what Russians would be reconciling from. To use the colloquial—what's the problem? It is not, of course, that Russia does not have its share of problems. The difficulty is quite the opposite, for there is a superabundance of problems, but they are overlapping and poorly delineated one from the other. Indeed, merely to ask the question—what might Russians be reconciling over?—is to see immediately the difficulty in thinking about reconciliation in the Russian context, for the list of events that could qualify is very long, indeed. One could start at almost any point in the last two hundred years of Russian history (indeed, probably much earlier) for the kinds of events which have given rise to, and which continue to give rise to, the kind of dispute for which reconciliation might be called. Was the 1917 Revolution a good thing? Were the agents of revolution heroes or traitors? What about the Russian Civil War? What about the virtual extermination of the bourgeoisie in the years following the Revolution and the Civil War? Did Lenin try to stop the ascension of Stalin or did he not? What about the forced collectivization of agriculture? What about the political terror? What about the preparations for the Second World War? Was it the case that Stalin was actually planning to attack Germany? Was

Stalin essentially good for the USSR, or did he have an overall bad influence? If the latter, was it simply Stalin, the individual, who went wrong, or was his evil a natural outcome of the system established under Lenin? Was Lenin himself a "Stalinist"?

Was Khrushchev saving himself when he exposed Stalin's "excesses" in the Secret Speech, or was he really trying to move the country forward? Did the USSR remain a repressive, totalitarian dictatorship after Stalin? Did Solzhenitsyn write the truth or were his books all lies, as many Russians seem to believe? What about Gorbachev and the dismantling of the USSR and the end of the Communist Party's monopoly on political life? The war in Afganistan? Yeltsin? What about privatization and the subsequent impoverishment of the people? The wars in Chechnya? The apartment block bombings that brought Putin to power? Putin? The sinking of the *Kursk* and the Russian government's handling of that disaster?

The list of possible candidates is very, very long, and continues to grow. So what can we say, is the alienation, or rupture in their relationship, from which Russians would be reconciling? There is no clear answer to this question.

A related difficulty—which may be the other side of the same coin— is the problem of defining Russia as a country and Russians as the citizens inhabiting that nation, as Hosking and others have noted. How can Russians even begin to succeed in national reconciliation when they do not know what it means to be Russian (apart from the strictly ethnic definition of "Russianness" which, in a multiethnic society such as the Russian Federation, obviously will not do)? It is likely that the two processes—definition of nationhood and reconciliation at the national level—are inextricably connected. But at a minimum, we cannot expect national reconciliation without some much better sense than Russians currently have of who they are and what Russia is, or what it ought to be.

Grievances, Complaints, and Laments

The result of all this confusion is a fabulous lack of coherency to the discussion of issues in the public realm in Russia. The lack of coherency is so acute that one is tempted to say that there are not even disputes. Unquestionably, there are grievances. It seems that every region, every city, has a host of its own grievances. It seems that every group, no matter by which characteristic you identify it, has grievances.

The specificity and bitterness of these grievances are well dramatized in Tony Kushner's play *Slavs*.[10] A scene in a doctor's office in Siberia illustrates the phenomenon. The action takes place in 1992. A bureaucrat has been sent from Moscow to investigate the extent of environmental contamination in the region and the resultant health problems. The doctor working in the clinic "tears a strip off" the bureaucrat about the region's horrendous environmental contamination and its neurological consequences. The doctor points, as an example, to a young girl in the clinic who has been catastrophically impaired by the pollution: it has left her unable to speak. The doctor leaves in a huff and the mother of the girl remains on stage with the official who proceeds to pull a political pamphlet out of his pocket and tries to recruit the mother to the nationalist movement he supports. At one point, in explaining the party's program, he says to her, "speaking to you as one Russian to another, may I suggest that we have got the right solution." After he makes this appeal, there is a long pause, and then she lashes out with an extremely vitriolic diatribe, an angry rant that has nothing to do with the big issues at stake, neither the region's environmental problems, nor the nasty nationalism that he has on offer. Her hate is not directed against the system that has ruined her child and led to such horrific, systemic degradation. Instead, it is an ethnic attack on him as a Russian. The gist of what she says is, "I am no Russian, I am a Lithuanian and I am only here because my grandfather was exiled here two generations ago. Her speech conveys a deep, wretched anger that this man mistook her for another Russian, but nothing by way of a response to the substantive issues at hand.

The example is fictional, but not unrealistic.

Grievances and Laments

In my experience, conversations in Russia on political themes—and many other topics, as well—often end in grievance, that is, in expressions of great dissatisfaction that have no practical direction. Because they have no practical focus, they seldom inspire action, let alone hope. Rather, they usually deepen the gloom and sense of powerlessness. The notion that personal initiative could lead somewhere, or that one should try to do something about societal problems on the assumption that one's efforts could bear fruit is not widely shared.[11]

Indeed, the airing of grievances might be seen as having evolved into something of an art form in Russian culture. I had concluded this on the basis of my own experience in Russia, but later discovered some of the literature on the topic, including that of American anthropologist Nancy Ries. In her book *Russian Talk, Culture and Conversation during Perestroika*, she examines the patterns Russian conversation tends to take. Several of these patterns amount to what I refer to as grievances (she often uses the terms "litany" and "lament"). She advances the view that the language of hopelessness so often used by Russians actually reinforces and helps perpetuate their powerlessness:

> in certain ways the particular logic of power and powerlessness in Russia was reproduced by the very lamentations and narratives that denounced it.
>
> The existential question that inspires my own work is the same question I heard a thousand times in Moscow: Why is Russian experience so full of suffering and misfortune? This book examines the possibility that the regular posing of such key rhetorical questions helps sustain the kinds of social and cultural institutions which perpetuate that "suffering."[12]

A profound sense of powerlessness and resulting hopelessness is encountered time and time again in Russian speech. There is, I think, something even constitutive about this hopelessness and the lament-like characteristic of Russian speech. Ries reports that when she felt herself compelled to interject with an encouraging or optimistic—at least practical—suggestion, she was met with dismay by her Russian associates: she, Ries, had obviously missed the point. The object was not to look for solutions—which by Russian hypothesis are not available—but to vent strong feelings and to establish closeness with those who share the Russian experience of hopelessness. I have had the same experience in Russia: part way through one of these laments, I well-meaningly offered a practical possibility—have you tried this or that?—only to be met with complete incomprehension. The purpose of this kind of talk is not to come up with ideas for overcoming the difficulties described, because the difficulties are insurmountable.

An aside: it is often at this point in discussing Russian affairs with the uninitiated that someone observes that it must be consummately depressing to witness this kind of behaviour repeatedly. Were it not for Russians' wit and often marvelous sense of humour, this could, I suppose, be the case. But their self-deprecating humour and appreciation of the absurd more than outweigh the frustrations some of us may feel with these incantations of powerlessness and hopelessness. Nancy Ries reports the following particularly lovely example:

> At a small gathering over tea one afternoon in 1990, conversation turned to "the complete disintegration" (*polnaia razrukha*) of Soviet society. As people traded examples of social chaos and absurdity back and forth, and the conversation reached its climactic pitch, Volodia, a writer, turned to me and delivered a punch-line, with a sardonic glee typical of certain kinds of Russian pronouncements: "You know what this country is, Nancy? This country is *Anti-Disneyland*." He was justifiably proud of his precise symbol for Russia, one that described quite well the sense of inhabiting a mythical land where everything was geared toward going wrong: a gargantuan theme park of inconvenience, disintegration, and chaos.[13]

Encouraging Signs? Reconciliation at Other Levels

Are there no encouraging signs? If there are, and I think there are some, then they are to be found on a smaller scale than national reconciliation. Let me briefly describe two possibilities with which I have had some personal experience in Russia—reconciliation at the (1) institutional and (2) regional levels. The problem is that the successes of both are very much limited by dysfunction at the national level.

It is clear that some substantial reconciliation has taken place within certain Russian institutions. Examples with which I am somewhat familiar are found in the departments of some Russian universities. Under the totalitarian regimes of the past, which operated on a divide and conquer mentality, individuals were forced into mistrust of each other. Conformity was the name of the game and informants were everywhere. Now many, especially better-educated people, are aware of the damage done to them by the mechanisms Soviet authorities used to keep them fearful and mistrustful of each other. Some of them have been able to develop more trusting relationships with colleagues and to cooperate with them in establishing ways of working together that are mutually beneficial. To be sure, some Russians developed and maintained networks of trust throughout the Soviet regime.[14] However, with the lifting of much of the repression, it has been possible to extend such networks further, beyond the intimate circles of carefully chosen friends and some family to larger social units. But those extensions have not gone so far as encompass even whole institutions such as a university, let alone a whole sector of the economy or the whole of Russian society.

As well, in some regions of the country, there has been a degree of reconciliation reached amongst the political entities that constitute that region. One might want to say, for example, that some of the policy and legal reforms in western Siberia would not have been possible without some degree of reconciliation amongst the various "provinces" and "sub-provinces."[15] There is no doubt that these organizational units have come together, overcoming some of their previous differences, in order to struggle more effectively against the central government that seeks to dominate them as in the past.[16] Whether this counts as reconciliation I am not sure, but I think it could, especially if one keeps in mind "quantity" and "content" of reconciliation, as explained by Govier and Verwoerd in "Trust and the Problem of National Reconciliation."

Other Points of View

I have concluded that it is, at best, premature to talk of national reconciliation in Russia. There is a lack of coherency to the myriad grievances articulated by Russians and a related lack of national self-knowledge or self-definition, which combine to preclude a serious possibility of reconciliation at the national level. But it has been suggested that one could, and in fact should, go further, to contend that reconciliation is impossible. After all, this argument would posit, it is not clear that there is even a desire for reconciliation in the general population or among the elites. No one was put on trial at the end of the Communist regime; there was no housecleaning. Consider the trials of the conspirators in the abortive coup of August 1991: none of them was severely punished for participation in that event. The question can legitimately be asked, are there advocates of reconciliation? There seems to be no shared acknowledgement of any kind of wrongful action. That might well lead one to think that national reconciliation is impossible, rather than just premature. Fingers are pointed in various directions and the biggest problem is that nobody is to blame. Even the ethnic Russians, that is, those who are seen by the minorities as having repressed them, say—"we too suffered under the Soviet system." So, some amorphous *Soviet system* was to blame, not particular individuals. There are even those who say that Stalin was not at fault: perhaps, the terror was not so good, but Stalin himself was all right.[17]

What would it mean to conclude that reconciliation in Russia is not just premature but actually impossible? If reconciliation is necessary in order that true progress be made in turning Russia into a more humane society, and if reconciliation is impossible, then there is no possibility of progress in this sense. For practical reasons, I think, one has to recoil from such a conclusion. On the other hand, if Russia is, as some people say, an already failed state, or even as has been suggested a state that never was, then perhaps it is more truthful to accept the conclusion that there is no hope for a (morally) better Russia.

My own view is that in its present form Russia is ungovernable, except perhaps by repressive means—although I doubt that extreme repression would work to keep the country together for long. However, I also think that Russia's form will change over time. Perhaps some of the parts of the present Russian Federation that are most anomalous will separate from it, although this is unlikely to occur in a very civilized way. More hopefully, a form of federalism will evolve that facilitates the healthy development of the various political subdivisions of the Federation and allows the country as a whole to go forward.

Another approach to questions about reconciliation in Russia would be to look at what is transpiring in Russia from a psychological perspective. It has been observed that the state of Russian society, as I and some others describe it, sounds like post-traumatic stress syndrome in individuals. One of the forms that post-traumatic stress disorder takes is a kind of marble-like indifference. Judith Herman, a psychiatrist at Harvard, has shown that people whom one might think are irreparably "messed up" and will never live as normal human beings again can, given the right, gentle, and patient kinds of environment, regain health. But the process they must go through is very painful. These patients have to relive some of the trauma in order to articulate it; they must turn the trauma into words, instead of mute suffering. The thought, then, is that perhaps something comparable can take place at the societal level.[18]

Apart from the questions that always arise about the appropriateness of drawing analogies between individual and group processes, there is a problem applying this model to national reconciliation in Russia. The problem is a crucial one: the preconditions for such "therapy" are missing.

There is simply no agreement in Russia on what the trauma is from which Russians should be recovering.

Some Concluding Thoughts about Cross-Cultural Reflections on Hopefulness

I would like to conclude with some thoughts on cross-cultural explorations of phenomena such as reconciliation. Eventually, as even a brief paper such as this one shows, our talk of processes such as reconciliation comes around to grounds for hope, or its absence. This was beautifully stated by Wilhelm Verwoerd, who said in conversation, "I have a life-long commitment to try and make hope practical instead of despair convincing." I well understand that motivation, but I am compelled to observe that my Russian friends almost never speak in terms of hope. They have the verb in their language, but they do not often choose to use it, and I have noted a certain alarm on their part when I use it about something significant. As the work of Nancy Reis and others shows, hopelessness figures very prominently in Russian conversation.

I think the explanation for this is not difficult to divine: Russian history is so miserable that hope is dangerous. Those who relaxed their guard long enough to hope for something were destroyed, one way or the other. Russians are very, very conservative people; they are extremely risk averse.[19] History has taught them, above all, caution.[20] As happy as they would be should it occur, they do not hope for much better. One dare not hope for better and one certainly *never* expects it.[21] A sort of corollary to this is expressed in the maxim a good Russian friend often uses: "The good things are a gift," he says, "the rest is just the way it is."

These reflections on the Russian fear of hope, even if sociologically accurate, do not speak to the desirability of change in Russia. At some level, Russians want better, much better, and their right to live in dignity is the same as those of any other people. I would not want to be taken as suggesting the contrary, because human rights are human rights and we must do what we can to advance their guarantee in practice wherever they are threatened or have not yet been accorded proper protection. I want only to observe that the psychological processes in individual Russians, and the sociological processes in the society at large, are not the same as those that drive, or may be assumed by, our exploration of themes such as the presence of hope or the possibility of reconciliation.

Notes

1 The Canadian Institute of Resources Law, for which the author is the Director of Russia Programmes, has been engaged in projects focused on regulation of natural resources development in Russia since 1993. Most of this work has been funded by the Canadian International Development Agency.

2 Trudy Govier and Wilhelm Verwoerd, "Trust and the Problem of National Reconciliation," *Philosophy of the Social Sciences* 32, 2 (June 2002): 178-205.

3 Ibid., 180-81.

4 Ibid., 185.

5 Ibid., 182.

6 Sergei Witte, cited in Geoffrey Hosking, *Russia, People and Empire* (London: Fontana Press, 1998), 479.

7 Ibid., 486.

8 Richard Rose, "Getting By without Government," *Daedalus* 123, 3: 58.

9 Executive Summary of the Conference Report (Washington: National Intelligence Council, June 1, 2001, CR 2001-02), as published in Johnson's Russia List, # 5375, July 31, 2001, <davidjohnson@erols.com>, 15.

10 Tony Kushner, *Thinking about Longstanding Problems of Virtue and Happiness* (New York: Theatre Communications Group, 1995). The play *Slavs* can be found at 81-185 of this book; the passage referred to at 172-73.

11 For a beautifully written illustration of Russian passivity in "action," as it were, see the first three pages of the chapter entitled "Vorkuta—To Freeze in Fire," in Ryszard Kapuscinski's *Imperium* (Toronto: Vintage Canada, 1995), 142-44.

12 Nancy Ries, *Russian Talk, Culture and Conversation during Perestroika* (Ithaca and London: Cornell University Press, 1997), 42. She also documents her experience in an article "The Power of Negative Thinking: Russian Talk and the Reproduction of Mindset, Worldview and Society," *Anthropology of East Europe Review* 10, 2: 38-53.

13 Ries, *Russian Talk*, 42.

14 A good reference on these networks and related phenomena is Alena V. Ledeneva's *Russia's Economy of Favours* (Cambridge: Cambridge University Press, 1998).

15 This is not what the political subdivisions of Russia are called, but the precise terminology does not matter for present purposes.

16 The literature on federalism in Russia has been growing steadily, although most of it is in Russian. The notion that developing a more effective federalism is key to solving some of Russia's major problems has received considerable recognition both in Russia and abroad. Because of our own struggles since 1867 to find a form of federalism that works for our vast and culturally complex country, Canada is viewed by many as having a unique ability to assist Russia with the process of developing a genuine federalism. Canadian technical assistance to Russia is increasingly focused on questions associated with federalism.

17 This argument has been advanced by Bohdan Harasymiw, professor of political science at the University of Calgary.

18 This view was advanced by Tom Scheff, professor emeritus of sociology, University of California at Santa Barbara.

19 On Russians' conservatism, or risk aversiveness, see Yale Richmond's *From "Nyet" to "Da"* (Yarmouth, ME: Intercultural Press, 1992).

20 Rose, 58. "Low expectations [of government] are not grounds for optimism, but they at least prevent frustration, and the acts of aggression that may follow."

21 This may be, of course, one of the reasons why things do not much improve. See again, Nancy Ries' "The Power of Negative Thinking." Thinking, for example, of governance, low expectations of corporate executives, politicians, or civil servants, indeed of almost anyone in a position of leadership, will almost certainly be self-fulfilling.

CONCLUSION

13

What We Have Learned

Justice Richard J. Goldstone

In this paper I shall be addressing what we have learned over the past decades about human rights abuses and the law. But before I get to what we have learned, I think it's important to set the context and also to put the whole question into an appropriate perspective.

It is natural and justified to feel pessimistic when we are talking about the worst atrocities that have happened on four continents during the last half century, and perhaps most tragic of all, over the last decade. One would have hoped that after the Holocaust, as humankind progressed, these horrors would have become less and less common. Unfortunately, they've become more prevalent and the pessimism is understandable, if not inevitable.

However, I remain an inveterate optimist. I would like to justify this optimism by placing the whole issue of war crimes and human rights violations into a broader context. It's important for another reason, because I can't think of a worse catalyst for action than pessimism. I think pessimistic people are frozen people. Pessimistic people are people who don't get involved in any activity. Pessimism is something that one has to shrug off if one is going to ensure that this new century is going to be a less bloody one for humankind than the one that has recently passed.

There have obviously been tremendous developments in many fields of human endeavour, but I wish to address the field in which I've been involved for the past few years: international human rights and the field of international humanitarian law—what used to be called the law of war.

I will address, in particular, the invasion of national sovereignty that has come about in the wake of international jurisdiction.

Before the Second World War, there was no such thing as international jurisdiction. Human rights violations were really a national affair. Human rights violations in Country A could on no account be prosecuted or investigated in Country B, even if it was a neighbouring country. National sovereignty was inviolate; the League of Nations was built on the assumption of sovereignty; and individual human beings were not the subject of international law. The only people who had recognition in international law before the Second World War were government officials. In the International Court of Justice, only governments have standing.

The Second World War, and particularly the Holocaust, brought with it a completely new approach, when individual human beings became recognized as the subjects of international human rights law. The key that unlocked the door was the recognition, for the purposes of the Nuremberg trials, of "crimes against humanity." This was a key that opened a Pandora's box in many ways, because the idea of crimes against humanity was that some crimes are so huge or so shocking to the conscience of humankind that they are truly offences against all human beings, no matter where they live. The sorts of crimes that are committed in Country A or Continent X can be investigated and can be punished in any country where human beings live, because if a crime is committed against humankind, any members of the human community are entitled to assume jurisdiction in respect of those crimes. That was really the idea that was born with crimes against humanity, and it was quickly taken up in the international legal world.

In the Universal Declaration of Human Rights and in the Charter of the United Nations, the rights of individuals were at the forefront for the first time. In the first international human rights covenant, the Genocide Convention, one immediately saw this international jurisdiction being taken up, because the Genocide Convention not only creates the jurisdiction but obliges all nations that ratify the convention to investigate any alleged commission of genocide by anybody, no matter where. If there was evidence that an immigrant coming to Canada had been involved in genocide in another country it became the obligation of the Canadian government and the Canadian legal authorities to investigate and if the evidence proved to be true, to indict in a Canadian court such a person suspected of committing genocide. It became the obligation of Canada and of virtually every other nation in the world to ensure that their own domestic laws enabled them to carry out that obligation.

That was in 1948. It was in the following year, in 1949, that the International Committee of the Red Cross called yet one more international diplomatic conference, and in 1949 four Geneva Conventions were passed. Again, virtually every country of the world ratified those conventions. These Geneva Conventions of 1949 contain a new species of international crime, called "grave breaches" of the Geneva Conventions. Every nation that ratified the Geneva Conventions of 1949 undertook to investigate, bring to trial, and punish any person suspected of committing grave breaches, no matter where.

And the Geneva Conventions went further. If a government that has ratified the Geneva Conventions refuses to investigate and put on trial such a person, its obligation is, as soon as possible, to hand that person over to a country whose authorities are prepared to prosecute.

This idea of international jurisdiction caught on very quickly in the international legal world. It was carried over a few years later in the Torture Convention, and became relevant when the extradition of General Pinochet was being sought by the Spanish government. To have told an international lawyer fifteen years ago that a former head of state of Chile could be arrested in England at the request of Spain for crimes committed in Chile twenty years ago would have been a matter for mirth, an unbelievable scenario.

So this international jurisdiction has become an important reality because, as the Pinochet case has indicated, it's become unsafe for leaders, whether military or political, to travel anywhere outside their country, where they are protected.

The other convention that recognized this international jurisdiction, interestingly enough from my own perspective, was the convention that declared apartheid to be a crime against humanity. That convention also required any country that ratified the convention to investigate and prosecute any person suspected of having committed the crime of apartheid. It's a matter of regret, and I'm sure the history books will bear this out, that very, very few Western nations ratified the apartheid convention. They did not undertake to investigate the many South Africans who came within their borders, who should and could have been arrested and punished for having been complicit or involved in committing the crime of apartheid.

It's a matter for regret because it's not too far-fetched to assume that had the Western nations taken that convention seriously, apartheid might well have come to an end a decade earlier than it did. If South African ambassadors, if South African businessmen, if South African politicians had feared arrest in Canada or Western European countries or the United States, I don't believe that the system could have survived as long as it did. But that wasn't to be, and it was due to other less direct methods that apartheid was eventually crushed.

The growth of international jurisdiction penetrated the iron curtain of national sovereignty. Governments safeguard and look after national sovereignty as if it really was their own crown jewels. It's something almost mythical, something that has almost a religious significance, but this has changed. I remember as a student at the University in Johannesburg and in my early days of practice that South Africa could and did put up an acceptable argument against the international community getting involved in the anti-apartheid campaign. It wasn't the right at all of any other country, of any international organization to get involved, least of all to criticize the way South Africa dealt with its majority black population.

China is now one of the exceptions when it says "Look, the way we treat our people is not your business; it's our business." The most extreme illustration of this change is in Kosovo. After all, Kosovo is in every way legally a province of an independent nation. Kosovo is a province of the Federal Republic of Yugoslavia. But nobody questions the right of the international community, the right of the European powers, the right of NATO to interfere. What is questioned is the means. What is questioned is whether bombing is an appropriate reaction. What is questioned is whether ground forces shouldn't have been sent many, many months ago to protect the Albanian/Kosovan population. Few question the right in law of the international community becoming involved in the terrible human rights violations that have been perpetrated against the Albanian population of Kosovo.

Unfortunately, one of the main advocates of the inviolability of sovereignty is, of course, the United States. The United States Senate for many decades has safeguarded its sovereignty with the sort of fervour to which I've referred—the sort of fervour that is now personified in Jesse Helms, the chairman of the Foreign Relations Committee of the United States Senate. But unfortunately it is mirrored in the Administration. It is mirrored, too, in the opposition to the Rome Treaty of the International Criminal Court. One of the main objections put up by the United States to the International Criminal Court has been that it is not prepared to send its troops to foreign shores as the "supreme peacekeeper" if its troops, its citizens, are going to be subject to an international criminal court without the consent of the United States. My successor in the Hague, Justice Louise Arbour, has astutely pointed out that the United States, soon after objecting to the Rome Treaty, voluntarily involved itself in Kosovo. It committed itself to air strikes and possibly committed crimes that could be investigated by the International Criminal Court for the former Yugoslavia. It's done exactly the thing it said it would never do if there was an international criminal court. Maybe that will have a positive influence in convincing policy makers in Washington of the emptiness of that objection to the International Criminal Court's jurisdiction.

What have we learned? I'm sure everybody could draw up their own checklist. This is mine.

The first is that if we've learned anything since the Second World War, it's that any people on any continent are capable of committing the most terrible evil and any people on any continent are capable of the most wonderful deeds. No people on any continent can claim a monopoly over good or evil. There was a myth after the Second World War, certainly in many Western countries, that there was something peculiar about the German people, about the German psyche. It was a belief that, notwithstanding their culture, notwithstanding their artistic contribution, their contribution to humankind, there was something about Germans that enabled them to commit the most terrible atrocities during the Second World War. But that myth, unfortunately, perhaps, for many millions of people, proved not to be true. I don't need to mention the terrible human rights violations, the terrible massacres and murders and tortures that have been committed in tens of countries since the Second World War. Over a hundred wars since 1945 have been responsible for the murder of tens of millions of people, for the rape of tens of millions of women, for imposing refugee status on many tens of millions of innocent women and children and men.

Second, we have learned that past hate, past revenge, and the failure to investigate and bring some justice to victims has fueled violence and death and misery. Yugoslavia, perhaps, is the prime example. When one goes, as I did, to Belgrade and Zagreb and Sarejevo, one is treated to long, long history lessons, by cabinet ministers in particular. The history lessons begin in the fourteenth century in Kosovo, and moves to lessons about the terrible things that the Croatians or Ustashe, did to the Serbs in the Second World War—the deaths of hundreds of thousands of Serbs at the hands of the Ustashe. How far does one go back to begin to understand this hate?

I was reminded of it by a report in the *Globe and Mail* that a small Serbian community in Quebec is beginning to move out because they read that the Canadian government was going to resettle some fifty Albanian refugees from Kosovo. They were moving out because they feared that they would be attacked and murdered by these fifty Albanian refugees who were being given homes in that little town. It reminded me of the tremendous legacy of hate that exists in the former Yugoslavia between people who speak the same language, people who come from the same ethnic group, but who, through the quirks of history, happen to have three different religions. It's that legacy of hate that gives rise to violence.

I was reminded of it again recently when visiting Belfast in Northern Ireland. During our stay there, my wife and I were guests of a retired judge of the court of appeal in Northern Ireland, and during my visit I was contacted by a young solicitor who was acting for the family of a young woman lawyer who had been murdered in Belfast because of her involvement in political cases for Catholic activists. He asked me my advice with regard to an investigation that the British government had authorized into that killing. He asked my advice particularly because it's a small world. The very senior policeman whom the British government sent as the chief investigator, Colin Port, happened to have been on my staff in the Hague and in Arusha. I felt the anguish he felt, this young solicitor, towards a British policeman investigating an incident in Northern Ireland where there was no confidence at all on the part of the Catholic community that there would be a fair investigation. I gave him what advice I could, and suggested that there should be at least some international people acceptable to both sides to assist in the investigation.

When I went back for dinner to our host and hostess, I asked if they had heard of this solicitor, and they said they hadn't. I showed them his card and they said "Oh! He's a Catholic." I asked, "How do you know that?" and they said, "From his address. He lives in a Catholic area." It reminded me so much of my home, South Africa, where people's addresses determined one's attitude to them. I asked our hostess if she had ever been to that part of Belfast. She said no, she'd never been in that street. We also hear from another contributor to this volume about his surprise that white people he had spoken to in South Africa have never been to Soweto, some fifteen minutes from the city centre. It's the same fear of the unknown, a fear of anybody who is different, and an inability to come to grips and to take that extra step in getting to know people across that border, whatever it may be. It's those past hatreds that have to be overcome if there's going to be any solution to these sorts of problems.

The third thing I would suggest we have learned is the danger of stereotyping people. I know from my own experience at home that people make assumptions because of colour, religion, and too, too frequently, gender. People stereotype, and there is even a legal presumption that women are not reliable witnesses in gender-related crimes. So when people are charged with rape, it requires more than one witness to have a convincing case. There needs to be corroboration only in respect of those sorts of crimes. I'm happy to say that in South Africa, under our new Constitution that outlaws any gender-discrimination, our Supreme Court of Appeal has recently held that the requirement of corroboration is unconstitutional and no longer the law.

In the Rwanda tribunal, fortunately, rape has been recognized in the judgement of the court as being a war crime. It has become routine, in many, many indictments issued by the prosecutor and confirmed by judges to recognize rape and other gender offences committed against women as war crimes. One judgement from Arusha was written by a woman judge, who I'm proud to say is a South African, Navi Pillay. Judge Pillay was one of three judges, and her two male colleagues had no difficulty in concurring with her judgement.

The fourth and perhaps most controversial thing that we have learned is the power of leadership, the power of leadership for good and bad. The power of an Adolph Hitler for bad, the power of a Nelson Mandela or F.W. de Klerk in South Africa for good. I would suggest that we have had unfortunately few good, strong leaders prepared to use their leadership in recent years. I have no doubt that if Western leaders had explained the moral and legal issues, decent people would have approved of NATO troops going out and arresting mass murderers such as Karadzic and Mladic. There was an assumption that people wouldn't accept that, that people would object. I really have little doubt how decent people of the United States, Canada, France, or England would react if they had a leader who went on television or radio and explained the position of victims in Bosnia, and how victims would react if they read that Western troops, the best armed troops in the world, were not prepared to go and arrest people responsible for the rapes and deaths of their loved ones. How must they feel when they read and hear, as we all do, military leaders saying "it's not worth one life of our people to go and arrest the people responsible for the tens of thousands of murders and tens of thousands of rapes with which they have been charged"? It's the victims who have been relegated to the bottom of the agenda, and sometimes they are not even on the agenda at all.

The fifth lesson we should have learned is to recognize the importance of modern technology in the commission of huge crimes. Without the radio, even in the technologically backward country of Rwanda, nearly a million people could not have been massacred in virtually hand-to-hand, eyeball-to-eyeball murders in a hundred days. It would have been inconceivable. Nazi leaders would have been green with envy because they never, ever got anywhere near the killing of nearly a million people in nearly a hundred days. It was done in Rwanda because of the use of propaganda and the use of the radio. In the former Yugoslavia, there has been no shortage of fabricated evidence and propaganda and particularly on the state-controlled television and in the state-controlled newspapers.

The sixth lesson we should have learned I have already alluded to— the frequency with which victims are ignored. I've referred to the failure of the Western nations to give appropriate orders to arrest war criminals. In 1999 I feared that the victims of Kosovo would be ignored if Milosevic were allowed to continue to be the president and to be in control of his country. I cannot think of any worse position for victims, who no doubt want to go back to their country, to be told that the person responsible for kicking them out is going to be the person in charge of bringing them back. It really would be a ridiculous scenario and it's going to have another consequence. On what basis could the KLA give up their arms if Milosevic were in charge of his army and his security forces? And if the KLA did not lay down its arms it's going to be a much less safe environment for the NATO and Russian troops. We don't learn from lessons as recent as yesterday. Decent leaders shouldn't be dealing with people who have been seen on our own television screens committing the kinds of offences that Milosevic has been responsible for. The fact that he's been indicted made it perhaps one step worse, but this man was not morally worse since the indictment than he was before the indictment. From a legal point of view, such a leader as Milosevic is entitled to the presumption of innocence. But the evidence is so strong, so overwhelming, the evidence from victims, the evidence from human rights organizations, international and national, to make it quite unacceptable.

The seventh lesson is the importance to victims of acknowledgement. Trudy Govier has noted all that needs to be said on that issue and I needn't dwell on it. I think those of us who've been involved in dealing with victims, of meeting and talking to victims in South Africa, Rwanda, and in the former Yugoslavia, have seen at first hand how the acknowledgement in many cases is the beginning of the healing process.

The eighth lesson is that acknowledgement and reconciliation are essential to allow societies to move forward. I have in mind the experience of South Africa. In this volume Wilhelm Verwoerd used a wonderful medium, political cartoons. It is a very serious means of pointing out what would take much longer to explain in words. It's all there. It's a sort of shorthand: children respond to it as quickly and as well as adults.

But the importance of the Truth and Reconciliation Commission in South Africa is, I believe, that it has played a vital role in allowing us to move forward in a number of areas. I'll just mention one. The Truth and Reconciliation Commission has enabled South Africa to move forward with a common history. Without its work we would have many histories. We would have a white history, generally one of denial, because the denials were there. No sooner are human rights violations committed than the cover-up begins. It's more comfortable to believe that these things are not being committed for you because the crimes of apartheid were committed for all white members of the South African community. People felt more comfortable with the denials than with the admissions, so there would have been a white version with the denials. There would probably have been an Afrikaans-speaking version that would have been more protective and defensive. There would have been at least two or three black versions, depending on the political stance of the black group concerned. The Truth Commission has produced a single history from the overwhelming weight of the testimony it heard. That overwhelming evidence appears in those five volumes.

The ninth lesson, and an important one, has been the development of democratic values and norms and the increasing recognition of the emptiness of claims for cultural relativism, particularly in the human rights field. It is one of the benefits of the end of the Cold War. There is generally, throughout the world, East and West and North and South, a recognition that democratic values are the important values for which countries should strive. Some countries cannot afford to do so. Rwanda can't have elections for a number of reasons. They haven't got the infrastructure, they can't afford it, and unfortunately, since there is a minority government, an election would result in a new government. So from a political point of view, it's not going to happen today or tomorrow or the day after. But there's a recognition of its importance, nonetheless, by the Organization of African Unity, and by Asian governments, with a few exceptions. Who are the politicians who claim cultural relativism? Who are the politicians who claim that human rights is a Western notion? They are the politicians who trample on the human rights of their people. The way victims react to torture, to murder, to rape, to human rights violations, doesn't depend on the colour of their skin or the continent on which they live. The human reaction is exactly the same. This whole idea of cultural relativism, I would suggest, is very short-lived and not going to be with us for too long. It exists again in gender issues. There are some fundamentalist nations that still don't accept that woman are entitled to full human rights and full human dignity, but they are becoming fewer and fewer. And in many of those countries, it is the women who are standing up for their own rights and forcing governments to recognize them.

The tenth and last lesson I would suggest is perhaps the most important, and that is that individuals can make a difference. It's in civil society that these changes are becoming more and more important. It's non-governmental organizations that are changing the views of their governments. It's Amnesty International, Human Rights Watch, and national human rights organizations that are making their voices heard. The Rome Conference on the International Criminal Court is a wonderful example of that. Many, many governments complained of the power of non-governmental organizations, the fact that their representatives were present at the most confidential, private meetings. The International Committee of the Red Cross was represented. Over 120 NGOs were represented at Rome and formed a most important bloc, and, to their credit, it was like-minded nations led by Canada that did the same thing with regard to the Landmines Treaty. They did the same things at Rome, and they were able to muster from around the world 120 nations that formed the majority in

Rome, voting in favour of the International Criminal Court Treaty. A mere seven countries voted against the statute. It is a matter for great regret that the United States found itself in the company of those seven nations. I predict that sooner or later the United States is going to become one of the parties to the Treaty for the International Criminal Court. The citizens of the United States will not want their country to stop being the leader it should be of the international human rights movement. The people of the United States want it, they deserve it, and it's this concept of sovereignty which I believe is going to be overcome, particularly because non-governmental organizations in the United States are demanding it, and will get more and more support.

Let me conclude with a reference to the important role that Canada played in my country in the fight against apartheid. It might be important for Canadians to examine for themselves why they are concerned about people so many thousands of miles from their own shores. It's not because they have a good life, or because they come from a wealthy country. There are many wealthy countries, and many comfortable people who really don't care too much about people in other countries. It is something to be proud of and it's something that's certainly taken note of, as any Canadian visiting South Africa would experience. There is a special welcome and special warmth from South Africans, and particularly black South Africans, who recognize what Canada did in the anti-apartheid movement.

Many people ask me whether I'm not pessimistic, how I managed during the last eight or nine years to continue dealing with the most horrible crimes imaginable, in my own country, in Rwanda, in the former Yugoslavia. And really the answer I've given, without any hesitation, is that I've become more optimistic rather than less optimistic because of my own involvement. I've become more optimistic because of the reaction from victims, positive response from people who have had the most terrible crimes committed and perpetrated upon them. I've come into contact with wonderful people who are concerned with other people's human rights—the people who worked in my office in the Hague, in Arusha, particularly in Rwanda. These are people who are committed and sufficiently concerned to leave their comfortable homes in their comfortable countries to come and work in a genocide-torn country—no tarred roads, security problems, being cooped up in unpleasant, smelly hotels, no concerts, no cinemas to go to, very little television to watch.

People prepared to sacrifice their own comfort to go and assist people in countries with which they have no connection. Many of them are from Canada, from the United States, and from very comfortable Western European countries. It's working with people like that, as well as the contributors to this volume who are concerned and are bringing their own intellectual powers, their own experience, their own disciplines to bear on finding solutions to these problems, that makes me feel there's reason for a great deal of optimism.

Index

aboriginal people (Australia), 113, 239-40

aboriginal people (Canada's First Nations), 11, 16, 67-69, 112, 128-29, 193, 223-44

aboriginal people (Guatemala), 279-306

aboriginal people (New Zealand), 112, 127-28

aboriginal people, 1996 Royal Commission Report (Canada), 6-7, 67-69, 77-80, 223-29

accountability (*See also* responsibility), 48-49, 120, 201-202

acknowledgement (*See also* confession, recognition), 13, 22, 27-28, 35, 45-48, 55, 65-89, 120, 122-25, 238, 351

acknowledgement, compromised, 82-83

Adenauer, Konrad, 28, 31

Akayesu, Jean-Paul, 48

Amery, Jean, 199

amnesty, 41, 248-49, 262-63, 265, 274-75, 312-13

Amnesty International, 51, 352

apartheid, 142-43, 245-78

apology, 22, 29, 41, 65-66, 69, 91, 106-107, 216

Arbour, Louise, 347

Arendt, Hannah, 31, 33, 208-209

Aristide, Jean-Bertrand, 177-84

Askin, Kelly Dawn, 147, 149

assimilation, 296-97

atrocities, 55, 198, 216

attention, 74-77, 80-81

Axworthy, Lloyd, 171, 177-78

Baier, Annette, 76-77

Barbie, Klaus, 213

Barkan, Elazar, 15-16

Bassiouni, M. Cherif, 139-40, 143, 151-52

Baumeister, Roy, 207-208

Benzien, Jeff, 248

Berkeley, Bill, 48

Berlin, Isaiah, 184

Bianchi, Herman, 115-16

bias, 256-57

Booth, Kenneth, 191

Boraine, Alex, 256-57

Bosnia, 10, 39, 41, 191-92

Boutros-Gali, Boutros, 171

Britain, 233